To all of those who lost their lives in Hip-Hop's treacherous crosscurrents.

Also by R.J. Bond
Tupac: Assassination
Tupac: Assassination II
Tupac–The Early Years

Also by Michael Douglas Carlin
American Federale
Rise a Knight
Peaceful Protests
A Prescription For Peace

Russell Poole's Story
Labyrinth by Randall Sullivan

TUPAC:187

THE RED KNIGHT

This Isn't A Grand Conspiracy; It Is About A Dysfunctional Family
That Commits Murder.

R.J. Bond
Michael Douglas Carlin
with contribution by
Russell Poole retired Detective L.A.P.D.

Martin Productions

Library of Congress Cataloging-in-Publication Data

Bond R.J.
Carlin, Michael Douglas
Poole, Russell
   Tupac:187: The Red Knight–This Isn't A Grand Conspiracy. It Is About A Dysfunctional Family That Commits Murder.

   ISBN-10: 0-6923--1784-8
   ISBN-13: 978-0-692-31784-6
   1. Murder–California–Los Angeles–Case studies. 2. Police misconduct–California–Los Angeles–Case studies. 3 Police corruption–California–Los Angeles–Case studies. 4. Tupac, 1971– 5. Notorious B.I.G. 6. Knight, Suge.

Martin Productions
11762 De Palma Road Suite 1C-448
Corona CA 92883

"You can spend minutes, hours, days, weeks, or even months over-analyzing a situation; trying to put the pieces together... or you can leave the pieces on the floor and move the fuck on." – Tupac Shakur

DEDICATION & ACKNOWLEDGEMENTS

My years as a homicide detective has taken years off my life. I was a husband and a father of three. A homicide detective in South Central Los Angeles during the 80's and 90's was a period filled with murder & mayhem. It was a genocide. I was a coach for all of my kids for their respective sports teams. I would be on the field coaching & would be called for duty many times. I want to dedicate this book to my wife Megan and my kids Kurt, Doug and Jennifer. I want to tell them I'm sorry for those times I was taken away from family events. I love them very much & hope to make up for those lost family times together. I did take an oath & promise to arrest those who committed murder. I'm proud of the work I've done & my dedication to truth & justice. Thank you, with lots of love!
  —Russell Poole

RJ dedicates this book to his wife, Athena, for the many disappointments she endured that ended up laying the foundation for this book. RJ also dedicates this book to Frank Alexander; "Wish we would have built that toll road in front of that house in Kentucky…" and to his dad, Don Erath, the greatest detective I know. (And Russ understands that, as my dad was one of Russ's T.O.'s at the Academy- what a wild coincidence!)

RJ wants to thank the following for their help: Frank Alexander (RIP), Michael Moore (RIP), Kenny Archer, Leslie Gauldin, Kevin Hackie, Leila Steinberg. Gloria Cox, Larry Spellman, Tracy Robinson, Russell Poole, Randall Sullivan, Peter Spirer, Perry Sanders, Jesse Surrat, Ric Hine, Robert Pavlovich, Josh Harroway, Jon Sheinberg, Marshall Ryan, Austin Michael, Athena Bond, Jimmy Remmers, Don Erath, Mike Allen, Jeff Braley, Ken Hawley, Mike Luppi and all who worked on the "Assassination" movies. Thanks to Greg "Shock G" Jacobs, Atron Gregory, Karen Lee. Charles "Man Man" Fuller and Lena Sunday, Ron "Money B" Brooks, and Yasmyyn Fula for allowing me to better understand Tupac before the Death Row era- that perspective was critical. BIG thanks to Chris Blatchford for helping Frank and I as well as Russell and I. Thanks to Michael Carlin for keeping me in check- steel sharpens steel, brother. Russell Poole is still my hero. Thank you to Afeni Shakur for hugging me the first time we met (and for signing my Assassination poster) and thank you to Voletta Wallace for teaching us all how to keep in the fight. If there is anyone I forgot, it'll be in the next book. RJ uses Zildjian Cymbals, and Fender strings…wait wrong kind of acknowledgement.(lol)

Thank you to Russell and RJ for inviting me to the party, to Chris Blatchford for sharing the letter and his story, to my attorney Meghan Maroney, my Chinese family as well as my American Family (you all know who you are), Tina Abeel, Chris Nassiff, Natalie Niewerth, Colin Finlay, Lincoln Phipps, and Chrome Cobra. All of you cheered me on. To children stuck in tough circumstances I would simply say, "Learn Mandarin! In today's world it is your ticket to a better life."
  —Michael Douglas Carlin

Contents

INTRODUCTION

I took my promotion to Robbery Homicide very seriously. I placed the Homicide Investigator's Creed prominently above my desk where I would see it every day. I often read those words out loud.

No greater honor will ever be bestowed on an officer, or a more profound duty imposed on him, than when he is entrusted with the investigation of the death of another human being.

It is his duty to find the facts regardless of color or creed, without prejudice, and to let no power on earth deter him from presenting these facts to the court without regard to personality.

—The Homicide Investigator's Creed

When Ennis Cosby was murdered I saw the fully functioning wheels of justice at work as we canvased America for clues. One tip that we received led to the case being solved. When we received that clue we emptied out the police academy and all of the cadets participated in the search and recovery of the murder weapon. A fully functioning department brought the killer to justice. The truth wants to seep out.

The murders of Tupac Shakur and Christopher Wallace continue to haunt me. I felt we were making progress many times only to have that progress halted by leadership within the department. It is difficult enough to solve a homicide dealing with witnesses that are reluctant or with evidence that has been destroyed. Opportunities to pursue clues met with internal LAPD roadblocks that were frustrating and as I sought to follow through on the Homicide Investgator's Creed by not letting any power on Earth stop me from learning the truth I was pulled off of the case. Through it all I have never lost hope that one day the case would be solved and the killers brought to justice.

We were not allowed to speak to members of the media while I was at Robbery Homicide unless the brass approved it but I always had an admiration for Chris Blatchford as he covered stories in some of the roughest neighborhoods. I met Chris Blatchford many years ago on the telephone and then in person. When my son needed to complete a project for school by interviewing a journalist I reached out to Chris and my son received an "A" on that assignment.

One day I contacted Chris and asked him if we could meet to discuss the murder of Tupac Shakur. On that call he shared with me that he received a letter in 1998 that had never been publicly shared. I invited RJ Bond to that meeting. We sat in awe as he shared the letter and revealed how he had obtained it. He spoke of his telephone conversations with Malcolm Patton and the attempt to drop off the murder weapon at Fox 11 Studios. I invited Michael Carlin to have a follow-up meeting where he heard the very same stories.

Is this the break that will solve the case? I don't know but it needs to be investigated; so far that hasn't happened. I know that if the LAPD would treat this case in the same way they treated the Ennis Cosby Case, we would bring the killers to justice. When the wheels of justice are fully functioning the truth will seep out. I hope that Tupac:187 leads to prosecution and conviction of the killers of Tupac Shakur and Christopher Wallace.

—Russell Poole, Former Detective LAPD

FOREWARD

Las Vegas Police complained that they could get no cooperation from witnesses in the Tupac Shakur Homicide in spite of several people coming forward and many more being willing to provide information. Those that did come forward to do the "right thing" and testify were handed over to criminals in both the Shakur and Wallace killings. Yafeu Fula said to Las Vegas Police that he could identify the driver of the white Cadillac. That information is passed on to Death Row Insiders. Michael Robinson aka Psycho Mike is promised he would remain confidential. His name is leaked and he is severely beaten by the Bloods in retaliation. Mario Hammonds is promised that he will remain a confidential informant but his name is leaked. This pattern happens over and over as those who attempt to do the right thing are penalized for doing it with Kenneth Boagni, Kevin Hackie, Antoine Sutphens, Paul Lewis, etc.

Frank Alexander speaks to the Los Angeles District Attorney's office where he is asked to testify against Suge Knight; the D.A.'s office feels compelled to tell him that his confidential police interview has been handed to the defense team. The D.A.'s office tells Alexander several times that he should be aware of this because it accuses Suge Knight of a clear probation violation. He hints that Alexander's life may be on the line but also makes it clear that Alexander is on his own to protect himself and his family. Where is Frank Alexander now? Dead! Michael Moore? Dead! Michael Robinson? Dead! Yak Fula? Dead! If there is anything to be learned from the tale of Shakur, Wallace, and Death Row Records it is that those who try to do the right thing in our society are penalized while criminals are allowed to break laws at will and are rewarded for their behavior. If you learn anything from this book it should be that if you witness a crime it isn't in your best interests to come forward until something deeply rooted in our society changes. Two citizens took a confession letter to LAPD that names the alleged shooter and not only was that information leaked by one of the four cops in the room to a former cop but it ended up on the Internet naming the people involved—instead of being investigated. Tupac fans have posted death threats leveled at the alleged shooter.

80% of homicides occur with offenders known to the victim. The murder of Tupac isn't some grand conspiracy involving the U.S.

Government. It is a family affair. When the dysfunctional family members include sworn officers all bets are off. Cops don't want their dirty laundry aired in public.

A witness came to us and told us that she was at the Petersen Museum the night of Wallace's murder and that she saw one of the LAPD Officers suspected of participating in the killing at the museum the night before the shooting and the night of the shooting. When she saw the officer's face being broadcast on the evening news she contacted a relative for advice about coming forward and was warned that it was too dangerous. We have kept her confidential information to ourselves because LAPD cannot be trusted until those that leak information are purged from the department. We believe that three out of the four cops that met with us are good people that want to see the right thing done yet they allow the fourth to continue working in the department. Until the majority of honest, hardworking cops squeeze out those that are corrupt; Police Departments in America will continue to deserve their notorious reputations. We know that the LAPD of the 80's and 90's was far worse than it is now and progress has been made but don't get a false sense of security about where society is today. Too many innocent people suffer at the hands of those that swear an oath to protect and serve, and too many criminals are never brought to justice.

Evolving toward "the more perfect union." —Michael Douglas Carlin

PROLOGUE

Frank Alexander was ready to kill Suge Knight. I was there! Suge's words, "What'cha gonna do Frank, what'cha gonna do Frank?" were echoing through Alexander's mind. Those were words Suge used to ask Frank if he had the guts to take a human life. Back in the day, Frank had declined Suge's offer to begin a life of contract killing. That day this wouldn't have been contract killing but it would have been cold-blooded murder. Frank un-holstered his sidearm; his Concealed Carry Permit was current and he also had a backup firearm with a total of 18 rounds to carry through on his intention. Frank Alexander was no longer objective when it came to Marion "Suge" Knight. We were at the 2009 Magic Apparel Show in Las Vegas working for a clothing vendor. Word had spread that Knight was one row away in the exhibition hall, and was headed our way. Knight had no idea how close he came to being killed that day.

I am 100% convinced that Frank would have died in prison happy that Knight was no longer a threat to him, rather than spend one more day in fear. Knight escaped summary judgment that day by not turning down our aisle. But I think that fear was, in the end, what drove Frank to his death in 2013; he just wanted to be free from that constant worry. Frank had a lot to worry about, largely because the people who wanted to silence Frank had a lot to worry about themselves.

Frank now has nothing to worry about; I buried my friend in May of 2013.

But Frank left me an amazing charge; one born out of his desire to not let disinformation and mistruths sway public opinion. He charged me with always asking, always searching, always challenging the dogma that has for so long misguided the homicide he was witness to.

The story of Tupac's and Christopher Wallace's murders is one of the most suppressed crime stories in American history. It is almost axiomatic to say that historians may lie but history cannot. Starting with Russell Poole's groundbreaking work on the homicide(s) through Frank Alexander's heart and into the amazing words of Michael Doug-

las Carlin, this work is a formidable and meticulously researched expose about one of the most shocking crimes of the last century. In the
work of this book, over 15,000 pages of evidence were read. Over 30
witness and associated interviews (video and audio) were reviewed and
transcribed.

We lost many, many sleepless nights in the preparation of this
book; it will disturb and challenge the reader. It will thrill at times,
but probably astound and anger you in-between. Within these pages,
official lies are witheringly demolished and the stark truth, however
uncomfortable, begins to take shape. You see, this is not a conspiracy
theory, it is a conspiracy. The highest levels of the media are involved
and shown to be in league with the worst culprits in the LAPD who
buried and obstructed their own investigations.

This book is what you get when you combine the work of the
LAPD Detective that found justice for Bill Cosby's son and who broke
the infamous LAPD Rampart Scandal to the world, the journalist who
dared to follow the Mexican Federale that killed drug lord Pablo Acos-
ta and the award-winning filmmaker who produced the classic "Tupac:
Assassination" documentary? You get a whole new group of suspects,
motives that support a completely new understanding of the Tupac
Shakur and Christopher "Biggie Smalls" Wallace homicides ("187" of
the title is the California Penal Code section for Murder) that some in
the law enforcement community would rather you not know about.

In this last year Michael and I discovered that these two homicides have been cast aside by law enforcement in both Las Vegas and
Los Angeles, victims of police bureaucracy and cover up. The current
Wallace investigation in Los Angeles has been left to one man, whom
we have reason to believe the LAPD left to make sure it stayed buried.

Las Vegas Metropolitan Police may know who their man is, but
are themselves victims of the work of a media smear campaign machine
designed to invalidate their work and destroy the credibility of any
witness that might have come forward with compelling testimony on
the Shakur homicide. This same media machine was equally effective
against the witnesses in the Wallace homicide; even now agents for
those responsible are still trying to turn the credibility of key witnesses
into "unreliable" sources. What we saw was a literal graveyard of dead
witnesses and others either to scared or too influenced to step forward.

"Tupac 187: The Red Knight" goes back to the beginning of

the investigations—the original police files—and re-examines the people and evidence who have been previously corrupted or ignored. We decided to strip the Death Row Records disinformation machine of its fallacies, and re-paint the witness disparagement campaigns by the Los Angeles Times with the color of truth. When all is laid out raw and exposed under the book's harsh light, "187" clearly evidences the power of the media—both of 1996 and of today- to not only report news—but to make it. It is interesting, because Russell, Michael and I are all old enough to still remember a time before the internets' reach surpassed that of the LA Times.

I personally do not believe that the Shakur and Wallace cases would have remained unsolved had they been committed today. Everywhere we look, we find ways of double—checking the fact; as if our society has sadly resigned itself that no one can be trusted. Ironically, it was the public trust that was abused by a few select people who had the money and power to influence the media—and therefore the world. It was an influence that today would be fact-checked and challenged faster than the time it takes to arrive in your "in-box." In other words, the unwitting guardians of the truth—the SmokingGuns, the TMZ's, or Radar Online's may seem like tabloid outlets to many, but one can be sure that if bad information crosses their desk, they will have public counter right back out.

Tupac: "187" exposes leaks in the Los Angeles Police Department that may have fatally crippled the investigations in both cases; covert operations to collect up investigation notes and findings, key credible witness testimony hidden in detective's desk drawers, complaints of Los Angeles Police employees of their work literally disappearing from their computer files—along with their computers—it's all brought to light. Even in the last year, Russell Poole and I took new information to a meeting with four key L.A.P.D. brass, only to see the body of evidence leaked by one of those in the meeting, to end up on the Internet—risking lives and attempting to sabotage the new information.

And yes, there is new information. In the absence of any other forward moving investigation, we try to pick up the case where it was supposed to have gone before the witness tampering occurred, and identify new persons of interest, new motives and identify a simple group of suspects who were doing everything they could to cover up what was effectively a "heist job" gone terribly wrong—a cover up that in our opinion covers all relevant events up to and including the most recent attempted murder of former Death Row Records head Marion "Suge" Knight in 2014.

The ghosts of over twenty dead witnesses and participants haunt the pages of our book (and my mind.) Michael Moore, Frank Alexander and others I knew who have been lost gave to "Tupac: 187" a clear message: in spite of the best efforts of the saboteurs, key, and even new leads, information and credible witnesses still exist that can grant closure to both infamous homicides; if—and only if—the right people care enough to put these cases to rest. Those responsible have had a great laugh at the 18 year misdirection, and now that we can lay it out in "187", the "word on the street" is that no one is laughing anymore; I am now called a "snitch" and have had death threats from the camps who have an interest in protecting a secret. A secret worth killing for. And as long as the public was misguided, they were safe.

But my father taught me that the only way to get a rodent out of a hole in your yard is pour gasoline down the hole. Plug one hole if you want to see them run out the other end—plug both ends if you just don't want to see them again. We spent the last year plugging holes in the Tupac and Wallace investigations' back yards, and the vermin still want to stay underground.

So it's time to get out the gasoline.

This book may not be what you expect. You may be looking for the reasons that Shakur and Wallace were killed. We'll give you that. But what we want to do more than anything—and I believe it is our responsibility to do so—is to also tell you the reasons why no one has ever—or may ever—bring the case to justice.

We can stop the abuse of our trust in the "establishment" and the media. You can help. Or we can let Afeni Shakur's or Voletta Wallace's child be your (or my) child. I watched my son ride his bike without training wheels today; it will not be my child. What about yours?

I hope you enjoy the book! —RJ Bond

CAST OF CHARACTERS

DEATH ROW RECORDS

Marion "Suge" Knight, Owner: Death Row Records, Victim of Vegas Shooting 1996
Sharitha Knight, Suge's Estranged Wife, manager of Snoop Dogg and Kurupt–Knightlife Entertainment
David Elliot Kenner: Criminal Attorney, Business Partner of Knight
Norris Anderson: Suge's Brother, ran Death Row for period while Knight in Prison
Michel'le Toussaint: Death Row Artist and Mother of some of Knight's children
Tammy Hawkins: Mother of some of Knight's children
Jewell: Death Row Artist
George Pryce: Public Relations for Death Row, known as "Papa G"
Larry Condiff: Front Desk
Kevin Lewis: Can-Am Studio Manager
Nina B: Death Row Photographer

WRIGHT WAY SECURITY

Alexander, Frank
Archer, Kenneth
Atwell, Jerry
Ardwine, Lawrence
Barritt, John
Black, Marcus
Criner, Glenn
Coatney, Michael
Dallas, Jason
Edwards, Gerald
Ellison, Philip
Ferriri, Robert
Ford, Paul
Gauldin, Les
Glover, Monique
Hackie, Kevin

Hernandez, Richard
Hernandez, Manuel
Howard, JB
Johnson, Donnie
Johnson. Marcus
Jones, Brian
Kinsley, D.
Knox, Kendred
Lee, David
Love, David
Martinez, David
Mattox, Marvin
Miller, Solomon
McCauley, Richard
McMichael, Jerald
Moore, Michael
Nealy, Darrin
Nichols, Ernest
Real, James
Robbins, Derek
Rojas, Rene
Smith. Rodney
Storay, Cedric
Thompson, Marcus
Washington, Andre
Williams, Tim
Wright, Reginald Junior
Wysinger, Howard

DEATH ROW ARTISTS

Andre "Dr Dre" Young: Co-Founder of Death Row records, artist: "The Chronic" forced out by Knight,
Calvin "Snoop Dogg" Broadus: Artist "DoggyStyle," Founder of "Dogg Pound" Long Beach Crip Rep.
Tupac Shakur: Artist: All Eyez on Me, Makaveli. Killed in Las Vegas September 1996
Daz Dillinger

DEATH ROW ARTISTS (continued)

Daz Dillinger
Kurupt
Danny Boy
Nate Dogg
Mc Hammer
Mopreme Shakur: Tupac's Half Brother
Gina Longo: Only White Artist Signed To Drr And Daughter Of Assistant District Attorney Larry Longo

DEATH ROW ASSOCIATES

Jimmy Iovine: Co-Founder Of Interscope Records, Teamed With Andre Young To Form $3Bil "Beats"
Michael "Harry–O" Harris: Drug Kingpin And Initial Investor In Death Row, Rep'd By David Kenner
Lydia Harris: Wife Of Michael Harris
Oscar Goodman: Mob Attorney, Las Vegas Mayor
Dick Griffey: Owner Solar Records
George Kelesis: Criminal Attorney representing Marion Knight
The D.O.C.: Hip Hop Artist
David Chesnoff: Criminal Attorney, Marion Knight
Ted Fields: Owner Interscope Records
Mcpherson Law Firm: Attorneys Replacing Kenner
Amanda Metcalf: Attorney Representing Dick Griffey
Chuck Philips: Writer For Los Angeles Times

TUPAC "OUTLAWZ"

Mutah "Napolean" Beale
Yafeu "Kadafi" Fula
Katari "Kastro" Cox
Malcolm "Edi Mean" Greenidge
Bruce "Hussein Fatal" Washington
Tyruss "Big Syke" Himes

SHAKUR ASSOCIATES

Afeni Shakur: Shakur Mother, Sued Death Row after son's death for masters and royalties
Yaasmyn Fula: Shakur Office Manager and Aunt; fired David Kenner—Yafeu "Kadafi" Fula's mother
Gloria Cox: Shakur Foundation Founder and Aunt; friend of Frank Alexander and Katari Cox' mother
Tracy Robinson: Shakur's Business Manager and Friend
Leila Steinberg: Shakur's Manager (Pre Death Row)
Gobi Rahimi: Shakur's Videographer and Friend
Watani Tyehimba: Shakur's Attorney (Pre Death Row)
Atron Gregory: Shakur Manager (Pre Death Row)
Lena Sunday: Can-Am Artist and Friend
Greg "Shock G" Jacobs: Digital Underground Artist
Ben Ogletree: Shakur's Attorney (Pre Death Row)
Nzasi Malogna: Shakur's Tour Manager
Charles "Man-Man" Fuller: Road Manager, Friend

LOS ANGELES POLICE DEPARTMENT

Bernard Parks: LAPD Chief of Police
William Bratton: LAPD Chief of Police
Charlie Beck: LAPD Chief of Police
Kirk Albanese: LAPD Deputy Chief of Police
Russell Poole: LAPD Wallace Case
Fred Miller: LAPD Wallace Case
Steven Katz : LAPD Wallace Case
Sgt. Ya May Christle: LAPD Wallace Case
P-III Kenneth Knox: Death Row Surveillance

COMPTON POLICE DEPARTMENT

Hourie Taylor: Chief of Police
Reginald Wright Senior: Lieutenant Gang Unit
Tim Brennan:
Robert "Bobby" Ladd:
Sgt. Kenneth Roller: CPD internal Affairs
Sgt Frederick Reynolds: CPD internal Affairs
Jerry Patterson:
Captain Steven Roller

OTHER LAW ENFORCEMENT
Lawrence Longo: Assistant District Attorney
Timothy Searight: US Attorney Office

LAS VEGAS METRO POLICE DEPARTMENT
Kevin Manning
Brent Becker
Mike Franks

DEATH ROW GANG MEMBERS
Buntry
Neckbone
Herron
Poochie
Travon
K-Dub
Danny Patton
Malcom Patton

OTHER GANG MEMBERS
Duane Keith "Keefe-D" Davis
Orlando Anderson
Darnell Brim

PART ONE:

THE MURDER

Life for Tupac Amaru Shakur had not always been one of wine and pearls. He had it hard like so many other inner city youths. However, a manager named Leila Steinberg—who has garnered a solid reputation for working with artistic inner city youth—saw something unique in Shakur while he lived in Marin City, a section of Northern California near Oakland.

"We had this place called the 'Top Ramen Shack,'" remembered Larry Spellman, a backup dancer that was close to Shakur in those early years.

"This was the most 'ghetto fabulous' little spot that you could possibly ever be in. We had all these cabinets with no food.

"You know what Top Ramen noodles are? That's why they called it a 'Top Ramen Shack.' The 'Top Ramen Shack,' it just basically had noodles. Everybody ate noodles. If you didn't have a bowl, you took your powder and put it in your bag and shook up the bag and ate the noodles right there. Nobody had no food in there... the refrigerator maybe had a couple of 40's, Kool-Aid... maybe.

"Playing dominoes was the thing, that was like, playing bones was the thing. I don't remember him (Tupac) being real good at bones and so we used to go at it for hours.

"While everybody was playing bones, he would be writing. You know, he always had his little notebook and writing and writing and writing and then he'd throw it away. I look back now and I say, 'Man, I wish I had kept some of those things he threw in the garbage,' because he would throw away so many songs.

"Well, Tupac and all of us got kicked out of the 'Top Ramen Shack.' Eventually, we got kicked out of 'Top Ramen Shack' because we got raided! Leila said 'come and stay.' She already had five kids. So you're talking about five kids and five grown men or more sleeping with—all we can sleep was on her living room floor.

"Those who remember back in the day remember this with Pac they will know, we all slept on the floor. You just had to get your spot on the floor. But at least we had a spot. When it was raining, when it was cold—and it got cold in the Bay—we had a spot."

Leila Steinberg confirmed Spellman's thoughts: "I can't remember how many people who lived with us. People will remind me they stayed with me, at one point or another. That's part of me; I will always be a mother to many."

"We had a mutual manager, a lady named Leila Steinberg," said

Spellman. "Leila had contacts all over the Bay Area. It didn't matter East Bay, North Bay, South Bay, she just had connections."

"They formed a group, and I would drive them to Oakland every day," echoed Steinberg, "and I would drive the guys in Shock's group to the studio a lot, but they were working on their album, and I was trying to help Pac and Ray with their group record, and I was probably the only one with a car and a legit license plate at the time, so I would like chauffeur, the person who did all the hands-on work!"

Tracy Robinson, who was Tupac's video producer and future business partner remembers, "Tupac introduced us and he was like, 'You've got to meet Leila! You guys have to work together.' She was managing him when we did the Mac Mall video, which is probably one of my most favorite videos. It was this video where we had to have them be old men playing dominoes on the porch."

"I was a young mother with my own artist's dreams," remembers Steinberg "and I met someone who was not afraid to scream out and let everybody know who he was, what he was going through and what he wanted to effect.

"From the moment that I met Tupac at the age of 17, he was one of the most startling individuals I've ever met. He was and still is just one of the most amazing voices. I loved Pac instantly."

To Steinberg Tupac was not the Death Row type. "Tupac knew absence," she said. "He knew affection. He had a mother who planted amazing seeds in him, who loved him dearly. He kind of appointed me. I always felt like I'll do what I can to help them and I love them soul and mentally but I wasn't really interested in managing."

According to her interview done with Atron Gregory, Steinberg admitted that ultimately she had a choice between managing Tupac and managing Ray Luv and she and Gregory decided that Tupac was too much work for her. She asked Atron to manage Tupac and she managed Ray Luv.

Tupac lived on the periphery of the Gang community, not unlike Marion "Suge" Knight whom he would meet later in his life. However the key difference between Tupac and Knight is that a) Tupac did not grow up surrounded by "street gangs," and b) Tupac never claimed, in his entire life, a "gang affiliation."

"He knew gangsters, what they would perceive as gangsters; tougher guys then a Suge," said Gloria Cox, Tupac's aunt.

"He just didn't know 'gangstas'—those 'gang' people. But the people in the Black Panther party that did 99 years was also some tough asses and they schooled him on revolutionary tactics and how you do this, etc. After a while, he didn't want to hear that no more because he would tell them, 'Mama now take off your Kenta cloth.' He wasn't a nationalist like that. Do you understand?"

Tracy Robinson added to the depth of Shakur: "He was on a mission, I think even when I met him back in '93 he was on a mission. He meant what he said. It was not a shallow conversation.

"I met him on a video set. The first time I met him I think he was doing 'I Get Around' or something. It was being shot at one of my friend's house. The guy was like shining.

"You've got this energy that God has given you and people recognize it, good people and bad people, and they pounce on your energy. They pounce on your history that helps make you who you are and they want to smother your fire."

While Tupac Shakur had many problems legally and socially (always looking for a home) he had a "larger than life" personality that more than compensated for it, according to friend Ray Luv. To Luv, that was where Tupac, when things did not go well for him, expressed it outwardly and loudly. But his feelings and loyalties ran deep into his family roots.

"He couldn't stay hidden," said his Aunt Glo.

"How could he? You know what I mean? He was not that person. He spoke his mind to his credit and to his detriment. He said what he felt and sometimes those feelings were "hmmph" and sometimes those were 'Oh, my lord.' But they were his feelings and they were true."

"He would call his mom up with nonsense pretty much. You know sometimes, 'Guess who I went out with? Guess who I did it to?' You know and she didn't want to hear about it—but I did.

"We were out there one time to Vegas and we go into his room and he got the big room with the bathtub in it and we are duly impressed. He's walking around with his little mink slippers on and everything and telling us stop begging people for money because we're in the casino. We had never really gambled before and somehow or another he heard about it.

"So we sit down like this, get chastised—again—and then he says that some woman had called him that was talking to him. I kind of chaffed at him. He looks at me because now he got to prove to me, his auntie—who I tell you, he was the apple of my eye and he knew it—that he's a man.

"Now he's telling me that he went out with this older woman and I said 'Oh, really?' to this he says 'Yes. She's almost as old as you!' I said 'what!? Really?'

I played along, 'Okay, little cute thing, so ain't he cute?'

"He was laughing, but that was to put me in my place; to let me know that now he's grown and I can't tell him, 'You can't tell me what to do now. You can't be giving me all this advice. I don't want to hear it.' But it was cute.

"Then of course, when we go back to the moment at hand: could we have some money so we could go back to the casino?'"

AUGUST 27—SEPTEMBER 3, 1996:
LOS ANGELES CALIFORNIA

By August of 1996, Tupac Shakur was at the top of his recording game: worries about lodging and food long behind him. He was out on bail from prison by this time and had signed with a new and promising record label—Death Row Records. He had already sold in excess of thirty million (30,000,000) copies of his earlier efforts, whose successes went supernova while Shakur cooled his jets in prison. There were royalties stocked up and Tupac, being from meager means, had not worried about the money—he believed it was waiting for him.

With that in mind, it was Shakur's burning desire to make sure he had enough tracks laid down and recorded so that if he did end up going back to prison, he would still be a money earner for his family.

But Shakur had made it clear to his staff, and they knew, that Shakur did not intend on being a long-term money-earner for Death Row. Knight had a signed contract with Tupac for three albums. Knight had nothing to hold over Tupac's head and Knight knew that at one point Tupac's lack of allegiance to Death Row would become a public affair.

And even though Tupac may have wanted nothing to do with Death Row in any way shape or form, he was smarter than to broadcast this feeling publicly. A woman named C. Delores Tucker was a perfect example of what happened when one attempted to speak negatively against Death Row.

Many people who know the Tupac/Death Row story know about C. Delores Tucker. To the uninitiated, during the early 1990s, Mrs. Tucker became troubled by the growing popularity of "gangsta rap." Of particular concern to Mrs. Tucker was the genre's influence on African-American youth, who she feared would adopt the music's violent and sometimes misogynist perspectives.

At the National People of Color's biennial meeting in 1993, Mrs. Tucker enlisted the help of well-known artists Dionne Warwick, Melba Moore, and Terri Rossi, along with lobbyist Voncier Alexander, to form an Entertainment Commission that would support African-American entertainers, and in particular, women. The Entertainment Commission adopted a mission in part to put pressure on music producers and distributors to halt the sale of gangsta rap to minors.

Among Mrs. Tucker's more high-profile efforts in pursuit of this goal was an appearance at a 1995 Time Warner shareholder's meeting, where she offered Time Warner executives $100 to read aloud gangsta rap lyrics from albums distributed under its name, and a protest against the sale of gangsta rap albums outside a Tower Records store, for which she was arrested. She was publicly "dissed" by Shakur for her beliefs and efforts.

What many people do not know is that on August 15, 1995, Interscope filed a complaint, "Interscope v. Tucker," in the United States District Court for the Central District of California, charging Mrs. Tucker with inducement to breach contract; interference with contractual relations and prospective business advantage; attempting to induce breach of fiduciary duty; unfair business practices; and unfair competition. Interscope sought an injunction enjoining Mrs. Tucker from interfering with the Death Row contract.

Moreover, Death Row filed its own lawsuit. On August 17, 1995, Death Row filed a complaint, "Death Row v. Tucker," in the United States District Court for the Central District of California. The complaint charged all defendants with racketeering and/or aiding and abetting racketeering under 18 U.S.C. 1962(b) and (c); conspiring to violate 1962(b) and (c); conspiring to interfere with advantageous business relationships; extortion; unfair business practices; and abuse of process. The complaint also sought to enjoin all defendants from engaging in extortion, interfering with Death Row's First Amendment rights, and "any other unlawful act alleged in this complaint." Attorney David Kenner, business partner of Knight, was listed as counsel for

Death Row.

Death Row and Interscope took the matter of public disparagement and their rights very seriously; slander and business interference are big legal theories and recorded slander is pretty compelling. Tupac's announcement that he was leaving Death Row might arguably affect Death Row "stock" in a negative way. It could also hurt record sales.

One understated negative affect this kind of publicity brings, is that it can adversely affect the ability to borrow or leverage (mortgage) the master tapes of the artists, which was clearly what Death Row was doing at the time. Recent court documents from artists who have sued Death Row in the last few years speak of the trend that Death Row was holding on to master tapes and mortgaging them; both the documented loans and the statements of Death Row artists show this pattern as fact.

In short, if a lender doubted the commercial profit potential from an artist, then the value of the collateral Master Tapes would decrease. The lender would realize that with that kind of negative "noise" the likelihood of recoupment on the investment might be a risk they did not want to take.

Of course, unaware of the these concerns, on or about August 27, 1996 Tupac visited his frequent recording studio and remote Death Row headquarters, Can-Am Studios, to pick up some of his master tapes. He was refused access to them by security guards from Wright Way Security who worked the door at the studio.

Tupac contacted many people about accessing them but was turned away. Tupac was concerned about his denial of access; there were approximately 200 songs stored on those master tapes; some were complete and some were rough but all of it, the sum of the work, he had done since his release from prison. It was becoming a library that could be used to sell while Tupac turned his attention to producing and acting in motion pictures. And Tupac knew what he needed if he were to breakaway.

"He sent us to the studio to get cassettes of what he'd done the night before—he wanted to listen to it" said Gloria Cox.

"I got a call from Al Giddens" (another security staffer for Death Row) said Frank Alexander.

"I was at home, I live in Orange County, and Al Giddens says to me, 'Hey, you need to get to the studio because Pac has been trying to take masters out of the studio and Suge has told us that no one is to take masters from the studio anymore.'

"He called me specifically knowing that I was Pac's bodyguard and said, 'Hey, you need to get down here, you need to talk to him, you need to calm him down, he's CUSSIN' he's going off, he's going crazy.'"

Yaasmyn Fula agreed, stating that "Pac went crazy" when he could not get his master tapes.

Gloria Cox, interviewed later, was in LA during this time. "It just was going to be ugly because we had already heard on the phone, driving around in LA, a call, Tupac is at Death Row pissed off. He wants his shit.

"If he was there, it was confrontational—he was going to get whatever what he was going to get, if he was asking for his masters, asking for the paper that he signed because he did those three albums. It didn't take him long. So that's the completion of that obligation, as I know it. You know, the three albums. I tell you, he had movie scripts and he was truly interested in that. People were talking to him about it."

But there was no way that Death Row was letting him have the masters. It was simply a matter of too much exposure—from the potential controversy on who really owned the copyright and more so, the fact that Tupac would then know he was being used. And the truth was that Tupac's account had been charged studio time for the creation of those songs; so there was arguably a clear chain of title to the songs that were over and above the songs he had promised to deliver in his Dannemora Contract. Unfortunately, that distinction would never be proven in his lifetime. Had he lived long enough, Shakur would have tried to release those masters and he would have realized that he would not have been able to "clear" his own title as the compositions and the physical rights to his work had been mortgaged and were "tied up." Of course this understanding, should it have happened, might have been trouble for Death Row Records.

Tupac, as angry as he was, even then, did not disparage Death Row. And even if Tupac was right and publicly put Death Row's antics out in the public forum, he is still going to face the risk of litigation costs, should Death Row treat him like Tucker. Remember that the truth is a great DEFENSE and for a defense to be heard it takes a lot of money.

To wit, here are some "Hollywood" lawsuits; certainly if these lawsuits moved through the courts it wouldn't be hard for Death Row Records to make a claim against Tupac that he hurt their record sales:

- David Schwimmer sued former Hollywood fund-raiser Aar on Tonken alleging that Tonken told the National Enquirer that two Rolex watches were required by Schwimmer in or der to attend the charity dinner;
- Sharon Stone sued plastic surgeon Renato Calabria alleging that he falsely told reporters that she had undergone a face lift;
- Cameron Diaz sued The British Sun over a story that implied Diaz was having an affair with a married man;
- Nelson Mandela sued a former associate in order to protect his name and a number of original paintings that he had signed alleging forgery by his former associate;
- Famed British couple, David and Victoria Beckham, sued their former nanny for telling the tabloids that their marriage is in trouble;
- Charlie Sheen, star of "Two and a Half Men" was sued by a woman who is claiming that the wacky, stalker lady next door is modeled after her;
- Jane Pauley sued the New York Times for invasion of privacy in divulging her struggle with bipolar disorder.

In Los Angeles, implication alone is enough to get one sued. Maybe Tupac had learned this from all the legal troubles he was having. There is no conflict reconciling that Tupac was leaving Death Row yet saying nice things about them. It's just good business to speak nicely about someone you wish to amicably divorce. Tupac also knew that Death Row had a reputation for violence against those exiting.

Yaasmyn Fula stated that it made sense to keep things "civil"; Tupac would want or need, at some point, to leverage resources or art-ists from Death Row in some capacity. And it is prudent for Shakur to avoid becoming adversarial with his record label when they were hold-ing his money.

That is not to say that Tupac necessarily knew when to be quiet. But at that time, and leading up to the September 4, 1996 MTV Music Award Show in New York, there was no public beef with Death Row, just a personal dissatisfaction about accounting and access to his master tapes; issues that Shakur hoped to get straight with Knight when he returned from his trip out of the U.S.

Tupac knew that hype sold records and he wanted to make

money. He hyped Death Row because it sold records. Tupac did an advertisement for St. Ides lager right around that time because it made him money. Was Tupac's favorite beverage St Ides? Many close to him doubt it. And that's the point: you advertise so that you make money.

To his end, Knight was happy to keep that unified appearance. He even publicly commented, "I loved Pac then, I love Pac now, he loved me, that's my little homie and it's always going to be that way you know, and it's never going to change."

But remember, Tupac was only beginning to understand the depth of the theft happening to him. And it would have been equally foolish to say negative things unless he knew exactly what was going on.

Meanwhile, Marion "Suge" Knight's legal trouble for assault with a concealed weapon was ongoing. He was in a position to persuade the Stanley brothers with an enticing record deal in order for them to support his request for a suspended sentence. Lynwood and George Stanley were given $1 million recording contracts. Larry Longo, the Los Angeles District Attorney prosecutor on the case recommended probation for Knight. The net result: Marion Knight "got off" with five-years probation after a one-month stay in a halfway house.

Knight was also trying to disavow himself from the partnership of incarcerated cocaine kingpin, Michael "Harry-O" Harris. Not so easy given that his new business partner, David Kenner, had previously been Harris' attorney. They conspired to cheat Mr. and Mrs. Harris out of their rightful share of the most profitable rap label in music history, Knight would eventually close the door on them, provoking a multi-million dollar lawsuit from Lydia Harris for Harris' share. Around this time, "Harry-O" was transferred from Lancaster State Prison to a downtown L.A. Detention Centre. This placed Harris much closer to the action and the "heat" that Knight's hubris was creating.

Disruption in the drug trade, and excessive and unwanted attention did not bode well with any of the gangs; many of whom were distribution conduits for the very products men like Harris put out. If Knight was distancing himself from Harris, might this have affected the flow of drugs on the street?

Obviously, Knight was burning bridges. Without direct "protection" from the gangs (a rather loose affiliation via his friends), Knight was exposed. And Harris would need to find an alternate means to protect his drug trafficking—with little attention and insurance against what is known in business as "shrink"; product loss due to external factors, like police actions—which was a sure outcome of the harsh light Knight was bringing to bear on the trade.

Whether or not he knew it, or would ever allow himself to admit it, Knight was in trouble. Knight should have seen that his course of action could only have a bad outcome; his dirty dealings with Tupac would cost him Death Row. Knight was known to be estranged from his wife, Sharitha Knight, which by that time had become more of a marriage of convenience and had also reduced itself to public arguments over money. An angry wife, law enforcement shining the harsh light on Knight's thug image and gang affiliations; and now Knight was making moves to stiff and evade a major drug "King Pin" who used the very gangs Knight associated with as distributors!

Clearly, the house of cards was built, but who was going to knock it over? Tupac? Harris? John-Q-Law? The only thing Knight could control was Tupac; he didn't seem to acknowledge or fear the rest. He should have.

Consider the case of "Bugsy" Siegel. Opening night in the launch of Las Vegas, everything that could have gone wrong did. Bad weather forced most of the stars to remain at home; many of the rooms were unfinished, forcing guests to spend the night elsewhere. Worse still, the casino lost money, and within its first month of opening, the Flamingo closed.

After Meyer Lansky pleaded with irate Syndicate leaders to give his friend a second chance, he was given a few months to fix the Flamingo and begin generating profits.

And, after borrowing more money from fellow mobsters and making renovations, the Flamingo reopened in March 1947. By the end of its first month back in business, the hotel was finally turning a profit. But it was too late for Siegel. His body, riddled with bullets, lay on the floor of his girlfriend's apartment.

Minutes after Siegel died, Syndicate leaders took over the management of the Flamingo. The eventual success of the hotel spurred the development of the Strip and cemented the Syndicate's increased investment into Las Vegas.

Why was Siegel killed? He was foolish with other people' money.

Knight had to take some responsibility for a lot of the foolishness that he brought upon himself. When Knight started running

Death Row like a gang instead of a label, artists started to feel uncomfortable and started to either leave (Dr. Dre) or refuse to sign (Fredro Starr). The 2006 Bankruptcy Court Trustee made the condition at the time vivid:

"The representation… in this Case has been particularly complex due to the individuals involved in the company's operations and intentionally illicit, 'gangster-styled' business operations of the Debtor.

"Knight asserted sole ownership of Death Row, and exercised muscular, exclusive control over the Debtor's operations. Knight was notorious for his business practices, including alleged physical assault of competitors, contempt for contractual obligations and legal proceedings, and failure to pay corporate and personal taxes.

"Recordkeeping was lax to non-existent. Contractual agreements, whether they were with artists, producers; or distributors were frequently not memorialized, signed; or otherwise adequately documented. As Knight's financial problems grew, he often took moneys from multiple parties for ostensible grants of the same rights in digital or other forms of distribution of Death Row compositions and recordings."

In other words, Knight used a lot of that intimidation to screw artists out of their publishing and keep their masters. They would be afraid to negotiate with him out of fear of either being killed or beaten up.

It was clear by August of 1996 that Knight was a liability and he had to go. He'd brought the wrong kind of attention to the mob, the gangs, the music labels, Harry-O, himself, his spouse, and partners, in one of the most crooked and dishonest businesses in the music industry.

For his part, the head of Death Row Security, Reggie Wright Junior had stood steadfastly beside Knight. But Wright Junior always thought of himself as better able to run the label than Knight.

Moreover, those like Sharitha, were tired of Knight bullying the likes of her boyfriend, Los Angeles Police Officer Kevin Gaines, while Knight ran, according to insiders within Death Row, a virtual harem; many of whom Knight would go on to have children with.
Everyone was done with him!

But how practical was this plan? The question became who would operate the label in the absence of Knight? Could Sharitha Knight actually run the label with help from Reggie Wright Junior?

Could Wright Junior arrange a coup d'état to take over the record label and kill Knight? As investigators would learn later, that was clearly the case and Wright Junior was more than suited for the job.

"It would have been easy for her to take over," said Simone Green former Death Row photographer and friend of Sharitha. "But I don't think she had the experience to that was necessary to keep a multi-million dollar record company running like that. I think he gave her Knightlife Entertainment to give her some experience. She was young, you know."

And Knight had been grooming Sharitha by setting her up with Knightlife Entertainment, which was the management "entity" for Death Row artists. If you were an artist signed to Death Row, you were generally, managed by Knightlife. Neither Knight, nor the artists and investigators to come years later, would actually understand how well, in fact, Sharitha had learned.

"She was a bitch with a dick," said Death Row Dave.

SEPTEMBER 4TH AND 5TH, 1996:
NEW YORK CITY

Michael Moore was one of almost forty (40), security personnel hired by Wright Junior to work contract security under his firm Wright Way security. He was assigned the personal protection detail for Tupac Shakur for his trip to New York at the MTV Music Awards show.

Moore was witness to a series of events that occurred prior to the awards show and later that evening, starting with a series of comments from Calvin Broadus aka "Snoop Dogg," regarding the much-ballyhooed "East Coast Rappers vs. West Coast Rappers" rivalry. Knight remembered, in an interview with Source Magazine, that Snoop Dogg had alleged that Shakur was not into the "East Coast-West Coast bullshit" and that Snoop Dogg would "gladly record" with Sean "Puffy" Combs, a prominent east coast rapper at the time, or with his protégé and rising rap star Christopher "Biggie Smalls" Wallace. He just did not believe that East Coast animosity was there.

Broadus later confirmed that he was doing a radio show interview with Angie Martinez. He was asked point blank how he "felt" about Combs and Wallace. Broadus states that he said what he felt and what he felt was that Combs and Wallace were his "homeboys" and that "he loved them."

Knight told Source Magazine, and Moore confirmed, that Shakur "went crazy" when he heard that interview. "He was like," Knight said speaking for Tupac, "'I'm covering this Muthafucka's back when he was out there promoting that video for "New York, New York." Muthafucka's shot up the trailer. They was cryin.' I went and smashed for them. I'm doing all this good, and here he is speakin' about hookin' up with my enemies? Me and him gotta get down.'"

Years later, Knight claimed that Tupac told him that Shakur had actually taken the time to write a whole new version of his Combs/Wallace bashing and Billboard Chart juggernaut "Hit 'Em Up." Only this time the song was bashing Snoop instead.

Of course, there is no proof that such a track exists. Other than a video shoot, none of the bodyguards interviewed made a claim that Shakur was in the studio at all on the 5th or 6th of September 1996. Tupac was healthy for only 2-3 days more, so there just wasn't a lot of time to go back to the studio.

Still Knight conveniently tied it up and put a bow around his claim by telling Source that he had never released that obviously uber-lucrative track to the public because he thought the only reason Tupac wrote or recorded the song (Knight was not clear) was because Tupac was angry and that he was simply "venting." That, says Knight is the reason he had "no intention" of releasing the song. The entire claim seems dubious as that would be the Tupac fans' most oft "wished for" track, because of that very significance.

"After the MTV Music Awards, prior to us going home," said Moore, "there was an altercation about what Snoop had done, Mr. Knight was very upset, and they got to yelling at each other back and forth.

"They confronted each other basically face to face and this is the first time I'd ever heard of Makaveli before it even came out to be a CD record. Tupac stated he was going to give Knight all the rights to Makaveli; he just wants his freedom and he wants off Death Row.

"I was in a limo, me and Tupac, we were driving around in Harlem and the radio came on was Snoop Dogg saying that he had no beat with New York, which sent Pac into a rage. We immediately spun the limo around and we went back to the hotel to confront Snoop. We couldn't find them but we found Mr. Knight.

"Tupac was displeased about what had happened. Mr. Knight was very upset and they got to yelling each other back and forth, they confronted each other basically to a 'face-to-face.' I did slide in between them and said, 'Hey, we can't do this while I'm here.'"

At this point, Moore opens the door to the internal workings at Death Row. "Normally," Moore adds, "I'm asked in every situation that I can remember while working with Death Row when there was altercations, fights, or some type of discipline was going to be passed out doing Death Row, I'm usually asked to step outside the room. But on this occasion, I think Mr. Knight had me stay for the safety of Tupac.

"I've been asked; the reason I was there (was) because, I think, Mr. Knight, with me not being there, he would have put his hands on him (Tupac). He was that upset!

Pac's words were, 'I'm going to cut out Makaveli and when I cut out Makaveli, I'm the hell up out of here. You got your money, I don't want nothing else to do with Death Row—I'm out.' And, that's how we left that day."

So in testimony unrefuted to this day the proverbial "cat was out of the bag" about Tupac no longer desiring to do business with Death Row. But to what degree this disinterest held was unknown. Of course Shakur was upset and wanted to get away but Knight had no idea how much Tupac knew about the issues he would have with Death Row when and if a separation were to occur.

But Tupac was furious. Moore adds, "He was screaming Makaveli at the top of his lungs!"

As history and videotape show, Shakur and Knight did go on to attend the MTV awards show that night. Tupac did several interviews; one with Snoop, who clearly held himself as someone who would have rather been ten other places than right there—right then in the studio with Shakur, and another interview in one of the hastily made and clearly never worn "Death Row East" T-Shirts given to him. And, as a good employee might, Tupac animatedly talks about Death Row East and what that "chapter" of Death Row may contribute to the rap industry.

This "promotion" was thrown together to take advantage of the media attention that the MTV Awards drew naturally. It also might have looked like a contradiction; Tupac was so enraged about what

Snoop Dogg had told the radio about his willingness to work with the East, but then later actually promoted a start-up label that would work with East Coast talent.

But there was no contradiction to Knight; this was a business move made to smear the names of the East Coast "giants" Combs and Wallace, and start to steal talent from them. And with his usual zeal and gusto, Shakur promoted it. But when remembering this the haunting voice of Shakur's friend Ray Luv stirs in the background; Tupac used his outward projection often to mask his inner pain.

Wright Way Security guard Kenneth Archer, assigned to protect Shakur and Snoop Dogg in New York, suggested that privately, Tupac's frame of mind after that event was not encouraging; a clear sign that Ray Luv may have been true in his observations. Whatever the case, Shakur's inner discouragement and frustration guided his next decision about his travels; he was going to stand down from running around with Knight and Death Row, for the immediate future.

"The time in New York," said Archer, "I think we just finished doing the MTV, and he had to come back to LA, I think, to do a video and he didn't want to go because he was like uneasy about going and he said he didn't want to go."

"He had told us," added Michael Moore, who was also there, "that he was not going there with his words—'them sell–out niggas.'"

Frank Alexander, in the 2002-taped interview he did with Archer, stated it more directly. Alexander alleged that Archer quoted Shakur's last words before getting on the airplane.

"I'm a dead man walking!"

While Archer began to "waffle" on his accounting of Shakur's comment, the tape shows that it was clearly uncomfortable for Archer to be directly confronted on camera about this matter. The bewildered and betrayed look on Alexander's face at that moment, staring at Archer in disbelief, said it all.

Archer was showing signs of an illness that would taint the investigation of the events of that evening years later; an illness that erased memory and often created impossible, fantastic new memories in their place. This illness would later be referred by Los Angeles County Assistant District Attorney, Patrick Frey in his web moniker "Patterico" as the Death Row Derangement Syndrome.

SEPTEMBER 5, 1996:
BETWEEN NEW YORK AND LOS ANGELES

The plane ride to Los Angeles must have been very interesting. In a 2013 Satellite radio interview, Broadus confirmed Knight's and Michael Moore's claims; claims that Wright Junior later challenged publicly in a 2007 attempt to smear Moore's credibility. More importantly, Broadus continued Archer's story about the trip from New York to Los Angeles—a particularly long flight back.

According to Broadus, Shakur thought that Snoop was a traitor for siding with Combs and Wallace with whom Tupac was, at least lyrically, having a dispute. Broadus claims that after that interview Tupac treated him differently, even to the point of Shakur sending a delagate to Broadus to get pot, instead of the normal course of business wherein Shakur and Broadus would directly interact.

"So I felt funny," Broadus stated.

Broadus goes on with the story; when he was about to board the plane from New York to Los Angeles, Knight gave orders to have Broadus security detail stripped from him. Because the detail worked for Wright Way, Wright Junior removed Broadus' security detail, to the point of even refusing to let them ride on the private jet.

The message was clear (and something investigators would see as a pattern of behavior later); when you were on the wrong side of Knight, the first thing he did was hobble your personal protection. And with his strong-arm bodyguard, Wright Junior, Knight could do exactly that.

This was the last time Broadus relied on Wright Way to influence his complete personal protection detail. Broadus actually did what Knight made a practice of doing—surrounding himself with gang members he trusted.

Meanwhile, Broadus is having no fun on the plane as Shakur is still steaming from the Martinez interview and Shakur's subsequent fight with Knight. Broadus stated that that the only occupants of the private plane were himself, Tupac, Knight and Knight's entourage.

"It was the most uncomfortable flight I had been on in my life," Broadus recalls; Shakur said nothing to him the entire five-hour flight. Apparently the tension on the flight was so bad, that at one point, Broadus actually feared for his life.

"I walk up to him," said Broadus, "maybe three hours into the flight, sit next to him like, 'You goin' to Vegas, cuz?' He turns [away from me], starts talkin' to somebody else.

"I'm like, 'alright', I go in the back, put the blanket on my head, knife in my hand, fork in my hand, and just sleep the rest of the ride, because I feel like they finna [fixing to] try to do something."

One question that Broadus tried to ask Shakur seemed to be about an impending trip. "I'm like," Broadus asked, "'Cuz, you goin' to Vegas?' He do me like" and gave a dismissive gesture.

It wasn't all about Snoop Dogg at that point. Knight was not one to break surprise news to. He hated surprises. Tupac knew that. Simone Green made that very clear in her book "Time Served." According to Green, Knight was okay with honesty in the negative (a.k.a. bad news) so long as it did not come as a surprise to him. A surprise piece of bad news was as bad as it got for Knight and he would react accordingly. One need not imagine the reaction to Tupac's announcement that night of bad news—and a surprise.

It is hard to understand why many are skeptical to believe that Shakur was not completely jettisoning Death Row. David Kenner was Death Row—every bit as much as Knight was. The ink was still wet on the notice, to David Kenner terminating Kenner's representation of Shakur, when Shakur made his announcement to Knight. There is a copy of an identical termination notice to Wright Way making rounds in the fan community, but it looks like a forgery. Surely Shakur would have said something in Vegas about it; he never did and that is all the proof needed to write it off.

However, the "declaration of independence" in the New York hotel room along with confirmation of the termination of Kenner, spoke volumes of not only Shakur leaving Knight's empire, but that Shakur's move was a premeditated move at that. Perhaps that was what was really hanging in Knight's mind like a dark cloud, over the entire flight.

To his part, Shakur made some other telltale comments that may indicate his frame of mind, not only generally, but in light of his recent actions; "Believe in yourself," he said, "and don't let nobody stop you from doing what you gotta do."

SEPTEMBER 6, 1996:
LOS ANGELES; AVERSION TO VISIT VEGAS

Frank Alexander and Michael Moore had gone ahead and arrived in Las Vegas the day before Shakur was supposed to have arrived. However, to most of the inner circle close to Shakur, his arrival in Vegas was not "a sure bet." In fact, so convincing was the belief that Shakur had other things to do, that Michael Moore was startled by Shakur's actual appearance.

"He did not want to go to Vegas," said Moore, "as a matter of fact, he fought off going to Vegas all the way to the last second and when I got there, I was surprised to see him there."

Tupac was already making excuses for not going on the upcoming September 7, 1996 trip to Vegas. According to later interviews with Wright Junior and George "Papa G" Pryce, Death Row's publicist, Death Row had already spent an inordinate about of time and money advertising Shakur's appearance at Club 662 later that evening; the event was to be a fundraiser for a retired Las Vegas policeman's boxing club—Barry's Boxing.

This new hesitance on the part of Shakur was disturbing on more than one level. Plans were made far enough in advance to the point where Wright Junior knew everyone's locations for the entire weekend, which he would convey to others. The only factor no one had planned on, was that Shakur was "just not feeling it." As investigators would learn later, this created a snag in more than one plan.

Tupac's excuses for not going to Las Vegas were pretty flimsy, but had an air of legitimacy about them. Kenneth Archer, the Wright Way bodyguard from the New York trip just a day earlier, cleared the air about Tupac's overall recurring feelings; feelings Archer attributed to the conversation Michael Moore claimed Knight had with Shakur.

"After we did the MTV Awards," offered Archer, "I don't know what went down but he wasn't too happy about it. He didn't care about going anywhere. So he didn't want to go to Vegas. I don't even think he wanted to do the video."

The flimsy excuse Tupac had established came through his aunt Gloria Cox's recollections.

"Pac's cousin," said Cox, "my son Kenny (Lesane); he was on drugs. He had taken one of Pac's rifles, and Pac heard about it. And he didn't want to go to Vegas."

"The most important story is the fact that right before he passed away, September 6th (he got shot on Sept 7th) he had left a message on my answering machine" revealed Kendrick "Kenny" Lesane, in an interview July 15, 2013.

"He found out I had pawned his AK-47. He had left it in my aunt's closet in Georgia, and I was snooping around, and I found it and I pawned it to my best friend. And when the family found out it was missing, I denied it. But then my heart couldn't take it. So my heart had to tell the truth.

"So my heart came to the family and said 'look, I was the one who stole the gun, I'm sorry I'm a dope fiend and I need your help.' I got checked into a program but I gotta wait 'cause there's a long waiting line. My family was understanding, you know? And they told me they wasn't going to tell Pac, they was like 'look we ain't gonna tell Pac, but you gotta get the gun back and you gotta make the shit right. So, I'm like 'okay, no problem.'

"So I called the dude; he wasn't willing to send the gun back because he'd already drove it back to Detroit. But the next day Pac went to the fight. Pac really wanted to come to Atlanta to deal with me. I was the one who when you look at any interview, from like the bodyguards that were with Pac that night he got shot, they all tell you that Pac was itching to go to Georgia for some reason. They didn't know, but I was the reason he was itching to go to Georgia. He was tired of people smoking crack and stealing his shit."

Kendrick's mother Gloria Cox, summed it all up nicely; "So he didn't want to go to Vegas but this was a good reason for him not to go because he was going to come out here, kick his cousin's ass."

She also stated that Tupac had another reason for leaving the Death Row "life"; he was spending most of the time not on the video shoot at home with Kidada Jones. "He was with Kidada" said Cox. "He had a thing going on. He had a fantasy that he wanted. He wanted to get married. He wanted to have kids."

According to Cox, there wasn't truly an urgency to come to Atlanta to "beat his cousin's butt" or to go to Vegas.

"That was a smokescreen," said Cox, "he could fly to Atlanta and kick his cousin's butt anytime. He did not want to go because he was with Kidada."

According to an article in the New Yorker Magazine, through most of the summer, Shakur friend Shawn Chapman remembered

Shakur driving away from his room at the Peninsula Hotel in his midnight blue Rolls Royce with the top down, playing Sinatra's "Fly Me to the Moon." As if to acknowledge his changing interest in less "womanizing" Chapman was clear to point out that their relationship went no further than a friendship. To those who knew Tupac, this was really saying something.

"It wasn't so much Vegas as his girl and that thing that they were doing together and that dream that he was into," Gloria Cox said, "as opposed to the thing in Atlanta as a family thing. It's a gun. The guns and his cousin is on drugs again… whatever."

In the audiotapes of Tracy Robinson, Tupac himself confirms his mindset on Chapman at the time and his evolving views on "tomcatting"; "I know niggas like me," said Shakur.

"I can fuck everybody's girl. I can fuck them all for real but I can never have one for myself because the thing that they love so much is the mystery. Soon as they know me it's like they want the mystery. Do you know what I mean? It's like they like the bad guy more than they like the real guy because once you know who I am as a human being it's not as exciting because you can figure it out."

SEPTEMBER 6, 1996:
COERCION TO VEGAS

There are plenty of people who have speculated on the matter of what finally motivated Tupac to go to Vegas, but there is only one witness interview on record that might actually shed some light on the matter: it comes from Lena Sunday. Lena was a jazz singer who had worked with Tupac ever since the days of Tupac's performing with the group Strictly Dope.

Sunday and Tupac had become very close friends and Sunday's jazz/R&B influence was obvious in Tupac's "more mature" recordings.

"I got a call the night before 'Pac went to Vegas, said Sunday, "telling me everything was going to be all right, that he and Suge Knight were going to work everything out; Suge was going to give him everything that's owed to him, and had invited him to come down to Vegas, and kind of clear things up between them, that Suge had accepted that he was leaving…

"And I remember saying 'Pac you made him a lot of money off that last album, I mean your first album, I should say, you made him a lot of money. I don't see somebody taking it that easy… that you're leaving. And that you're leaving… letting it be known that he didn't pay you. That's not a good rap to have in the business, because other rappers will hesitate to go—so if you leave him, you know that's not a good thing for his company—or him.

"And he said 'Oh no, no. Suge said 'Come to Vegas, we'll squash everything; everything will be clear.'

"And I told him 'I have a bad feeling' again… the same feeling I had when he went to Death Row. And I remember saying 'Just let the lawyers handle it'… 'Just let the lawyers handle it… don't go! And he said he really wanted to see the fight; it was Mike Tyson, I think, fighting.

"And I was like 'Watch it on TV like the rest of us!'

"And he said that there was nothing like being there in Vegas. And I just said, 'Well, take care of yourself—I just don't have a good feeling about this—but if that could happen, great—that's a good thing… But just be really careful, because something just doesn't feel right, something doesn't sound right…'

"And that was the last time I talked to him."

Lena Sunday's testimony is powerful on a number of levels; it clearly evidences what dozens of friends and family knew about Tupac's plans. But it does more than that. It is important to understand that Lena Sunday and Michael Moore had never ever met and did not know each other. Lena Sunday's interview was conducted by one interview crew in 2006 and Moore's by another crew in 2002. No single person from Moore's interview had anything to do with the Sunday interview.

Nonetheless, Tupac's statement that Suge and he were "going to work everything out" directly references and cross corroborates Moore's testimony of the events of September 4th. There was only one reason Sunday could know that this "smashing" of the issues between Death Row and Shakur—he told her about it!

Sunday also validates Shakur's statement about his understanding of whether Knight was clear that Tupac was going to leave Death Row (he was). This is something that no one else has ever directly testified about or corroborated independently! Not until Lena Sunday's interview had anyone been able to corroborate Michael Moore's account that Knight actually had any understanding that Tupac was leaving Death Row.

Also of importance is that this corroboration aids in clarifying Knight's independent understanding of Shakur's motives. Many until then had only the letter sent to Death Row business partner and attorney David Kenner by Yaasmyn Fula, terminating Kenner's service contract as Shakur's attorney, from which to merely suggest that Knight may have been notified about that letter. This of course was never proven, so it could not be assumed that Knight even knew about Kenner's dismissal and from there the relevance of Sunday's testimony gains traction. That said, it was probably not a wise move on Tupac's part to fire Kenner and remain in the company of the Death Row Records entourage.

Moreover, Sunday testifies that Tupac directly told her that Knight had promised that they'd "squash everything" indicating that there was something that needed to be "squashed." Aside of Moore's testimony about the confrontation in the hotel room, publicly there appeared to be nothing to squash.

And while Sunday may not have understood the need for Death Row to cover up what had been misappropriated from Tupac at that point, she inadvertently suggests that it was common knowledge by September 5, 1996, that Tupac's leaving Death Row had to do with money. In her mind, Shakur was leaving Death Row "letting it be known that he (Suge) didn't pay you." This is the clearest and sharpest corroboration that money issues were key to the Shakur and Death Row split.

SEPTEMBER 7, 1996: 12:00 P.M.,
GEORGE KELESIS OFFICE—LAS VEGAS

Frank Alexander had just come back from a vacation, after having provided personal protection for Shakur on a recent trip to Italy. He had arrived the day prior to Shakur's anticipated arrival in Las Vegas, and was in the car with Wright Junior on the way to an improvised security meeting.

"Reggie Wright asked me to ride with him to the meeting that we were having," said Alexander.

"It was about 12 noon and we were going to George Kelesis' office in Las Vegas. When we arrived there, there were 23 other security personnel for Wright Way Security at this meeting along with the attorney and Reggie Wright.

"When we got there, they started going through the meeting and what the meeting was about and one of the main issues and the main points were we were not to carry our weapons. We were told that we could not carry weapons and no one should have a weapon on them.

"We had never had a meeting like this before where an attorney in his office would have been in charge of a meeting and will be telling us that we couldn't carry weapons, so that right away brought up the issue of 'why not?' The topic of discussion about the weapons was 'why not, who were going to carry weapons, why we're not going to carry weapons.'

"At Club 662, it was a benefit for a retired boxer and the reason that it was a benefit for this retired boxer is because the feds and the police had been watching 662 every time we would come in town. I was told that 'they' (law enforcement) kept looking for a reason, I guess, to shut it down and we were not allowed in that weekend. So they had this benefit for this boxer going on and that was going to get us into the club for that night.

"We were told to either leave them in our room or in our car and how we got to the car is that it was going to be three of us. Myself, Michael Moore and Al Giddens were going to be the only three that was going to have weapons."

According to the majority of the bodyguards that were working for Wright Way, the trips to Vegas always included armed personnel. "Death Row Dave" Matthews, a Death Row Insider and driver for Knight says that typically "everybody had guns." The trouble was that this information could have easily been conveyed prior to departing for Las Vegas. So, why is this information only coming now, unannounced?

"We had never before had a meeting at an attorney's home or in his office," commented Alexander. "We would have security meetings where we would be told 'okay this is what is going to happen' at Suge's home in Las Vegas or at the studio. "But for us to have a meeting at an attorney's office? On a Saturday? First time! Out of the ordinary."

Las Vegas Detective Brent Becker added his own take on the matter: "For them to have a meeting at an attorney's office... I don't know why..."

The Nevada Rules of Professional Conduct provide one good

reason that an attorney was involved; everything discussed between his office and any client, or even a potential client, is and will be treated as confidential information, protected by the "attorney-client privilege" against disclosure.

The idea behind the attorney-client privilege is that society benefits when a client is permitted to be completely honest with an attorney, since one really cannot do their job without knowing the facts of a client's situation. So the "privilege" guards all communications to the attorney, or from the attorney, against being divulged, voluntarily or otherwise, by the lawyer. It is generally inadmissible in Court.

Michael Moore confirms, "One, we were told not to carry any weapons to Club 662; two, we were told not to have any weapons on us at any time while we were in Las Vegas."

Many of the security personnel had conceal carry permits of their own or were legally allowed to carry because of their off-duty police status. But even these bodyguards were asked to leave their weapons in their cars or hotel rooms.

SEPTEMBER 7, 1996: 1:25 P.M., T.G.I. FRIDAYS

Michael Moore was one person that made it clear that he would not follow the new rules that had been laid down. He was going to carry his weapon. His refusal led to him being removed from guarding Tupac.

"At our lunch meeting" said Moore, "prior to the fight starting, I was told that I'd be taken off Tupac Shakur.

"You put Tupac at risk when you remove one bodyguard and say, 'Hey Frank, you have them.' So, for most of the day, all this went on and Tupac did not have a clue that was what we were doing. I was a little upset that I was taken off of him and I got into a little argument with Reggie Wright at lunch over it.

"He said, 'Mike, I'm putting Frank back on him and I'm taking you, back off.'

"I said, 'Reggie, that part doesn't make sense, why not leave me and Frank on Tupac.'

"He said, 'Michael Moore, do what you're told, I'm going to put you at Club 662 and you're going to handle the security along with Al Giddens at the club.'

"I think the reason they removed me from Tupac is because I was one of the few people that wouldn't buy into not carrying your weapon and during no part of that day did I take my weapon off and Mr. Wright knew that.

"So, they removed me off of Tupac so there wouldn't be a weapon there."

SEPTEMBER 7, 1996: 2:30-4:00 P.M., THE LUXOR HOTEL

Tupac Shakur arrived by car in Las Vegas and checks in at the Luxor Hotel, where Death Row had reserved over twenty (20) rooms. According to "Death Row Dave" Matthews there was a lot of shuttling of Death Row people back and forth from the Luxor Hotel to Knight's home in Las Vegas.

"Earlier, after the meeting at the attorney's office." Frank Alexander said, "Reggie said, 'Hey, Pac is back at the Luxor, I'm going to go drop you off, go meet up with him.' So he dropped me off, I saw Pac and other Outlawz, went over, hugged them, greeted them and everything.

"And you know Pac, 'Frank, how was your vacation, man?' I said, 'It was cool, man.' So, he had been gambling. He was actually shooting craps at the Luxor.

"Pac is Pac; he said, 'Let's go.'

"We go, 'Where we're going?'

"He goes, 'We're going to go over to the MGM.'

"I'm like, 'Well, are we going to get a cab or how are we going to get over there?'

"He said, 'no, no, we are going to walk over there.'

"So Michael Moore, myself and all of the Outlawz with Tupac, walk from the Luxor to the MGM."

"There's plenty of times he was alone without a bodyguard," said Mutah Beale, one of the Tupac Outlawz, "we'd walk in the malls without bodyguards. He wasn't always relying on the bodyguard. He wasn't like that."

Bodyguards however, was the topic of the moment for Wright Junior who, because of the extended security staff, which included off duty California law enforcement and Las Vegas Metro Police officers, had to hold a second security meeting. "Death Row Dave" tells of a meeting with security at the Luxor between 3p.m. and 4p.m. where

Wright Junior says to security guards present, "no one is to carry his weapons."

He commented that in all the times he had gone to Las Vegas that this had never happened. This was the second time the bodyguards were asked not to carry weapons. They had travelled to Vegas on many occasions to attend club 662 events or to just party in Las Vegas and at no time had they ever been asked to disarm and now they were being asked twice in one day not to carry their guns.

SEPTEMBER 7, 1996: 4:50 P.M., MGM HOTEL

"We get to the MGM," Alexander continues, "again he goes for the crap table and MGM was a little bit more crowded that evening while he was gambling. He was gambling, he was winning on his own and Pac said to me, 'Go over, call Reggie and find out what time Suge wants to meet to go into the fight.'

"Tupac asked me to go make the call. I didn't have a radio; I couldn't contact Reggie, so I had to go to a landline phone. So I go to call. As I went to call on a landline phone, I came back to the table and they were all gone. So, I walked all over the MGM looking for him before I even realize he isn't even in the building."

And while Tupac was in transit Moore was in tow.

"During our conversation on the way back from the MGM Grand," Moore said. "I explained to Tupac that Mr. Wright was taking me off him earlier that day. He was a little upset; he made a couple of phone calls. As I explained, he's a real impatient person. I walked him to his room and my understanding was that he was supposed to wait there until another security got to him."

SEPTEMBER 7, 1996: 5:20 P.M., THE LUXOR HOTEL

"I get back over to the Luxor and I'm looking all around for him," Alexander said. "I'm on this phone, got a call and trying to find him and Pac walks up behind me. I'm like, 'Pac, where have you been, man? I'm looking all over for you guys over at MGM.' He said, 'we walked back over here. I was ready to go.'"

SEPTEMBER 7, 1996: 5:30 P.M.,
CLUB 662

People start lining up at Club 662, 1700 E. Flamingo Road, where Tupac Shakur and Mike Tyson are to appear after the boxing match.

SEPTEMBER 7, 1996: 6:00 P.M.,
LUXOR HOTEL

Michael Moore and Frank Alexander had an issue with their clothes. They had on short pants that day, and needed to change their clothes to get in the right clothes for the fight.

"But there were some problems there because with me not really being on Tupac" said Moore. "The person who really needed to change his clothes was Frank.

"So, I went to my room and that was actually the last I saw of Tupac."

SEPTEMBER 7, 1996: 8:10- 8:25 P.M.,
LUXOR HOTEL

Shakur and Alexander are in their rooms changing clothes and preparing to leave for the MGM hotel. Michael Moore has an entirely different experience—in his room he begins to receive a series of unusual phone calls.

"I think Frank had no idea that I received four phone calls prior to Tupac getting killed," said Michael Moore. "Three of the phone calls came from Mr. Wright and one phone call came from Al Giddens, who was head of Club 662 security.

"I asked them, I go, 'Al, why are you calling my room at 10 after 8 if I'm not supposed to be there until ten?' His answer was, 'Reggie just called me and told me to call you.'

"I said, 'Well, don't call me no more.' Then after that, all my phone calls came directly from Mr. Wright.

"I think there was a reason for that and I think the reason was making sure that no one carried a weapon."

When Shakur and Alexander finished changing their clothes

they headed down to the Luxor lobby. Alexander was apparently still under the impression that both he and Moore were "on" Tupac, as they were in Italy at the Versace Fashion Show some months before.

Alexander said, "So, I called Michael Moore on the house phone," said Alexander. "I said, 'Hey, get back down here because Pac is getting ready to take off and everything and he's upset about Reggie, have you talked to Reggie?'"

"I didn't have the knowledge that he was downstairs in the lobby," admits Moore, "until Frank Alexander called me and said, 'Hey Mike, watch Tupac down here.'

"I even believe on the phone, I explained to Frank even then, I am not on Tupac. I kept trying to say that the only person that was assigned to Tupac at that time was Frank Alexander. But Pac said, 'Michael, come over to the MGM and meet us over there.'"

Moments later, Shakur and Alexander begin the journey over to the MGM Grand Arena where the fight will take place. Alexander says that they took a cab to save time; it was about a 5-minute drive across the intersection.

Michael Moore explained in his interview that Shakur was not aware that security arrangements were being altered—without his knowledge. This began to resemble what happened to Broadus' security, when they were similarly dismissed on the September 4th plane trip from New York.

"To this day I believe that Tupac was under the impression that I was going to be going to the MGM Grand with him," says Moore. "But that wasn't the case; when I went to my room, I knew in my heart, I wasn't coming back because I had been instructed to go to Club 662 and that's what I did."

Michael Moore confirms Alexander's testimony about Shakur's dissatisfaction regarding personal protection after he was told about Michael Moore's reassignment.

"He got a little upset," Moore suggests, speaking about the earlier conversation prior to heading up to his room.

"Now when I think back on it, he [Tupac] said, he's paying for this shit and that he's telling us where we're going.

"I remember him saying that real loud that day in the lobby that 'I'm paying for you, you go where I say go.' Then I said, 'Frank, you need to make a phone call to Reggie.'"

Strangely, in spite of Shakur's being the artist, celebrity, star or whatever label you wish, he was clearly not in charge of his own security; again remarkably similar to Calvin "Snoop Dogg" Broadus' security arrangements. After finding out about Moore's reassignment. Shakur himself tried to get to Wright Junior while in the hotel room to no avail.

"Tupac even called Reggie," explained Moore, "and had Frank get in touch with Reggie to find out where Michael Moore was at. So the problem was festering and I knew something wasn't right. I told Tim Williams, 'something is not right here, Tim. What we have to do is find out what's going on.'

"So I said, 'let me go downstairs and I'll change clothes and I'll work with Tupac until Reggie says something.

"Tim said, 'Mike, don't do it.' He goes, 'you're going to piss Reggie off, don't do it.'

"I go, 'Tim, Frank's going to need some help.'

"He said, 'Don't do it.' To me, that's the beginning of our downfall."

SEPTEMBER 7, 1996: 8:15 P.M., MGM GRAND GARDEN ARENA

Meanwhile at the MGM Grand Garden Arena waiting area, Shakur and Alexander are stuck, alone, in the crowd, with no radio or weapon.

"Now people saw Pac, they were 'Tupac. That's Tupac!' We're waiting for Michael Moore to show up. At that point in time, I lost all communication with Michael Moore. I didn't know whether he was coming, what was going on or anything.

"Pac was real antsy. He was like, 'Where's Suge? Where's Suge? How come Suge isn't here?' He was looking at the time and stuff and it's getting closer for the fight to start at this point. People are going in."

SEPTEMBER 7, 1996: 8:30 P.M., OUTSIDE THE MGM GRAND HOTEL

Michael Moore was having a crisis of conscience. Anyone who takes pride in their ability to bodyguard is all too familiar with scenarios that are more high risk than other ones; they have an instinctive clarity that tells them when to increase and decrease security. Michael Moore knew that one person providing personal protection for Shakur was not enough, but was helpless to do anything about it and face losing his job if he did do something about it. These thoughts occupied Moore's mind when they sat in front of the MGM Hotel.

"Well, we got down to the MGM right in the front of it," said Moore "right where the fight was at and I was getting ready to get out of the car. I rode Tim Williams over there.

"He goes, 'Mike, what are you doing?'

"I said, 'Tim, I should just get out because if Reggie yells at me, and I'm covering Tupac, how bad can that be?'

"Well, at the last second, I decided to just stay in the car, I went to Club 662."

SEPTEMBER 7, 1996: 8:30 P.M.,
MGM GRAND GARDEN ARENA

Alexander finally saw Knight appear. "Suge got there with a couple of people that was with him with the tickets," he claimed "and we went in to the fight right as the National Anthem was playing."

SEPTEMBER 7, 1996: 8:36 P.M.,
MGM GRAND GARDEN ARENA

Mike Tyson knocks out Bruce Seldon in one of the shortest Heavyweight championship fights in boxing history, lasting just one minute forty-nine seconds. From the opening bell, Seldon tried to weather Tyson's barrage of punches, but Tyson was able to dodge Seldon's attempts.

Oddly, at around one minute twelve seconds in the fight, Bruce Seldon got knocked down by a Tyson punch that seemingly only grazed Seldon. Seldon would answer the referee's count at eight and continue the fight only to almost immediately get knocked down again by a punch that didn't seem to land at full force. Seldon slowly got back on his feet but was unable to maintain his balance, causing referee Richard Steele to stop the fight and award Tyson the victory by way of knockout.

While Shakur and Alexander follow Knight out of the arena

past security toward the Tyson dressing room, the audience began shouting "Fix!" having thought Seldon took a dive in order for Tyson to win the championship and move on to face Evander Holyfield. The crowd would continue to serenade Seldon with chants of "Fix!" as he remained in the ring for an interview.

SEPTEMBER 7, 1996: 8:45P.M., MIKE TYSON DRESSING ROOM

Shakur and Knight arrive at the dressing room, with Alexander in tow but Tyson is not yet there.

"Did you see Tyson do it to 'em??" Tupac asked a film crew. "Tyson did it to 'em!" He leaped around.

"Did y'all see that?" He became more agitated. "Fifty punches! I counted! Fifty punches! I knew he was goin' take him out! We bad like that. Come out of prison and now we running shit."

But as that same video shows, with one eye on the door, Knight is seen visibly tugging at Shakur's shirt. They were there to see Tyson, who had not yet arrived. Even still Knight is seen pressuring Shakur subtly, seemingly for no reason—other than a timetable that was being dictated.

They had no idea the real post-fight entertainment was just about to begin.

SEPTEMBER 7, 1996: 8:49P.M., MGM GRAND HOTEL ELEVATOR AREA

As Tupac Shakur leaves the MGM Grand, he gets into an altercation with a young black man believed to be a member of a gang—the Southside Crips. MGM security video catches the incident on tape. In the ten-second fight Shakur's chain breaks on his Medallion. The scuffle is stopped by security. A man involved in the scuffle with Shakur is held for questioning and then let go. His name was Orlando Anderson. Anderson is shown on security video after the fight talking calmly with Las Vegas Police and hotel security without appearing seriously harmed. He is not favoring anything and is not walking with a limp.

SEPTEMBER 7, 1996: 8:53P.M.,
LUXOR HOTEL

The Death Row entourage leaves the MGM Grand and stops by the Luxor Hotel on the Las Vegas Strip so that Tupac can change his clothes. In that time Alexander repairs Tupac's Medallion.

The parties are rushed out of the hotel. Alexander explains that he is going to take his car, but is told instead to leave it there. Alexander is not able to walk the forty minute round trip to the public parking to get his weapon. Anyone who has been to Las Vegas understands that to get from one side of the casino hotel in Las Vegas to another. At a dead run, it would take the better part of twenty minutes each way.

In his book, "Got Your Back," Alexander said that the possibility of getting his gun "would not happen" in spite of Wright Junior clearing security to have their weapons in their cars.

The plain truth is that bodyguards generally do not chauffer their clients using their vehicles. Personal Protection bodyguards generally ride along with their clients. Rarely does a bodyguard act as a driver. Alexander would sometimes follow Shakur in his personal vehicle, and in fact said that Shakur would try to "shake" the bodyguards from time to time.

Alexander had a plan but it wasn't optimal. His experience had told him that generally incidents happen in the moment and rarely are people told, "hang on a moment. I need to go out and get my gun." And as silly as that sounds, it's the reason that the closer the weapon is, the better.

Alexander said the plan of the night was to park his own car outside of the 662 Club so that if anything "jumped off" he could run to his car and get his weapon.

"And me, knowing I was going to the club," said Alexander, "stuck my gun in my car up under the seat cause that's where I was going to go and park my car in the front. The plan was that we were going to leave our cars up in the front. We had three open spaces and our cars would be there. If anything jumped out our weapons was right there and we could get at them."

But by this point in the evening, Frank Alexander knew it was a moot point about getting to his weapon. Since they were ordered not to carry a weapon, his weapon might as well have been at his home or on Mars. He was not to carry a gun on his person.

Sadly, in later years, the LA Times and others would rewrite history to imply that the decision to go and get his gun was an arbitrary and hastily made decision. It was not; getting to his car meant a significant delay and holding up the procession.

And, not everyone is clear on what a concealed weapon is. As an example of this historical revisionism even the issue of the concealed weapon was not clearly understood. Cathy Scott, reporter for the Las Vegas Sun, in less than eloquent penmanship, tries in vain to point out, "Well if you don't have it on your body that's a concealed weapon yeah they couldn't carry a gun, they could have a gun but they couldn't carry a gun." Based on that logic, it is easy to see how quickly things can get confused.

The press also does not indicate where else the bodyguards were supposed to put their weapons. The bodyguards are not at home. They are remotely located. They cannot take a weapon home. Therefore they have a few options:

- They could dispose of their weapons;
- They could take the weapons back to their hotel room;
- They could leave their weapons in their car.

The bodyguards were left with a problem on what now to do with their guns.

Alexander was not able to access his weapon that was in his vehicle, due to the fact that he was never able to retrieve the vehicle from the hotel parking lot. More importantly no one has ever explained why the gun prohibition was not conveyed prior to the trip to Vegas.

SEPTEMBER 7, 1996: 9:30 P.M., THE JOURNEY TO KNIGHT'S HOME

Inconsistency and apparent defiance of common sense are the key markers that make clues stand out as to relevance. It's almost as if they call themselves out.

One example is the allegation in the Patton Confession Letter that Wright Junior was able to tell the alleged shooters where Knight and Shakur were going to be in Vegas. Most people speak in vague generalities; for example "I am going to go to the store in the afternoon." The head of security, of all the people privy to the Vegas agenda, would likely be the only one who might have a full and complete picture of where people might be at a given time of day; knowledge is power.

As a typical security "expert," Wright would have handed out pieces of the itinerary that impacted a particular guard; "Okay, Michael Moore, I need you at Club 662 from nine to midnight, because Tupac will be there at that time." Moore may not have, and it looks like didn't have, any more information than that. Consequently, Moore would not be able to give an overview of where everyone is going to be. It's fortunate for the shooters that they coincidentally and allegedly had access to the top guy. What made that clue stand out was that the only person who could give that information out was Wright.

To be clear, the Patton Confession Letter does not imply the shooter knew who Wright was. It just documents that Wright Junior was there representing the itinerary. It wasn't the shooter's job to make the association. So we have that. Once attention is focused on that distinction, it begs the next question on how Wright could assure shooters that someone was going to be here or there. Was he capable of influencing the schedule? The answer to that question is a resounding "yes" because not only did Wright Junior know in advance about the fight and the like, but he was likely the one who set up the meeting at Kelesis' office for Saturday. So we can be assured that Wright was in a position to influence the schedule. He also manipulated the guard rotation as well, in contradiction to what Moore and Alexander knew to be best practices for security. That clue called itself out as well.

In a similar fashion, Knight's activity after the scuffle with Anderson also calls itself out, because the clue starts with Knight's behavior running counter to what most would consider to be "usual" under the circumstances. How Knight reacts after the attack of Anderson is key.

Not a stranger to violence, it is not clear that Knight wanted to avoid being arrested that night. Who would? But, the fact is, he had just skipped out on felony battery in a location covered with more cameras and security than most places in the world. His image was recorded and security was clearly trying to stop them inside the MGM; the camera surveillance tapes show this.

What makes this clue stand out is that Knight didn't run out of town; he had just fled the scene of a crime, which could be another charge in and of itself, and Knight should have been concerned about police pursuit. He seems not to be bothered with that worry.

Instead of cooling off in a discreet location, Knight chooses to flee to the first place the police may likely look for him. He flees to his house. And he does this with a procession of cars that leaves the Luxor to head to Knight's home southeast of downtown so that Knight "can change clothes."

Apparently Knight is somehow irrationally confident that Anderson would not say anything to the police, nor would he press charges. He was equally confident that the police would not show up at his house, where anyone else would have been picked up, to arrest him for battery or fleeing the scene of a crime. Compton policeman "Bobby" Ladd confirmed in a phone interview with Internet Anarchist, Anthony Battaglia, that the police did not like Knight. This should have been a "slam dunk" arrest. So why wasn't it?

Nostradamus himself never could have predicted what Knight apparently knew: that Las Vegas Metropolitan Police would not go to Knight's home that night to arrest him or even question him about the MGM incident.

How would Knight get that knowledge without actually having control over it? Like the shooter clue, generally certain outcomes cannot be predicted without knowledge of why something may happen or may not happen. Unless you are personally in control of the situation, you just can't go on a 50/50 chance like that. So we look at what elements might allow Knight to reasonably predict that he could commit battery, flee the crime scene, go to the first, most likely place he could be found, and then expect nothing to come of it.

SEPTEMBER 7, 1996: 10:33 P.M., THE JOURNEY TO KNIGHT'S HOME

The 10-car Death Row entourage leaves the mansion en route to Knight's Club 662, located about 10 blocks east of the Las Vegas Strip at 1700 E. Flamingo Road. Tupac Shakur and Knight ride in his black BMW 750. "There was a black BMW, a black Lexus 400, a white Suburban, a black BMW station wagon, a light gold Mercedes" and according to Las Vegas Police, they stood out.

SEPTEMBER 7, 1996: 10:55 P.M.,
THE JOURNEY TO CLUB 662

Gate logs indicate that the Death Row entourage was not at Knight's home for very long, and it appears mind boggling to think they would have driven all the way to Knight's home for a ten minute break—unless it was done to buffer a time table, instead of making an excuse for not being on time for the shooting.

Tupac Shakur, oblivious to the slaughter he is being lead into, rolls down the passenger side window to allow someone to take a photo at a red light. This is the photo that Cathy Scott uses on the cover of her book, "The Killing of Tupac Shakur." And though Scott tells Internet Anarchist, Anthony Battaglia, that Tupac gave his location away to a shooter because he had been "making himself known," neither the photo itself or any other evidence would seem to indicate that Shakur himself was making his presence known, however batty all of the other drivers in that procession were.

Tracy Robinson saw in Tupac's face, the pressure he was under when she looked at that last photo of Tupac in Knight's car. "You look at those pictures, that last photograph of him, the deer in the headlights photo and he just looks sad." Indeed, the picture does not look like someone out to have a good time.

And primary witness Frank Alexander was literally behind Tupac's car and claims no knowledge of Tupac ever leaning out any windows. Yes, the music was loud, Alexander recalled, but that was the extent of the action in the vehicle.

SEPTEMBER 7, 1996: 11:10 P.M.,
KNIGHT IS STOPPED BY POLICE

"As we're going down the Strip" said Alexander, "just before we got to Tropicana, couple of a bicycle cops stopped Suge."

The BMW was stopped by Las Vegas Metropolitan Police bicycle units on the Las Vegas strip for not having a license plate on the car (the plates are in the trunk) and for playing music too loud.

If Las Vegas only had known, according to "Death Row Dave" Matthews, Knight owned a body shop named One Stop for a short period of time. During this time, in addition to making modifications to vehicles owned by Death Row (lowering them and the like) some more sinister modifications had been made to some cars, including the BMW Knight was driving.

Matthews states that the BMW was originally supposed to have been a gift for Norris Anderson, Knight's brother-in-law. Knight liked it so much he asked Norris to drive the car, and Norris allowed it. But what Knight did not know, or may have known but it was unimportant once the BMW was inoperable, was that the "Asians at One Stop," according to Matthews, had ripped all the airbags out of most of the Death Row vehicles, and replaced that cavity with "pop out" compartments that were opened by a solenoid triggered by using a combination of seemingly random objects in a sequence. (Push in the cigarette lighter and push "5" on the radio, and the compartment would open.) And amazingly, no one knew that there were, on that particular night, according to Matthews, at least two Glock pistols in the car's hidden compartment. Matthews also offered that once the car became inoperable those solenoids would not work.

"He opened up his trunk and there was nothing in there." said Alexander. "It was a brand new car. He got back into the car."

No ticket was issued.

SEPTEMBER 7, 1996: 11:15 P.M., FLAMINGO ROAD AT KOVAL LANE

On Flamingo Road, near the intersection of Koval Lane, a white 4-door car with Nevada plates rolls up to the passenger side of the BMW.

"When I saw the white Cadillac pulling up to Tupac and Suge," said Alexander, "you know I mean, it was no different than any other car that was going to come up to a red light and stop. The only thing different about the Cadillac pulling up is that I noticed that it was getting a little bit closer to the car, no alarm because there was other cars pulling up to him and you know, 'Tupac!'—the groupie kind of situation."

The BMW was pinned into a 3-point block leaving only the right lane open. The Cadillac pulls alongside completing the 4-point block just the way many hits are made around the world including the hit on Biggie Smalls. The arm emerges from the window and 12–13 shots spray the BMW. Shakur suffers only one mortal wound. A bullet ricochets off of Shakur's finger up through is upper body cavity and into his lung. The pattern of bullets was a very loose spray in spite of the shooter only being four feet away.

"The arm came out," said Alexander, "fired into the BMW and we were like (mouth drops open)—myself and the three Outlawz was in the car with me.

"We were just in awe and it look as if everything was in slow motion. I mean, it's clear as me sitting here right now talking about it, my memory will always remember and the way I envisioned it, was in slow motion, even still now."

SEPTEMBER 7, 1996: 11:17 P.M., CLUB 662

All of the security men with the exception of Frank Alexander were pulled off of the caravan. They had been sent to wait at Club 662. "Death Row Dave" Matthews confirms that he was there waiting with the rest of security for the caravan to arrive.

Michael Moore was standing in front of Club 662 with Wright Junior. Michael Moore: "While I was working at 662, I heard something over the Nextel Phones that we all carried for security... and what I heard was 'got 'em!'"

Brent Becker explained that he had never heard about Nextel phones "No, that's news to me, the only phones I know, I think they were all through AT&T," he said later.

To clear the air of the details, Alexander had the ability to explain: "These radios that we keep talking about, the Nextel telephones two-way radios, they had pretty much just come into play because originally, all we had were the regular radios: just the radio itself.

"Probably, closer to around the time of us coming out to Las Vegas, around the time of the shooting I would say that those Nextel phone radios had just come into play for Wright Way Security. This is a guess, there was probably only four or five of them, but it was enough to go around to the people the matter this should have handled."

Moore continued: "The voice was definitely one of our security staff that works directly for Mr. Knight. Right before me and Mr. Wright got on the vehicle to go get to the hospital, someone else came on the radio and said, 'Hey, don't say nothin' over the radio.'

"Maybe, the police should have concentrated more on Death Row, the Nextel phone bills and other things that could have helped them investigate it more in-depth. I would definitely look more at Death Row than I would look at Mr. Anderson and that's from what I've gathered when I was at New York, what I heard at the hotel, the arguing with Suge Knight and what I heard over that radio that night after the shots were fired.

"Mr. Wright and I were talking about what had happened and I just clearly heard somebody say, 'Don't say that over the radio.' But the person who said it was not homeboy security nor was it one of our security guards, it was to me, would be like a stranger. Someone; and the person that said that was Caucasian, definitely not African-American."

"They got word that Tupac and Suge had been shot," said Alexander.

"So, Michael was with Reggie and they went to the hospital together. Michael talks about hearing something over the radio while he would have heard it over Reggie's radio because he wouldn't have had a radio that night."

SEPTEMBER 7, 1996: 11:17 P.M., FLAMINGO BOULEVARD

Knight makes a U-turn on Flamingo, races west to Las Vegas Boulevard, makes a left turn. After encountering heavy traffic on the strip Knight's car hits the median blowing out a third tire and comes to a stop near the intersection of Harmon Avenue.

"Right after the car sped off," said Alexander, "I jumped out of the car and I ran up to the back of the BMW. As I was approaching the BMW, as I got about to the trunk, the car did a U-turn. There was absolutely no way I thought that the car was moving because with all the rounds fired that went through that car, they were dead. (Even he thought the shooters had 'got 'em.')

"When the car did a U-turn, the other cars that was with us in the entourage, a car that was in front of Suge and the car that was next to Suge, all did a U-turn."

Cathy Scott, in a 2007 interview, talks about two Las Vegas Police officers on bike duty, who heard the shots: "Two bike cops, who were in the parking garage right above, on the second floor of the parking garage above, the shooting hear 'bang, bang, bang,' they jumped on their bikes, take the bikes downstairs and boom, they're on the scene immediately—so quickly that they're able to follow and then hit their little shoulder radios that there's been a shooting at Koval and Flamingo.

"Yet both cops; two bicycle cops, not one of them stays at the scene, both of them leave the scene."

"We got back over to Las Vegas Boulevard," Alexander continues, "turn left on Las Vegas Boulevard jumping curbs, blowing his tires, messed up his rims and all of that as the pictures show, with this crime scene tape being put around his car and it happened so fast like I can't even believe how fast it was.

"This tape was up as myself and the Outlawz and the other two guys which was with Suge, try to go into the crime scene tape, we were told not to at that point in time, put us down on the curb, put us down on a prone position and I said to the one cop that I was the bodyguard and he allowed me to come in.

"When I got up under the tape and Suge was laying on the ground in a prone position and I told the cop, I said, he is the CEO of the record label and that's Tupac in the car. That's when Suge, they let him up off the ground and Suge and I ran around to the passenger side of the car with the cop and we were all trying to open the door and Suge said, 'It's my car, I know how to open the door' whatever, so he opened the door and asked one to pull Pac out of the car and laid him on the ground."

The first official words from the scene of the shooting came from a press briefing done by Sergeant Greg McGurdy, then an information officer with the Las Vegas Police. In its raw form, quoted here, was the confirmation of the Shakur family's worst fears.

"We Rolling?" McGurdy asked. "About 11:17 p.m. tonight, we had several vehicles travelling eastbound on Flamingo. Officers were, um, at the Maxim Hotel, to investigate a stolen vehicle, when they heard several gunshots being fired down below. They saw a caravan of about five cars that were travelling eastbound, heard the shots—again approximately 12 or 13 shots were fired.

"The officers saw the black BMW, followed by a black BMW station wagon and three other cars make a U-turn on Flamingo from the Maxim hotel, and made a U-turn, proceeded westbound—uh—coming on to Las Vegas Boulevard, where they were driving very erratically. They radioed that they heard the gunfire and saw these vehicles travelling in such erratic fashion.

"Other officers who were working the strip area were able to get the vehicle stopped here as you see. The black BMW was travelling on the rims on the right side. Once they got here they found the passenger in the BMW had been shot four times, and the driver appeared to be hit with a fragment, ah, in the head area.

"At this time the wounds aren't life threatening; they're in serious not critical condition at this time. And the person, as you're already aware who the passenger in this vehicle was is a known rap performer known as Tupac Shakur. The driver, we, uh, haven't released his name yet. They're both being treated at University medical center, and we are looking for a suspect vehicle, which was described as a white or off white Cadillac, newer model Cadillac.

"That's all we have on it right now. We know the suspects described as one, possibly two black males that was in that vehicle. Um, again this, an unfortunate situation; we're lucky that no one else was hurt. There doesn't appear to be any other injuries to any other citizens. As you know this is very busy with a lot of pedestrian traffic."

McGurdy goes on to mention an overlooked fact; there may have been other cars that were shot in the Maxim hotel parking lot; a result of the "erratic fire." To date there has been no confirmation that any other vehicles had been hit.

Tupac Shakur arrived at the hospital in serious condition and Knight had only received minor injuries. What investigators would learn later was that for all the mayhem that ensued, the shooting was a complete surprise, the shooting was a complete fulfillment of the Kenner/Wright/Sharitha Knight plan at the time, and the shooting was a complete failure.

But that understanding was a long time in coming; for now, the debris had to be cleared.

By 11:30 p.m., up to twenty Las Vegas Metropolitan Police officers had arrived and there was a great deal of confusion at the crime scene. This is not uncommon in situations like this: a public location, multiple crime scenes and police unfamiliarity on what people's various involvements were. Greg McCurdy, now Police Department Deputy Chief, was then the Press Relations Officer. He told the media, that they were looking for a "suspect vehicle," which had been described by several witnesses as a white or off-white "newer model" Cadillac.

Frank Alexander had been the most immediately vocal about the description of the car. One witness, one of the four girls in the car next to Shakur's had said it may have been a Lincoln Continental. But Alexander was adamant about the matter even when the police had stopped a new model white Nissan in the confusion.

"Where the car broke down, all of the cops were right there, and there was a lieutenant," said Alexander. "He walked over to me and we were talking and I said, 'That's not the car!'"

"I said, 'that's not the car, it was a white Cadillac,'" repeated Alexander. But the officer was apparently not convinced.

"He was telling me," Alexander said, "'you don't know what you're talking about, shut up!'"

It is not clear if an "all-points bulletin" was issued, but Don Erath, retired Robbery Homicide Investigator for the Los Angeles Police Department says that doing so would be pretty common.

"Suspect vehicles that have left the scene at a high rate of speed that would draw attention to themselves," said Erath "if there are vehicles noted by the witnesses, the preliminary officers and sergeant or supervisor on the scene will issue an all-points bulletin describing the vehicle."

Former Hamilton Township police lieutenant Jeff Braley, also agrees that this would have been typical. "I know, our standard operating procedures or procedure that we follow is basically that," Braley comments.

"If we have a witness come forward and say, 'I saw this, it was this type of vehicle,' the first thing we're going to do is get on the radio and start having every agency in the area look for that vehicle; put out the word, 'This is what we're looking for, this is a vehicle of interest, they can be considered armed and dangerous! Let's find this vehicle! This is the vehicle you want, this was the last direction of travel that is known to us!'

"Now, being in control and alert, I'm looking for that particular vehicle, I'm setting on the side of the road waiting for that vehicle to drive past me. You give the description, the direction of travel that you know of, you're going to have many agencies start to look for that particular vehicle to cover those roadways."

According to former Las Vegas Sun reporter Cathy Scott, there were helicopters available at police headquarters downtown, which wasn't very far; perhaps a couple of miles away. She opines that the police could have dispatched almost immediately and was sure some were, in fact, on call almost immediately. She added that there also could have been news crews in the air."

"It just didn't feel like a typical murder investigation," said Scott. "They could have closed I-15" Scott continues. "I mean, they close it for an accident and not even a small accident, not even leave a lane open for motorist, so it's not like they're worried about the motorist.

"They could have closed I-15, they could have closed the Strip, could have walled the place off. You had Nevada Highway Patrolman on extra duty, you had Metro Police on overtime working; it's a Tyson fight.

"At state line, the Nevada Highway Patrol has an office that's manned and so all they would have to do was radio thirty to forty minutes away, that's how long it would take to get to the state line, they could have road block that thing so fast, it won't have been funny.

"Las Vegas Metropolitan Police also has a sub office at the airport. So the airport police, Metro Police are ready on the scene at the airport, could have been on alert for the shooting coming out of there too."

Ultimately police were unsuccessful in locating the Cadillac, which frustrated many, including Frank Alexander.

"They're looking for the Cadillac and doing the things that they should have done to find that Cadillac," said Alexander "obviously they weren't doing that because they didn't get to find it."

Mutah Beale, of the Tupac Outlawz, summed up the general feeling of the victims' friends and family at the time, regardless of if it were actually true. "No, I don't think the police really care to be honest with you, I don't think nobody really cares."

Beale's statement does not ring true. The pain and frustration was obvious in lead detective Kevin Manning's voice as he held a press conference to update the media on the Shakur shooting. He gave an appropriate response to Beale's contention that Vegas Police did not care.

His counter: no one was helping or providing them any reliable information.

While it appeared that Manning was particularly hard on Alexander, who had provided the most information and was the closest eyewitness to the shooting, he was expressing the overall lack of cooperation by Death Row and the victims.

"It amazes me" an exasperated and tired Kevin Manning stated "that when we have professional bodyguards, as parts of this entourage that they can't even give us an accurate description of the vehicle."

SEPTEMBER 8, 1996 1:00 AM,
UNIVERSITY HOSPITAL

In an interview Knight did with ABC news sometime later, Knight was asked about his election to make a U-turn, which he did after the shooting.

"Do you think any person gets shot in the head thinks of the quickest way to the hospital?" Knight replied. "The average person, I think, would be dead."

Cathy Scott, in a 2009 interview with Anthony Battaglia, the Internet anarchist blogger, discussed a common misconception about Knight's condition (including her own):

"In fact everybody is like no big deal," she said. "No, he had a piece shrapnel at the base of his skull... right at the top of his neck at the base of his skull—the shrapnel.

"I don't believe it was removed and he had a piece, I think it's still there but he had a piece of shrapnel and he was in the ambulance with Tupac and he wasn't just riding to the hospital with Tupac, he was also being taken to the ambulance!

"You don't hand a semi-automatic weapon to somebody and say 'hey shoot Tupac and don't hit me' you know it's so ridiculous… I talked to the doctor about it, who absolutely said he had a piece of shrapnel on his head, at the base of it; can you imagine at the back of your head at the base of your skull?"

In spite of Scott's accounting or the credibility of its source, the hospital spokesperson, clarified that the media was talking about Marion Knight, said that he was treated for a "minor injury to the head."

Over time, Knight has changed his story on the incident. He claimed to the Washington Post on June 17, 2007 that he had a bullet in the back of his head from a .45-caliber gun that was used that night.

"I got a .45-caliber bullet an inch into my skull," Knight says, grabbing a reporter's hand and placing it on his baldpate.

"There's the bullet," he says, "and there's the shrapnel."

The reporter feels the lump and something that feels like a bullet, something hard and circular. Is it? Or just bone? But there is no scar at what would be the slug's entry point.

"I never scar," Knight said as justification.

But Knight was already contradicting himself. A .40-caliber Glock cannot fire .45-caliber shells. Is Knight so impaired by the "bullet in his head" that he can't remember what kind of gun he was shot with? Knight told MTV on September 19, 1996, "I got the bullet still in my head I got shot in the head, got grazed some other places, but I still got the bullet in my head. It's still here..."

Of course both of these statements contradicted an interview that was completed shortly after Shakur's death. The reporter remarked that she could see Knight's injury. For that matter, many people could. It was on the top of his head.

> Knight: "I got the bullet still in my head."
> Interviewer: "The bullet is still in your head?"
> Knight: "Yeah. The doctor told me that they did a brain scan and all kinds of stuff, and it went in and cracked my cranium; and it stayed there. He said there was more chance of damage trying to take it out than to just sew it up. I was hit there, grazed in some other places. I got a deep graze where the bullet grazed the back of my neck."

So to recap the confusion; Cathy Scott claimed it was shrapnel, Knight claimed it is a whole bullet and his cranium cracked. Compton Police claimed the weapon used for the shootings was a .40-caliber. Knight claimed he was hit with a .45 and it is a .45 slug in his head. Then, Scott writes in the article "10 Years Later," "Knight, who was grazed in the back of his head, was rushed to University Medical Center's trauma unit."

Head injuries are very serious, especially ones allegedly lodged in the back of the head. According to FC Vinas and J Pilitsis in their

2006 article "Penetrating Head Trauma," (Emedicine.com), penetrating injury from any missile such as a bullet has a mortality rate of 92%. This is their explanation of true bullet shrapnel injuries from a semi-automatic weapon:

"The automatic weapon, with its increased requirement for ammunition, necessitated lighter-weight ammunition. To compensate for the loss in missile mass, if wounding power was to be maintained, it was necessary to increase missile velocity.

"The penetrating missile or fragment destroys tissue by crushing it as it punches a hole through the tissue. This hole or missile track represents the so-called permanent cavity. After passage of the projectile, the walls of the permanent cavity are temporarily stretched radially outward. The maximum lateral tissue displacement delineates the temporary cavity. Any damage resulting from temporary cavitation is due to stretching of the tissue.

"Firearm injuries have become much more common with ready availability of the firearms in the society. The management of these injuries needs to be studied in detail in order to intervene during the course of the treatment at the right moment. The cases need to be treated on individual basis with few basic guidelines. Most of the decisions are dependent upon the course of the recovery within the hospital.

"Bullet injuries to head need special attention in view of the ballistics and requirement of prompt decisions regarding surgical removal. The neurological status at time of presentation and the location of the bullet often dictates the decision regarding surgical removal. However an important though uncommon complication of retained missiles is that of spontaneous migration."

Now that we see the seriousness of the problem with head trauma; especially trauma to the brain caused by a bullet fragment, let's look at the events. Knight, with an alleged bullet fragment in the back of his neck made a U-turn and drove a mile. He then had the presence of mind to talk with the police, get down on the ground and then get up and get around to the side of the car where Tupac was."

Knight is examined, treated and released by the next morning as if it was an outpatient surgery: less than 8 hours—in and out. That is far from a standard treatment for any head injury.

Club 662 was crowded. All available security was directed to the club and they were waiting. According to "Death Row Dave" Matthews once the call came in, shortly after the shooting, and news spread quickly, the club was immediately closed down.

George Pryce, public relations for Death Row, was entertaining press members at a buffet where he was planning to announce Death Row plans that included Shakur. If Tupac and Suge had both been killed could a telephone call have sent them all scrambling to break the story? Instead Pryce is called by Kenner with the news of the shooting and summoned to head quietly back to Los Angeles. Of note, is the fact that even though David Kenner received written notice of termination of his services by Shakur, Kenner never mentioned it to Pryce.

Gloria Cox and her husband were in route to Los Angeles having sold everything they owned except for what they could fit in their car. Their plan was to live with Shakur at his Calabasas home and to subsequently move across the street to remain close. They elected to drive to see the United States and make an event out of it. They were traveling through the State of Texas when they got the news.

"At the club, Pac was going to introduce," said Cox, "Mike was going to come out to one of Pac's songs and so we were real excited about hearing it.

"So we're trying to find a station, we keep turning, we don't hear any sports. Finally, we get the public radio station and what we hear is, 'Rapper Tupac Shakur, shot in Vegas.'"

"Now we're stunned, nervous, I am a wreck because I'm driving," continues Cox.

"We had to go another two miles before we see a gas station; no cell phone.

"So we pull off at a gas station, I call his office and Molly's sister answers the phone and tell us, yes, he got shot and that he was in the hospital but it look like he was going to be okay. That he had gotten shot. I think they had to take out, she didn't even say the lung then.

"We drove a little further, a couple of miles, nervous, stop, call again and that's when they told us they had to remove a lung. But that people could live with the lung and that one of his fingers had gotten shot off. But we still don't get the scope of it. My husband was singing songs to me, trying to keep me up, trying not to get into the emotion of it."

Tracy Robinson explains where she was when she heard the news. "We were in the cab," said Robinson, "and we heard 'something happened, Tupac, something.' It was like over the radio, all of those rappers, 'Tupac something. People been shot.'

"I was like, 'Oh, no.' I'm like, 'Pull over.' I'm calling Yaasmyn (Fula). I'm like, 'Is everything okay?'

"She calls us; 'No, go to the hospital.'"

"We finally get to Vegas and we get to the hospital," says Gloria Cox. "We get to the hospital, my daughter is there, Molly is there and my sister is there.

"My sister comes out and tells me that, 'you all can go in. You and Tom can go in.' When we got out the car my husband, all of that holding in, when he stepped out the car, he slumped out. It was like all of the weight now had fallen and he was now, you can see the 'crushed-ness.' (It was) like he had aged 50 years.

"We go into the hospital and they take us into his room. He's in a coma; he has the tube in his mouth. I look at him and I'm really afraid and I start (doing) all the old things that the women do, 'What have they done to you?' and all of this.

"My husband says to me, 'Don't do that because he can hear you.'"

What Shakur couldn't hear or see was Knight filling out his discharge paperwork at about 6am—a mere few hours in the hospital—in total.

But Tracy Robinson did see Knight in the hospital.

"I also remember seeing Suge roll by in a gurney with a little Band-Aid on his head," recalls Robinson. "I was like, 'What happened?'"

Gloria Cox also saw Knight the morning of his discharge "Pac is in the isolation room, intensive care, and some of the Death Row people, the gangs really, were outside.

"The first day I think when I saw Suge I was really, I didn't want to see him because they say, 'Look, Suge got shot.' I don't see that. I don't see the shot. I see something but it's not a shot."

Gate logs show an early morning arrival by Knight at his home in South Las Vegas. He is there for about a day.

"Tupac Shakur underwent another operation," Hospital spokesperson Dale Pugh told MTV, "He has been conscious." On Monday he was still in critical condition, his injuries now described as severe. He was likely to survive, the UMC spokesperson said.

Tupac's backup group, the Outlaw Immortalz, held prayer sessions with his fans. A large group gathered and rebuffed the media. One photographer across the street raised a camera; supporters rushed over and pushed his lens aside.

In the book "Have Gun Will Travel" by Ronin Ro, the author wrote that Las Vegas police had gang units patrol the area near the hospital. When these officers stopped a car to question its driver things took a turn for the worse.

"We had pulled up to see how things were going," said a Las Vegas Police sergeant. "It was completely in a friendly mood. One guy misunderstood and wouldn't cooperate."

The officers were shocked to see twenty of Tupac's distraught friends charge across the road, "The crowd came not knowing what was going on and got in the way and were pushing some of the officers."

Luckily, one of Tupac's female friends helped police calm the group; four handcuffed men were released despite the fact that butts of marijuana cigarettes were found on two of them.

"We let them go because they were grieving," said the sergeant. "Besides, it was such a small amount. These people are human. We detained them, hoping to get their emotions calm and logic rolling. At first they wouldn't listen, but after twenty minutes, when we explained where we were coming from, they were very easy to get along with.

SEPTEMBER 9, 1996 8:30 AM,
KNIGHT'S RESIDENCE

Knight does a very strange thing on September 9th; he goes back to LA. Let's review his "condition" (depending of course on who you believe as to his injuries).

Knight said he had "a bullet in my head"; Knight had been discharged from the hospital less than 24 hours before and had been shot at less than 26 hours previous; Knight owned a home in Las Vegas, where he could rest and recuperate from his professed injury. Meanwhile Shakur remained in a fragile and uncertain state.

Knight doesn't just take his head injuries to Los Angeles. He goes back to work. According to author Ronin Ro in the book "Have Gun Will Travel," Knight was seen at Can-Am studios in Los Angeles. He was attempting to complete "Christmas from Death Row," a Nate Dogg Album and a few other projects. Knight was now late on his deliverables to Interscope records. He was to have delivered 5 albums by this time, but had only delivered 2.

With Knight only gone four days, it seems like the albums' delivery was the last thing on Knight's mind even before New York.

Checking the math: Knight had a home to go to in Vegas and a business associate and core breadwinner for the label in the hospital, in an unstable state, who was hundreds of miles from LA. Knight has done dozens of interviews on how close he claimed to be to Shakur. "Pac fell in the water and he was drowning, so I jumped in and I put him on my shoulder and told him it's ok little buddy... you're alright now."

So, in spite of being able to be close to his "friend," Knight goes back to L.A. with a "bullet in his head."

The Las Vegas Detectives Franks, Manning, and Becker have been extremely busy processing clues from the shooting. They were not forthcoming to the press, but this is not that unusual. Detectives in open and fresh murder investigations tend to be tight lipped about clues.

The Las Vegas Police are conveying to all interested that they are looking for Knight but he is "unavailable" according to Death Row attorneys. This became a constant thorn in Las Vegas Investigators' sides; Death Row was not making anyone available, for an unknown reason. The lone cooperating witness was Shakur's backup singer "Outlawz" member Yafeu Fula. He assured police he could identify the driver if shown a photograph. So instead of detaining Fula, the Las Vegas police let David Kenner persuade them to release the rapper by promising to set up an interview that never happened.

This interference from Death Row did not stop Vegas investigators from pursuing matters; they were simply not making their work public. In Los Angeles Police Officer Kenneth Knox' Log, it is revealed that the LAPD had received a telephone call from Detective Paul Page regarding Knight. It appeared that in addition to investigating the shootings, they were also seeking information on Knight to try to build a case against him for gaming violations, as they related to Club 662.

Of course Knight did not own the club. The club was leased to him by Helen Thomas and her attorney… George Kelesis, the same attorney that attended the meeting disarming the guards. Paul Page alleged that both of Thomas and Kelesis were reputed to have ties to organized crime. But this curious relationship between Knight and Kelesis was not lost on Page, who wrote "Suge Knight has obtained Mr. Kelesis for his Vegas dealings."

Another thing that Page noted was that at this same time, Knight also obtained a Public Relations Firm (Rogich Communication Group) to promote Club 662 and Death Row Records in Las Vegas.

Finally Page also mentioned to the Los Angeles Police that Death Row Records had started yet another management company by the name of "Mookie Management" whose CEO was to be David Kenner, Esq. who Page noted, was "Suge Knight's personal attorney."

SEPTEMBER 9, 1996 1:30 P.M., LOS ANGELES OFFICES

Meanwhile, back in Los Angeles, Knight is trying to make sense of what happened. Why was he being shot at? What happened to get Tupac shot? By this time in the chronology of events, Knight was in LA attending to Death Row business while the people of Las Vegas are about to read about what a great guy Knight is.

Michael Moore recalls the aftermath of the shooting in a Los Angeles security meeting held by Death Row Artists, some who were in Vegas the night of the shooting and many others who were not. Wright Junior was present at this meeting, and Frank Alexander was conspicuously absent. Moore said, "We were also instructed to lie by Reggie Wright to Suge and the reason we were instructed to lie was because Reggie Wright told us not to carry any weapons.

"Suge called the meeting, all the artists were instructed to come to this meeting and certain security was invited and I happened to be one of them but prior to going into the meeting with Suge and all the artists from Death Row, Reggie met with us out front in his own meeting and instructed us to say certain things.

"When I got into the meeting, the meeting was basically about what happened and the artists were drilling security about what methods we had used and what was some of our tactics.

"I looked around and no one said it, no one was speaking up for security," Moore continued. "So I seen it was more… and I've been in this type of meetings before even at the fire station, some were like similar to a 'political type' meeting about what was going on. So I was one of the few people that spoke up and said, 'Wait a minute! We were instructed not to carry weapons!' None of the artists knew that. And it looked like Reggie wasn't going to give that information to them.

"So I spoke up and said, 'No, we were instructed not to carry weapons that day, and that's why no one in security with probably with exception of me, had a weapon.'"

Alexander did not understand why he was not at the meeting to explain his actions that night, but he was still working for Wright Way.

"At that time, Suge wasn't even aware that I was still doing security. Reggie had taken me to another job that he was doing, security at a church up in Inglewood from 6 AM to 6 P.M.. Suge wasn't even aware that I was still working with Wright Way.

"I remember Michael telling me that Reggie had told Suge that I was no longer working with Wright Way Security and I often wondered what he would have done or how he would have felt to know that I was still working for Wright Way all the way up until the end of November."

But Knight had bigger things on his mind. He had no idea what happened and yet he needed to convince Las Vegas Police that he was innocent. His Public Relations machine was in full swing; the Death Row Records executives were well aware how influential a well-placed article could be. By September 10, 1996, with Knight back in Las Vegas, Rachael Levy of the Las Vegas Sun does what is in effect a "fluff piece" on Knight.

Carefully planned to coordinate its timing with that of Knight coming to Vegas to meet with police, the article makes it a point to attest that Knight was never really into all the "gang" activities and was generally a nice likeable man. The author even takes the time to make sure the readers know that his nickname was based on "Sugar Bear."

This article also features three former UNLV football coaches praising Knight, who the article said had come to "personify all that is controversial about gangsta rap." The three men, a New Orleans Saints coach, a sports radio personality, and a junior college instructor claim to see "the goodness in the top producer of music that critics say corrupts the minds of children, degrades women, and glamorizes violence."

Ironically, the reporter also states in this article that Knight was "grazed by a bullet. This is yet another reporter that does not print that Knight had a "bullet in his head." But in this article there is no mention of any other victim. A perfect opportunity to promote "Makaveli" Shakur's newest album, there was no similar article about Shakur! Why single out Knight as the source of praise? Tupac was the bigger "star," so why not even mention him and what a great guy he was? Simple! Knight needed the court of public opinion.

SEPTEMBER 10, 1996 1:30 P.M., LAS VEGAS POLICE OFFICES

Knight arrived back in Las Vegas on September 10, 1996 and reported to the police department immediately. Of course arriving at the police station with three attorneys in tow seems excessive. And this was not lost on Las Vegas Investigators, who distinctly noted on their interview reports, that there was a noticeable tension between David Kenner and George Kelesis.

But in the end, Knight came back to Las Vegas with an alibi and his attorneys. About 6 p.m. Wednesday night, Metro's homicide division detectives questioned Knight for about an hour.

In this interview, Knight is advised that at that point, he was not a suspect in the shootings, but they want to know what he saw. They asked the wrong guy. Knight burned though an hour's worth of questions with lack of memory and a deflecting fixation on Alexander and why Alexander did not have his gun.

Detective Kevin Manning would not comment to the press why Knight, with two flat tires, makes a U-turn on East Flamingo with two bicycle patrol officers in pursuit. Knight's interview proved worthless. He had no idea about many details of the shooting. Manning stated that they had "no reason to interview him again," clearly expressing his continued frustration at the "dodge ball" being played.

This comment by Manning was not a conclusion on the part of the Vegas Police, but a statement of helplessness. Knight made it very clear that he was not willing to help the Vegas Police even if he had information. "It's not my job," Knight said. "I don't get paid to solve homicides. I don't get paid to tell on people."

Manning took the time to clear this up in an article in the Las Vegas Sun several months later. "This once again," said Manning "it comes back to that until somebody has the courage to take the witness stand and put themselves in front of the prosecution and defense attorneys to answer hard questions, the case is at a standstill."

SEPTEMBER 12-13, 1996 4:03 P.M., UNIVERSITY HOSPITAL

By this time there were many who believed that Shakur would overcome his injuries, and Las Vegas Police at least had to consider the fact that this was not yet a homicide case. No one had died at that point. A shooting that Shakur might walk away from, as he did in 1994 is a shooting that the investigators do not have to put much effort into.

And as of September 12, 1996, now five days later, Tupac is still in very critical condition, struggling for his life. He is still on life support.

His family and thousands of fans around the world hold out hope. Gloria Cox added "So the last day, the day before I had went in to see him and when I went in to see him that day with my niece, it was like I knew but I didn't know.

"I looked at him, it reminded me of my mom when she was in a coma. So I cried real hard that day."

On September 13, 1996, the crime was reclassified from a "gang related" or "random shooting" to First Degree Attempted Murder and First Degree Murder.

Gloria Cox recounts the last moments of Shakur's life, "The next day we went, me and my sister went, and they had called, we went, then we went back (to the hotel). Then they called us, said to come.

"When we got there they told her that his kidney was failing and they wanted to put him on dialysis before. It wasn't there yet but they wanted to put him on dialysis. Okay. Then they come back and say that every time they tried to hook him up his heart would fail.

"My sister was not really hearing him and they kept saying it and she said, 'What did you say?' He said, 'We did it and we had to resuscitate him three times.' When she heard that she said, 'don't do that. Don't do my son like that. Leave him alone. Let him go.'"

Frank Alexander said, "Have you ever played the 'what if' game? What if I could have done this, what if I could have done that? What if I would have had my gun, what I would have done? I have put myself in this position in my mind many times to say what if I would have my gun, what I would have done. I've put myself in my mind imagining jumping out of the car and taking a firing position and firing back into that Cadillac, disabling the Cadillac to where it wouldn't have been able to have gotten away. I would have shot back and hit one of the assailants that shot Tupac, whatever would have happened.

"The 'what if' game. I've played that game for 12 years."

At 4:03p.m. on September 13th Tupac Shakur quit fighting. He died as a direct result of the injuries he sustained from the Las Vegas shooting. He was three days from celebrating his one-year anniversary of the signing with Death Row Records.

And the Las Vegas Police Department realized that because of the nature of the crime, the lack of cooperation by witnesses and the lack of any real evidence, even by September 13, 1996, the investigation was almost over before it even started. They wouldn't admit it to the media, however, until about eleven days after the shootings. On September 18, 1996 a clearly upset Manning echoed this inevitable truth. "Our official stance is it is still unclear as to a motive or suspects. We are not getting any substantial new help from the Tupac group, so anything we are doing now is pretty much on our own."

PART TWO:

PERSONS OF INTEREST

The recording industry is full of false promises and broken hopes. Only a few "make it" the rest simply food for the machine. Andre Young aka "Dr. Dre" lied telling Eazy-E "they were going to work it all out" and asked him to come over to Galaxy Studios where Suge was waiting. Suge told Tupac that "they were going to work it all out" and asked him to come to Las Vegas where Wright Junior had people waiting according to the Patton Confession Letter.

Suge Knight and Tupac are shot while driving from Suge Knight's home in Las Vegas to Club 662 on the night of September 7th 1996. Michael Moore, a former Tupac bodyguard, tells of standing right next to Wright Junior at the time of the shooting and hearing, "Got 'em" come over Wright's radio. With 13 shots fired the shooters would have believed that they "Got 'em" but nothing could have been further from the truth. Suge is injured in the shooting but walks away. Tupac is shot four times and is given a 50%/50% chance of survival but is only able to hold on for a few days. He dies on September 13, 1996. If the recently uncovered evidence is correct and this was an attempt on Knight's life as well as Shakur's life, there would have to be a cover-up. People that knew about the plot would have to be silenced or killed. So who were the conspirators? Who had the means? Who had motive" Who had opportunity? Who had all three?

WHO IS MARION "SUGE" KNIGHT?
KING OF HIP-HOP?
RED KING OF THIEVES?

It has been said that if boxing's most ruthless promoter, Don King ran his own record label he would be Suge Knight. The same way King ran his stable of primed battering studs of the ring, Knight ruled his roost of rappers in the same feared manner. Hip-Hop's most brutal pimp had everyone within Death Row Records under his cast-iron thumb, dancing and rhyming at his beckon call. Knight turned one of the music industry's fast-growing records labels into a wild-west street gang. From 1992 until the crumble of an empire began in 1996, west coast Hip-Hop was Knight's for the taking. Knight has been one of the most feared and formidable business opponents in the battle of Hip-Hop's hierarchy.

Suge Knight was born and raised in Compton, California—ground zero for Los Angeles street gangs Bloods and Crips. Marion

Knight was nicknamed Sugar Bear, shortened to Suge, for his sweet disposition. Suge was only ten when Compton was desolated by the loss of its manufacturing plant bringing despair and unemployment into the community.

Unlike most children in his neighborhood, both Suge's parents were gainfully employed, his father was a janitor at UCLA and mother worked on the assembly line at an electronics factory. Suge had grown up north of Alondra Boulevard and west of Wilmington Avenue, a patch held by the Leuders Park Piru Bloods. By the time Suge reached his teenage years he was exempted from joining the destructive forces of the street gang, because at six feet, two inches tall he was a talented athlete. He earned letters in both football and track all four years at Lynwood High School eventually achieving a football scholarship from El Camino Community College after graduation in 1983.

In 1985 Suge transferred to the University of Nevada in Las Vegas wearing number 54 and starting at defensive end, he was a powerful build, listed on the program at 260 pounds. He was voted UNLV's Rookie of the Year, elected defensive captain and won first-team all-conference honors. On campus he carried due respect as a promising athlete with all-American smiles. He socialized in College party circles with drugs, sex, and alcohol, while teammates committed armed robberies, carjacking's, and sexual assaults. He earned honest money as a bouncer for the Cotton Club.

His senior year Suge's reputation took a change of direction, earning enough money for his own apartment and a series of late model sedans. With regular visitors from Compton, it seemed Suge had now earned a title of being possibly the biggest drug dealer on campus. He was drafted by the Los Angeles Rams NFL team, Suge promptly dropped out of school and moved back to L.A. He made the run-on roster during the NFL lock out season in 1988-89 crossing picket lines to play as a 'replacement' player. As the strike ended, so did his short football career with professional players returning to their positions.

Suge's criminal record began almost immediately after leaving the field. A restraining order was placed on him after several altercations with his girlfriend Sharitha Golden. He was arrested for assaulting her and cutting off her ponytail in front of her mother's home. Two weeks later on Halloween night Suge was again arrested in Las Vegas for shooting a man in the leg and wrist whilst attempting to steal his Nissan Maxima. When the LVPD arrested him he was found with a .38-caliber Smith & Wesson revolver in his waistband. Extraordinary events influenced felony charges to drop down to misdemeanors by way of a well-connected lawyer and reputation as an All-American football athlete. He was released with a $1000 fine and three years' probation. In 1990, Suge used a pistol to break a man's jaw. He pleaded guilty to felony assault with a deadly weapon and yet again managed to walk away with a $9000 fine and two year suspended sentence.

At this stage Suge Knight was working as a bodyguard for R&B sensation, Bobby Brown, where he learned the fundamentals of the entertainment business. It wasn't long before he found a new employer involved in entertainment management by way of Beverly Hills sports agent, Tom Kline who was very interested in getting involved in the music industry. He hired Suge as a driver and bodyguard and soon evolved him into a talent scout. He soon used Kline's office for auditioning local rap acts with the intentions of soon forming his own record label.

His first interest was in a young talented rapper, The DOC, who was already signed with Eazy-E's Ruthless Records working alongside the emerging legends of Ice Cube and a radical and prolific producer named Dr. Dre. Knight gained the reputation as a ruthless businessman using gang tactics to create the most successful rap record label in the history of music.

It cannot be disputed that Knight had motive to kill Shakur. Many have speculated that Knight was even brazen enough to put himself in the car when shots rang out. But recent evidence suggests that as Las Vegas police stated Knight and Shakur were "victims" not "suspects."

REGINALD WRIGHT JUNIOR:
THE RED KNIGHT

While we are still contemplating the means motive and opportunity in the Shakur Homicide, a peak into the future reveals that Wright Junior was considered a Person of Interest in the murder of Christopher "Biggie Smalls" Wallace. He was mentioned in the discovery of the civil suit between the Estate of Christopher Wallace and the City of Los Angeles.

On November 20, 2007 a motion was filed by the Wallace family to compel the LAPD to produce clues that were missing from the previous disclosures and hidden. An agreement was struck to provide that information in a secretive way. All "Closed Clues" or clues that had been exhausted and were no longer considered viable, had been provided. Revealing "Open Clues," or clues that were not exhausted at that point and still viable, was fought by the LAPD because disclosure of the clues could potentially cloud the case.

According to the LAPD, the following Persons of Interest, or suspects were identified as "Open Clues" in the Wallace homicide: Suge Knight, Reggie Wright Junior, William Fletcher, Wesley Crockett, Tyruss Hines, David Mack, Rafael Perez, Nino Durden, and Harry Billups aka Amir Muhammad.

So who is Reggie Wright Junior? From his deposition in the Brian Watt vs. City of Compton litigation of March 12, 2002, we learn that Reggie Wright Junior completed high school at Lynwood High. He graduated in 1989, from Cal State Long Beach, got a Bachelor's of Science degree in criminal justice. His major was law enforcement and a minor in Black studies. He also attended Compton Community College, Long Beach City College, and Rio Hondo.

Prior to becoming self-employed with Wright Way Security it is clear that his being the son of Lieutenant Reggie Wright Senior from the Compton Police was a good path to getting into the Compton Police Department, but many believe that because his tenure as an officer itself was short, Wright Junior's exposure to the landscape of the Compton Police and penal system was brief. It wasn't. In fact, prior to starting Wright Way in 1995, Wright had completed his ten-year relationship with the Compton Police Department and its officers.

First employed in January of 1985. Wright Junior was a Community Service Officer or more commonly known as police cadet for the City of Compton. He primarily took cold police reports and worked in the communications center. "Cold" police reports refer to "not-in-progress" police reports, or reports when a crime has been committed but the act itself already over. Wright held that job for about eight months.

Wright Jr next worked as a jailer for the city of Compton; a job that would have placed him right in daily communication with the street hoodlums and drug dealers in the area. He was not yet a sworn officer, but was at the jail for about four years.

The next stop in his career was as a police recruit until the end of 1989 and Wright graduated from the police academy in August of

1990. Following his graduation from the academy, he was hired on by the City of Compton as a police officer, where he remained a trainee for about eighteen months.

Interestingly, according to his deposition in Watt, Wright Junior was given some unique and special treatment.

"The whole time because I was placed on loan. I was never officially assigned to a bureau, so I was in patrol my whole career. I worked the street crime suppression unit—like the gangs, narcotic unit. That was toward the end of my career in '95. I pretty much specialized in the gang members and the gang problems of the city, working for the homicide detective units trying to help with the shootings that were going on in the City of Compton and mainly intelligence units, just trying to gather the younger guys or the guys that were in the city that were active gang members, trying to get to know them, take pictures, identify them, F.I. (Field Interview) them—I was pretty much hand-picked by the chief of police."

The chief of Police for Compton at the time was Hourie Taylor.

Wright ended his position with the Compton Police Department in May of 1995 but not his relationship with the City of Compton, because he was given a "medical retirement" due to an ankle injury. In a later application for a Temporary Restraining Order against his girlfriend, Wright reported that he received about Two Thousand a Month from his "retirement." Apparently there are no desk jobs in the City of Compton, even though Wright claims in the same deposition to have worked the dispatch desk, likely a "sitting job," for several months prior to being injured.

Wright explains the cause of his disability, "They called me in and I was reprimanded for–I think it was for failure to look both ways. I was in an intersection, I was in a pursuit and got sideswiped by the car. I think they found me on failure to look both ways or something. That was the reason I got reprimanded."

From the jail, to the gang suppression unit, to the head of security for a record label with gangs in their midst, it is safe to say that by 1995, Reggie Wright Junior was likely a walking rolodex of gang members who wielded power and influence. Wright had the drug trade lines mapped out and was rumored to control drug trafficking within Compton.

In May of 1998, Kevin Hackie was interviewed by Detectives Russell Poole and Fred Miller. It is recorded that LAPD Detective Miller stated, "that Reggie Wright, Junior, controlled the dope trafficking in Compton, California and Wright's father, Reggie Wright, Sr., who served on the Compton Police Department, was concealing his son's involvement with the street crimes and that he believed that Reggie Wright, Junior, was calling the shots and having people murdered over drug transactions."

DAVID KENNER:
ALCHEMIST TO THE RED KING OF THIEVES

"David Kenner once directly worked with Suge, and in my opinion damn near ran the company" said Wright Junior.

It is true that Kenner was a big part of The Red King of Thieves' life especially since Kenner possessed a unique skill set that The Red King needed for his own legal troubles was well as the troubles of many Death Row Artists.

According to his own website, Kenner was admitted to practice in the State of California in 1968 and has handled literally thousands of State and Federal criminal matters across the country. In addition to all criminal matters he has handled, Mr. Kenner has developed a large part of his practice devoted to civil litigation most typically opposing government counsel. His website boasts that he has tried cases against US attorneys, district attorneys, attorneys general, and has confronted in litigation the FBI, DEA, CIA, ATF, organized crime, OCIDEF Task Force cases, government contracting fraud, and many others.

Kenner was uniquely versed in money laundering operations, and how to beat them. Kenner was defense counsel in the first Federal drug king pin case brought in the United States, including the largest DEA undercover money laundering investigation called "Operation Polar Cap"; it was a $700-million jewelry district money-laundering probe leading to three previous major sets of indictments in Los Angeles. In that case, Kenner won a dismissal for his client.

In his career, Kenner has handled nearly every kind of Federal crime including white-collar crimes, weapons charges, federal homicide cases and CFTC and SEC matters.

However smart Kenner was, he could not save himself from his own misdeeds; which came back to pay him a visit. According to his statements in a 2002 federal indictment for tax evasion, Kenner admitted he made $4.1 million in the year 1994 alone; income that prosecutors said he intentionally failed to disclose to the Internal Revenue Service.

Kenner has been universally known by anyone involved with Death Row as never being far from The Red King or The Red Knight. And even though he denies it, in 1997 Kenner, along with Red King Knight and his wife Sharitha also known as The Red Queen of Thieves, charged up $1.7 million dollars on their American Express Cards; a debt that was never paid.

Kenner had met Knight through Michael Harris aka "Harry-O" who was known to have created the largest cocaine distribution network in North America. Money to start-up Death Row flowed from Harry-O through Kenner. At some point the relationship between Suge and Kenner deepened; the relationship with Harry-O became collateral damage. Lydia Harris writes, "At the heart of the problem stood Kenner who played Suge and Harry-O against each other."

David Kenner was an important part of the Death Row Records machine as rappers only developed street credibility through problems with the law. Those legal entanglements gave artists free publicity that was great for revenue, but inhibited an artist's ability to perform. Having David Kenner to steer that side of the ship brought a new twist to the defense of criminal investigations; it worked on any problem, no matter how big or small.

Known to the investigation as the "Five Element Strategy" which is perfect for an Alchemist of his skill, Kenner devised a process that was used time and time again.

The First Element involved the incident itself; what happened. It would then be cast into the Second Element; a preliminary investigation and initial findings of fact. If the Second Element proved to be detrimental to Kenner or his clients' interests, Kenner would activate the Third Element: intervention in the form of witness tampering, misleading newspaper articles, rumors creating disinformation, smearing credible information sources, general misdirection, and causing evidence to disappear. All of these components would work in concert to create the Fourth Element: a derailed, hijacked, or redirected investigation. The final act of illusion was the optional—if necessary—Fifth

Element: the Act of Furtherance, which involves an overt act or acts that galvanize the image or theory put forward by Kenner as if it were cast in stone. This is what the public will remember as the "irrefutable truth" even though it is a lie.

Death Row would perfect this alchemy to an art form, using it on ever more high profile cases that began with cases such as Andre "Dr. Dre" Young's notorious and brutal record party release assault on Dee Barnes, host of the syndicated Fox TV rap show "Pump It Up." Kenner would also apply this equation to Broadus' murder trial for the killing of Philip Woldermariam. It was also most evident in the murders of Shakur and Wallace.

David Kenner sat at a very interesting intersection. He had represented the biggest money launderer, the biggest drug distribution outlet and now he had a seat at the table of Death Row Records that afforded him unparalleled access to the music industry known to launder money and rife with drugs.

Through Knight, Kenner was able to represent a steady stream of clients that needed his criminal representation. His vast knowledge and connections into the criminal world were possibly quite useful in creating the criminal enterprise known as Death Row Records. He could hide behind Attorney Client privilege as the voice whispering in The Red King's ear. He exhibited a pattern of betrayal, playing the people around him; many of those people were unaware they had even been played. Was the betrayal of Suge Knight and the murder of Tupac Shakur his crowning achievement?

SHARITHA KNIGHT:
THE RED QUEEN OF THIEVES

Was the idea that Knight was also a target in the Shakur killing not far from Vegas Police minds? In an interview done for Tupac Assassination in 2006, Brent Becker stated that this was not the "typical homicide," and then compared the shooting to "a CEO" of a company. This may not have been a coincidence; in this moment of thought Becker may have been thinking about Knight being in the car, and how it affected the investigation. There is no evidence that investigators pursued this line of thought.

What happens in a "typical homicide" involving a married person? Isn't motive one thing looked at? According to the F.B.I. report

"Topical Crime Studies Released with Crime in the United States" (2003) homicides in the Nation can be divided into two basic catagories. The first, murders in which little is known about the offender, accounts for approximately 30 percent of homicides reported to the FBI. The remaining homicides are those where the victim and offender typically had some prior relationship. 80% of homicides are committed by someone who knows the victim. 14% of all murders in the United States were committed by an intimate partner. That risk increases if the victim recently separated from the offender.

This is a short way of saying what many investigators know; the spouse of a "CEO" or other executive who is the victim of an attempted homicide is on the short list of persons of interest to be examined. If there is any sign, circumstantial or otherwise, that the spouse may be involved, investigators frequently examine this theory.

Wright Junior remained in the shadows for years. Sharitha Knight was also not very visible publicly. Sharitha did a great job of staying in the background. She is absent from the limited documents released about the Shakur investigation. Not that anyone would characterize the Shakur murder investigation as thorough. But what if they would have turned that investigation into the attempted murder of a music label head? What if that was all there was? Take away Shakur for a moment, and what do you have? You have an attempted murder of Suge Knight!

Sharitha Knight was married to Suge Knight and separated. According to this article at Thugmusic.net, daring to call Knight a "mama's boy," they claim Suge Knight suffered from separation anxiety. According to this article, Sharitha Knight adapted to Suge Knight's street hardened personality, she spoke slang, resented the rich, was wary of the police, and was driven by an ambition to escape Compton's demoralizing poverty. And while she has remained out of the line of fire as to all the sordid Death Row story, research and a litany of documents state clearly that while Queen of Death Row, her hands may have been every bit as dirty as Suge Knight, as to how Snoop Dogg and other artists were treated. Sharitha Knight ended up owing at least one hundred sixty thousand dollars ($160,000.00) back to Calvin Boadus that was wrongfully taken.

Bankruptcy Court documents (Box B-044) entitled "Sharitha Knight Amex" were filled with American Express credit card receipts as part of the $1.7 million dollars allegedly owed to American Express by David Kenner, Sharitha, and Suge Knight. Apparently the Court and Amex never bought Kenner's contention that Steve Cantrock was responsible for the debt.

There is not one shred of evidence that Sharitha was in the Cadillac the night of the shooting but Sharitha's motive to have Suge killed is undeniable. She stood to gain all of Suge Knight's shares in Death Row Records. At the time Death Row Records was valued at hundreds of millions of dollars. Sharitha Knight was estranged from Suge and was in a long-term relationship with LAPD officer Kevin Gaines. Arguments about the direction of Death Row Records were a regular occurrence and money seemed to be a constant issue.

Ultimately, a divorce from Sharitha Knight in 1999 lead to a battle and a court order that Suge Knight pay her $735,000 in owed child support. The Baltimore Sun reports that sources claim a court-created receivership siphoned about $600,000 in October of 2002 from Knight's company to go toward that debt.

Death Row Dave said, "She was a straight up hood bitch, but with fancy clothes on, and you can take the bitch out of the hood but can't take the hood out of the bitch. There was always big fights about money; she was concerned about her future, and I got the impression that a lot of her stuff was taken care of and sorted out. I remember him buying a house; they bought the fucking house—paid cash for the house so that she was taken care of, purely from the perspective so that she wouldn't run her mouth. Because she knew a lot, I mean she knew a lot of the inner workings of Death Row, unlike Michel'le or Peaches.

HOW DID DEATH ROW RECORDS BECOME THE KINGDOM OF THIEVES?

He thinks too much: such men are dangerous. —Caesar

A single event can ripple through time. On March 3, 1987 Eazy-E paid Lorenzo Patterson to set up a meeting with Jerry Heller. Eazy-E paid Lorenzo right in front of Heller and then played Heller NWA's song "Boyz-n-the-Hood."

"Cause the boys in the hood are always hard. You come talkin' that trash, we'll pull ya card."

Jerry Heller asks Eazy-E to play it again and after that, Jerry cancels all of his other client's contracts and agrees to only represent Eazy-E.

"Two spins of 'Boyz-N-the-Hood' and I was convinced," said Heller.

"I prepared to jettison my whole life and devote myself to this music. If this song was the only one he had, I would devote myself to that one song."

Jerry Heller and Eazy-E would create an extremely profitable record label but the vultures would soon swoop in to topple what they had created.

NWA consisted of Eric "Eazy-E" Wright, DJ Yella, O'Shea "Ice Cube" Jackson, Arabian Prince, and Andre "Dr. Dre" Young. Eazy-E and Jerry Heller would create Ruthless Records to distribute the albums. The early 90's, Ruthless Record, release of the now-classic NWA album, "Straight Outta Compton" would make stars of Ice Cube and Dre, and would change the landscape of the music industry.

According to the documentary, "Welcome to Death Row" Eazy-E posted bail for Dr. Dre on the condition he lay down tracks for the album in repayment. Dr. Dre would go on to become one of rap's greatest producers. The revenue stream they created would become a target of powerful forces. A single event started the label and a single event would also bring it down. Jerry Heller wrote about the regret of letting ambitious young Suge Knight enter his world.

The music came from the streets. The artists came from poverty where life was hard and stories told through their music connected with America. The struggle that was previously playing out only silently in the streets would enter center stage and continue to play out in the boardroom.

The drama unfolding inside the record labels and on the streets is intertwined. Understanding any single high profile Hip-Hop murder one must look, in context, into the entire Hip-Hop movement. People do strange things when there is money involved. In Hip-Hop there was so much money so fast—and in the Hood, you only ever own something if you can keep it.

At that time, Shakur was in obscurity. He began with Digital Underground as a backup dancer and roadie. He took a low level position just to tour with the group. His break would come during the tour when he appeared on stage without his shirt and the crowd connected with Shakur. His songs would come from his upbringing associating with members of the Black Panthers, Tupac would detail their struggle and life on the streets. His solo career would take off when his single "Brenda's Got a Baby" was released.

According to Nzasi Malogna, Shakur's Digital Underground's Tour Security Director, "Tupac was a prestidigitator of drama." His antics created the controversy that drove album sales but created legal entanglements. Shakur was loved! He was hated! As a Hip-Hop artist, Shakur's music polarized America. His music and lyrics attracted the attention of the leaders in the Republican and Democratic parties. His music brought the once hidden inner-city struggles into the limelight. Gangs that operated in the shadows were thrust onto center stage. The culture of gang life was glorified.

As the youth of America began listening to and singing along with Shakur's songs, a campaign gained traction to suppress the Hip-Hop movement. Shakur's album, "2pacalypse Now" would draw fire from sitting Vice President, Dan Quayle, who said, "There's no reason for a record like this to be released. It has no place in our society."

But this would create a flurry of album sales and make Shakur a target of powerful forces. The backlash from leaders throughout America would soon come to bear on Shakur and the entire Hip-Hop industry. In a relatively short period of time he would rise from obscurity to superstardom. But many stars that burn bright get extinguished before their time. On a September night in Las Vegas, Shakur met a tragic end.

The story of Shakur's murder in the context of the story of Death Row Records becomes the tale about the perils of "New Money." It is a tale about avoiding the consequences of crime. It is one of the most gilded stories ever to be told about rags to riches—money over bitches—about unfettered greed—about friendship and betrayal. Those themes would play out over and over again. Circumstances would change but human behavior would remain.

Andre Young aka "Dr. Dre" opened the door for Suge Knight. Dr. Dre asked The DOC to come out to Los Angeles. When he arrived he was sleeping on the couch of Andre "LA Dre" Bolton who considered Suge Knight to be his brother. Knight and The DOC began clubbing together. When Knight formed Funky Enough Records, it was because of The DOC's song, "It's Funky Enough."

The DOC used to go to clubs and sit in the women's bathroom. He wanted to be where the ladies were. Knight would guard the door so nobody bothered The DOC. Some of the women were irked and some thought it was cool. But you can't fault the logic... the women all come through the restroom. When Knight and The DOC got tired of that they moved to the dance floor and The DOC would slap a woman's ass and wait for what came next. Sometimes the woman liked it but most times when men saw this it led to a fight. Knight and The DOC would begin a brawl in the club and fight four or five people at a time. At one point they were banned from nearly every club in Hollywood.

Eazy-E made the mistake of not valuing Dr. Dre properly for his work. As a result, Dr. Dre fell in with Knight, who had a thug reputation from a story that he had dangled Vanilla Ice over a balcony to force him to pay royalties. Vanilla Ice denies the story, but says he paid up regardless. It was the beginning of Knight's legend and a glimpse of the street gang business tactics to come.

"I'm gonna make him an offer he can't refuse."—Don Corleone

Eazy-E and Jerry Heller were irritated that The DOC would bring Knight around but they were also afraid. He was intimidating at 6'4" and 315 pounds. They heard about the Vanilla Ice incident. They also knew that lots of money was flowing into Ruthless Records but a small percentage of that money was filtering down to the artists.

A pattern Knight would use later to good effect, when Knight asked to see the artist's contracts he was refused. He stormed into the offices of the Ruthless Records' attorney and rifled through filing cabinets until he found the contracts. Armed with information, The DOC recruited Dr. Dre and his girlfriend Michel'le to exit Ruthless Records. Knight negotiated all of them out of their contracts with Eazy-E albeit using gangster methods straight out of the Godfather.

According to Jerry Heller, Eazy-E was invited to Solar Studios by Dr. Dre to work it all out. When he arrived, Dr. Dre wasn't there but Suge was—with two of his henchmen. Knight told Eazy-E that he was holding Jerry Heller hostage and if he didn't sign away the three artists, Jerry was dead. Eazy-E signed away The DOC, Dr. Dre and Michel'le.

"My father made him an offer he couldn't refuse." Kay, "What was that?" "Luca Brasi held a gun to his head and my father assured him that either his brains, or his signature, would be on the contract."—Michael Corleone

The DOC created the name for Death Row Records. He originally imagined it as Def Row Records until Jewell misunderstood and called it Death Row Records and the name stuck. The original deal for the company was 35% to The DOC, 35% to Dr. Dre, 15% to Suge Knight, and 15% to Dick Griffey. The DOC was involved in a car accident after leaving Knight's house tripping on ecstasy pills. That accident nearly cost The DOC his life, but the accident damaged his vocal chords. He was in the hospital for a month and when he emerged his stake in the record label vanished along with his career as a rapper. He continued to write lyrics but was never valued in the same way as when he was able to perform.

Death Row was the Kingdom of Thieves, and Knight appointed himself as The Red King. If his kingdom was to become successful he would need funding. About that time Lydia Harris approached Suge and Dr. Dre about recording a demo for her. She was married to Michael Harris, or "Harry-O" after the 1970's television show, about a private investigator starring David Janssen. Harry-O was incarcerated at the time for attempted murder and dealing drugs. His conviction doesn't really paint the picture. His network of dealers spanned from Los Angeles to New York and he was dealing directly with the Columbian and Mexican Cartels to supply such a large volume of drugs.

According to Mrs. Harris, Knight seemed more interested in her husband's money than in her music. But Dr. Dre, a hotshot producer affiliated with the record smashing rap group NWA listened to Lydia's demo and told her he could remix it. Lydia Harris' album never materialized but Harry-O introduced Suge Knight to his criminal defense attorney, David Kenner.

Each king had his "Merlin": the sorcerer and conjurer of record, who could influence with his words men of power and judgment. The Red King had David Kenner who became legal council for Death Row. David Kenner had "entertainment attorney" qualities, flamboyant sharp and looking "mafia-ish." David Kenner became an important part of the Death Row machine as rappers only developed street credibility through problems with the law.

In late 1991, Knight, Lydia and Michael Harris, along with the lawyer Kenner, founded a company called Godfather Entertainment. Michael Harris bought 50% ownership of the venture with a $1.5 million investment. David Kenner brokered the deal while Harris was in prison.

Incarcerated, Harris relied on Kenner and his wife, Lydia Harris, who had little business experience. As a result, Lydia Harris says, Kenner was able to ingratiate himself as her confidant, and became integrally involved in the business while remaining the sole point of contact between Suge Knight and Michael Harris.

Harry-O's $1.5 million gave Suge the leverage he needed to take a bigger stake in the record label than when it was imagined as a partnership with Dick Griffey, Dr. Dre and The DOC. It also provided money to purchase a recording studio from Dick Griffey. When it was originally formed Death Row Records was a subsidiary of Godfather Entertainment with Michael Harris as a silent partner.

The launch party for Death Row Records was held at Chasen's in Beverly Hills creating the atmosphere that would set the tone for Death Row Records. The party marked the beginning of a stupendous rise in fortune for Suge Knight. At the party, David Kenner, during a videotaped toast, raised his glass and said, "Special thanks to Harry O!" The FBI confiscated that tape.

The record label "Death Row Records," Kingdom of Thieves, was born. The label had no problem finding talent. Every Hip-Hop artist on the West Coast wanted in. Knight, The Red King, had created a "family" company at its Los Angeles office: its environment underlined by a constant and oddly paternal threat of violence. Knight ruled his empire with an iron fist.

The Kingdom of Thieves became a lightning rod for talent, drugs, corruption, and vast fortunes. In a relatively short period of time the label sold forty million albums. They transformed the music industry just before peer-to-peer sharing would completely decimate it. The money that sloshed around the company was used to promote records, keep artists out of jail, record new music, and influence officials in the private and public sectors. There was a machine that was put together that has never been matched for the influence they wielded or the swath they cut.

Alongside The Red King was The Red Queen, Sharitha Knight, mother to Suge Knight's children and the actual "manager" of Calvin Broadus aka "Snoop Dogg" through Knightlife Entertainment, which The Red King had founded and The Red Queen ran. At the time, Kenner, the Alchemist was dealing with six pending cases for Death Row, including murder charges against a bodyguard that implicated Calvin Broadus.

For a year or two, it seemed that the "Untouchable" predicate The Red King placed before the name Death Row Records sometime later, actually seemed to fit. Death Row's albums went platinum, hype exploded and Knight became a folk hero to the African American youth who all sent in their demo tapes hoping to be discovered.

Folklore has it that Kings are born from being given swords of invincibility by a lady in the lake. In other stories a sword gets pulled from an unrelenting stone to bestow its new owner the royal grant. The Red King also pulled something out to gain his kingdom; but it wasn't a sword. It was money. The Red King was practiced in one special kind of magic, one that held his kingdom together for some time through wars of urban legend. Knight's special magic was that he knew how to make other people's money disappear without a trace. Some of it voluntarily and some of it by Knights own brand of sorcery—lies.

Years before the The Kingdom of Thieves was born, the "record" industry was always known for being an easy target for criminals. There have been suspected links between the record industry and the Mafia, which has much to do with the nature of the industry as with the nature of the Mafia.

"The record business is a natural vehicle for organized criminal activity because you can make a lot of cash very fast and the producers of the goods—the artists who make the records—can be easily controlled by contracts and through their personal managers," said one FBI agent involved in the 1986 Newark murder case, which was tied to the mob.

For example, gangsters have long been involved in record counterfeiting. More recently, however, investigators say they are discovering a growing number of organized crime figures that have obtained interests in pressing and duplicating plants that frequently are used by the major record companies to handle their excess production when other plants are operating at capacity.

Organized crime's recent increased involvement in the record industry "can be equated somewhat with its traditional infiltration of other industries," said one FBI official. Once the mob penetrates an industry, "even if it's through legitimate investments, they often develop a competitive advantage through their willingness to resort to extortionate practices," he said.

Harry-O was dealing with Knight and Kenner from prison. Harris claims to have been suspicious as he saw a shift in the way Kenner was carrying himself. It is said that the entertainment lifestyle was hindering Kenner's representation of Harry-O. Kenner was, and had been, friends with Lydia Harris and Harry-O. But Harry-O saw it differently. "The business became more dominant than the legal situation," he said. "The legal situation got put on the 'back burner.'" Lydia Harris stated that Harry-O started to hear rumors that Knight was trying to get a distribution deal through Interscope, but when Kenner would visit Harris in prison, no mention of any pending deal was made. Harris would have already read it in the newspaper, but Kenner insisted that it was not true.

It was at that time that Kenner taught his apprentice Knight his first magic trick: he made Harry-O's money disappear from Godfather Entertainment. Kenner and Knight formed Death Row Records, Inc., a company distinct and separate from Godfather Entertainment, and basically left Godfather Entertainment and its subdivision Death Row Records devoid of assets. They moved everything they were working on to Death Row Records, Inc. as a 50/50 deal between Dr. Dre and Suge Knight.

When Knight refused to admit to Harry-O that the distribution deal was closed, Harry-O again asked Kenner, according Lydia Harris. Kenner lied to Harry-O and said that Knight made the Interscope deal behind Kenner's back.

"Once Suge got a taste of the spotlight," said Harry-O "he wanted it and he wanted it by himself...

"If Suge didn't want to be my partner, I didn't have a problem with that. But at least compensate me for the time and money that I have invested."

It appeared that David Kenner "played" Harry-O against Knight from the middle. And, when the rift between Knight and Harry-O became too large, Kenner had to pick a side. He chose the money. He chose to side with Knight. And even as Knight was going around saying he had, on his own, started Death Row Records, Kenner was visiting the prison telling Harry-O that this was not the case at all.

Ruthless Records had filed a lawsuit against Death Row Records and blocked their distribution deal with Sony. Knight approached Jimmy Iovine who made his name as a producer on albums by Bruce Springsteen. Iovine interceded with Jerry Heller and Ruthless Records and settled the lawsuit against Death Row. As part of the deal with Interscope, Ruthless would get 10% of Dr. Dre's fees and 15% of all revenue from his albums. This agreement allowed Death Row Records to become a steady supplier of albums and rely on Interscope as a funding source to finance growth.

The DOC and Dr. Dre had received a $1 million advance on a publishing deal that they used to create "The Chronic," which became the first album released on the Death Row Records label. Interscope released the album through Priority Records. So think about how many companies interrupt Death Row Records revenue stream. 15% off the top goes to Ruthless. Priority gets a distribution fee, Interscope takes a fee and pays themselves back from any advances given or expenses incurred before any money is paid to Death Row Records. Suge Knight, Sharitha Knight, David Kenner and the expenses of Death Row Records, get paid before there are any distributions given to artists. Even with $60 million, grossed on "The Chronic" there is little to be able to pay Dr. Dre. Dr. Dre would approach Jerry Heller asking to come back to Ruthless complaining that he didn't have money for Christmas. Heller gave him a check for $40,000 and arranged a twenty million dollar advance from Sony Records. At the last minute Sony killed the deal fearing litigation from Death Row Records, David Kenner, and The Red King.

When The Red King began appearing on the covers of magazines alongside his artists, Harry-O told him he was making a mistake; high exposure would only increase his vulnerability. Knight ignored his incarcerated partner's advice and eventually began ignoring Michael Harris altogether. Harry-O suspected that his own lawyer was spending more time defending Suge Knight and Death Row's stable of legally troubled artists than he was trying to get him out of prison.

Sometime later, Harry-O got a hold of the original paperwork for Death Row's incorporation. What he learned shook up even a man as world-weary as Harry-O. It didn't reflect the original plan, where Death Row Records was to be a subsidiary label of Godfather Entertainment. The paperwork Harry-O held showed that Knight and Kenner had gone out and incorporated an entirely distinct and separate entity from Godfather, and that entity was Death Row Records, Inc. "They had both crossed me," said Harry-O, "the person who had brought them together."

Death Row Artist "Pretty Ricky" states that Harry-O was the one who discovered Knight, liked him and asked that Kenner talk to Knight. Knight was kept out of prison, on constant probation, allegedly at Harry-O's request and through Kenner's work.

"But when the money came in, they acted like 'what?' They went all 'Scooby Doo' on them, like 'Huh? What money?'"

When Harris inquired about the money and payback, he was told that it would be months before they saw a royalty check, according to Lydia Harris. She also said that the "sixty to ninety days" turned into years.

Doug Young, a record producer with Death Row, told the producers of "Welcome to Death Row" that the phone line to the prison at Death Row was never blocked. There were always people calling from prison.

"But later, and I think it was because of Harry-O that they blocked the phone." "I would send my representatives to the offices of Interscope, to make arrangements to collect." said Harris.

When Harry-O's representatives visited Interscope they were basically and flatly told they were not getting money from Interscope because Harry-O had no contract with Interscope. Knight also tried to disavow himself from a partnership with Harry-O. Kenner and Knight conspired to cheat Harry-O and Lydia out of their rightful share of the most profitable rap label in music history. With Kenner, Knight finalized construction of the walls of the kingdom and shutting the doors to Harry-O. The new unclouded entity formed by Knight and David Kenner was created just in time to receive the revenues from "The Chronic."

Distancing the company from Harry-O may have had advantages. As profitable as the music industry can be drugs can be even more profitable. The fact that cocaine was worth $18,500 a kilo on the west coast and $26,000 on the east coast is all that anyone needs to understand to put the entire Death Row Records enterprise into perspective. Private jets were being hired to move the party from one city to another. What else was on those jets? Ties to Harry-O might bring the wrong type of attention.

"Det. Arnwine heard that Los Angeles Crips and Bloods were transporting kilos of cocaine to the east coast, buying it in Los Angeles for $18,500 and selling it to artists in the east for $26,000. Suge Knight was never really a street gangster he started out as a narcotics dealer who would rip off Latino suppliers." —From LAPD Robbery Homicide Police Report

Everybody talks about the cash that was sloshing around at Death Row Records. It was as if someone was going down to the bank and cashing a check for $250,000 and getting hundred dollar bills.

Although Death Row Records criminal enterprise was likely built using Michael Harris drug connections, the money from record sales was the legitimate portion of the business. Whenever the criminal enterprise needed a check from a legitimate source, Death Row Records would write the check based upon a cover story. Cars were purchased and sent to Knight's customizing company where secret compartments were installed to hide small amounts of drugs, guns or other contraband. If a large shipment needed to be moved from Los Angeles to another city a private jet would be hired and a "business trip" would be planned. The artists were brought on board and the party would provide the reason for the trip.

Cooperation was the business arrangement between east coast and west coast but competition and contention a distraction. Crips and Bloods were at war, but seemed to have territories clearly marked for drug sales. The East Coast/West Coast feud was created as the fuel that drove album sales and diverted attention away from drug dealing.

Leaving Harry-O could not bode well with certain gangs loyal to him. If Knight was distancing himself from Harry-O, what might have been said about the following of Harry-O's former network? Remember, Knight was burning bridges. Without a direct "protection" from the gangs that Harry-O could muster, Knight was exposed.

Knight needed a "backdoor man." He needed soldiers. The "backdoor man" could shield Knight from blowback of the soldier's activities. Suge Knight, The Red King, fancied his business structure to imitate the mob. Who were some other "backdoor men" within organized crime?

Frank Nitti, for one who came to the attention of Chicago crime boss Johnny "Papa Johnny" Torrio and Torrio's newly arrived soldier, Al Capone. Al Capone's family lived nearby, and Nitti was a friend with Capone's older brothers and their criminal gang, the Navy Street Boys. Similarly, Knight turned to Reggie Wright Junior whose friendship went back to the same schools in Compton. Their families lived close by in the same neighborhood. But Compton wasn't like other neighborhoods. Compton was the birthplace of the Bloods Gang. The Bloods were outnumbered three to one by the Crips in that neighborhood. Growing up in Compton created much stronger bonds than growing up in a random neighborhood in America. King Knight created back door man, The Red Knight Wright Junior.

Under Torrio's successor, Al Capone, Nitti's reputation soared, as did Wright's when Knight invested $300,000 to "front" Wright's business, Wright Way Security. Nitti ran Capone's liquor smuggling and distribution operation, importing whisky from Canada and selling it through a network of speakeasies around Chicago. Wright arguably ran all of the security operations for Death Row, but more recent interviews now indicate "Junior" was much, much more invested in the music business operations of Death Row including taking the reins in the Winter of 1996.

Nitti was one of Capone's top lieutenants, trusted for his leadership skills and business acumen. Wright was Suge's most trusted confidant.

Capone thought so highly of Nitti that when he went to prison in 1929, he named Nitti as a member of a triumvirate that ran the mob in his place. Nitti was head of operations, with Jake "Greasy Thumb" Guzik as head of administration and Tony "Joe Batters" Accardo as head of enforcement.

The lawsuits against Death Row Records by Clear Channel and McPherson confirm that Reggie Wright Junior was put in charge of Death Row when Knight went to prison.

Coincidence?

Nope. In earlier days, Nitti had been one of Capone's trusted personal bodyguards.

And despite his nickname, "The Enforcer," Nitti used Mafia soldiers and others to commit violence rather than do it himself.

Salvatore "Sammy the Bull" Gravano, born March 12, 1945, was a high ranking member of the Gambino crime family. Originally a mobster for the Colombo crime family, and later for the Brooklyn faction of the Gambinos; Gravano played a key role in planning and executing rival mob figure Castellano's murder; the conspiracy would elevate Gravano's position in the family to underboss under Gotti.

It is worth mentioning Gravano and a similar tale of Frank Nitti for Al Capone, because both of them were men who took orders from the "boss," and both of them maintained a position of anonymity at the time; each had the position at one time or another as an "enforcer" within their respective crews.

As former FBI agent Joseph D. Pistone a.k.a. "Donnie Brasco" notes: "The thing is, wiseguys do not go around killing people for no good reason... it is very unusual for people with no mob dealings or no connection to the mob to wind up dead at the hands of a mobster... If, however, you are a wiseguy or a guy with some association to the mob, and you do certain things, you will get whacked…

There is nothing romantic about what they do. Understand what we're talking about here— bad, bad men. Are they funny? Sure. Kind to their mothers and children? You bet. Generous to the help? You bet. But the same day they tip the valet $100 they might stick a meat hook up a guy's ass." Suge was known to give away turkeys at Thanksgiving and toys at Christmas but from everything we have seen he could be brutal in business.

A Day at The Office

The Red King and The Red Knight set up a DBA company called "Wright Way Protective Services." There is no listing for this in the California Secretary of State register as either a LLC or Corporation; the listing for the FBN (Fictitious Business Name) in LA County states two dates for the filing of the DBA—19950110264, filed 1/23/1995 and 19950290783 filed 2/22/1995. In other words The Red Knight was paid personally, using an alias "company" and was without a corporate shield for liability.

Licensed by the California Bureau of Security and Investigative Services in December of 1995, in spite of civil judgments against The Red Knight for the beating of Duane Baudy and The Red King for violence in their role(s), Wright's company maintained a "clear" status with the bureau.

The Red King had his inner guard consisting of childhood friends and associates who were known for their gang affiliations. They were affectionately known as "homeboy security." Meanwhile, The Red Knight delegated the protection of the artists to former and current police officers and fire department officials—men with badges.

The Los Angeles Riots, in the aftermath of the Rodney King beating and acquittal of four officers charged for the crime, had created a vulnerability within the Police Department: a vulnerability that Death Row Records would exploit. Management inside of LAPD was reluctant to make arrests or investigate crimes that were perceived to potentially ignite racial sensitivities. Knight would capitalize on this weakness through his arm's length relationship with Wright Way, having them employ off duty police officers who would see crimes, but not "see" them. Their extra paychecks came from The Red Knight but The Red King called the shots to further his iconic "gangster" stature.

And even though the majority of Wright Way officers were Compton, Inglewood, Hawthorne, and other small city police officers, the "Murder Rap" investigation on the Shakur and Wallace Shootings and its lead detective wanted to be adamant that no Los Angeles Police Officers other than Officer Rich McCauley ever worked for Death Row or Wright Way. But that is incorrect. Per Los Angeles Police Department Internal Affairs Report #96-1408, we learn that Hurley Glenn Criner, David Love, and "possibly" Kenneth Sutton were also on the payroll of Wright Way Protective Services while working for LAPD. Of course the illusion that no LAPD were on "Death Row's payroll" has to exist, because it clears the way for an emphatic denial that Raphael Perez and David Mack could also have been working on Wright Way's payroll.

The Red Knight—Wright Junior's relationship with Death Row officially looked to be arms-length. Wright Way was "contracted" to run security for Death Row. The security team was never directly employed by Knight, which provided each of them plausible deniability. Many companies do this and The Red King was no exception. Even when the security staff was interviewed they claimed that Wright Junior was simply a contractor for Knight.

But "Death Row Dave" Matthews, who has never been interviewed before, not only had the distinction of being the only Caucasian working security for Death Row, but also had intimate knowledge of Death Row's inner workings. He was trusted to install the "safe room" where money and guns were stored. He put in all the security. He would run "payoff money" around Los Angeles. Dave knew the intimate relationship between The Red King and The Red Knight. "Reggie Wright was a go-between between Suge and all kinds of crazy shit. I am surprised that Reggie isn't in prison."

Frank Alexander wrote, "Although Reggie Wright 'owned' the company, Suge had set him up and called all the shots. Knight's first specification was that all members of security had to be retired or off-duty policemen... Period! Even Reggie had been a Compton police officer before he began working for Suge.

"Suge wanted the guards to be able to keep them out of trouble and to neutralize situations. It was always instilled in us that we were there as credible witnesses when they 'f-ed' up. This was the main reason they needed off-duty police officers. They weren't looking for the average person."

The reason that it is important to establish this relationship is because it speaks directly of the betrayal; a plot to have Knight killed, involving Wright Junior would almost be a matter of instinctive denial from Knight.

Of course, as legend goes, The Red Queen, Sharitha Knight, stayed very active in The Red King's life by having children with him and helping run The Kingdom of Thieves through "Knightlife Entertainment." The Red Queen obtained the right to "manage" Calvin Broadus aka Snoop Dogg on September 3, 1993, a day after he was arrested for murder. The special, and expensive, skills of the Alchemist Kenner came at a price; one must yield to the wishes of the royalty in The Kingdom of Thieves. The price of The Alchemist was an "exclusive management agreement" between Broadus and The Red Queen, Sharitha.

In an excerpt from the "unconventional" contract, other than "management," which was undefined in the agreement, The Red Queen was obligated to do little else:

> "Artist agrees that Manager is not expected to, nor shall Manager procure or secure employment for Artist. Manager is not to perform any services which, standing alone shall constitute Manager a talent agent or artist's manager, and Manager has not agreed or promised to perform such services except to the extent permitted by any applicable laws. Artist agrees to utilize proper talent or other employment agencies to obtain engagements and employment or other employment agencies to obtain engagements and employment for Artist after first submitting the names thereof to Manager, and not to engage or retain any talent or other employment agency of which Manager may reasonably disapprove in writing." (Broadus v. Sharitha Knight, 1997)

Obviously having Broadus in a weekend position, The Red Queen convinced him to give her signatory power of attorney over all of his business affairs with the promise "to advise and counsel" him in his pursuit of success in the entertainment industry. But it is important when looking at The Red Queen's experience with Knightlife to understand that it was only after The Red Queen signed that contract with Broadus, that Knightlife Management, Inc. was formed (12/22/1993).

Writings of the California Labor Board reveal that shortly after that contract was signed, a one hundred sixty thousand dollar ($160,000.00) commission was paid to The Red Queen, a product of Broadus' royalties from his music, which was a product of Death Row and paid to Knightlife directly. As The Red Queen, of course, she had the ability to completely ignore section (11) of the contract which said that:

> "Manager shall not be entitled to commissions from the artist in connection with any gross monies or other considerations derived from artist... from the sale, license or grant of any literary or musical rights to Manager or any person, firm or corporation owned or controlled by Manager."

And of course, a conflict of interest that obvious is going to become a problem at some point. There eventually became a controversy between Broadus and The Red Queen, over the Queen's desire to be paid in spite of contractual commitments. And to make sure Broadus knew she was sincere, in spite of the apparent illegality of the contract, The Red Queen sued Broadus on or about May 27, 1997 alleging that somehow he had not paid her a 20% "managerial fee due her" for service between August 3, 1993 and August 3, 1996.

Concerned over The Red Queen's over-reaching allegations of entitlement to "royalties," Broadus took The Red Queen to the State of California Department of Industrial Relations Labor Standards Enforcement Division in an attempt to have their agreement nullified.

The Red Queen appeared, and admitted that she was never licensed by the State Labor Commissioner as a talent agency, but had clearly booked events and taken money for them without Broadus' knowledge: fitting behavior for royalty in The Kingdom of Thieves.

In fact, in one 1994 series of performances in Japan, Sharitha Knight wrote: "Per our conversation, I am sending you this letter to confirm Snoop Doggy Dogg will perform in Japan on April 1-7, 1994 at $100,000 USD for five 35 minutes performances (venues to be announced). To close deal, I require fifty percent ($50,000 USD) in advance. The remaining fifty percent ($50,000 USD) is due upon our arrival in Japan."

The Red Queen was asked about this damaging evidence. She alleged she did not create the memo to Japan. But, Labor Standards was not moved. Calling The Red Queen's statements "not likely," they noted that in all of the contracts for appearances and bookings made on Broadus' behalf, not one document contained Broadus' signature. In fact, he claimed that he had never even seen one of the contracts.

"I did whatever I was told to do, said Broadus. "I trusted Sharitha. She was family."

In the end, Labor Standards voided the contract and called it out for the conflict of interest it was.

"Here, Petitioner's record company is 'Death Row Records,' owned and operated by Respondent's (now) ex-husband. When the 1993 commissions were paid, respondent was still married to Death Row's owner.
"It is difficult to imagine how in good faith respondent could charge petitioner commissions on royalties derived from record sales where she also owned the record company. Though no evidence was presented with respect to 'Death Row Records' profits, one can only assume that respondent benefitted twice at the expense of the petitioner and breached section 11 of the Personal Management Agreement."

In short, Sharitha Knight ended up owing at least one hundred sixty thousand dollars ($160,000.00) back to Broadus that was wrongfully taken. But that was only what Broadus knew about. If Broadus never signed contracts and never saw contracts, just how many deals like the Japan deal The Red Queen had enriched herself with before anyone caught on. But it would appear that there might be a ratio between the number of times you get away with something for each time you admit to doing it. No one knows but Broadus probably lost a small fortune.

DEATH ROW:
THE KINGDOM OF THIEVES

It was a great time for The Red King and The Kingdom of Thieves; they ripping their artists off blindly. The Broadus embezzlement was only an indication of a much bigger heist that was underway inside the record label. The Red King and Queen were taking money, it appeared, largely for, shall we say "romantic interests." For in the Castle, things were a bit of an internal mess.
Back in the early days of the Kingdom, around 1992, Simone Green became the chief photographer for Death Row Records. While there she captured some of the most often displayed images of Dre, Snoop and Tupac.

In doing interviews for her later book, "Time Served: My Life on Death Row," Simone Green was asked some very straightforward questions by interviewer Jesse Surratt. Death Row "dalliances" were openly discussed in her book, but she added some very direct information as it related to The Red Queen and The Red King's indiscretions:

"I knew what he did outside of Death Row Records, like I knew he had a relationship with the girl... ah... Marilyn Woods at B.E.T... "But when Sharitha found out about it—he had the utmost respect for her. Because as soon as she would find out something that had happened, Knight send the girl home. They were done... He didn't 'play that' with her. I guess it was like it's either me or them, and I'm not giving up child checks."

But that ultimatum was really a smokescreen. The Red Queen had her own personal Lancelot—The Blue Knight. She was dating a man by the name of Kevin Gaines whom she met in 1993 at a Chevron gas station at La Brea Avenue and Adams Boulevard.

The Blue Knight (Gaines) was a Los Angeles Police Officer who was rather flamboyant. He drove an expensive steed, a Mercedes Benz, wore $5,000 suits, $1,000 Versace shirts, and lived his off-duty life in the fast lane of L.A. and Las Vegas nightclubs, a lifestyle he obviously didn't maintain on his $55,000-per-year policeman's salary. Author Brian S. Bentley contends in his 2003 article for Streetgangs.com that Gaines had money saved from a relative's lawsuit award and that this fact was ignored. The Blue Knight had many credit cards with expenses like the $952 he had dropped just the month before for lunch at Monty's Steakhouse in Westwood, a favorite hangout for black gangster rappers. The Blue Knight had been separated from his wife, according to court papers.

"He was kind of flashy, over abundantly flashy for a police officer," The Red Queen admitted in her deposition for the civil lawsuit brought by Johnnie Cochran, who sued the LAPD for wrongful death on the Gaines family's behalf.

Former lead Christopher Wallace homicide investigator Russell Poole had more to offer about The Blue Knight. He said that Kevin Gaines was apparently given to violent outbursts, causing his wife to file several domestic-abuse complaints. Investigators learned that he had been involved in other road-rage incidents, and in at least one case he had allegedly threatened to "cap" a motorist who had annoyed him.

Russell Poole had also been handed another case to investigate—the evidence that disappeared from the Pacific Division's evidence locker in Calvin Broadus' trial for murder. The missing evidence weakened the case and probably led to the acquittal of Broadus. Poole believed that Kevin Gaines, who had access to the Pacific Divsion's evidence locker, was responsible for removing the evidence.

Gaines had a run-in with the LAPD the summer before his altercation with Detective Frank Lyga; Lyga was the LAPD narcotics officer who shot and killed Gaines.

According to police records, the LAPD responded to a 911 call regarding a shooting on the grounds of a Hollywood Hills mansion. Gaines, off duty, pulled up to the scene and got involved in an altercation with the responding officers.

The LAPD's account was that Gaines became verbally abusive and provocative, and had to be handcuffed. "Tell these motherfuckin' assholes to take the cuffs off of me, motherfucker!" Gaines shouted. He taunted the officers, saying that he hated "fucking cops."

By contrast, Gaines's account was that he'd been mistreated by the police. He hired an attorney and filed a notice of claim against the city. When the incident was investigated by the LAPD's Internal Affairs division, it was discovered that the 911 call had been made by Kevin Gaines himself.

"The evidence suggests that he did that to engage LAPD in a confrontation and basically wanted to secure a pension or whatever by filing a lawsuit," said Poole.

Of significance was that this happened at Sharitha Knight's Hollywood Hills home.

In the course of investigating the road-rage incident, Detective Poole discovered that the S.U.V. Gaines was driving, a green Mitsubishi Montero, was also registered to Sharitha Knight.

There were two documented "run-ins" between The Red King and The Blue Knight. The first incident was, allegedly, when Suge Knight found out about the romance between Gaines and The Red Queen. According to her deposition in the Gaines vs. the City of Los Angeles lawsuit, Gaines, Sharitha Knight, and several of her relatives had just come out of a performance in Las Vegas.

The Red King materialized seemingly from nowhere. Sharitha Knight claimed The Red King pushed his way into the van driven by Gaines, in which she and her family were riding. She said Suge Knight, who had another man with him, asked for a ride to his hotel.

"Where you guys want to go?" asked Gaines, who had put his gun in his lap.

"I'll tell you. Just keep driving," Knight replied, according to the deposition.

"Kevin's driving. In the back Suge is in my ear, threatening me basically," Sharitha Knight testified. "By now [Suge is] really mad... so we're driving to this deserted spot."

This is not to say The Red Queen was in any way afraid of The Red King. Simone Green made that clear. The Red Queen instead played the "cop card" with Knight when she told him: "That man is a police officer, and I don't think we're going to play games with you."

Sharitha Knight then told Gaines to turn the van around, and they dropped Suge Knight and his friend off. Gaines went straight to the airport and flew back to Los Angeles.

Apparently this threat did not sit well with Suge Knight. Remember, no one questions The Red King.

This lead to a second run-in with Gaines. According to a Death Row bodyguard at the scene, Gaines was allegedly taken to "the middle of nowhere outside of Lake Los Angeles" in late November 1995. He remembers this because it was during the video shoot for "California Love," which featured an area known for being largely uninhabited desert.

At that time Gaines was told to stay away from The Red Queen and was confronted by an empty hole in the desert. Gaines was stripped naked and even though he feared that he was soon going to be the dead occupant of the hole, Gaines was left stranded dozens of miles from anywhere—naked—with a long walk back to think about matters.

Sources did not know if Sharitha Knight found out right away or shortly thereafter, but Gaines made it back to LA and continued his relationship with The Red Queen to his death in 1997... completely ignoring The Red King.

Queen Sharitha's fling with The Blue Knight didn't erode her position. Cathy Scott stated in the Las Vegas Sun that when Suge Knight was imprisoned, Sharitha Knight took over the day-to-day operations of Death Row Records and the operation was very complex.

Operations included a substantial legal presence.

• George Kelesis, the attorney that advised the guards to disarm while in Vegas, was involved with the "Friends of the Las Vegas Metropolitan Police Department" as a director. In fact, so entrenched with the Las Vegas Metropolitan Police Department was Kelesis, that he formed a personal and business relationship with the former Sheriff of Clark County Nevada, who oversaw Las Vegas Metropolitan Police Department operations. They joined forces on the board of directors of "Hookers for Jesus," an organization started by an ex-prostitute to help other prostitutes find the error of their ways.

• Oscar Goodman, Mayor of Las Vegas had already defended Tony "the Ant" Spilotro a mob enforcer who actor Joe Pesci, caricatured in the motion picture "Casino." Goodman also defended several other major criminal defendants including Meyer Lansky. The Prosecuting Attorney Office was no doubt aware that Goodman had said he personally knew Knight and called Marion Knight a "genius." The local paper quoted Goodman that it was his desire to see Knight move his recording business to Las Vegas.

• David Chesnoff, former US attorney and Goodman's law firm partner, represented Knight on criminal matters. Chesnoff is no stranger to mob figures; as late as July of 2013, Chesnoff's offices represented to Vincent Faraci and formerly represented Rick Rizzolo. Rizzolo was linked to Joseph Cusumano, former lieutenant for Spilotro. Rocco Lombardo, brother of onetime reputed Chicago mob boss Joseph Lombardo, worked with Faraci. Recently, suspected Bonanno mob associate John Venizelos, worked at Faraci's Brooklyn nightclub, Jaguars III, alleged to be tied to a Canadian drug lord.

It is an understatement to think that there wasn't much Knight needed to worry about with that kind of legal firepower. A simple brawl in a casino was hardly the caliber of crime the likes of Chesnoff, Goodman, or Kelesis would handle; they could do those kinds of crimes in their sleep and the Las Vegas Police Department knew that. Perhaps that kind of "political" arrest; one for which Knight would likely skate from or at best be right back out on bail, was not worth an immediate reaction. Knight knew with the likes of those attorneys, he would walk out of the police station, worst case, before the ink was dry on the fingerprints.

To illustrate this point, fast-forward 13 years. In 2009 Knight is surrounded by Las Vegas Metropolitan Police, weapons drawn. Knight is caught brandishing a knife right in front of them at his girlfriend, whom he had clearly just beaten. Any "normal" person would have gone straight to jail for that, and many have been arrested and charged for far less.

However, in Knight's case, police action was completely sidelined.

Knight suited up his legal "bulletproof vest" and in spite of having police personally witness his behavior, Knight, facing mandatory probation and up to four years in a Nevada state prison on each of the felony drug charges for possession of "Ecstasy" and Hydrocodone, a misdemeanor battery charge, and one felony coercion charge, was given the opportunity to strike a deal. His attorneys got Knight to plead "guilty" to the battery; the felonies were all dismissed. Per Clark County District Attorney David Roger, who spoke with the Las Vegas Sun, it turned out that since the beating, police "lost contact" with the victim who happened to be the key witness. The prosecutors, actually having to prove their case, couldn't proceed without this testimony. She was "disappeared" along with Knight's troubles.

And in 2009 Knight had a small fraction of the money and control he exercised in 1996.

Remember in 1996, a media storm was brewing over the Death Row stable's raunchy and violent lyrics. The controversy swirling around Knight and Death Row made Time Warner's shareholders nervous; so much so that in late 1995, the company divested its entire stake in Interscope Records. Conservatives and centrists like Former Drug Czar, William Bennett; Former Vice President, Dan Quayle; Senator, Joe Lieberman; and bolstered by support from the National Political Congress of Black Women rallied Washington DC to apply pressure on gangsta rap ultimately convincing Time Warner to sell its stake in Interscope back to Jimmy Iovine and Ted Field, the young team that had founded the label.

In contrast to its intended consequences, the daily life in the early days of The Kingdom of Thieves was good. Andre "Dr. Dre" Young, formerly of N.W.A., by that time had released "The Chronic"; in 1994, "Nuthin' but a 'G' Thang" and "Let Me Ride" were nominated at the 36th Grammy Awards, with the latter winning Best Rap Solo Performance for "Dre." "The Chronic" was included in Vibe Magazine's "100 Essential Albums of the 20th Century" and it was ranked at number six in their "Top 10 Rap Albums of All Time." Rolling Stone ranked it at number 137 on their list of the 500 Greatest Albums of All Time.

Similarly, Calvin Broadus aka Snoop Dogg's debut album, "Doggystyle," was released in 1993 under Death Row Records, debuting at No. 1 on both the Billboard 200 and Billboard Hot R&B/Hip-Hop Songs charts. Selling almost a million copies in the first week of its release, "Doggystyle" became certified platinum in 1994 and spawned several hit singles, including "What's My Name" and "Gin & Juice."

In 1994, Broadus released a soundtrack on Death Row Records for the short film "Murder Was the Case," where he also starred. Tupac recorded a track for the album and was paid $200,000 by Knight. Sadly, even though the track was recorded it wasn't released on the album.

Shakur meanwhile was generating his own controversy and stacking up lawsuits in nearly every state. He had shot two off-duty police officers in Atlanta that created notoriety but he also drew attention to himself from law enforcement. In late 1993, Shakur was charged with nine counts of sexual assault and in early 1994 he is sentenced for his attack on director Allen Hughes. When law enforcement and the prosecutor had a chance to put Shakur away for the alleged sexual assault they acted carefully. Ayanna Jackson, the alleged victim, in her interview with The Source Magazine, stated that it wasn't about her as a victim as much as it was about getting Shakur.

"They wanted everything to be fresh and documented and they had their own reasons." Shakur was sentenced to prison in "Dannemora" also known as Clinton Correctional Facility.

The Clinton Correctional Facility houses or has housed the likes of Lucky Luciano, the Brooklyn Strangler, Joel Rifkin—referred to as "Joel the Ripper" by tabloids after murdering 18 women, John Jamelske—Mass-kidnapper and serial rapist serving 18 years to life, John Taylor—who shot seven employees of a Wendy's restaurant in Queens, NY, Christopher Porco—Serving 50 years to life for the ax murder of his father, and Altemio Sanchez a.k.a. "The Bike Path Rapist" who murdered at least three women and raped at least 14 others in and around Buffalo, New York.

And in 1995, Tupac Shakur found his way there. Shakur was already a notable artist but he was in prison pending appeal for the conviction of the alleged sexual assault in New York. Shakur showed up to Court just after having been shot four times in a New York Studio. Tupac spent a good deal of time confined to his cell, but would see visitors often. The Outlawz were camped out at a hotel across the street and would rotate shifts on spending time with Shakur inside.

"Pac is now in Dannemora and everybody's visiting him back and forth, the guys," says Gloria Cox, Tupac's Maternal Aunt, otherwise known as "Aunt Glo."

"We want him out, nothing is happening. We tried to get an appeal lawyer. We did have the appeal lawyer, Charles Ogletree—but that's time."

By 1995, in the Kingdom of Death Row, one could not directly speak to King Knight; he had insulated himself to the world. There were only two people in Death Row that you approached if there was a problem—Prince Norris Anderson, a relative of Suge Knight and The Red Knight, Reggie Wright Junior.

Even controversy could not stop Death Row Records; Time Warner refused to distribute Death Row's release, "Dogg Food" by Tha Dogg Pound, which had been originally scheduled for release in June 1995. The album was subsequently pushed back, while Death Row and Interscope made an outside deal with Priority Records for distribution. Harry-O's money long gone, Knight now financed the label with funds from Time Warner's Interscope division under a novel arrangement that allowed him to retain ownership of Death Row's master recordings and song publishing rights. Advances were given to develop new artists.

In a recorded interview with Kevin Hackie by Los Angeles Police, Hackie then details more of the operating roles in the Death Row camp especially as it applied to Sharitha.

> MR. MILLER: You mean Sharitha?
> MR. HACKIE: Sharitha. Knightlife Entertainment, but that was actually the thing Suge set up. By law, it is a conflict of interest to have that. Basically we are getting all of these young artists, you know, buy them some jewelry, and give them $5,000 here and there. And then, of course, if 'the album didn't sell, keep all the money. Because a lot of times he would get big advancements from Jimmy Iovine (phonetic) over at Interscope, he would get the big advancements. He did that with all of his artists.

Knight received at least a million dollar advance for each act that he brought to the label, with the promise of a released album. If the album didn't do well, Knight was still paid and the artists never got paid. However Knight did not return the money to Interscope or Priority, he just had the understanding with the hungry labels that if you wanted the "40 million copy" money, you needed to eat a few million to do it. The labels were on board with that, and the artists were on bread and water rations. In one case, a producer threatened to quit if he was not paid immediately. Because Knight liked him, he broke his cycle and sent "Death Row Dave" with a quarter million dollar royalty payment to keep the guy working.

PART THREE:
THE INVESTIGATION

SEARCHING FOR LOGIC IN THE
ORLANDO ANDERSON SCUFFLE

The Shakur Investigation from the Point of View of Las Vegas Police was almost D.O.A. "Almost" is appropriate in this case, because while they were not sure who they "liked" for the shooting, they knew who they didn't like for the shooting almost immediately. This created an immediate tension between the Las Vegas Police and the Compton Police Department, for within a day or two of the shooting, Compton police were calling Las Vegas detectives and telling them that the shooting was the act of a single gunman, named Orlando Anderson.

Part of the skepticism about the Compton allegations came from a gamble that Wright Junior made in the immediate aftermath of the shooting. To understand this, the investigators had to learn about the "scuffle" with an alleged gang member—Orlando Anderson.

"Orlando Anderson is leaning up at the wall," Cathy Scott, former Las Vegas Sun reporter explains "watching people come out of the fight. This is near the food court and the lobby elevators, is where this happened and then you walk to the lobby, through the casino entrance and then to lobby.

"It always struck me as—that whole thing struck me as odd and they let him go. He did not have a ticket to the fight. He did tell people at one point and told the police that he had a ticket but he didn't have a ticket. He did not attend the fight. He's from Compton, He had no reason to be in Las Vegas."

Frank Alexander adds, "Travon (Travon Lane one of Knight's innercircle) whispered into Tupac's ear right after we walked out of the Mike Tyson fight. Pac took off running. I took off running behind him. The rest of the entourage was behind us."

"Maybe that was a set up," says Scott. "I mean, he was standing there waiting and waiting for somebody and then Tupac shows up and they start exchanging words with his entourage and everybody else they started stomping, yelling and doing their silly things but it was odd that—I keep saying odd, but the whole thing is odd."

According to the MGM video, Cathy Scott's recollection is incorrect. There was no time for anyone to exchange information with anyone else. They ran right up on Orlando Anderson and were immediately attacking him, looking much like a Black Sunday crowd at a Wal-Mart—all kicks and elbows. It was vicious and very short—less than 10 seconds.

From the moment that investigators understood the event and how the event happened, focus from everyone but Las Vegas investigators was on Anderson as the key suspect in the shooting. Vegas Police weren't buying it; but the collateral issue that arose was what finally sent Knight to prison—Knights involvement with the beating was a violation of his probation. And in a shortsighted gamble, The Red King and The Red Knight forced Frank Alexander to put forth a lie.

"If you swing to their story they won't hold you accountable" said Michael Moore to Frank Alexander on recorded telephone conversation. Their story was the fabricated story that Frank Alexander would tell Las Vegas investigator Brent Becker a week later. Alexander told investigators of a "chain snatching" by Orlando Anderson, where Anderson attempted to grab a Death Row Medallion chain off the neck of a Death Row entourage member. This was put forth to be the motive for the beating of Anderson later that day. Knight and Wright picked 6:30 p.m. as the time for the fabricated chain grab.

In an investigation, there is always a loose thread. It just so happens that in many cases when you begin to pull the thread, the sweater starts to become un-raveled. Depending on the size and strength of the thread, the entire sweater may dissolve. Anderson and the chain snatch was an immediate thread for investigators, simply for the fact that Death Row felt a false comfort in presenting a theory that admits culpability to a violent public crime but tries to evade responsibility by suggesting that it was "necessary" out of some weird code. And no matter how you look at it, the logic should not make any sense. How does a "gang issue" ever justify any violent act? Should the saying "two wrongs don't make a right" apply here? What made Death Row believe for a moment that this rationale would ever sell? Nothing excuses mob behavior.

KENNER ALCHEMY I:
THE EL REY THEATER SHOOTING

The pathetic truth is that Death Row had gotten away with using this failed logic chain or "rationale" successfully many times before as part of The Kenner Alchemy—and literally walked away from murder.

While the murder on March 14, 1995, at the Death Row Records "after party" for the Soul Train Awards, added to Knight's "gangsta" image, Knight wasn't ever a suspect in the murder. That said, many of his henchmen—including his best friend Jai Hassan Jamaal 'Jake The Violator' Robles—were suspects in the death of Kelly Jamerson at the El Rey Theater.

El Rey was pure Kenner Alchemy in action. The actual facts of the El Rey case itself make up The Kenner Alchemy's First Element. In the case of Kelly Jamerson's murder, it is impossible to ignore Death Row Records, as they sponsored the party. The Soul Train Awards "after party" was in honor of Calvin Broadus aka Snoop Dogg.

Security Guard, Eddie Shaw, gives an account of what happened: "David 'DJ Quik' Blake, a Tree-Top Blood, and the other guy, a Rollin 60 Crip, were throwing gang signs at each other. He was unsure who started the fight, but it was one of DJ Quick's bodyguards or friends. DJ Quick then picked up a chair and hit the first guy, while his bodyguards beat him. DJ Quick was also kicking this unknown person... the victim (who was not in- volved in this initial fight), then picked up a bottle and hit a guy in the head known as 'T-KO,' who was with Death Row. Between 12 and 15 suspects formed a circle around the victim and began kicking him."

Shaw said at one point he heard someone whom he knew as 'T-KO' say "We're going to kill this motherfucker! He and 'Tracy,' who worked for El Rey house security, then assisted in breaking up the fight. Shaw said DJ Quick was among the group that kicked the victim, and that the victim tried to get away, but the group wouldn't let him."

The beating lasted fifteen minutes. To put this into perspective the Orlando Anderson scuffle lasted 10 seconds.

Kelly Jamerson was attended to by paramedics, wheeled off on a stretcher, taken in an ambulance to the hospital and pronounced dead with- in hours. Kelly Jamerson endured a mob frenzy kicking, stomping, punch- ing and hitting him with chairs and beer bottles.

The Kenner Alchemy Second Element involved the initial findings by Los Angeles Police Detectives from Wilshire Division. DJ Quick was seen at the center of the beating and was clearly in the crosshairs of investiga- tors along with many Death Row insiders commonly known as Suge's inner circle.

Witnesses claimed that Quick grabbed a bottle from a bar and struck Kelly Jamerson. The investigation was closing in on Death Row affili- ates as the responsible parties for Kelly Jamerson's murder.

The Kelly Jamerson coroner's report would detail the extent of the damage and severity of the wounds that were literally all over his body. Many thought that the act of hitting Kelly Jamerson over the head with a full beer bottle was the blow that killed him. There was certainly a fracture and blood oozing out of his skull but the autopsy report was inconclusive. In fact, there were so many other blows, bruises, cuts, and severe tissue damage that there was no single clear-cut cause of death. That was a factor that complicated the investigation and clouded the prosecution but many eyewitnesses named names and sighted acts that were done and a case was coming together.

Two LAPD Officers were witnesses to the fight and murder that night. "Officer Meade stated that while looking into the lobby, he observed the victim (Kelly Jamerson) being hit over the head by a beer bottle. The victim fell to the ground and he observed blood coming from injuries to his head. He stated that approximately twelve male/blacks then began kicking and hitting the victim on all areas of his body." They were able to identify eight suspects that were submitted to the District Attorney's office for prosecution. Nineteen witnesses, some of which were police officers, gave statements that implicated MOB Piru Bloods, all were consistent, however, no charges were filed, no one was prosecuted, and there were no convictions in this brutal beating and murder. Why?

"If I had a world of my own, it would be nonsense!" said Alice from "Alice in Wonderland." Welcome to Alice's world, otherwise known as the Third Element.

The Kenner Alchemy Third Element is where the forces of the Kingdom of Thieves all come together and bring their powers and influence to replace the truth with a convenient lie or lies. The end result would be a sabotage of the findings in Element Two. One effective method was the use of the LA Times aka "Death Row Times" to manipulate existing facts or create completely fabricated facts—whatever it took, with the entire readership of Los Angeles and the Associated Press making those altered facts the public truth.

Another tactic was to make a witness face scrutiny or outright slander to discredit his or her testimony, or destroy the "messenger's" credibility. In the El Rey murder of Kelly Jamerson a telemarketing campaign was created to point suspicion away from Knight's "Homeboy Security." There was also information provided that Quick had previously been involved in an altercation with a Rolling 60's Crip.

And like the Orlando Anderson "chain snatch excuse" years later, some screwball logic is passed to Wilshire Division Homicide detectives: interference that was orchestrated and executed by Tim Brennan of Compton Police. He called over to Wilshire Division and recommended that the case be cleared without proceeding against the gang members or DJ Quick identified by witnesses, because Brennan stated, "this just boils down to a gang retaliation, nothing more."

Police know that it is extremely difficult to solve a homicide involving gangs; even harder to get through court with a conviction. Gangs do not turn on each other. Brennan and his mentor Reginald Wright, Senior, lieutenant for the Compton Police Department and head of the city's "gang detail" knew that a "case" would be hard to build against an amorphous entity like a gang.

And here was the false logic: "you won't get anywhere with this crowd, so it makes it alright to not challenge it and you might as well stop now." And that appeared to work, propelling the El Rey Investigation into the Fourth Element.

By the time the investigation achieved The Kenner Alchemy Fourth Element, it meant that the Third Element was successful; the train had become derailed. And a train wreck is a horrendous thing: the antithesis of a train gliding smoothly downs the tracks. As discussed earlier, the Kenner Alchemy formula is strict and structured and damaging.

The investigation was now confused and clouded. If the case went to trial, the prosecution would also have to release all leads in the investigation to the Defense. Keep in mind that any leads pointing away from the people charged with murder would create reasonable doubt. That is all any defense attorney would need to obtain an acquittal for his or her clients. Brennan's advice seemed the course of least resistance for the confused Wilshire detectives, and with that the investigation was closed. The case was cleared and no charges were ever filed in spite of so many credible witnesses.

KENNER ALCHEMY II:
MURDER WAS THE CASE (SNOOP'S TRIAL)

There was another murder case that was being sabotaged a mere month after the murder of Kelly Jamerson. As mentioned earlier this one involved Calvin "Snoop Dogg" Broadus. Broadus was on trial for murder; the result of the shooting of Philip Woldermariam by his bodyguard at the time.

The murder evidence possibly incriminating Broadus for this trial was being held at the Los Angeles Police Department's Pacific Division. Pacific Division was also where LAPD officer Kevin Gaines, the Blue Knight of Thieves, was stationed. At the time, Broadus was critical to The Red Queen.

The Blue Knight was The Red Queen's suitor, and Broadus one of her main sources of income. So, it came as little surprise to anyone but the Los Angeles County District Attorney that somehow, mysteriously, the evidence from the Broadus murder case disappeared from the LAPD Pacific Division evidence locker.

At the time the evidence disappeared, the case against Broadus was not looking good for the defense. The loss of evidence would turn the case around; the Kenner Alchemy applied again. The First Element was the shooting of Philip Woldermariam. The Second Element was the finding against Broadus. The Third Element became the alleged intervention through the theft of evidence. Evidence missing from lockers seemed to be a problem for police at the time, as if it was California building code to place revolving doors with no locks on the evidence rooms in all Southern California police stations!

The Kenner Alchemy Fourth Element became the derailed case against Broadus, wherein the prosecution's critical missing evidence, a shirt and shell casings, completely undermined their case. To galvanize the story for the public and the media, Kenner and his team of spin-doctors employed The Kenner Alchemy Fifth Element—the act of furtherance by actually going on the attack; poking fun at the prosecution who planned to use this evidence to demonstrate that Woldermariam was murdered in cold blood. The Los Angeles Times' Frank B. Williams galvanized the Fifth Element into the public's conscience.

"Defense attorneys have maintained," Williams wrote, "that the lost 9-millimeter casings might have been useful to match bullets found in Woldemariam's body. They also said the bloody shirt was crucial in determining if the victim was shot at close range or might have been twisting when he was shot. Defense attorneys contend that Woldemariam was reaching into his waistband for a gun when he was shot."

Woldermariam was shot in the back. As the Kenner Alchemy need only prove reasonable doubt, the ploy worked. Broadus was acquitted.

ORLANDO ANDERSON'S ALIBI:

In respect to the Shakur homicide it appeared that Las Vegas Police were quickly moving to exclude individuals. Las Vegas detectives interviewed Corey Edwards who was with Orlando Anderson after the scuffle. Edwards made this statement (Statement of: Corey Lamont Edwards (DR#97-0711963):

"I remember when Tupac got killed. I had driven to Las Vegas with my friends Red (Ken Johnson, late 20's early 301s), Polo (LaDale Watkins or Watson, 28-29 years old) and Pook (Calvin Winbush, 28-29 years old). Polo and Pook are cousins and are from Detroit. Red is from Ohio. Pook got us rooms at the MGM Grand Hotel. I can't remember what room numbers.

"I had tickets to the Tyson fight. I got them through my friend Gouchi (from Pasadena, nfd). He had an extra ticket. I told him I would pay him for it but he said that I didn't have to, to just buy him a drink. My girlfriend came up to Vegas later with some other friends... I know that there were some other Southside guys there too, but I never saw them.

"After the Tyson fight, I went to a bar in the hotel and drank with Gouchi and Stacy Augman (retired professional basketball player). That's when I saw some other friends of mine. I asked them what was going on and they said that Baby Lane and Tupac had gotten into a fight. I looked around and saw Baby Lane standing in the corner. Me and Gouchi walked up to him and asked him what had happened and if he was okay.

"He said that he had got into it with Tupac and Tupac's people, but that everything was cool. Baby Lane didn't appear to be injured or too upset about what happened. We walked away from him and continued to drink at the bar. A little time passed and that's when I ran into Lisa. We got into a big argument in the lobby of the hotel. We went up to our room and continued to argue.

"After a while, we came back downstairs and I saw my friends at the bar including Gouchi. Lisa left and went to where her cousins were staying at the Luxor. I hooked up with Gouchi and he told me that Tupac had been shot. I drank some more and then my friends Red, Polo and Pook came up to my room. We called some girls that we had met from Chicago. They came over and partied with us. I never saw Baby Lane again while I was in Vegas. On Sunday, I drove home and got home Sunday night."

Las Vegas casinos all have interior and exterior surveillance footage. Much of what anyone says about their whereabouts in Las Vegas casinos is verifiable with the "eye in the sky," the same type of surveillance footage that is used from the MGM Hotel during Knight's probation hearings.

The MGM footage was "leaked" publicly by an unknown party, much to the displeasure of Las Vegas Detectives. However, after it was introduced at Knight's trial it was public record, and neither MGM nor Las Vegas Police had anything they could say about it. It would be very likely though, after the MGM footage appeared publicly, as did other subsequent "leaks" surrounding the investigation, that Las Vegas Detectives sequestered any and all footage that validated or discredited the statements of key witnesses or suspects.

The important part of Edwards' narrative was regardless of where he was staying, his meeting with Anderson at the hotel bar subsequent to Anderson's scuffle with Knight, Shakur, and the entourage, was no doubt recorded by hotel surveillance cameras.

What's more, the MGM hotel security would have preserved ALL footage from the preceding 24 hours and the proceeding 24 hours from the event, solely because a felony battery had taken place and the event itself is subject to court action. It is irrefutable that the meeting between Edwards and Anderson was recorded and no doubt Las Vegas Detectives knew it. There is also a solid probability that the Monte Carlo hotel footage showed time-coded coming and going from Edwards' room. A later series of "communication issues"–matters of trust–would mar the open flow of information from Las Vegas, but more importantly Las Vegas would not want to risk exposure of its evidence to the leaking and conflicted police departments of Los Angeles and Compton.

As to Edwards, the failed 2006 LAPD "Murder Rap" investigation into the matter of the shootings, produced no new revelation into Edwards' statement. Its self-proclaimed lead investigator wrote about it in his book:

"But it was all wishful thinking, like Tray before him, Corey Edwards wasn't about to cooperate. He'd already given his statement, he told us. He was trying to go straight and start a new life as a boxing promoter. That was all he had to say on the subject. Like every criminal facing a prison sentence, he had done the math and was willing to take a calculated risk to find out what kind of time he would be facing back in Ohio. If the number came up right, he could wait it out. If it didn't, well, maybe he'd take us up on our offer to help him out if we could. We had hit another dry hole. We were now 0 for 2." (Murder Rap, page 102)

INITIAL FINDINGS EXCLUDE
A RANDOM EVENT

Las Vegas Police would also need to exclude that the shooting of Shakur and Knight could simply be a "random shooting." Brent Becker, Junior Detective on the case, felt at least at one point, it was. One way to eliminate this option was to visualize the map. Knight lived on Loma Vista Road and they were on route to 1700 Flamingo Road. A map of the location gives the "appropriate route":

- Start: Knight's Las Vegas house
- Head south on Loma Vista Ave toward Alamitos Circle (0.2 mi)
- Turn left at Mira Vista St. (0.3 mi)
- Turn right at E Warm Springs Rd. (0.5 mi)
- Turn right at S Eastern Ave. (4.0 mi)
- Turn left at E Flamingo Rd./NV-592 (0.6 mi)
- End: 1700 E Flamingo Rd. Las Vegas, NV 89119

Next, the question is whether this was a "normal" route to the club. Clearly the entourage was not interested in taking the "appropriate route" that night, because witnesses had made it clear that the entourage wanted to be seen. The revised appropriate way to access the nightclub was via Tropicana, then down Koval. But the entourage intentionally stayed in heavy traffic to approach the club from Flamingo straight down–past Koval. This is the route the witnesses testified to:

The trip up Las Vegas Boulevard:

- Head south on Loma Vista Ave toward Alamitos Circle (0.2 mi)
- Turn left at Mira Vista St (0.3 mi)
- Turn right at E Warm Springs Rd (0.5 mi)
- Turn right at S Eastern Ave (1.0 mi)
- Turn left at NV-562/E Sunset Rd (3.0 mi)

The course correction:

- Turn right at Las Vegas Blvd S/NV-604 (2.0 mi)
- Turn right at E Flamingo Rd/NV-592 (3.5 mi)
- End: 1700 E Flamingo Rd Las Vegas, NV 89119

The entourage had plenty of opportunity to access the club in a more expedient route, yet they took the most difficult route possible. It may have been a matter of expediency, without making multiple turns. It also was because, as stated by witnesses, they wanted to be noticed. The most direct publicly known route is on two streets; up Las Vegas Boulevard and down Flamingo. It is less confusing and one would not want the shooters to get lost going to or going away from the shooting.

One possible scenario, but apparently eliminated early on, and one that was tied to the Anderson scuffle, was one of revenge by gang members that were just driving around when they supposedly get a call from Anderson who says, "Hey this guy beat me up. We need to get him!" The other scenario that was likely eliminated early on, was that Anderson's crew left from Treasure Island, where Anderson's lawyer says that he was staying; the direct opposite direction from Club 662 and several miles from Knight's home.

The pristine "random shooting" theory suggests that there were some gang members with a serious desire to shoot at Knight and Shakur for some reason or another, who were in a car just driving around waiting for the Death Row entourage to come past them on the way to the nightclub. The theory also carries the conceit that these gang members would have had to have been in a location to "pick up" or acquire the entourage on its way to Knight's home, follow the entourage through the 3rd least probable route, and then find an opportunity to drive up and fire their weapons at a car that they believed had Shakur in it.

The issue with this theory is that it contradicts witness testimony. Shakur was not making himself known, as former Las Vegas Sun Reporter Cathy Scott points out. No witness, including the 4 girls in the car next to Shakur and Knight, who had the best view as witnesses, ever claimed that Shakur was drawing attention to himself. If anyone looking for Knight were to assume that Death Row followed "Death Row Protocol," witnesses stated that it was typical and common knowledge that Knight wanted to always be in the first car of the procession. "Death Row Dave" Matthews confirmed that this was the way Knight wanted it.

The next hurdle investigators faced was summed up in Brent Becker's sarcastic comment in his 2007 interview. "They would have to be pretty good, with all the traffic there." Becker referred to a random shooter knowing that Shakur was riding with Knight. How would they know that? Shakur had his fiancé's car, and Alexander was driving it. But to simply "guess" that Shakur and Knight were in the same car and not in the front seems, frankly, implausible. Becker is right–they would have to be "that good."

The truth investigators in Las Vegas already would have known by that time, was that anyone that would happen across a 20-car-plus procession would be in no way capable of knowing, without some intelligence handed to them, that Shakur was with Knight and not in his Kidada Jones' Lexus. It is doubtful that even most of the caravan actually knew which car Shakur was in; that was inside information.

Cathy Scott gets it right this time when she states in a 2006 interview, "Just coincidentally, some gunman sticks his arm out of the white Cadillac and shoots the biggest rapper in America. Why didn't they shoot anybody else?"

Unfortunately, the lead detective for the 2006 failed LAPD "Murder Rap" investigation put out a coerced interview with Orlando Anderson's uncle and current fugitive from the law, Duane Keith Davis. In this interview, with a pending 3rd strike on the line, Davis alleges that in spite of all the logic problems, this was exactly how it went down; It was a big stroke of luck. They just happened to be going the opposite direction on Flamingo at 50 mph and saw Knight and Shakur together in the same car, in their own moving vehicle at night.

LOS, or Line of Sight, is what allows a person to actually see what they are shooting at. Line of Sight says that we need to acquire a target at some point. Knight passed the following streets;

- East Diablo Avenue
- Giles Street
- East Reno Avenue
- East Tropicana Boulevard
- Rue de Monte Carlo
- East Harmon Avenue

Anyone wanting to catch the procession would have had to sit waiting to make a right on Las Vegas Boulevard. Similarly, if the shooters wanted to catch the procession, and were waiting for it, they would have been waiting to make a right on the following street:

• Audrie Street

As just stated, Duane Davis says that they "got lucky" and saw Knight and Shakur though lanes of traffic, and did a U Turn on Flamingo. This was not part of what investigators, at the time, were ever told by a single witness. As established, no witness ever claimed that Shakur gave his position away. Neither did any witness make a claim about anyone asking about it either. Under the Las Vegas Police, Becker's "that good" standard, it was not a credible option.

So what it the actual likelihood that the shooters would be "pretty good" and randomly acquire the victims en route? What were the odds that Knight's car was spotted and followed with random gang guys in a car or by Davis driving around?

This is the math:

- There was a 50% chance of leaving down Vegas Blvd from Suge's home;
- There was a 10% chance the shooter would be on a street with line of sight;
- There was a 50% chance they know what car Shakur is in: they either could or couldn't;
- There was a 50% chance they could actually intercept/ acquire the cars with Vegas "stopped" traffic: they either could or couldn't;
- 50% x 10% = 5%;
- 50% of 5% = 2.5%;
- 50% of 2.5 = 1.25%;

So, Becker's sarcasm is warranted, and it is no wonder this theory never publicly gained traction. There would be a 1.25 % chance of being "pretty good."

If there was no communication with the shooters who may have stumbled onto the procession, then anyone expecting to know the entourage's route would have had to follow them to, and from, Knight's home; the option of leaving from Treasure Island, with two streets, Las Vegas Boulevard and Audrie Rd, to acquire the target provides no better odds. How would anyone have had time to know what people, were in which vehicle?

That said, Las Vegas Detectives would have to consider that there may have been communication from someone in the procession. If that were the case the odds begin to shift: communication from the procession on intercept: add 1.25% as they still would have had to be in the spot to ask. If there was additional communication about any part of the route they were travelling, it increases the odds 50% to about 62%. And if there was communication from someone the whole way regarding the route being taken arbitrarily by the procession, the probability increases to 90-100% likelihood of the hunters getting to the hunted… and immediately closes the "random shooting theory" as not credible.

If there was communication from anyone to the attackers, it was no longer random or unplanned. It is planned and communicated. Now there are accessories, conspirators communicating with each other. And while Las Vegas Detectives would not know it at the time, a clue that would come in later, the "Confession Letter" of Malcom Patton, would become immediately important.

Patton's letter may very well have perfectly addressed the issue of the "line of sight" by stating that there were six "barricades" from which "no one was going to make it out alive." Could the six intersections of Las Vegas Boulevard have been the "barricades" referred to in the letter? More importantly how would Patton, not a geographer, know about that specific number of intersections, unless he had been there or had been told? This was a clue that would not re-surface for almost 20 years, and implicates The Red Knight in doing one critical deed: providing information on where the King of Thieves would be. We doubt it coincidental.

The final collapse of the "random theory" happens when evidence is presented that the shooter started firing from the rear of Knight's car. The shooter did not stop to make a positive identification of Shakur or Knight; a flaw that was corrected in the Wallace shooting. Someone already had that knowledge. And according to multiple witnesses, Knight's BMW was new; a gift to Norris Anderson that Knight elected to drive. In fact, the Las Vegas police stopped Knight for not displaying temporary plates.

So was this information communicated? Michael Moore hearing "got 'em" come over The Red Knight's radio is certainly damning testimony that there were at least three radios being used by Death Row members that night, and possibly countless more cell phones. Clearly someone was talking. And even when Las Vegas claims one can "beat the odds," it is rarely ever true and the entire city was built on that lie.

This left Las Vegas Detectives to begin to search for another motive.

THE PRICE OF FREEDOM

By 1996, Calvin Broadus and other artists were beginning to notice that in spite of astronomical numbers coming into The Kingdom of Thieves, somehow it wasn't coming down to the common folk or the knighted few. The magic of The Kingdom no longer seemed limited to fooling new artists into signing contracts that were not in their best interests. The sorcery of making money disappear now appeared to include artist royalties. But Snoop wasn't the first to notice.

Andre "Dr. Dre" Young, one of the artists in the Kingdom, was cast down from his spot when Kenner and Knight basically usurped his position. They were not sharing much with him as a partner in the business or as an artist; the magic was in full bloom.

However, when one dared to question The Red King of Thieves, there were severe and absolute consequences. Most of the time, The Red King would send one of his Knights of the Kingdom of Thieves; soldiers with nicknames of "Buntry," "Heron," "Neckbone," and others, to pay an unfriendly visit. The result of that visit usually involved physical violence and some recant of the person being visited. Such was the case with Young. While the details are sketchy, Young's home was broken into and it was made clear to Dre that no one should ever question the Kingdom.

And the threat apparently was so substantial that on March 14, 1996, Young relinquished his ownership interests in the Kingdom of Thieves and inconceivably forgave Death Row's obligation under the 1992 Agreement to pay him royalties due through December 31, 1995—all valued at sixty million dollars ($60,000,000). One must be very afraid to not only relinquish the interest in the Kingdom at its height, but to also completely walk away from any royalties earned from a Grammy award-winning album. But he did!

Young's 1996 contract contained a separate provision whereby he quitclaimed to Death Row his copyright in the sound recordings he had created and/or produced while at Death Row, and/or on which he performed, including "The Chronic," "Murder Was the Case," "Doggystyle," and "Above the Rim."

In exchange for Young's release, The Red King agreed that the sound recordings and albums would not be distributed or re-distributed in anything other than their original forms. Death Row would pay Young royalties, but only from and after January 1, 1996. As the name implies, previous royalties were the given up as tribute to The Kingdom of Thieves.

Young was not the only artist not seeing royalties. Broadus' attorneys shared some interesting facts with the 2009 Bankruptcy Court that shed light on this. They claimed that Death Row was obligated to pay royalties to Broadus for his work on some of Death Row's biggest selling recordings, including "Doggystyle," "Murder Was the Case," and "The Doggfather."

It is unclear just how many times Death Row re-released or licensed these recordings, but one thing is clear—Broadus received neither royalties nor accountings owed to him. And if that was the case for the larger artists, it was certainly the case for smaller ones.

In the 2006 Death Row Bankruptcy, many other artists came out the woodwork making identical claims about crooked accounting. Nathan Hale ("Nate Dogg") had this to say:

> "The Death Row Parties collected millions of dollars in record sales and record royalties and music publishing and music publishing royalties and never accounted to or paid Creditor (Nate Dogg) amounts he was entitled to in respect of his contributions to records and songs released by or through the Death Row Parties."

It appeared, according to Hale, that whenever he would approach the Death Row Royals regarding payment of monies he was potentially owed, he was either threatened with violence; told he was not owed any monies because no profits were derived from the venture because no monies had been collected; or told that he would be accounted to in due course.

The problem was that Death Row Records was constantly spending money before it was earned. Typically, the Record Distributor would own music masters. The Red King promised artists that they could own their own masters but they were pledged as collateral. Those masters would be mortgaged to strip cash out of them. "Death Row Dave" Matthews speaks frequently about the large sums of cash that was sloshing around the company.

The private jets would pick up partygoers and fly them around the world. Alcohol, cocaine, and marijuana were mere party favors. The most beautiful women from all over the world joined in the fun and lots of cash greased the wheels to keep the party going. Record albums were flowing out the front door and the back door led to criminal activities in the deepest secret places around the world. Concert tours took them to many American cities and new connections were established to give new life to the party. Death Row will be forever remembered as one of the pinnacles of opulence.

No matter how much money poured into the company the appetite for spending was insatiable. "Dogg Food" was supposed to be released in July of 1995. Death Row Records had already received an advance for the album. Because of turmoil at Interscope and Time Warner the release was delayed until October 31st and was distributed by Priority Records.

By the fall of 1995, The Kingdom of Thieves needed an infusion of cash and Tupac Shakur was languishing at the Clinton Correctional Facility. Tupac Shakur perfectly fit the profile of Death Row targets; he was successful and was embroiled in criminal troubles. Shakur's album, "Me against the World" debuted at number one on the Billboard 200 and stayed there for four weeks. Shakur sold 240,000 copies in the first week of its release. His royalty accounts were overflowing with money, that under his contracts would not be due to him for several months. Gaining power of attorney over Shakur would give Death Row Records immediate access to that money.

Knight worked out a deal with Interscope Records, who was interested for political reasons in distancing themselves from Shakur because he was serving a prison sentence for sexual assault.

Nina Bhadreshwar confirmed however, that Knight had wanted Shakur on Death Row for some time, but Shakur was not interested. "Suge had been asking Tupac to come to Death Row eighteen months or so before, but Tupac always refused, stating he wanted to do his own thing," Nina Bhadreshwar claims. "He told everyone he didn't want to go there."

"Throughout all of this, David Kenner sat staring at me with a slight smile, sometimes whispering in Suge's ear. David Kenner, his lawyer, stood nearby and, when Suge looked on the verge of flipping out over a particular issue, he would look over to Kenner for guidance and Kenner would say something which Suge would repeat loudly so it sounded like it originated from Suge."

Bhadreshwar also seems to allege that Shakur's addition to Death Row was not as important as the much-needed money such an addition would bring to the Kingdom's coffers.

"'What about Tupac?" Bhadreshwar asked. "Shouldn't we be helping or supporting him in some way? He's in jail and I've had letters from him. He's not doing well.'

"For a moment, Suge's face went black as thunder. Then he laughed and said, looking at David Kenner, 'Did he tell you about when he was raped?' I was nervous and confused. I just hooked onto the word 'rape' and not what he'd actually said. I thought he said something like ''Did he tell you about the girl he raped?'' so I automatically rushed to his defense. 'That's not true and you know it. He didn't do it.'

"Suge bristled slightly but carried on laughing. All the staff members stood in stunned silence. 'Tupac's been raped!' laughed Suge, looking at David Kenner who also chuckled. The more I ranted in Pac's defense, the more Suge laughed over me.

"Everyone heard him say this. I don't know how people could have worked up there when Tupac later joined Death Row knowing Suge had been so blatant with his malicious disrespect of him."

So, what was Shakur's motive for wanting to align himself in the Kingdom? Why would Shakur sign with Death Row?

For one, Shakur had made it known to his manager Atron Gregory, that he was interested in recording with Snoop Dogg and Dr. Dre. The only way he was going to be able to record with those artists was as an artist of Death Row; at the time Death Row did not let artists record with non-Death Row artists. Shakur's "Murder is the Case" recording never was released.

Gloria Cox confirmed that Knight had been "trying to get at him" for some time. Watani Tyehimba, Stewart Levy, and Charles Ogletree told the New Yorker Magazine in 1997 that they argued vigorously with Shakur about his decision to go to Death Row. "Tupac told us, 'The trouble with all of you is, you're too nice,'" Levy recalls.

But rumors about Shakur's New York shooting abounded citing it as an orchestrated hit. The manufactured myth about East Coast vs. West Coast put Shakur's life in danger while inside the predominantly "East" Dannemora facility. The East vs. West controversy may have existed to sell more albums, but Shakur needed the protection an alliance with the Kingdom of Thieves might provide.

From prison, Shakur threw down the gauntlet; he wanted to test Knight's desire to have him in the The Kingdom. According to Atron Gregory, Shakur's former manager, because Shakur was in jail, he could only experience the world via the television. So, Shakur asked Knight to show him a sign at the 1995 Source Award show that Knight wanted Shakur in the Kingdom.

On a hauntingly familiar date, September 7, 1995, Knight publicly addressed Shakur over the air telling him to "keep his guard up" and then dissing Sean "Puffy" Combs and the East Coast. Knight got up and did his famous "if you want a video without your producer in it, come to death Row" scene-stealer.

When Shakur heard about that, he was convinced that Death Row might be able to shield him from "the others" out to get him. It meant that Knight acknowledged Shakur's outrage about being the victim of a shooting in 1994, while in New York; a shooting commonly and misguidedly blamed on the rappers of the East Coast. This is sometimes why people turn to the mob, but quickly learn, as Shakur would, that there was quite a price to pay.

Most importantly this public spectacle was about all Knight could do for Shakur, which made Shakur feel good. But this was an illusion propped up for an audience of one. The truth was that no one from the Kingdom of Thieves had ever visited Shakur in prison. Knight and The Kingdom were completely remote from Shakur, and Shakur was going to be released from prison on a Certificate of Appeal regardless of what Death Row did; which was filed in March of 1995.

So Shakur invited Kenner and Knight to visit Shakur in prison. Within a week of Death Row's visit to Shakur and in a stunning coincidence, the New York Court of Appeals granted Shakur his Certificate of Leave to Appeal. As his bail had been posted months beforehand, he was releasable the moment the order was granted. That release took a lot of work, and it's important to detail out what getting out of prison involves. One does not wave the Kenner Magic Wand as Wright claims. It's a lot of paperwork and months of preparation.

In order to appeal a conviction in New York, the defendant must file a notice of appeal and Motion for Leave to Appeal within 30 days of the date he or she was sentenced. This means one has to ask the Court for permission to file an appeal. One just doesn't file an appeal. You have to be granted that right first.

Shakur was convicted December 1, 1994. He was not sentenced however until February 7, 1995. This means that the notice of appeal and Motion for Leave to Appeal would have to be filed no later than March 7, 1995.

Shakur's attorneys ordered a transcript of the trial, in order to prepare a written brief that included all of the arguments in the appeal. Once the brief was submitted to the court, the prosecutor would need to respond with a brief and the attorneys might have been asked to make an oral argument. Shakur, via his attorneys, requested he be released from prison pending the decision of the appellate court, which is known as an application for a stay of execution of sentence.

Shakur's bail was set at the time of the original sentencing. The bail was set very high compared to that of Charles "Man-Man" Fuller. Shakur's original bail was three million dollars ($3,000,000). Shakur's attorneys used that disparity between the two bails, as a way to re-negotiate a lower, more compromised bail of the one point four million dollars ($1,400,000) while in the middle of drafting the Motion for Leave to Appeal.

Since there is only one time that the Court was going to make a decision on the "leave" request, and the only time they can determine if the Shakur could be out of prison during those years, it made perfect sense to make sure a "bail bond" is already in place.

So, prior to the time the intermediate appellate court might issue an order staying execution of the sentence pending the determination of the appeal, and releasing Shakur on bail that had to be posted no later than March 7, 1995. Tyehimba and Gregory raised the bail and submitted it as a bond and package to the court with the Motion for Leave to Appeal attached. It is intentional that this March 1995 date is mentioned repeatedly. It is months before The Source Awards.

The "Motion for Leave" was considered by the Court, and the Court issued a certificate granting permission, or "Leave" to Appeal. Next the Court needed to decide on what to do with Shakur between the time they say it is okay to appeal and the time the appeal itself is filed and accepted by the Court. He can either stay in jail or be freed for the interim. Shakur was freed.

As to the bail itself, Atron Gregory said the "push was on" to get the paperwork in to the Court. They were under something of a time constraint; Shakur's appeal needed to be considered prior to the end of the current Winter/Spring session, as it would place the matter for review when the courts came in session in the Late Summer/Fall. Any delay in raising the bail that would cause the appeal to be delayed, and keep Shakur "on ice" for another year at least.

So Interscope advanced money; Interscope had the money to pay an advance because it was Shakur's money. At the time Shakur was in prison, his album is released at #1 on the Billboard Charts. There was plenty of money owed him. He actually paid a significant portion of his own bail. But had Shakur waited for it to actually get paid and not use an "advance" it could have taken several months to fund. Shakur would then still have to wait in prison between the time the "Motion for Leave to Appeal" package was filed and the hearing on that package. Interscope paid royalties before they were contractually due. But by then it was irrefutable that Shakur had earned the money.

Jasmine Guy, the actress, added money to the bail, and mythology insists that Madonna, the pop singling icon who had at one time dated Shakur, posted a portion of the bail as well. But this was not exactly true, and this among several other pubic misconceptions about the Shakur/Wallace relationship would haunt both the Shakur and Wallace homicide investigations for some time.

In truth, an attorney that did in fact represent several celebrity clients, including Madonna, fronted the part of bail money attributed to Madonna. However the attorney represented another noteworthy client: Christopher Wallace.

It is interesting to examine this possibility, in light of how wrong Shakur's observations about Wallace were during that period. Wallace was at the hospital in 1994 waiting for news on Shakur. Wallace helped Fuller remove weapons from the hotel room in the 1994 "rape" case; weapons that if discovered by prosecutors, would have spelled doom for the entire group. Wallace was openly upset about Shakur being shot, according to Gloria Cox who was in New York with Wallace. Many have come to the understanding that perhaps Wallace did not deserve quite the visceral hatred Shakur was broadcasting across the nation against Wallace: that the punishment may not have fit the crime.

It is possible that Wallace may have known about the bail being posted? His own attorney was posting the bail. Was it money received from Wallace? Is it possible that Wallace actually put up the money? Wallace knew that Shakur would not accept money for bail coming from his so-called "rival"; what would the press make of the East Coast/West Coast feud if Shakur accepts "charity" from Wallace?

At any rate on September 16, 1995 Knight and Kenner visited Shakur in prison where he signed with Death Row Records. Knight and Kenner had no previous business dealings in the bond posted in March of 1995, but because the appeal bond had already been proffered, there was no need to gather the money and post bail. Shakur was released immediately the moment he was awarded the Certificate from the Court.

However, The Death Row Times makes Shakur's release seem magical by tying it to Shakur signing with Death Row Records. The Kingdom of

Thieves made sure, like many other falsehoods, that this was part of public legend.

Even recently, in a 2011 interview done with website Bomb1st, Wright discussed why he "knew" Shakur was not leaving Death Row. The Red Knight proclaimed that the only reason that Shakur would never dream of leaving Death Row was because Death Row paid Shakur's bail.

> "Why would you want to leave somewhere where the people are controlling your freedom," said Wright. "David Kenner who once directly worked with Suge, and in my opinion damn near ran the company, was also the attorney doing his [Tupac's] appeal.
>
> "If David Kenner, Suge Knight or anyone else was mad at Tupac, what wouldn't they have done? Institutionalized Tupac! Had his appeals bonds revoked ultimately!
>
> "They didn't have any reason to kill him or anything like that. They'd have him go back to jail... if someone wants to do something like that.
>
> "This is all so stupid—he wasn't going to leave nobody knowing his appeal was going to be overturned! Why would you have people mad at you that's holding your freedom in their hands? Tupac had a four year jail stretch to do—he did not want to go back to prison... how long do you think it would be if he had to go back to jail?"

Wright Junior's comments are, to use his words, just as "stupid," largely because all of the evidence clearly proves that Death Row had nothing to do with the bail. If this statement had come from anyone else, there may have been some sort of an excuse for getting it this wrong, but not from Wright—who claimed to know all of the inner workings of Death Row—and in fact ran it for Knight. He was intimately involved in every aspect of the relationship with Death Row and Shakur, and knows that Death Row had absolutely nothing to do with the appeal or more importantly the bail posting. Yet the lie gets repeated: a poor and failed imitation of the Kenner Alchemy.

An interview with Shakur by Street Heat in November 1995 speaks about the matter and the myth of Death Row paying the bail:

> "So Pac, a lot of people want to know, since Death Row Records put up your bail money," asked Street Heat. "Is that why you left Interscope?

"It didn't have nothing to do with the money," said Shakur. "It had nothing to do with the bail. I was already, um, I hollered at Suge before the bail situation when I was still an inmate in the correctional facility and I was looking at serving three years, I called Suge and said, 'Yo, I want to be with Death Row. I want you to manage me because I'm in jail–and no one is handling my business while I'm in jail, nobody's putting it down like I want to put it down.' I knew he's a man that would put things down. I trust him, his word, you know, um. I really couldn't trust nobody in business no more, so I chose him, you know?"

"Wasn't it during the time that Interscope was rumored to be leaving Warners and all that?" asked Street Heat.

"Yeah, that was another factor," replied Shakur. "Because I was like, 'Dang, they don't care about us.' I mean, it's not Interscope's fault, but they really don't owe us anything and at any minute we could be you know, alone without a contract after you put all your heart on the line, your music on the line, you went out there and gave all your talent up and all of a sudden, it's not good enough anymore and they'll kick you off.

"So I was like, by going to Death Row, it's like two superpowers joining up. You know, it would be similar to the US and England teamin' up against anybody, you know what I mean? So I felt it was like joining two super powers. And if rap music was going to have to fight for its right to be uncensored, then this was the team for me to get on, to wage that battle."

A SIMPLE HEIST

Las Vegas Metropolitan Investigators had spent the first week of the investigation interviewing witnesses while Shakur was on his death bed. They were getting interference from Kenner and Kelesis about speaking to Death Row employees. People from all over the media have made claims that Las Vegas Investigators were not clear as to what they believed and that they were "not sharing" information. Las Vegas Sun Reporter Cathy Scott goes out on a limb about the matter to go public in her 2007 declaration that the entire matter was 'buttoned up at the top' of the investigation.

"Oh, I was regularly, regularly contacting the police," said Scott, "and I had sources within the police department saying, hey, they don't want this thing to go to trial, all these gangster rappers would come to town, it would be bad publicity for metro and for the city, it would be bad for tourism and I guess, justice comes second to tourism, but at least, that's what I was being told from within and these are sources.

"But basically, it was buttoned up at the police department. They would talk to me but they would tell me nothing."

Maybe they just didn't want to talk to certain people. Scott's appropriation of a picture of Tupac Shakur as he lay dead at the morgue was neither official nor part of the police file. The Las Vegas Sun, Scott's former newspaper employer, claims that Clark County Coroner Ron Flud has said the photo, which shows Shakur dissected on a table at the morgue, is not an official coroner or police photo. Metro Internal Affairs Bureau Lt. John Alamshaw also said it appears that it was not an official photo.

But contrary to Scott's perception, Las Vegas Investigators were clear on their direction of the case even a year later. In September 1997, Las Vegas police Sgt. Kevin Manning told the Review-Journal that Shakur's slaying was not motivated by a gang war or arguments within the rap world. "It appears to be motivated by a personal dispute, more than anything," Manning said. Since Las Vegas by that time had already advised Orlando Anderson that he was not a suspect, it immediately draws attention to the other personal dispute Shakur had: one about money.

"I got a phone call that Death Row had went to visit Tupac and that I think he is signing with Suge," said Gloria Cox, Shakur's aunt.

"Then she called back and said 'He did sign with Suge'... I was like quiet for a minute and then got scared and said, 'Wow!' I was really taken aback by it because I was a little afraid for Tupac; how he was going to maneuver himself through that deal."

On September 16, 1995, Knight and Kenner visited Shakur at Dannemora. They walked in with a three page handwritten agreement. Many people have the misconception that the letter was drafted "on the scene" with Shakur while Knight and Kenner were on-site with Shakur. The misconception comes from the fact that the contract was unusual in its brevity and format—it was handwritten, and hastily so, by its penmanship. A contract so prepared would hardly be the work of an attorney unless the attorney was doing the contract "on the fly" or at an opportune time.

The misconception is exactly that. The agreement was signed by Knight on September 15th, the day before the visit, and signed by Shakur on September 16th. That would indicate that this was not drafted during the prison meeting but rather before the meeting. Kenner and Knight arrived at the prison with a document already drafted. The terms of the deal must have been worked out prior to the meeting—perhaps on the telephone. David Kenner, seasoned attorney, drafted the agreement.

Hollywood legends abound with the hope that one can be plucked from obscurity, and the discovering party so moved by the moment, that they grab whatever instrument is close to them and something to write on, and drafts an agreement that catapults the talent to becoming a "star." Rap artists also send thousands of demo tapes to labels and give out countless more to friends and contacts with the same hope. So the story that Shakur was approached in prison by The Red King one fine day, and granted a three-page contract scratched out by Alchemist David Kenner is easy for hopeful artists to embrace; it's a dream come true.

And as the saying goes "if it is too good to be true, it isn't."

It is perfectly acceptable in Court and in depositions to answer the question "how do you know they wanted to do it?" by answering, "Because they did it." There were only two things on the mind of The Red King the day they visited Shakur; obligating him to producing revenue for Death Row and getting access to Shakur's money via a power of attorney signed by Shakur to David Kenner. Why else would Kenner and Knight, know they were flying across the US to sign a deal with Shakur, and arrive completely unprepared for a deal of that size? They did little more to prepare for the visit than write out a sloppy agreement in handwritten form.

So why do they show up with a sloppy and slight contract, signed by Knight the day prior? They did it because it benefitted them.

This sloppy business was not common for Kenner, nor was it just the way he normally operated. That's too hard to believe. Kenner was an attorney who defended murderers. Details—and attention to them—are his business. He knew contracts inside and out. Knight was also no stranger to what "industry" contracts looked like.

But are there actual contracts with Death Row that pre-dated Shakur's? Yes. Were they more formal agreements? Yes, they were. The contract between Death Row and Brodus weighed in at a staggering thirty-five pages.

The fact that Knight and Kenner wanted to foist this flimsy contract on Shakur may explain all there was to understand about their plan: a "game changer" in that respect. They wanted the power of attorney to do exactly what they did—call Interscope and get funds released from Shakur's earnings. They wanted to keep the contract vague. Shakur's very simple contract spells out some very basic tenants. It spells out what was important to Shakur… getting paid. It also spells out what was important to Death Row… getting control of and managing Shakur and most importantly his money.

What's blatant about Shakur's contract is what the "contract" doesn't contain. It just so happens to be missing a bunch of terms that would be critically important to Shakur's attorneys:

- Audit Rights;
- Rescission Rights;
- Termination Rights;
- Accounting Rights;
- Liability;
- Ownership of Masters
- Licensing Rights;
- Survivorship Rights.

What screams out at that time is that there no longer is an attorney like Tyehimba to care about those missing elements. Now, Kenner was Shakur's attorney and he wrote the deal. No one was in a position to tell Shakur anything, as they were not his legal counsel. This is not to say many didn't try; but Shakur believed in Kenner and The Red King of Thieves.

Unlike Shakur, in Broadus' 1993 deal there was no ambiguity. Broadus had no rights to the master recordings at all—section 7.01 of his contract made it clear: "Each Master Recording made or furnished to Company by you or the Artist under this agreement or during its term, from the Inception of Recording, will be considered a work made for hire for Company."

Moreover, in section 15.02 of his contract, Broadus knew exactly what would happen if Death Row failed to meet its obligations.

"15.02. If Company refuses without cause to allow you to fulfill your Recording Commitment for any Contract Period and if, not later than sixty (60) days after that refusal takes place, you notify Company of your desire to fulfill such Recording Commitment, then Company shall permit you to fulfill said Recording Commitment by notice to you to such effect within sixty (60) days of Company's receipt of your notice. Should Company fail to give such notice, you shall have the option to terminate the term of this agreement by notice given to Company within thirty (30) days after the expiration of the latter sixty (60) day period; on receipt by Company of such notice the term of this agreement shall terminate and all parties will be deemed to have fulfilled all of their obligations hereunder except those obligations which survive the end of the term."

Unfortunately, Shakur never had that kind of agreement and Death Row had plenty of time afterward to make one for him, but failed to do so. Why was that not done? It wasn't done because it did not benefit Death Row Records.

The contract in its entirety was summed up in the "Shakur v. Death Row" lawsuit in California Superior Court:

"Subject to written contracts, Tupac designated Kenner as his attorney and Knight as his manager. As manager of Tupac, Knight was to cause a contract to be drawn up between Tupac and Death Row.

"Tupac would record three record albums for Death Row. The first was to be based on material already recorded; the second would be released in 1996; the third would be released in 1997;

"Tupac would receive in advance of $1.0 million for the first record album, in addition to $125,000 for the purchase of a car, a $120,000 expense allowance over a twelve month period, a $250,000 legal fund to be spent as Tupac desired, and the legal services of Kenner on behalf of Tupac;

"Tupac would be paid a royalty of 18% for sales of the first record album, plus a bonus of 1% of sales if that album sold over 500,000 copies ("Gold"), and an additional 1% of sales if that album sold over one million copies ("Platinum");

"For the second and third albums, Tupac would be paid an advance of no less than $1.0 million, or $1.0 million for every million copies of the prior album which was sold; and,

"For both the second and third record albums, Tupac would be paid a royalty of 18% of sales, plus a bonus of 1% of sales if that album went Gold, and an additional 1% of sales if that album went Platinum."

Shakur's previous attorney, Watani Tyehimba, spoke about his last meeting with Shakur at the prison. He claimed that Shakur hugged him, wept, and said, "I know I'm selling my soul to the devil."

Shakur was right. According to 2006 Bankruptcy Court documents, within two weeks of Shakur signing that flimsy agreement and within a mere TWO DAYS from his release from prison, Death Row began siphoning money, diverting it for their own ends. For example, Shakur's royalty account was charged $23,857 for repairs to Knight's and Steve Cantrock's cars. Knight was already weaving that Death Row disappearing act on Shakur's money!

Why does a bank robber put on a mask? Maybe he is cold. Maybe he is fashionable. But more than likely the bank robber wears a mask because he intends to rob a bank!

Likewise, a flimsy contract that gives Shakur no recourse and gives transfer to all his money earned is the robbery. The people who put the contract out knew better, and took advantage of an artist while he was in a vulnerable position. Shakur just wanted to make money and get out of jail and he was having trouble being objective according to friends and family. The contract gives Death Row the ability to spend Shakur's money without any fear of Shakur having recourse.

To make matters worse, in California, the law is pretty clear on contracts. No other understandings are often given weight outside the contracts own words. But it takes an attorney to understand that. And both The Red King and Kenner definitely knew. It wasn't about loyalty or the future. They were covering up a heist job, and anyone who dared look behind the curtain to see the magic was a threat.

On October 10, 1995, Shakur was released from prison on bail pending his appeal. Tupac Shakur was completely oblivious to the money being taken from him in his first few months at Death Row. Keep in mind that he was only with the label a little less than a year. He was busy finishing his first Death Row album, "All Eyez on Me." He was on a mission to make money and he was having fun.

The spending charged to Shakur's account is mind bending. Shakur's money is found in these examples:

10-3-1995: $23,857 Shakur was charged for repairs to a Porsche automobile. Cantrock and Knight owned Porsches; Shakur did not.

1-4-1996 Check # 1154512105 $10,994 apartment located at 10601 Wilshire Boulevard not occupied by Shakur, but by other

Death Row artists.

1-4-1996 Check # 1154612106 $1,728 apartment located at 10601 Wilshire Boulevard not occupied by Shakur, but by other Death Row artists.

1-4-1996 Check # 12107 $1,828 apartment located at 10601 Wilshire Boulevard not occupied by Shakur, but by other Death Row artists.

2-1996: $67,596.70 (GL Reference No. 12300, Check No. 12497) Jewelry purchased from B.L. Diamonds a business operated by a close personal friend of Knight's accountant. (Not only had Knight represented that the jewelry in question was a gift to Shakur from Knight, but the bills were not even paid and the Estate was then being sued on those bills by B.L. Diamonds.)

2-1996: $15,599.00 (GL Reference No. 12301, Check No. 12898) Jewelry purchased from B.L. Diamonds

2-1996: $32,312.00 (GL Reference No. 12302, Check No. 12899) Jewelry purchased from B.L. Diamonds

2-7-1996 Check # 1234 $4,800 apartment located at 10601 Wilshire Boulevard not occupied by Shakur, but by other Death Row artists.

3-4-1996 Check # 1287713526 $4,800 apartment located at 10601 Wilshire Boulevard not occupied by Shakur, but by other Death Row artists.

4-8-1996 Check # 14400 $4,800 apartment located at 10601 Wilshire Boulevard not occupied by Shakur, but by other Death Row artists.

5-2-1996: Check # 1432315670 $14,500 Rental on Longo's Malibu House

5-2-1996: Check # 1432615073 $21,600 Rental on Longo's Malibu House

6-1996 $5,845 (GL Reference- No. 16029P, Check No. 15258) Jewelry that Knight purchased from XIV Karats Ltd

6-11-1996 Check # 1527116041 $100,000 Rental on Longo's Malibu House

6-12-1996 Check # 1531116087 $12,000 Rental on David Kenner's Malibu House

6-13-1996: $2,700 (GL Reference No. 16184, Check No. 15404) Charged child support paid on behalf of Nate Dogg, another Death Row performer

7-31-1996: $51,425 (GL Reference No. 17342P Check No. 16508) Purchase of a Chevy Suburban- title was taken in Shakur's name initially, but was then transferred by Knight to his brother-in-law, Norris Anderson. The second was costs in connection with the cost of transferring the car.

9-3-1996: $1,453.51 (GL Reference No. 96P, Check No. 1094) Expenses associated with Michel'le Toussaint's (Knight's Girlfriend) Range Rover.

Shakur was even charged over $100,000 for the cost of furnishing an apartment. However, upon his death, Death Row emptied the apartment and took the furniture to an undisclosed location, according to attorneys for Shakur's estate.

So how did Knight keep Shakur at bay? It was probably the smartest thing that Knight did. It was not unlike how Steve Jobs—yes that Steve Jobs of Apple computer—chiseled Steve Wozniak at the beginning of their relationship. Jobs took a position with Atari; he was offered a $5,000 bonus for completion of a game. Jobs recruited Wozniak, telling him that the job was worth a mere $700 which Jobs would eventually split with Wozniak. Jobs lied to Wozniak and Wozniak not being any wiser was happy with the meager sum he was paid because he believed it to be all there was to make.

Similarly, when Shakur would ask for money, Knight or his associates would say that there was no money owed to him. However Shakur knew better and would weekly ask Frank Alexander to go "get him five"—which indicated a cash payment from Death Row for his weekly "paycheck" in the amount of five thousand dollars ($5,000). Alexander would ask and the money would be provided to him. According to the many lawsuits against Death Row, this was a common practice.

And for a while Shakur was okay. However, when the math started to not add up, albeit sometime later, Shakur became suspicious. But that was not for a while.

In fact Death Row was so empowered at one point, that any claim that Death Row owed Shakur money was actually refuted. Afeni Shakur had to sue Death Row after Shakur's death to get any movement at all.

"When Tupac died, he never had a music lawyer," said Dina LaPolt, the attorney for the Estate of Shakur.

LaPolt stated that when someone is a recording artist, every royalty payment that goes to producers and other third party royalty participants—

people that perform on your album—comes out of the artist's royalty. If they write music with the artist, the artist has to do agreements with them, like song split agreements, and these people share in the publishing money.

LaPolt stated that when Shakur died, nothing was papered on his behalf. Under the terms of his recording agreement, she stated, Death Row was still allowed to release all of Shakur's albums. They just didn't pay him.

"They just froze all the royalty streams and kept their profits. When I got involved, there was literally over $13 million dollars in frozen royalty payments that belonged to Tupac, his producers, all his co-writers… it was just awful."

They were too busy spending the money. And Kenner was right there in the middle of it with Knight.

FINAL ACCOUNTING

No sooner did Las Vegas Police start to get some traction with the investigation when the proverbial "other shoe dropped." Star witness to the Shakur shooting, Yafeu Fula, was killed in a "gang related" homicide.

"Yafeu Fula was a name that a lot of people have thrown back in our faces," said Brent Becker, of the Las Vegas Police, "that we were derelict in doing things. Yafeu Fula was interviewed the night of the shooting. Yafeu Fula gave a statement. People say we never interviewed him. He was interviewed. The big thing is everybody says that he said, he could identify the shooter. No, he did not. He never said that to us. He said, he might be able to identify the driver—that is what he said.

"We tried to re-interview him, the problem was, this is a big country, and people go wherever. We don't have tracking devices on them. So we have to depend on people that we know we can get in touch with to try and reach out to them."

On November 10, 1996, police in Orange, N.J., notified Las Vegas Lead Detective Manning about the killing. Fula lived in Montclair, N.J. He was shot once in the head in the third-floor hallway of an apartment where he had been visiting a friend. Officers found Fula at 3:48 a.m. after receiving a report of a shooting.

Orange Police Capt. Richard Conte said that they didn't believe the murder of Fula to be related at that time to the Shakur killing. Perhaps he should have spoken with Los Angeles Police Officer Kenneth Knox, who at the time and for several previous months had been conducting surveillance on Death Row Records. Knox and two LAPD sergeants as well as 7 patrol officers filed reports that linked an altercation at Can-Am studios, Death Row's Recording Studio, where Knight himself had an office, to an East Coast New Jersey Crip group.

Knox says he received word about an altercation at the studio October 1, 1996, between a gang member and a security guard. The Can-Am night manager wanted the gang members who infested the studio to be removed at once. NO less than seven (7) uniformed LAPD officers and two (2) LAPD Sergeants joined Knox in an effort to exterminate the studio of its unwanted pests.

Removed were a group of gang members, both from an East Coast Crip set and Mob Piru Bloods who were associated with Knight, pretty even in number. They were working or partying together in the Can-Am studios, and had become boisterous. In case that sounds odd, it bears repeating: Within days of Shakur getting killed, ten LAPD officers removed Crips and Bloods working/partying together. The report specifically mentions "The other suspects were from the Bronx, N.Y., Newark, New Jersey, & Brooklyn N.Y."

As discussed later, this incongruity between Crips and Bloods meeting and working/playing together and the Death Row/Compton Police sponsored "gang war" theory is more obvious when, for no good reason, the Blood gang members in the Kingdom of Thieves invite Bronx, N.Y., Newark, New Jersey, & Brooklyn N.Y Crip gang members to hang out. This kills any hope of claiming a "gang war" which Manning had said they ruled out anyway.

And as of now, no one has had a decent explanation as to what (in the middle of an alleged gang war) east coast gang members were doing at Death Row offices as observed by Knox. And five weeks later, the main eyewitness to the shooting of Shakur ends up dead in New Jersey. We do know information was exchanged when Knox received a call from Brent Becker on October 7, 1996 less than a week later.

Las Vegas Metropolitan Police Lieutenant Larry Spinosa told the Las Vegas Sun rather heartlessly that Fula "wasn't coming forward anyway. We didn't know where he was until he turned up in New Jersey dead on Sunday."

Spinosa also said that after talking with Metropolitan Police, Fula went to the attorney for Death Row Records, David Kenner. "All our contacts after that were from Kenner in California," Spinosa said.

Meanwhile, Las Vegas Police were still developing motive and otherwise very quiet about their theories. Brent Becker of the Las Vegas Police, did say, however, in a 2007 interview "There was all kinds of alleged baggage involved as far as Tupac wanting to leave Death Row Records."

Shakur was well aware of the history regarding Dr. Dre's departure from Death Row—and it was not particularly exciting to him. It was pretty common knowledge within the industry that Dre left because he was un-comfortable with Knight's "business practices." Dre abandoned his interest in the company in return for a relatively modest financial settlement, and Interscope facilitated the divorce by giving him a lucrative new contract.

By February of 1996, Dre was gone. So was the money, from what folks around Shakur were being told. And they were still not getting any accounting. "We'd ask for them, and they'd send a present—like a car" said Yaasmyn Fula.

"I felt like there was this dark cloud over us. I knew so much was wrong—but Pac would say, 'Yas, you can't keep telling me things, I know what I am doing.'"

It was within days of Andre Young's departure from the Kingdom that Shakur decided to start his own production company, called "Euphana-sia." He asked his old friend, and honorary "aunt" Yaasmyn Fula to come to L.A. to run it. Fula began trying to organize Shakur's business affairs.

"We weren't getting copies of the financial accountings," said Yaas-myn.

Yaasmyn was joined by Molly Monjauze, Yolanda "Yo-Yo" Whita-ker, and Tracy Robinson. Between Fula and the other three, Shakur's social and business activities were handled.

Shakur did right by putting Yaasmyn in charge. Yaasmyn Fula was no one to screw with. From 1976 to 1982 Yaasmyn Fula "worked as a para-legal by the Bronx Legal Services Corporation and as a word processor op-erator in a private New York law firm. Since 1976, she has also worked as a paralegal with the National Task Force for COINTELPRO Litigation and Research ("Task Force"), described by Fula as a collection "of lawyers, paralegals, and law students who are attempting to expose the racism and hypocrisy of the policies of the United States Government and, in particular, its law enforcement intelligence operations directed against Black organiza-tions."

Several pieces of evidence linked Fula to an attempted armored truck robbery in New York. One of the suspected robbers was Nathaniel Burns, a former member of the Black Panther Party (and therein her ties to Afeni Shakur, who was also a member of the party).

Fula stated to the Court that Burns and an accomplice stayed at her Bronx apartment for an unspecified period following the robbery attempt. When Burns was captured and the accomplice killed in a shoot-out with police on October 23 1981, they were driving a car registered to Fula. A bullet extracted from the accomplice's body was traced to the gun of one of the police officers killed during the Brinks incident. In addition, a third suspect in the Brinks robbery, Anthony LaBorde, was a co-worker of Fula at Bronx Legal Services.

So when a federal grand jury was empanelled in the Southern District of New York to investigate the robbery and to question whether it was a part of a larger pattern of criminal activities. Fula was subpoenaed to appear. She was not personally convicted of any wrongdoing in the matter, other than to annoy a judge enough to breach protocol in a civil contempt citation to Fula. The judge put her in jail in contempt without a public hearing on the matter.

"It was an irresistible time for a young man growing up in the literal birthplace of Hip-Hop: the Bronx. All of the young people were gravitating to Hip-Hop; it was the voice of their generation dealing with every issue that confronted them. Tupac lived in the heat of the times, the South Bronx Projects, Africa Bambaataa, T. La Rock, DJ Jazzy Jay, Kool Moe Dee, White Plains Road/Cross Bronx Expressway, Black Panther Party—all of these cultural phenomenon's were fusing into a musical tornado that attracted every outlaw element, especially amongst the youth.

"Many of the housing projects in the South Bronx is where we did a lot of our organizing and so being in the nucleus and a witness to all the elements that were fusing together made it impossible not to succumb to the lure of Hip-Hop. Tupac was imbued with a spirit of revolutionary consciousness from our Panther days so he was instrumental in always keeping the elements of Hip-Hop that flourished in the Bronx alive in the household–b boy, DJ, MC, break dancing and graffiti. He understood it very well and translated it constantly to Yafeu (her son). It was difficult for some of the older family to comprehend it… today it has become incomprehensible, having lost its historical perspective… Yes, the Bronx was a virtual Mecca for young boys dreaming about becoming a rap star."

Preston Holmes, the president of Def Jam Pictures who had worked with Shakur in the movies "Juice" and "Gridlock'd," said that Shakur always wanted to be a leader, not a follower. Holmes said Shakur had to act a certain way—screwing the most women, stomping the most guys, talking the most shit.

However Homes was quick to admit that Shakur was also trying to distance himself from the negative image by saying that "Gangster Rap" was dead.

Meanwhile, Shakur's attorney Charles Ogletree was trying to settle the many lawsuits against Shakur for his exploits. Ogletree would have to call the record company to get money. Ogletree claimed that Shakur came out of jail with no money.

Shakur would tell Ogletree to go get the money from Death Row when he would negotiate a settlement for Shakur. Ogletree said that when the check didn't come, he would call Kenner. Kenner would tell Ogletree that the check was "in the mail," and when it never arrived, Kenner would claim he was sending it FedEx. Again, when it didn't arrive, Kenner would promise to wire it. Ogletree felt that they should have been able to close settlements, but it was never possible. He always had to go through the record company.

Fula goes on to claim that in lieu of a record deal Shakur would always look out for the "group" (speaking of the Outlawz) as they were his "family." They were going to be his first act that he signed on Makaveli, after his contract was up with Death Row.

"The plan was to fulfill his contract with Death Row and move on. 1996 was one hectic year. It was a strategic move, not a business move, but one he thought he could control… Yes he was leaving Death Row once his contact was up. It was in August that I typed the letter to David Kenner, Death Row attorney, releasing him of his services representing Tupac. I remember clearly the day I faxed it to Kenner, I celebrated with a bottle of wine!

"Tupac finally understood what I and others had been saying to him. David Kenner's' representation of Death Row and Tupac was a conflict of interest. It was like a cloud was lifting from over us, especially as I began the process of interviewing other attorneys in August 1996."

Shakur later repeated this awareness to others in typical Shakur style. In an interview done in 2013, engineer Lance Pierre (the sound engineer for the Makaveli Sessions) remembers telling everyone, including those he was on the phone with, that he was "tired of paying Nate Dogg's child support." Pierre clearly stated that Shakur was not happy about it.

> "Everything was happening so fast and Tupac was under an enormous amount of pressure. He was fulfilling his contract with Death Row and at the same time doing movies, meeting with directors for future movies, videos, etc. making his plans to be independent, something that was very important to a young solider."

Gloria Cox, in her direct approach style, minced no words. "That wasn't his plan. He wasn't going to be wedded to no Death Row. Guaranteed you he was bigger than Death Row. His ideas were bigger than that because he wanted to go further than that and he wasn't dragging a Suge behind."

Fula also claimed that she felt Afeni had been influenced by Knight's attentions and largesse. Shakur's signing with Death Row had transformed the lives of his extended family, even more than his contract with Interscope.

Fula said that previous to Death Row, Shakur's family had lived lives of what she called "scarcity"; worrying about the next meal and worrying about how to pay the rent. After Death Row they stayed at the elegant Westwood Marquis hotel for several months, and charged up an "astronomical" bill. Toward Shakur's end, Fula claimed that Shakur felt cursed with what she termed a less "dysfunctional" family.

Nevertheless, Ogletree claimed that Shakur was carefully plotting his escape by the spring of 1996. "He had Euphanasia, he had the Outlawz, he had his movie deals–he was building something that was all to be part of one entity... He had a strategy–the idea was to maintain a friendly relationship with Suge but to separate his business."

Meanwhile in the spring of 1996, Death Row still tried to collect Shakur's money for him.

> "It seemed like he always had a tough time getting his money on weekly basis" recalled Gobi his videographer.

"So, whether it was him or Yaasmyn Fula making the calls, there always seemed to be a struggle getting the loot. A few times I heard Yaasmyn, a few times I heard him, just asking for his money."

"They weren't happy," replied Gobi when asked if the calls he overheard were confrontational. "I think once even one of his

Gridlock'd checks got sent to [the label], or Death Row was asking for his acting checks to be sent to [them]. So he was a little [upset] about that as well."

Frank Alexander, Shakur's personal bodyguard, also said that the more important element of the problem between Shakur and Death Row was still the credibility gap between what Death Row was saying they owed Shakur and what they truly owed him.

"Yaasmyn who was Yak Fula's mom, was Tupac's assistant," Frank said. "She had called me that evening and said, 'I'm going to come down to the set. I need to talk to you and Kevin Hackie about some things that's going on with Pac and Death Row and I'll talk to you guys when I get there.

"She arrives and she started telling us that there's some serious problems; that Pac is going to be leaving Death Row and that he wasn't happy and that there was an audit that was about to be performed on the record label.

"She didn't go on to any great details about anything and she told us basically to step up our game and watch him because of these things that were about to occur. That's the first time that myself and Kevin was told that there was problems with Tupac and the record label."

Not everyone understood what a record label audit is. Apparently the lead detective for the failed 2006 LAPD "Murder Rap" investigation did not either. "But as far as these rumors," said Greg Kading "about him getting killed over those matters that he was going to leave, or these rumors that he was having Death Row audited, it's all bullshit. There's nothing to substantiate that. It's all pure speculation. We know why the IRS audited Death Row. It had nothing to do with Tupac."

Obviously the two have nothing to do with each other. Shakur was not interested in the tax structure of Death Row—he was interested in a reconciliation against all sales of his albums to date. Billboard Magazine certified his album sales and his payments were not reflecting those sales.

"At that time his aunt," said Kevin Hackie, "her son was the one that was killed in New Jersey, accidental shooting, okay? Basically they start questioning the accounting of all the money because, of course, Suge, you know, basically said that he was still in the hole,

Tupac was still in the hole with them 2, 3 million dollars, although the first album, "All Eyez on Me," grossed over 70 million by six months.

"And so basically there was a problem, there as far as the money, because he would have to beg and plead, this and that, to get a couple hundred thousand sent over to Euthanasia. He was still living out here in Woodland Hills, Calabasas area.

"And, so, like I said, the problems were mounting, and mounting, and Suge knew as time went on, especially with Yaasmyn here now, his aunt, that she wasn't going to allow him to screw him over, and he knew that all the questions, of course, Tupac was asking, requesting for this and that, wasn't coming from him. Because the way Suge was, I can see with all of these artists, Suge was a bully. He was a bully in a sense, and that was, at the time he had Knightlife Entertainment, quote, unquote, which his wife ran, and basically knows it is a conflict of interest. You can't own a record company and also manage somebody; it is a conflict involved."

Back in The Kingdom of Thieves, The Red King enjoyed a monopoly over The Kingdom's creative assets, managing the careers of his artists and controlling the rights to their compositions and recordings. Prior to this, artists typically signed over the copyrights to their songs and master recordings in exchange for a royalty of about 12% of sales. Major record labels and music publishing companies reaped the bulk of the profits, often collecting millions of dollars annually by packaging and repackaging the same music. Death Row kept 100% of everything, from the looks of it. Quite a tax!

Shakur also was running quickly into a block wall relating to his control over his "master tapes." Master tapes are the lifeblood of the music industry. From these original recordings, copies can be made for distribution. Master tapes are very important to an artist. Control of the master tapes means control of the revenue they generate.

It is not unusual for a record company to hold tapes as collateral or own them outright—as was the case with Snoop. This is sample language from a real record label Contract:

"For good and valuable consideration, the receipt and sufficiency of which are hereby acknowledged, you hereby grant to Keylite a continuing first-priority security interest in all of your and your Affiliates' right, title and interest of any kind, nature and description (whether now owned or existing or hereafter acquired or arising) in and to the Collateral (as defined below) in order to secure the complete payment and performance of all of your obligations to Fontana pursuant to the Distribution Agreement.

"As used in this Agreement, the "Collateral" shall mean all of the following items, tangible or intangible, in every stage of completion, wherever the same may be located:

• all audio-only and audio-visual recordings embodied in Records sold or distributed under, or otherwise subject to, the Distribution Agreement (collectively, the "Masters"),

• all photographs, liner notes and other graphic and textual material used or created for use in connection with the packaging, sale, distribution, marketing or other exploitation of the Masters or Records derived therefrom (collectively, the "Artwork"),

• all other materials used or created for use in connection with the marketing, promotion, sale, distribution or other exploitation of the Masters or Records derived therefrom, including music videos and other audiovisual materials (collectively, the "Materials"),

• all rights in the Masters, the Artwork and the Materials, including all copyrights and other proprietary rights therein and further including all renewals and extensions thereof,

• all rights (including name and likeness rights), powers and benefits of you and your Affiliates under any and all agreements, instruments and documents relating to the creation of, or the acquisition or exploitation of rights in, the Masters or Records derived therefrom, the Artwork or the Materials,

• all Records derived from the Masters and all other derivatives or duplicates of the Masters, including all inventory now owned or hereafter acquired by you, all claims and causes of action relating to the Masters or Records derived therefrom, the Artwork or the Materials, whether previously accrued or hereafter accruing,

• all of your rights under the Distribution Agreement, including your rights to receive any monies thereunder,

• all of your trade names, trademarks, service marks and logos, together with the goodwill of the business symbolized thereby, as utilized on or in connection with Records derived from the Masters,

• all books and records relating to the foregoing,

• all accounts and general intangibles relating to the foregoing, and

• all proceeds, products, rents, income and profits of the foregoing."

In the music industry, and other industries, the idea of "mortgaging" the masters is not just the physical tapes themselves, but the intellectual property associated with them.

The trouble for Shakur stems from what was already discussed about his vague contract: none of this specific language regarding ownership of the master tapes was in the contract; the paradox caused by Kenner's and Knight's desire to keep the contract's terms obfuscated.

For Death Row, the contract with Shakur was a double-edged sword; the ambiguity of the contract worked to Shakur's advantage as well. After all, Shakur paid for the sessions, the engineers, and the tapes. He was charged for them. Death Row appeared to have written the check, but the money was not, in the end, a Death Row asset.

In many other artists' cases, the absence of a contract right, may have been a problem—but not for Shakur. If there was a "work for hire" then Shakur was the one paying for it all. Not Death Row; Death Row was advancing nothing; they were paying the bills off Shakur's Royalties.

Of course, Shakur had no idea that in addition to siphoning his money, over the course of time, Death Row had gone out and mortgaged the masters for most of Shakur's songs.

Wright Junior gives his version of events in which Shakur is alleged to have to asked "permission" from Knight to take tapes from the studio:

"Suge and I were in Miami at the time. Umm. I remember we were at the Canterbury Inn when the incident happened… I don't know why we were in Miami at the time… And the issue was… uhh… the issue was, no one–no artist could bring out any DATs or cassettes or anything, and take it home, because something (could) get leaked. It wasn't like it was then. You know you purposely leak stuff. Now, you purposely leak stuff. Back then, you hold stuff like gold. You didn't let stuff get out, until you was ready for it to go out.

"So the rule was that you listened to it, without Suge's permission, you couldn't take any cassettes or DATs. It wasn't reels, no one was trying to take reels out of the studio. It was DATS back then, the little DATS. And the thing was before you go in or out of the studio, you got searched—you got pat down. But there were certain people who didn't get searched or pat down. And that was Tupac, Snoop, Suge—of course—and security. But everybody else was subject to a pat down.

"Engineers had informed us that Tupac had taken some DATs that they'd made some DAT's and he was trying to leave with the DATs or the cassettes. And I called him and told them he couldn't leave the studio with the DATs or cassettes in his possession without Suge's permission.

"Of course, I was right there with Suge, so before I contacted or said anything to Tupac I had already gotten per... given my orders from Suge–and Suge did not authorize Pac to take any DATs or cassettes out. And that did happen.

"This was probably sometime in August or something like that.

"And the thing was... Pac was thinking about leaving because he knew the rules? He was probably one of the ones who created the rules for Suge!"

Yet in spite of owing Shakur money, in spite of no contractual right to ownership of the Masters or Recordings, studio sessions, tapes and engineers which were being charged to Shakur's "account," along with seemingly everything else, Death Row was not giving up those master tapes without a fight. Why not? They could use Shakur's money against him!

But Shakur was growing discontent asking for more money and an accounting. Also, he viewed himself as more than just a rap artist. His ambition was to continue his music career while creating a separate revenue stream from movies.

By August of 1996, Tupac Shakur was completing what he felt was the last of his commitments to Knight. He had already caused a scene in wanting to get his master tapes. Yaasmyn Fula had made it clear that in similar fashion to the Harry-O conflict, David Kenner had a conflict in representing both Knight and Shakur.

Shakur was on a roll in the motion picture game. Gloria Cox claimed that he had no less than two scripts in front of him at any given point in time. Shakur was surrounding himself with true professionals like Quincy Jones. He was realizing that he was being limited by the Death Row arrangement.

The real problem for Death Row was the inevitability of the pending train wreck; it was only a matter of time until Shakur found out how badly he had been taken from a monetary perspective; not only how much he was being underreported, but then to find out what actually did happen with the money he made.

This revelation to Shakur would have been the personal insult that would have severed the personal side of the relationship with Knight as well as the business relationship.

And typical with Shakur's flair for airing his dirty laundry publicly, as he did to "Yo: MTV Raps," relating to his admitted assault on the Hughes Brothers, Shakur would have made it known that he had been disrespected. This would have been calamity for Knight.

Knight was already feeling the castle walls closing in. Harry-O was threatening Knight with legal—and other action—for allegedly cheating him. Knight was taking money in 1996 for himself and paying bills of other artists with Shakur's earnings. Knight was one of the only labels to hold master tapes and until that time no artist had been successful in wrestling those tapes from Knight. They were beaten and violently acted upon for even challenging the Death Row label.

As for Shakur, he was forming his own business interests. Shakur was terminating the mediator between Knight and Himself—David Kenner, and hiring outside counsel to protect his interests. Shakur was hiring his own recording artists to sign under him.

Even if we assume that Shakur would have left his music interests with Death Row, how long would that have lasted once the information about the misappropriations would have surfaced? Knight hid and did not disclose the location of the master tapes of Shakur for 10 years. Good lawyers pursued those tapes. Would Shakur's attorneys have any more luck had he been alive?

Remember that each time the Shakur Estate pursued Knight and Death Row, there was an agreement to make those masters available—Knight volunteered the tapes. There were no judgments to hold him to—he was too smart for that. Knight agreed to settlement agreements specifically so that there would be no Court enforcement. So, even when Knight voluntarily agreed to something, that agreement was a lie.

And the lie would have happened in the "sunny days" of Death Row, when they and Interscope were predominant music labels, not an afterthought as Death Row has become today.

Another reason that the unspooling of Death Row's financial affairs in 1996 would have been disastrous for Knight was because many of the artists were still actively participating with the label. They were still recording. The ink on half of the fraudulent checks written on Shakur's bank accounts was still wet. Investigators would have day's old information and not year's old cold leads for fraud and conversion. Artists would have fled. The civil dockets would have been crammed to capacity with artists trying to get a piece of the Death Row pot–and this is important—before Interscope, the apparently legitimate accounting source, would have paid Knight. In theory, the money could have been attached and levied before it got into Knight's hands.

Certainly Shakur's direct personal relationship with Interscope would have allowed him to at least make the argument that funds be diverted from Knight, as they did later with the Estate—how much more with Shakur himself. Interscope did not want to lose the earnings from Shakur and might have used their clout over Knight to allow that to happen, as they later did: no different with the other artists.

In short, the stranglehold over the artists of Death Row would have ended and so would the cash flow to Knight. This might have also exposed a means to address the issue of monies owed to Harry-O.

Should his claims be true, it is a fair assumption than the whole house of cards would have collapsed by mid-1997, had Shakur lived.

Citing that Shakur was leaving Death Row Records doesn't really paint the true picture. In a relatively short period of time he had created over 200 songs. But whose songs where they really? Many of the songs he and other artists created were stolen by the Death Row and reworked by the entire team of people that were employed by Death Row Records. Shakur was part of that team and he was the artist at the front with his voice on the tracks. By the very nature of the sheer volume of work that he completed, we know that many of those tracks were not completely authored by Tupac Shakur. When he came for his masters Knight and Wright Junior had a legitimate reason not to release them.

Was Shakur being paid all that he was owed under the contract? Was anyone? Shakur received $5,000 in cash every week. He was running up huge hotel bills and leasing expensive cars and houses through the label. It is quite possible that a good portion of the Death Row payroll was being paid in cash or drugs.

No artist at Death Row ever really got paid his or her fair share. Shakur was in the throes of renegotiating everything. He really did fire David Kenner and he was moving toward creating his own label. He was a quick study. He learned from Digital Underground and learned more from Suge. But he wanted to control it all. However, the world of gangster rap can be a scary place for an independent operator.

STRAIGHT OUT OF COMPTON

Even though Las Vegas Investigators, by September 18, 1996 felt like they were not getting cooperation from Death Row insiders, they were hearing about peripheral events being blamed on the Shakur killing. These peripheral events were not occurring in Las Vegas, but in Compton, California, where Knight and Wright grew up.

Compton California was a city founded early in the development of the greater Los Angeles area, and was an ironic part of Los Angeles history. The current racial makeup of Compton is predominantly African-American and Hispanic. The ironic fact is that Compton made Los Angeles history by being the first city to ban "all white" housing tracts, which meant that for years in its history, Compton, California was predominantly all Caucasian.

As its own city, Compton had its own schools, police, fire, emergency services and government. It interacted with other cities like Los Angeles, but had its own police and jail, as well as its own jurisdiction. Hourie Taylor and Reggie Wright Senior were in charge for many years. Wright Junior had time to get to know the jailed and the jailors, the cops and the robbers, the good guys and the bad guys. It was all he had to do, so of course he was good at identifying the people likeliest to be trouble for the law-abiding citizens of Compton.

About 72 hours after the Shakur shooting, news got back to Vegas Police that in Compton California, gang members were shooting at each other. Normally most police who hear the words "gang" and "shooting" pay it little mind, it is such an everyday part of that lifestyle.

Las Vegas Police were primarily uninterested, though the police reports were clear that they were at least talking with both the LAPD and Compton Police. The reason Las Vegas police were uninterested about the Compton shootings is because they were pursuing where the evidence took them; and the evidence did not, as Manning would make clear, tie Shakur's murder to gang related issues.

Darnell Brim, a high-ranking member of the "Crips" who were a rival to Knight's "Blood" gang affiliations, was shot along with an innocent bystander first. He was not killed. Brim knew Orlando Anderson and both belonged to the same Crip gang, so it was of note to Compton Police, simply because Anderson's name had been mentioned as being in Las Vegas.

In fact, word on the "street" was that this shooting of Brim was somehow "payback" for the shooting of Shakur; this is specifically indicated in Brennan's affidavit—the rumor started by someone who wanted the incidents to gain traction as related. Several other gang members got shot in back and forth shootings, until the noise from the street was so loud—correct or not—that someone needed to simply address whether or not the two—the shooting in Vegas and the shootings in Compton—were related. Las Vegas Police did not believe so.

It is true that there are only so many magic tricks in the world: perhaps less than a hundred. But the reason that there appear to be so many is because of their alternate elements. For example, consider an effect in which a magician shows four aces, and then the aces turn face up one at a time in a mysterious fashion. This effect, as it is explained is called "Twisting the Aces," but it is based on the "false count" trick, invented by Alex Elmsley, which features magically appearing cards, you simply rename the trick. In another example, the trick that makes the mouse disappear has the same mechanics as the trick that makes the elephant disappear. There may just be more moving parts, but the trick is the same.

What Compton Police generally didn't know and Las Vegas Police didn't believe, was that each and every one of them were unwitting participants in the biggest Kenner Alchemy trick ever performed. And in case it needed calling out, the First and Second Elements—The Crime Itself and the Initial Findings—were already being played out. There was one last initial finding that stood of relevance.

Tracy Robinson best summed it up: "He was done. He was done. He was done.

"There were meetings with attorneys. Yaasmyn and I—yes, he was done. He was done. He had fulfilled his obligation with Death Row and no intentions of renewing any sort of paper agreement."

Remember what Yaasmyn Fula had said? "Yes he was leaving Death Row once his contact was up... It was in August that I typed the letter to David Kenner, Death Row attorney, releasing him of his services representing Tupac. I remember clearly the day I faxed it to Kenner, I celebrated with a bottle of wine!"

Ogletree told the reporter in New Yorker Magazine that Shakur waited to make the move from Death Row much longer than he would have preferred. But, to Shakur's more streetwise friends, firing Kenner seemed impossibly rash.

"Syke (a rap artist that did some recording with Shakur) didn't know that had happened until I told him, and when I did he looked at me for a long moment, as if he was having difficulty processing what I had said. Then he murmured—repeatedly— 'He fired Kenner?'"

The trouble was that beyond a certain point; you don't just "fire" the Alchemist of Thieves. In an interview done for the movie "Welcome to Death Row" Michael ("Harry-O") Harris described David Kenner as smooth and vicious.

According to the movie, David Kenner, a criminal defense attorney, was the only one that would work as a go-between between Interscope and Death Row. He was also the only attorney that would be up at 2 a.m. when these rap artists would have their troubles. The only real advantage Death Row flaunted to many inner city aspiring rap artists was that they had a home-grown "legal team" that could get them out of trouble.

Truthfully, it is an academic point about whether Shakur was worth more to Death Row alive or dead, at least from a "future earnings" stand-point. It is a worthless discussion that leads to the counter-argument that other artists left Death Row and were not killed. And it isn't the point. Shakur wasn't killed because of money he might make in the future, he was killed because of money already stolen.

Death Row benefitted in Shakur staying in The Kingdom, because it would keep the fraudulent accounting secret—at least for a time. But that was a short-term gain. No one would have stayed, knowing what chicanery was happening behind the scenes.

And Fula was on top of the matter; no stopping her. Shakur would have found out and exposed the cover-up; and he would have done so before Death Row could "re-coup" the money from anywhere, or anyone else. Fula would help Shakur, the copyright holder, lien the music to collect his royal-ties.

What's worse, Shakur's announcement that The Red King "had no clothes" would have sent shock waves through the industry. Shakur was just a messenger, a really loud and uninhibited messenger. This would have made bad PR for Death Row and worse PR when the media found out and the hidden agenda was revealed publicly. No Death Row artist had ever been able to take masters from Death Row. Andre Young was too quiet a personal-ity to vent the dirty laundry publicly.

In reality, Shakur had become a liability, the kind that Time Warner stockholders worried about and avoided when they ditched both Interscope and Death Row on September 25, 1995; the kind that Interscope worried about and avoided when they allowed Shakur to move to Death Row.

Yes, Shakur was the kind of liability that Death Row needed to worry about. The problem was there was no one left to pass Shakur off to. They had to deal with Shakur; dissuade Shakur from doing any snooping on the financials, keep Shakur generating positive cash flow and use the opportunity to take advantage of both.

Horse owners have an interesting saying: you can give the horse the carrot or the stick. Metaphorically, Knight knew that Shakur may in fact need the "stick," but if Knight could make the stick morph from the carrot, perhaps Shakur might reconsider his position. It would have to be one hell of a big stick. And Knight knew only one way to solve his problems.

Sometimes a fate worse than death is embarrassment. And we all know what happens to the messenger 8 out of 10 times.

So what was the exposure, exactly? What fights off a big "so what" when Shakur elects to "divorce" Death Row and Interscope?

We go back to Shakur's sloppy, handwritten contract. A contract can be declared void, otherwise known as a contract "rescission." You have to give everything back to their rightful owners, spent or not. So what might this have meant to Shakur, Death Row, and Interscope, once Shakur was onto the diversion of his money?

From just the examples, and that is not a full accounting to be sure, of the fraudulent conveyance shown in the later court filings, at least three hundred fifty thousand ($350,000) dollars was converted, misappropriated, or whatever term fits best, from Shakur. It looks pretty provable and documented.

Let's suppose that because of the fraud that has apparently occurred, the contract to Shakur was rescinded. Then, let's also suppose that Death Row and Interscope have sold 10 million (10,000,000) units of Shakur's albums. We'll offset any reduction with the fact that Shakur was on "Above the Rim," "GridLock'd," and a few other "one-offs" that made Death Row some major money, not forgetting "Greatest Hits." That number sounds good.

Next remember that Shakur came around at the dawn of the "digital" era before MP3's. Consumers were still paying $14-$20 bucks each for a CD, especially a double album; a concept lost on most young adults 18-25. Now how old do you feel?

We'll also knock off marketing and manufacture costs, say 25%. That leaves us hovering at anywhere between one hundred twenty million dollars ($120,000,000) and one hundred sixty million dollars ($160,000,000) give or take a few million. All that money would need to be returned to Shakur,

"To Make Parties Whole," the term used in Court.

But let's not stop there.

While Interscope and Death Row have to reach into their pockets for the money, the Court would then factor the "fraud" used to obtain the contract, the conveyance afterward and the inability for Shakur to have use of those funds. The general formula is provable damages. Some might argue that the exposure would be equitable with what Death Row and Interscope made and used in the interim, so we'll stack another 120-160 million on top.

That leaves exposure to Death Row and Interscope at about two hundred forty million dollars ($240,000,000).

And because its fraud, let's talk about punitive damages. To find a reference for possible punitive damages, let's look at the "one that got away"; Harris v. Death Row. Michael Harris and his wife, who allegedly formed Death Row with Kenner and Knight received a rather large judgment against Death Row, which put the label under: $45,000,000 in economic or real damages, $2,000,000 in "non-economic damages" (pain and suffering) and an incredible Sixty Million Dollars ($60,000,000) in punitive damages.

So if Harris's got roughly 1.25 times the economic damages as a punitive award, apply that same formula to Shakur.

Three hundred million dollars ($300,000,000) in punitive damages plus 240 million in actual damages or $540,000,000 were on the line? $107 million had knocked out death row. Think about who is up line from there?

One more thing: a 1996 judgment for $540,000,000.00 is worth about $804,930,401.53 now.

Shakur was a billion dollar problem for Death Row!

Of course neither party would have let it get to that point. Interscope would have likely settled; Death Row was not willing to let it come to that. But at any rate, Shakur's reaction to the conversion and diversion was basically the end of the road for Knight and Death Row—possibly even the crippling of Interscope revenues.

"He wanted to make money." Gloria Cox explained. "He would tell us, 'You all ain't got no sense. You don't know how to make money. Use me. You all can't make a t-shirt. You can't do a t-shirt business?' So we started trying to make t-shirts. 'Use me. I'm a commodity. You got the best thing to make money right here.' So why would he be stuck with a Suge Knight?"

In fact, Shakur's attorney Ogletree told the New Yorker magazine he felt Dre was a brilliant, creative musician; he stated that Dre started Death Row, and in order to get out, Dre had to give up almost everything. Taking it a step further, Ogletree asked what it would take for Shakur, the hottest star around, whose success was only growing, to leave. Legally, Ogletree stated, it was not tough to get out of Shakur's sloppy handwritten contract, but his concern was more pragmatic. "But you have to live after that... It was a question of how to walk away with your limbs attached and bodily functions operating."

Not wanting to take on the scrutiny that plagued Time Warner, MCA too initially refused to distribute many of Interscope's Death Row releases; most notably "All Eyez on Me," Shakur's first album, which was later certified "Diamond" in the U.S by Recording Industry Artists Association. This forced Death Row and Interscope to strike a deal with Island Records to distribute that particular album outside of its home base. That meant a new relationship and more complications.

Death Row was feeling squeezed from all sides.

The bank accounts were drying up. The walls were closing in.

The Red Queen—Sharitha and The Red King were arguing about the direction of the company and about money. The FBI was visiting the 8200 Wilshire Offices investigating Death Row Records. The police were a constant presence at the Can-Am Studios, in Tarzana. Dr. Dre had already left, Snoop was leaving and Shakur was making noise about leaving and trying to gain possession of his masters. The bank accounts that were once overflowing were beginning to dry up. Harry-O was sending rival Blood sets over to harass Knight about the start-up money he had provided.

There are many opinions on what happened at Death Row but all agree that September 7, 1996 was the turning point for the record label… the night Shakur was shot. The party was over and they knew it.

When Shakur was shot some think that a Crip was the gunman who pulled the trigger that night. Some think the Bloods were hired. Some think Suge was behind the shooting in spite of being in the passenger seat that night. And some think that the entire Las Vegas shooting was arranged by Death Row to scare Shakur and remind him that he needed the protection that Suge Knight could provide. They may have wanted to send the message that, "there are evil forces lurking out there" and nothing, like a drive-by-shooting, can remind an artist that he needs protection from nefarious forces.

But sometimes truth is so much more interesting than fiction. The truth of the drama surrounding Death Row Records is absolutely way too preposterous to ever be believed. Yet, the truth often has that ring. When you hear it you know that no matter how unbelievable it might be, that it is, indeed, true.

It was time to turn Death Row into a "bust out" and kill off those who could be blamed for it.

BUST OUT

In its 1988 publication, "Subversion by Organized Crime and Other Unscrupulous Elements of the Check Cashing Industry" the State of New Jersey Commission of Investigation defined a "bust out" as follows: "A 'bust-out' is a scheme customarily employed by organized crime to deplete the assets of a legitimate business, thus forcing it into bankruptcy."

In Martin Scorsese's now classic film "Goodfellas," there is a scene where wiseguys Henry Hill (Ray Liotta) and Tommy DeVito (Joe Pesci) burn down the Bamboo Lounge, a nightclub the gangsters had been using as a way station to house cases of liquor, food, and expensive clothes that they then "flipped" or sold, on the street. Watching as the U-Hauls pull up and unload the merchandise, Henry Hill sets up the scene with the following voice-over:

"As soon as the deliveries are made in the front door, you move the stuff out the back and sell it at a discount. You take a two hundred dollar case of booze and sell it for a hundred. It doesn't matter. It's all profit.

"Sonny, the club's owner, is unable to make the payments and soon the debt is insurmountable. The gangsters have been profiting and now they will score one last huge gain by burning the place down and leave Sonny, the owner, with a huge load of debt impossible to repay.

"And, finally, when there's nothing left, when you can't borrow another buck from the bank or buy another case of booze, you bust the joint out."

Suge Knight was "Sonny"; the figurehead owner of Death Row, The Red King of Thieves sat at the helm. He earned his place and became royalty in the seat of power. He brought with him The Alchemist David Kenner and The Red Queen. His best friend and closest confidant became his right hand—his enforcer—The Red Knight of Thieves. Knight clawed his way to that throne with the help of The Red Knight.

Soon jealousy and opportunity born out of depleted options would dethrone The Red King; his backers were done with him. But The Red King had the Knights of the Kingdom of Thieves. His enemies could not hurt him. Only The Red Queen and The Red Knight had the ability to blindside The Red King and shatter his power into a million pieces.

The Alchemist was already orchestrating the biggest Kenner Alchemy he had ever conjured. It was necessary to shield all royalty of The Kingdom, regardless of their fate. So, The Red Queen would conspire with The Red Knight to take everything that The Red King of Thieves had himself taken. The plan was in place to send both The Red King and "troublemaker" messenger Shakur to the grave. Shakur succumbed to his wounds received that night. When the bullets missed the primary target, The Alchemist, The Red Queen and The Red Knight would begin a campaign to send Marion Suge Knight to prison while at the same time appearing to tirelessly work to keep him free. By that time The Alchemist had summoned the forces of darkness to invoke the Kenner Alchemy Third Element.

One last thought: Michael Harris may have assisted The Red Queen and The Red Knight. He certainly had motive. LAPD Jailhouse informant, Waymond Anderson, though unreliable, seems to confirm that there was a plot to take over Death Row Records. He states that the plot was by Lydia and Michael Harris aka Harry-O, a known associate of Freeway Rick Ross. Robert J. Frank asks Anderson in his deposition, "you indicated that Michael Harris, I think you said Lydia Harris, and who—who else can you name as part of that conspiracy?" Anderson answers, "Those are all that I can do at—at this point."

"There was money that was laundered through Death Row Records by Lydia while Michael Harris was in jail, and then they later came back and tried to say that they gave Suge money to start Death Row Records, which is totally untrue. A lot of people don't understand the dynamics or the mechanics of how the record industry works.

"You can get one hit record and a record label will advance you 25 million dollars the next morning. So there was no reason for Suge to have to get drug money to start that. His "187 Cop" provided them with enough cash to develop his record label. But at the same time, when you grow up in inner cities the hard way, it's hard to walk away from the individuals you grow up with.

"So Suge still participated with individuals who were involved in criminal activity, and in doing so he laundered some money for Michael Harris, and then that later came back to bite him in the butt to where she and Michael felt that they should be provided profits from Death Row Records. And when Suge basically kicked her out, Michael and herself took that very personal, and from there it was on trying to get back at Suge Knight."

It isn't a stretch to think that Michael Harris could have easily reached back to people he knew from his drug running days to topple Death Row Records. He could have easily reached out to The Red Knight.

We know that a decision was made to gut the company of all meaningful information. Steve Cantrock the accountant was targeted, discredited, and coerced into signing a confession letter that he stole money from the company. There was now a reason the information would be missing with a clear party to blame. At the same time, they tainted him as a witness for the government. Anything he could testify to could be dismissed as a disgruntled employee who had stolen money from the company exacting revenge by using the judicial system and law enforcement as his tools.

The missing records would make it difficult for the government to prove that Death Row Records was a money laundering operation and front for criminal activities. By the time the police and FBI got around to executing search warrants the pertinent information was gone. The paper trail was erased.

PART FOUR:
THE INTERVENTION
MISDIRECTION

While the Royalty in the Kingdom of Thieves was preoccupied in trying to assure the King of Thieves that the shootings they had planned for the King were not really meant for him, Las Vegas Investigators were invited to take a trip to Compton, to watch the swift and powerful use of police power in a multi-jurisdictional gang sweep. Why were Vegas Police interested? Had they not already made it clear that the shooing, in their opinion was not gang related?

They had. There appeared to be two reasons, according to Becker, that they made the trip to California. One was because they were asked. The other was to see "if they might pick up some useful information" on the clues they were working. Did Vegas police tell Compton what their leads were?

It appears that not only did they, but they made it clear, before it was a homicide, that they believed the shootings were in some way tied to Knight. Kenneth Knox, LAPD officer making reports about Death Row said that Vegas Police were seeking any info on Knight to try & build a case on him on gaming violations due to his recent "purchase of a gaming club (662 Club 1700 E Flamingo Dr.)."

But there was more to it. Other agencies were also sharing information, but perhaps not with Compton. On September 10, 1996 Detective Page from the Las Vegas Metropolitan Police Department also informed Knox that the FBI, Agent Dan McMullen, had an ongoing investigation on Death Row Records and Suge Knight. Knox updated Las Vegas Police on the information about Knight. The next day, Knox received a phone call from FBI Agent Dan McMullen. He advised Knox that they had a current Investigation (RICO) on Death Row Records and Suge Knight. The FBI was primarily interested in any Death Row arrests made with gun violations, narcotics, extortions, or intimidation type crimes known by the LAPD.

It must have been clear to Las Vegas Police as they set foot in Compton that the information Compton Police wanted to share with them was not information they were interested in hearing; no evidence exists to state that Las Vegas Police ever went to Compton to pursue a lead, they went only on a "fact finding mission"—toward their own end. Why were they already skeptical?

They had read Compton Police's entire reason for the gang sweep and found that it lacked credibility!

As stated before, the Kenner Alchemy was in full effect; he

needed to make the Third Element (the derailment of the investigation) so large, that it would not only convince the media and the world, but it would more importantly convince Suge Knight. So Kenner and The Red Knight began to employ tactics that had worked for them previously.

First they needed to turn the state of the current investigation into an investigation that was worth walking away from or unable to be successfully prosecuted. The last good execution of that was the El Rey Theater, and they went with that tactic: "say it was a gang matter," that way no one will want to touch it, just as Wilshire Detectives abandoned the El Rey Theater investigation.

And to do that, they employed the person who was so convincing for the El Rey Theater detectives. But in this case a simple phone call would not work. With no disrespect, Kelly Jamerson was a "nobody" compared to shooting the biggest rap artist in the country and the head of the biggest rap label. A case would have to be made and it would have to be larger than Orlando Anderson, but Anderson and his gang affiliations were the key.

Compton Detective Tim Brennan wrote an affidavit in support of a search warrant—which also happened to be primarily a work of fiction. The Affidavit as it was written is very colorful and error-wrought. This document started the entire "Orlando Anderson was involved" theory:

> "Approximately 1–1/2 to 2 months ago, "Death Row Records" affiliate Travon Lane was in the "Foot Locker Store" in the Lakewood Mall, with other "MOB Pirus," Kevin Woods aka "K.W." and Maurice Combs aka "Lil Mo." Lane aka "Tray" was confronted by 7–8 "Southside Crips." They got into a fight and the "Southside Crip" gang members took "Tray's" "Death Row" necklace.
> "On September 7, 1996, after the "Mike Tyson Fight" at the MGM Hotel in Las Vegas, there was a large entourage of "Death Row Records" people and some "Blood" gang members. The entourage had seen several "Southside Crip" people and some "Blood" gang members. The entourage had seen several "Southside Crip" people at the fight. The "Death Row Records" people observed a "Southside Crip" gang member alone in the lobby. "Tray" recognized the "Southside Crip" member

to be one of the people who took his "Death Row" chain at the Lakewood Mall and pointed him out to Shakur Shakur (who had a fresh "MOB" tattoo on his arm). Shakur confronted the "Southside Crip" member, saying "you from the South?" and began fighting him. Several of the other bloods also began striking the "Southside Crip." The altercation was broken up by security, and the "Death Row Records" people left.

"The "Death Row Records" people were caravanning in several vehicles en route to the "662 Club." "Suge" and Tupac were in the first vehicle. Some of their people in the vehicles that followed were "Buntry" (Alton MacDonald), "Neckbone" (Roger Williams), "Hen Dog" (Henry Smith), "Lil Wack 2" (Allen Jordan), "Tray" (Travon Lane)– all "MOB Pirus"–and Shakur's security person, Frank. The entourage stopped for a red light at Flamingo and Las Vegas Boulevard, when a Cadillac pulled up next to Tupac and "Suge." There were at least two people in the Cadillac. The passenger got out "talking shit" and pulled a gun and began shooting, hitting Tupac and "Suge."

The suspects in the Cadillac left and were thought to be caught by the police, by the "Death Row Records" personnel. The "Piru" and "Death Row Records" people met at the "662 Club" (the numbers 662 coincide with the letters on the telephone to spell MOB) after the shooting. "Timmy–Ru" (Tim MacDonald), "Mob James" (James MacDonald), "Tray," and others were present. "Tray" was telling everyone that the shooter was the same person they jumped at the "MGM." "Tray" said that he knew the person and that the shooter was "Keefee D's" (Keith Davis) nephew from "Southside Crips." The gang members were saying "it's on" (gang war) when we get back to Compton (with "SSC"). Several of the gang member left Las Vegas Saturday and Sunday and came back to Compton."

As a sample of the creative narrative: without saying who actually confirmed this or where Brennan heard the information from, and not being there himself, Brennan declares under oath that he was told:

"Tray" recognized the 'SOUTHSIDE CRIP' " (Speaking

of Orlando Anderson) "member to be one of the people who took his 'Death Row' chain at Lakewood Mall and pointed him out to Tupac Shakur."

Frank Alexander, Shakur's personal bodyguard, does not confirm that Travon Lane recognized anyone. He merely says that Lane whispered something in Shakur's ear and they took off running. Alexander states emphatically that Shakur never made the often referred—to statement "Are you from the South?"

"Tupac didn't say anything when they were on Anderson," stated Alexander to Las Vegas Police. "Nothing."

The person closest to Shakur in proximity at the MGM was Frank Alexander. He made it clear that he did not hear what Lane said to Shakur. Only two people can confirm that anything was said at all: Shakur and Lane.

So where is this coming from? It comes from the creative narrative of a police officer that was looking to get a judge to sign a Search Warrant. It's really hard to believe that this narrative has become the dogma that it has become.

Inside the Tim Brennan Affidavit Orlando Anderson is painted as the most hard-core criminal. There are eye–witnesses that testify in the Brennan Affidavit to seeing Orlando Anderson with handguns and an AK-47, guns are discovered at another location where Orlando Anderson has his diplomas on the wall, a confidential informant told police that Anderson was responsible for the 1996 murder at 1409 South Burris, George Mack positively identifies Anderson as his shooter in the September 10th shooting, he is also identified as the shooter of Elbert Webb on April 12, 1996, a Deputy states that Anderson has four guns in his possession, John Hibler is an eye-witness fingering Orlando Anderson as the shooter in the Elbert Webb murder, and to top it off Anderson is claimed to be responsible for the murder of Tupac Shakur.

Yet, Orlando Anderson is never charged in any of these crimes; there is no evidence to hold him or prosecute him.

The Lakewood mall story is also a part of the document. There is absolutely no evidence that this is a true story, in fact, there are several indications that this story has been fabricated by Death Row Records. On September 12th at Suge's house, Frank Alexander was asked, by Reggie Wright Junior, to lie by telling the police that Orlando Anderson had tried at 6:30 p.m. on September 7th to grab Shakur's chain. This was prior to the concocted Lakewood Mall story that Tim Brennan publicized on September 25th. Frank reluctantly agreed to tell the police about Orlando Anderson grabbing the chain earlier in the night. Suge and Reggie seemed to think they needed a reason to explain why the altercation with Orlando Anderson had occurred at the MGM. Alexander told the Las Vegas Police on October 1st about the 6:30 p.m. "chain-grab."

"These lies that this Compton police officer wrote about me have put my life in danger and brought stress on my family. Don't they know how many fans Tupac had? I'm afraid to leave the house. I can't sleep at night. That affidavit has just about ruined my life."—Orlando Anderson (RIP: August 13, 1974—May 29, 1998)

According to Brennan's affidavit, two men got out of the Cadillac and fired 13 rounds from a Glock .40-caliber handgun at the BMW from less than 13 feet away. Tupac Shakur, sitting in the passenger side of the car, is hit three times, one striking his hip, another his right hand, with the fatal wound to his chest. Brent Becker asked Frank Alexander, "Did anyone get out of the car?" Alexander responded, "No one got out of the car."

According to Knight, Tupac Shakur attempts to jump into the back seat of the car as he is being shot but Suge pulls him down into the seat. Two tires are punctured in the barrage of gunfire.

Knight suffers a minor wound to his head or neck. Suge turns to Tupac and asks "Are you OK Pac?"

Tupac Shakur, after seeing blood on Knight's head says, "Me? You're the one shot in the mutha-fuckin' head!"

Sadly, not one single other account of the night's events corroborate Knight or Brennan's stories. In fact, the statements and testimony of Fula, Cox, Greenidge, and Alexander all contradict them. In conversations with Cox, Greenidge, and Alexander at the Shakur Foundation in August of 2008, the three witnesses unilaterally agreed that there was no person who got out of the vehicle at all. They certainly would have seen a person stand up in front of them and fire into the vehicle. The Cadillac also would have had a tough time taking off in that scenario without someone reacting.

In what has been erroneously accepted as the official account of what happened that night, Tim Brennan filed the preceding "Statement of Probable Cause" in order to obtain a search warrant. Keep in mind that this was filed less than two weeks after Shakur died and that Compton Police had absolutely no jurisdiction to investigate the murder. They preempted Las Vegas Police's investigation. Because this isn't a typical search warrant where law enforcement has a specific objective, their search turns up almost no evidence. If you don't know what you are looking for you may not find it. The affidavit was a giant "fishing expedition" full of half-truths, outright falsehoods and unjustified conjecture.

This is what Las Vegas Metropolitan Investigators read prior to their arrival in California. And this is what they knew they were walking into.

More recently, when asked by Anthony Battaglia, an Internet anarchist known as "Anton Batey," Orlando Anderson's former attorney was interviewed. The attorney was asked about the scuffle in the hotel. "I think that that's you know, what people just assumed" the attorney commented "because Orlando had been beaten, he had been beaten pretty badly, then he made his way from the fight to the hotel, but that's where he stayed because he was really injured.

"I mean, if you saw that tape, you'd have saw that he kicked him pretty hard in the ribs and all over, I mean, there were guys all over him and the fact that he was even able to get up and then go out revenge, I think was pretty, you know, if it had happened a couple weeks later then I think that would be more plausible, but not that night."

"The affidavit is full of fiction. There is nothing in there that's independently corroborated. We don't know why that particular Compton police officer wrote it, but it's full of lies."

Vibe Magazine interviewed Orlando Anderson about the beating.

"I really don't know why Suge would say something like that," said Orlando Anderson. "I don't even know Suge."

"As far as we're concerned," Anderson's attorney told Vibe, "whatever Suge Knight is saying, he's saying for his own gain. We've also named him in the lawsuit. There is no evidence against Orlando. If they would do a proper investigation, they would very likely find out who killed Tupac."

Vibe magazine then asked "On the stand, you said Suge was not involved in your beating; that he tried to stop it. Now you're naming him in the lawsuit for participating in your beating."

"At the time," Anderson replied "I was fearing for my life."

"You were fearing Suge's camp? Death Row People?"

"We don't want to comment on whom he was fearing," said the Attorney.

Where Compton Police failed to arrest, charge, and prosecute suspects or to collect evidence in relation to the Shakur killing, they did establish their concocted version of events as the prevailing theory about what happened that night. It should be noted that Tim Brennan was working for Reggie Wright Sr. at the time. Remember that name? Reggie Wright Sr. is the father of Reggie Wright Junior who, at the time, was supposedly just the head of security for Death Row Records. Isn't it a little ironic that the person that was ultimately responsible for the safety of both Suge and Shakur has ties through his father to influence the "official account" of what happened that night? Isn't it ironic that Death Row insiders had never before heard the "Lakewood mall Orlando Anderson medallion grab story" until a week after the Tupac Shakur shooting? And that the story had morphed from Anderson grabbing Shakur's chain at 6:30 p.m. on the night of the shooting? The lies were just beginning to take shape. They would continue to morph over the next 18 years.

To summarize the entire, ever-evolving Orlando Anderson story, we go to Cathy Scott: "Take Orlando Anderson, that beating doesn't make sense."

"Everything we had, came from Tim Brennan," said Brent Becker.

So did Orlando Anderson have enough sway within the Crips organization to motivate his buddies to jump in a car–or in a more far-flung scenario, pick up the phone and call in a hit? The second scenario would indicate a ton of weight, especially if he was not in the car himself.

It needs to also be pointed out that Las Vegas Police reasoned that there was not enough time for Orlando Anderson to make the moves to kill Shakur; though Manning would recant this statement for inconceivable reasons. Brent Becker still believes this to be the case. And he is well off to still believe this. The timeline scenario was refuted in a December 2002 VIBE story, which calculated that it would have been physically impossible for Anderson to have traveled back and forth to the specified locations on a title–fight Saturday night in Las Vegas during the two hours and 32 minutes between his scuffle in the MGM Grand lobby and Shakur's shooting on East Flamingo Road.

Ask a gang member and even the lowest of them can tell you what the "word on the street" is. The "word on the street" was that there had been a fight between Lane and Anderson at a Foot Locker. In fact, we do not know that it was also not common knowledge that Anderson was going to be in Vegas.

It is a bigger leap of faith, almost ludicrous; to believe that there was a set up at the Lakewood Mall. That was simply gang people doing what they do. But the ability to capitalize on the events by asking Anderson to come to the fight, or even setting him up to be waiting there for a friend he thought might show up is certainly possible. So it is easy to reject the argument that any theory involving Anderson needed to include a setup at the Foot Locker.

Cathy Scott adds, "I mean, he was kept and stomped a little bit and the police didn't do anything. They didn't even take him downstairs. The police didn't take or security, take Orlando downstairs at the MGM to talk to him about that beating. He just said, 'No, he didn't want to press charges,' and they sent him on his merry way."

Frank Alexander tried to put the matter into perspective on the timing of events. "Now, I never knew who Orlando Anderson was. It's just kind of funny, ironic, whatever you want to call it that from April to September, why would Reggie have told me about Travon getting into this fight at the Foot Locker in Lakewood Mall with Orlando Anderson and here we are, a few months later, Pac gets into the same fight with Orlando Anderson at the MGM and then everything just went from there."

The Red Knight and Compton PD were convincing enough to some, however, because at that time Las Vegas Detectives were not talking much. They also did not respect Afeni Shakur or the Estate, because no one from the family or Death Row put up a cent for a reward in helping to catch the killers, and they believed that this lack of support kept anyone who might have been financially motivated to talk from coming forward.

Orlando Anderson filed a lawsuit against the estate for the scuffle at the MGM. A wrongful death suit against Orlando Anderson was filed in retaliation. Shakur's attorneys ripped it verbatim–literally plagiarized Tim Brennan's affidavit. In addition to the basic recall of the Lakewood Mall incident, the allegations involving the shooting were identical to the ones Brennan made in his affidavit–and equally as wrong:

- Suge and Shakur were in the first vehicle, a BMW owned by Suge.
- Plaintiffs are informed and believe, and thereon allege, that some of the people in the vehicles which followed were Alton MacDonald, Roger Williams, Henry Smith, Allen Jordan, Lane and "Frank."
- The caravan stopped for a red light at Flamingo and Las Vegas Boulevard, when a white Cadillac pulled up next to Shakur and Suge.
- There were at least two, and possibly more, people in the Cadillac.
- Plaintiffs are informed and believe, and thereon allege, that Bonds was the driver of that Cadillac and Anderson was a passenger in the Cadillac.
- Plaintiffs are informed and believe, and thereon allege, that Anderson got out of the Cadillac and approached the BMW on the passenger's side.
- Plaintiffs are informed and believe, and thereon allege, that, upon approaching the BMW, Anderson pulled a gun and started shooting at the BMW, willfully or negligently striking both Shakur and Suge.

Other than being completely unimaginative in the preparation of the complaint, which seems odd considering the suit is for wrongful death, and being completely unsubstantiated in fact as to the events of the shooting, the complaint was filed a year after the shooting. Clearly there had to have been some information other than Brennan's report they could have used to file their complaint.

The attorneys didn't even get Alexander's name correct—in

spite of the fact that the Shakur Estate knew Alexander personally. The cited "Frank" as one "some of the people in the vehicles." The Estate ended up settling with Orlando Anderson for somewhere in the area of $25,000 net to him. Orlando Anderson filed suit against the Estate for the beating at the MGM. Donald David, attorney for the Shakur Estate, explained that Wright Junior was present for the depositions in the Anderson case, though no one really knows why, other than Knight being named defendant in the case.

If Knight is to be believed, then Wright Junior, who was only the security chief and not actually running Death Row, would have no reason to be present. But if Wright was the de facto CEO of Death Row while Knight was in prison, he might have a reason to be there. Kenner was best suited to determine the known decorum of Wright Junior and Death Row associates; specifically what armor they wear to depositions. It is likely that this information was also known to Orlando Anderson at the time he was deposed.

According to Donald David, shortly after the settlement offer was made, Orlando Anderson was killed. His recollection also jibes with sources who told us that Knight knew of the settlement and wanted a part of it; that within hours of Anderson rejecting Knight's offer and agreeing to the settlement, he was killed at the car wash. The AP reported on August 18, 2000 "His estate claimed that only hours before Anderson was killed his attorney was told he would receive a $78,000 settlement from the Shakur estate."

In October and November of 1999, the City of Compton conducted an investigation of the Compton Police Department. Sgt. Kenneth Roller, Sgt. Frederick Reynolds, and officer Jerry Patterson detailed in a internal 95-page report incidents of corruption that led to the City Council disbanding the Compton Police Department and the contracting the Los Angeles Sheriff's Department. Cited in the report was an incident of 60 kilos of cocaine being seized on April 23, 1997 that supposedly had been turned over the FBI. The FBI had no record of ever having received the drugs.

"It cited former Chief Hourie Taylor, former Capt. Percy Perrodin, former Lt. Reginald White Sr. and a handful of sergeants as being responsible in terms of a near complete lack of rules and regulations governing the vault and little to no oversight by department administrators."

In fiscal year 1994-1995 there were nearly two million dollars in forfeiture seizures that lacked any kind of documentation—a year before Shakur was killed. The corruption was clearly continuing throughout the Shakur shooting and investigation.

There is a sad irony here. It is well documented that Compton had fatal corruption issues regarding police personnel. The Compton Police Department was in effect absorbed into the Sheriff's Department. Many of the officers named in the 95-page report as corrupt were welcomed into the ranks of the Los Angeles Sheriff's Department. The legacy of corruption continued leading to the indictments of 19 Sheriffs and the resignation of Sheriff Lee Baca.

Is it reasonable to believe that the citizens who voted to disband the Compton Police Department actually intended for the Sheriff's to rehire the corrupt police?

To his own end, Wright was making it known that Knight was a candidate for the jail cell. On September 17, 1996 the following police log entry is recorded:

> "On their A.M. Watch Officers Jetter and Yamamoto were working a crime suppression detail to address gang activity problems @Death Row Records, 18730 Oxnard St., Suite 211. Officer Jetters spoke with the head of security @ Death Row (Reggie Wright) & was informed by Mr. Wright that since the death of Tupac, Marion Suge Knight was now using gangsters (Bloods) from Compton as his own personal body guards and that they were armed."

Why would Reggie Wright Junior tell law enforcement that Suge was using criminals for protection? Wouldn't this be a clear probation violation? Passive aggressive behavior?

INFLUENCE

The website run by former Compton Detectives Tim Brennan and Robert "Bobby" Ladd, explains that most everyone that worked for the Compton Police Department for a few years was an expert in gangs. They claim to have learned from "the ones that came before us, most notably, Hourie Taylor and Reggie Wright." Obviously Reggie

Wright Senior, Wright Junior's father, was on the Compton Police Department and was the Reggie Wright referred to by Tim Brennan.

Brennan explains that Taylor and Wright, Senior were from the South Central Los Angeles and Compton areas where the Crips and Bloods were formed. The website goes on to say that today's experts have adopted and now teach what Taylor and Wright Senior had to say. "They lived the history of what led to the forming of the black gangs."

This website also begins to give some narrative structure to Reggie Senior's involvement in the Compton Gang community. It turns out that Reggie Senior and Taylor started the Compton Police's first continuing gang unit. Brennan and Ladd write that the gang members respected Taylor and Reggie Senior for their knowledge of the gang community.

It seemed clear at that point, that if there was respect between the gangs and Reggie Senior there would be at minimum the opportunity for open and direct communication with the gangs, which begs the question of whether Compton Police, who were known to be corrupt, abused that respect to influence the gangs.

Brennan and Ladd claim that Taylor and Reggie Senior taught the gang officers that to truly be successful they had to "know the gang members." They were "in the street every day to observe and contact gang members." To Brennan it appeared that everyone in Compton knew Hourie and Reggie Senior.

While this is good information, it isn't strong enough to imply that Wright Senior was capable of exerting undue influence on the gangs of Compton. So it seemed shaky at the time to question that role.

In 2010, the 1999 Compton Corruption Report surfaced and settled any questions that Reggie Senior had the ability to unduly influence or even control the gangs. Before the 1999 report surfaced it looked like Reggie Senior was merely capable of helping Wright Junior with gang participation in the legal and illegal affairs of Death Row; as LAPD Detective Fred Miller alleged was the case.

It is no leap at all to expect that if gangs respected Reggie Senior, they would at least listen to Wright Junior out of that same respect; a theory not again corroborated for another 6 years.

The website's testimony confirms that Brennan's and Ladd's unflinching commitment to Reggie Senior and his agenda, may also make them, like the gangs, subject to undue influence and compromise. The Frank Alexander secret tape recordings provide some insight. "Reggie ordered the red carpet, he said, 'I tried to fly straight.'"

When the Compton Police department was annexed by the Los Angeles County Sheriff's Department, Reggie Senior continued to work in Compton. He has kept silent regarding anything he knows about his son's tenure or life after the Compton Police.

Ladd, Brennan, and Reggie Senior became part of a gang homicide unit in 1989 and remained in the gang unit until 2000. For its own part, it was important to note that the City of Compton and its key city functions were disbanded because of corruption... from the mayor on down.

Robert Ladd, Tim Brennan's partner on the Compton Police, was asked if he believed "that there would have to be a huge conspiracy" for Knight to have control and influence on the Compton Police, as well as Las Vegas Police?

Ladd affirmed, the thought would be "ridiculous" to say that Knight himself controlled or had the capacity to control that much manpower; it just seemed a bit much for one man. But to be clearer Knight's influence was more of a "networked" sphere of influence. Unfortunately, that distinction is lost on many, such as Ladd who indicates that Knight would also have to control the DEA and "everybody else."

Speaking of the DEA, Knight was being investigated by the DEA, generally. Knight was served with seventeen (17) warrants in two states related to several homicides and conspiracy to commit murder, when law enforcement served warrants at the offices of Death Row Records. Knight was convicted and spent over six years in prison on a successful prosecution of a probation violation charge.

However, the matter is more localized than that. The only law enforcement agencies Knight had to exert some sort of influence over by proxy were the Las Vegas Police Department and later the LAPD; Compton was arguably already in Wright Junior's sphere of influence. It was definitely under Reggie Senior's influence.

Knight had a history of violence that any other person would have constantly faced legal turmoil over. Knight was constantly dodging legal entanglements but not to the extent of he was committing. Police, the District Attorney's Office, and the United States Attorney's Office were after the "big conviction" and they allowed so many smaller infractions to slide. Police on the payroll of Death Row often looked the other way. Law enforcement agencies that "had something" on Knight, picked him up and charged him. Warrants were served but Knight was likely tipped off far in advance.

Boy are those days done!

Compton police dissolved. Reports were issued condemning Hourie Taylor and Reggie Senior's management of the police, challenging their personal conduct while executing their official roles and giving an overall pile of unanswered questions, most having to do with missing evidence—a problem they had in common with LAPD.

And whether or not one thinks that Knight controlled the actions of the entire body of the Compton Police and the LAPD, the term "influenced" is still completely relevant. And in certain circumstances, influence can equal de facto control. Kenner didn't control Larry Longo; he manipulated him. Reggie Wright Junior did not control the Compton Police department; he influenced it either directly or indirectly, with people like his former partner Kevin Hackie, who was still working for Compton Schools and working for Wright Junior at Death Row, or directly with Wright Junior working through his father who was extremely influential inside the Compton Police Department.

Influence happened at LAPD as well. Evidence disappeared from the Pacific Division in the Snoop Dogg's murder trial while Sharitha Knight was his manager and Kevin Gaines was Sharitha's boyfriend. Kevin Gaines was also associated with Death Row through his close association with David Mack and Rafael Perez.

Kevin Gaines' actions had influence on the LAPD. David Mack's actions had influence on the LAPD. Raphael Perez's actions had influence on the LAPD. Rich McCauley, a security guard at Death Row, worked for LAPD. LAPD has spent millions of dollars to bleach the taint the actions of these officers' "influence" caused. Each and every person who commits an act has influence on the body as a whole. It's because as a whole, we are often forced to react to information and influence.

Delores Tucker's actions had influence on Knight, Shakur, and Time Warner. Dan Quale had influence on Time Warner, Interscope, and Shakur. Any time a person has to react to what another has done, he has exerted influence over another's behavior. Knight, Wright, and Kenner clearly influenced LAPD, Compton Police, and Las Vegas Police.

Because of Death Row Records sphere of influence, Compton Police didn't stand a chance. And for their part, they admit themselves that they forwarded clues to Las Vegas Police and were ignored. This shows that Compton Police's influence on Las Vegas Police wasn't enough to motivate Las Vegas Police to act on Compton's beliefs. Compton Police may have "had enough" on Knight to mean something, but it's not fair to say that their evidence would have been strong enough to make an arrest; historically it wasn't.

Writer Cathy Scott claims that Knight had Las Vegas Police on his payroll while he was in Las Vegas implying that Knight had influence on them. Factually, police officers are hired to work security, close streets, and baby sit film crews, while off duty. Factually, the company, who hires these officers, pays for their services, most of the time through the city or county. Without any further supporting evidence in the form of documentation or specifics, it is reckless to say that an off-duty Las Vegas Police Officer was "on the payroll" for Death Row simply because they were working security for a public event or at Club 662.

But more importantly, influence over or on a police department only goes so far and is really not the place to have influence. The real spot to have influence is where the police send their cases to be prosecuted. And judging by the number of charges the police placed against Knight versus the number of actual convictions he has had, his attorneys have a broad influence on the prosecution of the claims.

The only exploitable flaw Knight's hubris gave him was that his reliance on Orlando Anderson agreeing not to press charges was sufficient to not bring the police to his front door. In Nevada, the victim does not have to press charges against the suspect in those types of situations. Las Vegas Metro Police did not need Anderson to press charges. They could have had Knight on a videotaped battery, which we now know was strong enough evidence to revoke Knights probation. So in and of itself, either Knight relied on the other layers of influence, or Knight himself knew he had influence over Orlando Anderson—enough influence to form a collusion or at least enough to not worry about going home.

REDIRECTION

In a rather overt statement, Brent Becker made it clear that Orlando Anderson wasn't a suspect. In a city like Las Vegas where there is a camera everywhere Orlando isn't a suspect due to video evidence that corroborates Orlando Anderson's alibi. Corey Edwards stated that Anderson came to the bar after the scuffle and Anderson said he went to his room. All of that is verifiable with the eye in the sky; the same type of surveillance footage that is used from the MGM Hotel during Knight's probation hearings. Tim Brennan and the Compton Police had given it their best shot and came up short—a pattern with those on the Gang War front. Kenner's Alchemy began to fail under the sheer weight of this investigation.

"Now, Compton got involved," adds Cathy Scott, "because they brought detectives there and handed a Crips member to them who they thought had information and Las Vegas Police did interview him. They talked to him casually, 'Hi, how you're doing?' that sort of thing but they didn't formally interview him and did not name him a suspect and let him go into the night."

When Becker was asked by Orlando Anderson if he was being questioned for the shootings, Becker responded "Why should I?"

The Kingdom of Thieves was still exposed. Kenner needed to change the chemistry. He resolved that The Kingdom needed to neutralize the Las Vegas Police and attack the character of Brent Becker in order to keep selling the "Orlando Anderson did it" theory. How to go about that in a "pre-Internet" world was the challenge.

The Kingdom of Thieves needed to be heard—they needed what is called "reach": the ability to influence thousands or millions of people with their dis-information. That way the noise from Death Row, would deafen the masses; that deafness would silence the Las Vegas investigation. They also needed to accomplish the fallback plan for preservation of The Kingdom of Thieves, at least until it was gutted successfully, and that was to get The Red King banished from The Kingdom; in exile so far removed from the world that he would have no voice, and would eventually become meaningless.

The reach Kenner needed was found at the Los Angeles Times, soon to be referred to as the Death Row Times. First published on December 4, 1881, The Times said its daily circulation in September of

1996 was 1,029,073 readers. By 2008, it was the largest metropolitan newspaper in circulation in the United States. Those numbers would help reach millions, and would no doubt be carried by the Associated Press and other major newspapers nationally.

According to Wikipedia, author Chuck Philips has written for the Los Angeles Times, Rolling Stone, Spin, Village Voice, The Washington Post, AllHipHop, the San Francisco Chronicle and Source magazine—and probably for Death Row.

Philips participated in doing the Kingdom's business: undermine the Las Vegas Police Department and attack of the character of Brent Becker in order to keep selling the "Orlando Anderson did it" theory. On February 10, 1997 Chuck Philips writes the article, "Rap Mogul's Lawyers Contend Detective Lied."

In the article, Philips rehashes the information from the Tim Brennan Affidavit—now getting that account entered as the official LA Times account of what happened. He also contends that Brent Becker is a liar–an assertion in a motion filed by Knight's attorneys to get the probation violation set aside.

Tim Brennan and Bobby Ladd posted on their website, "Detective Richardson testified to what Anderson had really told us about the assault in Las Vegas. Detective Richardson testified, and the Judge revoked Knight's probation and sentenced him to the maximum 9 years." So we know that Brent Becker wasn't the only one who testified at the probation hearing.

Kenner had, perhaps purposely, bungled Knight's probation hearing by introducing the MGM surveillance tape and by putting a scared Orlando Anderson up on the witness stand to recant his earlier statements made to Detective Richardson from Compton Police and Brent Becker from Las Vegas Police. Why would Suge's lawyers then file a motion to get Brent Becker's testimony stricken when they knew that had zero chance of success?

The motion was filed based upon the Chuck Philips and Alan Abrahamson article published in the LA Times on February 4, 1997, "Police, Shakur's Entourage At Odds over Investigation." That article sets up confusion between Brent Becker and Kevin Manning of the Las Vegas Police. In this article Manning is saying that Orlando Anderson is a suspect and Brent Becker is saying he is not.

They filed the motion because it gave Chuck Philips a story that could discredit Brent Becker and the Las Vegas Police and enter the story of Orlando Anderson as the shooter into the official record. In order to get the story believed by law enforcement (outside of Vegas) and the public they needed to make the Brent Becker statement that "Orlando Anderson wasn't a suspect" dissipate. They wanted to smear Brent Becker.

We get insight into how Chuck Philips works by listening to his interview of Frank Alexander for the February 28, 1997 article, "2 Say They Saw Attackers of Slain Rapper." Philips is heard selling Alexander on his "Orlando Anderson was the shooter" theory. He begins with the premise that "they know who shot Tupac" and is attempting to put this theory into Alexander's mind. This is known as witness tampering; Philips is feeding testimony to one of the few people that saw something.

Where was this coming from? Chuck Philips made it clear to Alexander that he is in touch with Knight and David Kenner. He tells Alexander about his December 29, 1996 article, "U.S. Probes Death Row Record Label's Money Trail." That article is a puff piece giving Knight a chance to steer the investigation from the official newspaper in Los Angeles. Philips lets Knight tell his side of the story to cloud the Federal Investigation and to play the race card.

On Alexander's recorded telephone call Chuck Philips asks three times if Alexander would participate in a line-up or if he saw the shooter. Alexander responds to the first question, "I would rather leave that question to law enforcement." When Chuck asks the second time, "Chuck I'm really not going to comment on that question there. That is a law enforcement question." The third time, "that's a question I'm not going to answer one way or another."

Yet when Philips article appears he contradicts what Alexander has said and writes, "Could I identify the killer of my friend Tupac Shakur if the police showed me photos or a lineup of suspects? Possibly so," Alexander said. "The thing is that the Las Vegas Metro Police never even tried to show me a photo of the shooter. Nor did they call me at any time for a lineup or to ask me anything concerning the shooting and death of Tupac."

We know from Alexander's written statements on the night of the shooting, and March 19, 1997 as well as the telephone statement of October 1, 1996 that he was fully cooperating with police.

Philips' article contains lots of Malcolm Greenidge quotes including, "I saw the driver." The trouble is that this is a flat out false statement, which Greenidge is all too happy to clear up for Becker when he is brought in a second time. This is the extent of what Greenidge saw, according to his Las Vegas Police statement:

> Q: So you guys are stopped at the light, when did you first notice this Cadillac?
> A: When it- when the shots came.
> Q: Okay; So when it had already pulled up?
> A: Looked in the direction of the shots, yeah.
> Q: Could you tell how many people were in that car?
> A: Nope. I can only see two individuals and I couldn't even really see 'em. Just seen two individuals on the side where the guns comin' from.

So why on earth would Philips make such an obviously false statement? And why does he continue to do so years later? Well, the simple answer is that Philips like Kading and others, rely on the fact that the readership's trust in them is strong enough that no source documents ever have to surface, and the odds at the time that they would surface are extremely slim. In a word, just trust us.

Brent Becker has a different story, "We would try to get in touch with people and would have to go through Death Row Records to try and locate them. Classic example, we ended up getting a lot of press about how Malcolm Greenidge said he could identify the shooter. We finally track him down to set up a re-interview and he says I'm not going to look at any photos because I can't identify him. Yet we got beat up in the LA Times over that, you know, and I'm thinking put up or shut up - Ace. But again, Reggie Wright Junior was the one that brought him to that interview."

The quotes attributed to Frank Alexander and Malcolm Greenidge were miles apart from what each of these witnesses officially said to authorities and Frank Alexander's taping of the Chuck Philips call leads us to believe that Alexander never provided Philips with any quote let alone a quote that said he could identify the shooter.

Philips wrote three stories to get the Orlando Anderson narrative placed as the official account of the LA Times, as part of the Death Row Records cover up and to obfuscate any investigation into the true perpetrators of the crime. The three Philips stories:

- February 4, 1997: "Police, Shakur's Entourage at Odds over Investigation."
- February 10, 1997: "Rap Mogul's Lawyers Contend

Detective Lied."
•   February 28, 1997: "2 Say They Saw Attackers of
Slain Rapper."

Previously on the night of Shakur's shooting Frank Alexander
told police about the white car calling it a newer 94 or 95 Cadillac. He
said he did not notice the plate. There were three young women in the
car next to Shakur and Knight. "Those, uh, ladies that were in that car,
uh, in my opinion, had the best view of the vehicle that did the shooting." —From Frank Alexander's Statement to Brent Becker hours after
the shooting.
Shelayne Lashaun Turner, Ingrid Johnson, Lauren Michelle
Hart, and Teneisha S. Fort were traveling in a rented Chrysler Sebring
right next to Suge and Shakur. They were interviewed after the shooting.
Lauren Hart said she saw a large newer model four door car, possibly a
Lincoln or Cadillac with Nevada plates nearby and heard several gunshots. "Ingrid estimated hearing about 20 gunshots during the incident.
Ingrid recalled that Tanesha, who was seated in the back, did not put her
head down and possibly saw more of the incident." Teneisha Fort saw a
large older white vehicle and heard several gunshots. A year later Lauren
Hart gave a statement to Detectives Katz and Martin:

"Shelayne drove off, almost hitting a white car which Hart
thought was a Lincoln Continental. The white car, which was on
their right (passenger) side swerved to avoid hitting them. Witness Hart stated that the white car was to their right and in front
of them, so she was able to see the rear of the car. Hart feels that
the white car had Nevada license plates (white with blue) and
felt the car was possibly a rental. Hart thinks the shooting came
from the driver's side of the white car and that there was four occupants." — Lauren Michelle Hart Statement 9-10-97

So where does the myth of California plates come from?

Chuck Philips seems to be the source of the "California Plates"
myth. He also has lengthened the window of the Orlando Anderson
scuffle to the shooting calling it three hours when it was two hours and
twenty-five minutes. In the investigation of a murder; thirty-five minutes
is enormous. He is giving his readers a story to believe and someone to

blame. Philips writes in his February 10, 1997 article, "About three hours after the fight in the MGM lobby, as Shakur and Knight were stopped at a red light just off the Las Vegas strip, a white late-model Cadillac with California plates pulled up in the lane next to Knight's 750 BMW." Philips rehashes it again in his February 28, 1997 article, "About three hours later, Shakur and Knight were sitting in Knight's 750 BMW at a red light just off the Strip when four men in a white late-model Cadillac with California plates pulled up in the next lane."

It may not seem like a big deal but when the LA Times prints something as the official account it taints an investigation or confuses a case. The Los Angeles Times is considered to be a mass media dis-seminator of information in the Los Angeles market. Any article that is published in the LA Times can change witness testimony or cloud a jury pool. When it comes to salient clues in any investigation journalists have a responsibility to get the facts right. The license plate of the murder vehicle is a significant piece of evidence. The most credible witness statements said the license plate was Nevada issued.

Popular theory has it that Orlando's cousin Jerry Bonds drove the white Cadillac into an auto shop on White and Alondra with another guy at 3 p.m. Afeni Shakur's attorneys, largely following the Brennan affidavit, also made the claim that Bonds was the driver of the vehicle. Does that mean that Bonds was also the contracting party on the rental agreement? Someone would have had to rent it, used their license, given a credit card.

In the case of Enterprise rent a car, where the rental allegedly happened, there was a policy for a number of years that you did not need a credit card to rent a car. In the event however, that you did not have a credit card, at least three verifiable witnesses to your credibility had to be listed on the application and they would've been verified by the agent at the counter. In addition to that, you had to provide proof of local residence, like a utility bill.

To date, no copy of the rental contract has ever been released by the Las Vegas Police or Compton Police for that matter. No one has ever identified a person who was under the contract to rent the car the weekend it was used.

However, according to the Chuck Philips via the Los Angeles Times, two days after the shooting, two Crips were seen in Compton driving a white 1996 Cadillac bearing a rental sticker. An "informant" told the Compton Police that Crips had visited a car stereo shop whose owner also did bodywork. They believed that the Crips brought the car to the stereo shop to have the damage repaired.

The Times also goes on to claim that the Compton Police found that a Carson Enterprise Rental Car agency had rented such a car to a man with possible ties to the gang underground. They took a photograph of the car and detailed their findings in   a report.

Compton investigators say they gave this additional information to Las Vegas Police. Manning said his detectives never received it. "We thought there was a possibility that we had located the Cadillac used in the crime," said retired Compton Sgt. Robert Baker. "It was a solid lead that should have been pursued."

Philips also broke the story about Suge Knight's conflict of interest with Deputy D.A. Larry Longo. He wrote that the D.A.'s office received an anonymous tip September 17th that Knight "is living in Assistant District Attorney, Larry Longo's Malibu Home" and Longo is placed on administrative leave.

Why make an anonymous call on the 17th? Remember that this was a failed attempt to kill Knight. So what is the next best thing to killing him? Get him put in prison. It had worked so well when taking Harry- O's money. It would work again in taking Knight's money. So why drop a dime on Longo? Because if there was the appearance that Knight was attempting to have influence over the D.A.'s office the judge would be sure to give Knight a harsh sentence. They burned Larry Longo because they wanted Knight to be gone for a long time. Larry Longo had met Knight socially after Gina signed her recording contract… he might be sympathetic toward Knight since Knight was recently the victim of a failed attempted murder.

No, Longo was removed to pave the way for Knight's incarceration.

So many conspiracy theorists have rewritten history to suggest that Gina Longo got a contract and payoffs were made to Larry Longo in return for suggesting probation for Suge Knight. They play with the dates in order to make their case. Larry Longo suggested probation for Knight before Frank Longo ever handed Gina's tape to David Kenner—before Gina ever signed a recording contract—before Frank Longo rented the house to David Kenner. Gina received a $25,000 payment and worked six months at Can-Am Studios recording six tracks toward a ten-track album. That money was advanced to her and would have to be paid back from album sales.

When Shakur was killed Gina Longo's record deal died too. The rental money paid wasn't a bribe as has been theorized, it was for the rental of a house in the Colony—a gated community in Malibu. It is really expensive to rent a house in the Colony. This was part of a smear campaign to dirty up Knight in a way that judges abhor. They wanted to make sure that Knight would be away for a very long time so that they could divert the revenue streams away from him.

How do we know all of this? From Philips November 12th LA Times article! He states that "On Sept. 17, the district attorney's office received a tip that Knight had been living in a Malibu Colony house owned by the Longo family. Gina's brother leased the house in May for $19,000 per month to Knight's attorney Kenner." How did Philips know that on September 17th a dime was dropped on Knight at the D.A.'s Office? How did he know that Knight was living in the house?

As a coincidence, September 17th was the same day that anonymous telephone calls were being made to the Las Vegas Police, claiming that "Orlando Anderson is the shooter." We know that at Knight's probation hearing, the Compton Police Interview of Orlando Anderson was used to revoke Knights Probation, especially since it directly conflicted with the testimony that Orlando Anderson was providing on behalf of Knight. The Chuck Philips article was preparatory to making sure that Knight wouldn't be able to conduct the affairs of Death Row Records.

The DA's office launched a criminal investigation of Longo. He was never charged with any crime. When you look at the timeline of events the Longos only did one thing wrong. They failed to notify the District Attorney's Office about the two contracts and Larry Longo failed to recuse himself from the related cases. They were played. A State Bar action resulted: "By his conduct," the stipulation says, "[Longo] placed himself in circumstances which created the appearance of impropriety in the mind of the public." In mitigation, however, the bar found that although Longo exercised poor judgment, he did not act dishonestly. He also had an exemplary 27-year career as a prosecutor.

"Longo was fired for conflict of interest and other departmental policy violations, but a California Justice Department investigation requested by the district attorney found insufficient grounds for criminal charges against him. Investigators said he never sought any special treatment for Knight."

PART FIVE:
THE DERAILED INVESTIGATION; WHAT A TRAIN WRECK LOOKS LIKE

There was an amazing wake left by Philips barrage of LA Times articles. In each and every article, there were two objectives: discount everyone else and promote the Orlando Anderson/Gang War concept to keep the public misdirected away from Death Row. It is important that we make a clear delineation between Suge Knight and Death Row—while they were intrinsically linked together in the media, for those on the inside "no player was bigger than the game itself" and Knight was not looked at by fellow insiders as Death Row for much longer.

According to the Patton Confession Letter, the Crips knew about the shooting because they were at the gang summit where Wright Junior cleared it with them for Shakur and Knight to be hit. Knight was alive and it was necessary to conceal the plan from him. Hitting someone high up in the Crips would send a clear signal not to talk. The killing was hardly knee-jerk, because 72 hours had elapsed since the shooting. The first person to get clipped was the head of the Crips section. Darnell Brim was high up and he knew about the meetings in which Wright Junior asked the gangs to "look the other way" and let Death Row deal with the shootings as "an internal matter" like the way the Mob seeks passive consent from the other families; to make sure their internal operation does not ignite a gang war.

Compton Police flip-flopped on their stance of Shakur's killing erupting a gang war (remember the Brennan Affidavit). Later they stated that 75% of the killings in that time span had nothing to do with the hit on Shakur. Brim was shot to send a message: Don't tell Knight he was set up. Don't tell anyone you were in on it, and it was an internal hit.

Remember, as of September 16th, 1996 "On their a.m. Watch Officers Jetter and Yamamoto were working a crime suppression detail to address gang activity problems @Death Row Records, 18730 Oxnard St., Suite 211. Officer Jetters spoke with the head of security @ Death Row (Reggie Wright) & was informed by Mr. Wright that since the death of Tupac, Marion Suge Knight was now using gangsters (Bloods) from Compton as his own personal body guards and that they were armed."

Wright Junior is making it known that Knight is violating his probation.

On a humorous note, according to police reports, LAPD Officers attempted to stop Suge Knight's vehicle coming out of Can-Am, studios in the Valley, but were interfered in making the stop by the rear vehicle, a Green Humvee driven by Rapper M.C. Hammer. Subsequently Hammer was Q&R (Questioned and Released)—with a warning only. Knight and the rest of the gang caravan eluded the Police.

The Death Row PR Machine, in conjunction with the Death Row Times has successfully split the media, the public and even some in law enforcement. Las Vegas Police are getting a barrage of phone calls from random callers who are claiming that Orlando Anderson is the suspect. The media is also entertaining Anderson as a suspect with wild applause because of the inherent drama. It makes for "good television" to have a story, and that is exactly what Philips gave them. "I don't know yet" is not such a great story.

As of September 25, 1996, the LAPD was getting word trickling in from Compton, and this time part of it was true. LAPD Captain Ibarra, Sergeant Bolton and Sergeant Ken Knox met with a Detective Caffeym who informed them that since the shooting of Tupac Shakur things have heated up in South Central L.A. and the Compton area between the Crips and Bloods.

He revealed that through sources and "confidential reliable informants" that there were "three separate hit contracts on Suge Knight's life." He set Knight's life expectancy to before Christmas. Caffey also related that the reality of Suge being killed in Tarzana was extremely high, due to the fact that Knight was an easy target at Death Row Records.

This is not surprising at all as Knight was supposed to have been killed September 7, 1996. The conspirators took great pains to make sure that Orlando Anderson and Bloods/Crips story had by that time escalated to East Coast/West Coast story of feuds. This time, because there was such a great push to confuse the public, the general acceptance was this would be a gang retaliation.

What is surprising is that with all of this noise, the Las Vegas Police are not shaken and are standing by their guns. In the "Death Row" Times article of October 4, 1996 "Man Found Who Fought With Shakur" Las Vegas Police Lieutenant Larry Spinosa says flatly that "at this point, Orlando Anderson is not a suspect in the shooting of Tupac Shakur."

The article goes on to state that Las Vegas police had previously contended that the Orlando Anderson could not have committed the crime. "Investigators in Las Vegas have noted that even if they do identify a suspect, they do not yet have a witness to the shooting to place the suspect there."

As previously identified, Knight was also under attack. There was already a tip to LAPD that Knight was using convicted felons as protection, which is a probation violation. Now from the same people who were notorious (no pun intended) for being unwilling to give out any information at all to law enforcement, on October 10, 1996 they volunteered to LAPD that Knight was out of the country—another clear probation violation. There was a concerted effort to make sure that Knight was going to see the inside of a prison cell. And it looked like Death Row was giving law enforcement more reasons than the prosecutor's office.

WITNESSES AFRAID TO SPEAK OUT

"We could have had Tupac meet us in the middle of the Mojave Desert if we wanted to but we going to conspire to have him shot on a Las Vegas Strip right after he gets into a fight? That's Crazy." —Reggie Wright Junior

The above Wright Junior quote implies, "we would take him out to a hole in the desert, you know like we usually do." There were way too many people that kept tabs on Shakur's movement so it would not have been easy to lure Shakur into the middle of the desert. But it begs a question; how many people did Death Row kill by taking them to the middle of the Mojave Desert? We know that Kevin Gaines was taken to the middle of the desert where a hole was already dug and he was stripped naked and left to die or make his way back. There was a rumor that a hole in the desert had been dug with Frank Alexander's name on it. On September 12th Alexander was asked to tell the Orlando Anderson chain grab story to the police and he had reluctantly agreed.

On September 13th, Frank Alexander received frantic messages on his pager summoning him to come out to Knight's house. Knight's inner circle, The Bounty Hunters, were all there. When Alexander arrived the first thing that Knight said was, "I bet you have your gun on you today." Alexander's gun was then taken from him. Wright Junior sat directly behind Alexander and Knight's Bounty Hunters surrounded him on all sides.

The conversation that day was extremely heated. Knight was still inquiring about what had happened the night Shakur was shot. Alexander was clearly the man that was taking the blame. Knight was disappointed that Alexander was not carrying a weapon that night.

Wright Junior was neglecting to inform the group that he had participated in disarming all of security that night. He too, was expressing his disappointment that Alexander was unarmed. Revelation about security being disarmed seemed to come as a surprise to Knight.

As the argument reached a fever pitch the telephone rang and Knight decided to answer. On that call he received the news that Shakur was dead. Knight threw his phone into the glass table and smashed it to pieces, "Now what are we going to do? Tupac is dead!"

The tension in the air was also smashed as everyone there was impacted by the weight of what was just said. Each of them took their own moment to come to grips with the reality of Shakur's passing. Their plans, the waiting plastic in the trunk of the car, the empty hole in the desert, and all of their differences could wait for another day. They all felt they needed to abandon themselves for a moment to pay homage to their fallen brother. In unison they all headed for the hospital. How ironic that Alexander was hired to protect Shakur's life and that Shakur's passing at that precise moment was the catalyst to spare Alexander.

Later that night Michael Moore warned Alexander to leave Las Vegas without telling anyone. Moore feared for Alexander's safety. On the ride home Wright Junior called and said Knight wanted to speak to him. Knight tried to get Frank to come out to a party with the boat and jet skis at Lake Mead. Alexander had heard about such parties on lakes with nefarious people where boating accidents claimed lives or where someone vanished without a trace. Lake Mead may contain many such secrets. Alexander politely declined that generous offer.

Alexander had lived to see another day. The day Shakur died he was no longer reluctant and had agreed to tell the story to Detective Becker of the Las Vegas Police that Orlando Anderson had tried at 6:30 p.m. on the night of the shooting to snatch Shakur's chain and medallion providing a reason for the scuffle at the MGM. On October 1, 1996 Alexander had a telephone conversation with Brent Becker.

What was really said on that telephone conversation was between two men and we may never really know the truth. Alexander told his lie about the medallion and Orlando Anderson... that much is clear. The report claims that Alexander told Becker who was doing the kicking, punching and stomping that night. Alexander denied that he ever told these things to Becker but they were published in Becker's report and that report was sent to the Los Angeles District Attorney and David Kenner. That report would once again put Alexander's life in danger as Suge was arrested on October 22nd for violating his probation and everybody sees Alexander as the swing vote that can put Suge away or keep him free.

When Alexander received the first hint of the danger directly from

Wright Junior, "life can become more complicated for you and your wife… that isn't a threat," Alexander then began recording his telephone conversations with everyone including: Reggie Wright Junior, David Kenner, Michael Moore, Larry Condiff, Kevin Hackie, and Chuck Philips. These calls give us tremendous insight into the Death Row Records obstruction of justice machine that was working overtime to keep Knight out of prison. Wright Junior was also working overtime to conceal his role in the attempted Coup.

The District Attorney's Lead Investigator, Bill Guidas, called Alexander and warns him that his statement had been provided to the Death Row Records team.

"I want to put you on notice," said Guidas confirming the danger, "that they have that report so I want you to know that for whatever reason. I think you better know that."

On a recorded call Larry confirmed the danger.

Larry Condiff: "They don't want you around. He said it right out of his mouth and his girlfriend confirmed it."
Alexander: "Who? Reggie?"
Larry: "Yeah"
Alexander: "What'd he say?"
Larry: "They want you dead."
Alexander: "He said they want me dead?"
Larry: "Yes. He said that you told a lot of stuff against Suge, and Buntry and Pac to the police. They got the police report that you said that Suge was kicking and Buntry was, and that Tupac was beating the guy up also."
Alexander: "I never said any of that."
Larry: "She said the people at DRR want you dead."
Alexander: "I never said any of that."
Larry: "That's neither here nor there. I don't know what to tell you… Maria said, 'You know they mad at him, they want him dead. Larry they want him dead.'"

It turns out that Alexander has become a critical witness for both the defense and prosecution. The prosecution has two Compton police officers who are going to testify that Orlando Anderson made statements to them about the scuffle implicating Suge and Shakur as the attackers.

Testimony from any of the rest of entourage wouldn't be as credible as they are all convicted felons. Alexander is the only one that can counteract their testimony. There is an attempt to coerce Alexander into providing testimony that can clear Suge from any responsibility. Death Row is in shock that Alexander refuses to lie for them. He had agreed to lie to the police about Orlando Anderson snatching Shakur's chain at the MGM hotel but he refuses to lie on the witness stand.

That makes him a potentially devastating witness for the defense. If Alexander won't get up on the witness stand and lie and they can't easily kill him especially now that everybody involved is under the microscope then the best they can do is to coerce him into not getting subpoenaed.

Much of the rest of the tapes deal with Alexander avoiding getting on the witness stand as a life preservation measure for both Alexander and his wife. We get an inside look at the cause behind Death Row Records Derangement Syndrome.

DEATH ROW RECORDS DERANGEMENT SYNDROME

Death Row Records Derangement Syndrome is a viral fungus which infects a witness. After the Death Row Records Derangement Syndrome intervention, witnesses who formerly have said one thing in a statement or on a witness stand before the "infection" by Death Row Records, seem to say something completely different when threatened after the infection. Death Row Records Derangement Syndrome will play out over and over as the investigations continue and the court cases mount. Others who would contract the Death Row Records Derangement Syndrome and recant their statements or testimony would include: Orlando Anderson, Waymond Anderson, Kevin Hackie, and even Wright Junior and Knight themselves when they provide depositions or get on a witness stand.

There was more to this call, however. Alexander was openly concerned about what he called "the can of worms" that he believed that even Kenner would not be able to protect him from. Alexander refused to physically see David Kenner at his office, and explained for about 20 minutes to Wright Junior that Kenner could just as easily hear his statement over the phone. They claim to want Alexander in person to watch the MGM video, and answer questions about it.

In a 2009 conversation with his business partner RJ Bond, Alexander made the statement that the reason that he was opposed to getting on the stand is because he was "being made the scapegoat" for Shakur's killing and he believed that the actual hearing for Knight was already decided, based on his conversations with Michael Moore which were already recorded as well.

Alexander told Bond that he was worried that Kenner was going to take advantage of Alexander being on the stand to get Alexander to admit to all of the shortcomings on the part of security—particularly why he didn't have his gun on him—a major point of Knight's in his Vegas interview.

Q: Since all this has happened, obviously you've seen all the media hype, but have any of your employees, uh, Frank Alexander or any of the other security people talked to you about anything that happened that they know happened?

A: Actually I've had some words with, uh, security (redacted) and (redacted) a little disappointed (redacted) A guy don't get paid to watch Tupac (redacted)

Q: But yet he's still watching him at the hospital.

A: Right. But I don't like (redacted) I found that out (redacted).

Q: Has anybody told you anything about what they saw happen that may have been behind you or around you?

A: ...Frank the body guard, was directly—directly behind us, so I'm just tryin' to prove it in my head and see that car came (redacted) was able to get there to do somethin' like that.

Alexander clearly told Bond that he was sure Wright Junior was going to use Kenner to shift the "blame" from what appeared to be Wright Junior's "irresponsibility" in guard detail assignments and make it appear in front of Knight that Wright Junior was still trustworthy and loyal to Knight; whatever happened was not Wright Junior's fault. Alexander believed that Kenner was going to "filet me like a trout on that stand and I was not going to let him do that."

Alexander may have been right, in what the true agenda was. In a 2007 interview, Wright Junior was asked if part of the problem back then with some of the body guards was that they were "not really focused on their job."

"It was always obvious to the artists and Suge that some Wright Way employees were more Hollywood then the artist. Now, I have to admit they were right… because even though we made a lot of mistakes that night… that white Cadillac and its occupants should have all met its maker seconds after the shooting into the BMW."

In fact in the recorded tapes made before the hearing, Alexander and Wright Junior got into a heated argument over the instructions about where the guns were to be left, and Wright Junior's instructions—not unlike the disagreement Moore had in the meeting with Wright Junior in front of the artists at the Death Row offices weeks earlier.

Alexander was well advised to have skipped the meeting, because the plan to take back Death Row, or "plan B," had not gone exactly as planned. Norris Anderson was in charge and that hardly served the agendas of those who wanted to take over. Wright Junior and Kenner would likely have directed the scope of the sworn witness testimony (in front of Knight) to place all the security issues at the hands of Alexander, and free Wright Junior to regain the trust. In fact it was Norris Anderson who finally reprieved Alexander from going to court at all, not knowing the real agenda had little to do with Knight getting out.

On November 10, 1996 in the middle of the Knight Probation Revocation drama, there is a devastating setback for the investigation.
The closest key witness to the Shakur shootings, Yafeu "Kadafi" Fula is gunned down in New Jersey in a housing project. He is visiting his girlfriend when two young men knock on the door. He appears to know them. They walk out into the hallway and a few minutes later a gun goes off and Fula is shot in the front of his face. The two young men flee the scene. Fula was able to identify the driver in the Shakur Shakur murder.

He got a clear look at the driver as he followed Shakur in the car behind Knight's BMW and he had said that he wanted to cooperate with police. Detective Manning of the Las Vegas Police Department said he was eager to interview Yafeu Fula but never heard from him in spite of leaving messages with the attorney for Death Row, David Kenner. Those messages may have pronounced the death sentence on Fula.

But how do you arrange a hit on someone and it happens in New Jersey? Weren't the East Coast and West Coast at war? Weren't the Crips and Bloods at war? To put this into perspective we look at the current writings of Brennan and Ladd of the Compton PD from their own website, ComptonStreetGangs.com:

"Tupac and Suge were shot the night of September 7, 1996 in Las Vegas, Nevada. Most of the Compton gang members involved had returned to Compton on September 8th, and 9th. As we were coordinating with LVPD, contacting informants, and gathering information, the City of Compton turned into a battleground. The next 5 days in Compton, the toll would be 3 murders and 11 attempted murders as a result of this feud."

We will forget that it was found not to be true later. But Brennan was still at this time running with that story and it was the "Death Row Times" who was still broadcasting the "Gang War" as if World War III had erupted in Compton. This "war" is what Brennan sold to a judge on September 25, 1996.

Within a few days on October 1st, 1996, right in the middle of the "gang war," LAPD Officer Kendrick Knox filed a field surveillance report. In this report Knox claims at 2:30 in the morning, LAPD Sergeant Buttita and LAPD Officers Gutierrez, Cormier, Velasquez, Dunn, Chandler, Rivas, and Townsend—eight officers—responded to a "Major 415" (Disturbing the Peace) call at Death Row Records on Oxnard Boulevard.

On arrival the security guard Paul Bailey exited the location and while acting reluctant, advised the LAPD officers that a verbal and physical altercation had occurred inside the studio and spilled outside into the parking lot area. Bailey stated at one point he was struggling over a metal chair with one of the suspects, identified as a Crip gang member from New Jersey.

The Crip gang member from New Jersey received injuries to his mouth, and Bailey had no injuries but was scared and reluctant to answer any of the officers' questions. The security guard then tried to cover up the incident by saying he did not know where the suspects were.

During the officers' investigation, the night manager of Can-Am, James Geiser approached Sergeant Buttita and advised the Sergeant that he was concerned because the suspects that caused the fight with the security guard were still in the back of the studio and that he wanted everyone to leave due to the incident so that he could assess the damage.

The LAPD officers rounded up 13 suspects and field interviewed them. Seven (7) of these suspects were identified as Piru Bloods. One of these suspects Allen Ray Jordan Junior was wearing a bulletproof vest. The other suspects were from the Bronx, New York, Newark, New Jersey and Brooklyn N.Y.

Seven Bloods and Six Crips… Two weeks after Shakur's death… Bloods hosting Crips at Can-Am–Death Row–studios… in the "back of the studio"… East Coast Crips and West Coast Bloods…

Saying it again. East Coast New Jersey Crips at Death Row, sleeping with the enemy… 5 weeks before Fula is killed in New Jersey? Wonder what they had to talk about? Didn't Wright Junior just say that Knight is now using Bloods as his security? In light of what is being represented 30 miles south in Compton, California either Brennan has grossly misrepresented the state of relations between East Coast and West Coast Crips, or there was a specific topic of agenda that would bring East Coast Crips into Death Row enemy camps.

From FBI report 194c-LA-232722-48, we read about the interview of an Orange, New Jersey Detective by the FBI.

"(Redacted) Detective, Orange New Jersey, Police Department, telephone number, (Redacted) was interviewed telephonically at his workplace. After being advised of the identity of the interviewing agent and the nature of the interview he provided the following information: (Redacted) stated back in late 1996 or early 1997, a 16 and 17 year old subjects were arrested in the shooting death of Yafeu Fula, aka Khadavi. The murder of FULA occurred in East Orange, New Jersey but the subjects were arrested in Orange, New Jersey (Redacted) This murder took place just after the shooting death of rapper TUPAC SHAKUR who was killed in September, 1996, in Las Vegas Nevada while sitting in a car (Redacted) Det. (Redacted) stated FULA was the key witness who evidently witnessed the TUPAC shooting. Det. (Redacted) added FULA was killed mob style as he was executed from point blank range by the teenagers, who apparently have an uncle or some other relative who lived in Los Angeles and was somehow involved with Death Row Records. Det. (Redacted) who stated he will pull this entire file from their archives and attempt to locate the two teenagers, recalls the murder of FULA was done professionally and wiped out the key witness in solving the TUPAC murder."

THE BANISHED RED KING

Back a few days, as mentioned earlier, Kenner, perhaps purposely, bungles Knight's probation hearing by introducing the MGM surveillance tape and by putting a scared Orlando Anderson up on the witness stand to recant his earlier statements made to Detective Richardson from Compton Police and Brent Becker from Las Vegas Police. Kenner is too good for this kind of junior plan.

The conspirators see their plan start to come together. On October

22, 1996, Judge John Ouderkirk sends Suge Knight to jail pending a hearing on a probation violation. The probation violation stems from the altercation at the MGM hotel where Orlando Anderson was beaten. He is placed in L.A, County Jail. Norris Anderson takes over management of Death Row Records.

Then inexplicably, after Ouderkirk sends Suge Knight to jail, Knight's lawyers file a motion to get Brent Becker's testimony stricken knowing they have zero chance of success. Kenner knew that the retraction of Becker's testimony had no future effect on Knight—there was enough information against Knight and that die was cast: on February 28, 1997, Suge Knight's suspended prison sentence is formally reinstated following the finding of the probation violation.

They filed the motion because it gave Chuck Philips a story that could smear Brent Becker. The motion, of course was filed based on information that Kenner had fed Chuck Philips, who in turn broadcast the Philips/Alan Abrahamson article via the LA Times on February 4, 1997—twenty four days earlier—"Police, Shakur's Entourage At Odds over Investigation." The article sets up confusion between Brent Becker and Kevin Manning of the Las Vegas Police. In this article Manning is saying that Orlando Anderson is a suspect and Brent Becker is saying he is not.

With Orlando Anderson and the East Coast/West Coast Crips/Bloods Gang War story continually evolving and gaining traction, they need only galvanize the story into the public's mind to make it legend. If in doing so, they can send Knight down a hole he may never recover from, then all the better. With Alchemist's sorcery, The Red King was banished and The Red Queen and The Red Knight were in charge. All that was needed to solidify the "gang story" and keep Knight banished far, far away from the kingdom, was the Kenner Alchemy's Fifth Element—the act conjured up to leave a scar on the public psyche so great that they would not dare question the "facts."

Ladies and Gentlemen, we give you the killing of Christopher Wallace!

PART SIX:
THE WALLACE
SHOOTING

There is a rash of violence tied to Shakur's murder including the slaying of Biggie Smalls on March 9, 1997. The similarity of the murders is compelling. There are three differences that stand out. The Shakur slaying was a wide pattern of bullets (bullets hit all over the car) with regular bullets being used. The Biggie killing is the same type of drive-by with a relatively tight pattern (bullets hit Biggie's door) and armor-piercing GECO rounds used seeming to indicate that this hit was done professionally.

The callers in the Shakur murder were mostly anonymous citing that Orlando Anderson was the shooter. The callers in the Biggie murder all provided their names and said that Suge Knight was behind the murder and that Wright Junior coordinated it. The shootings are identical except for an experience modification.

If the same person planned both murders, he would have learned something valuable from Shakur's killing substituting a shooter that spent time shooting for accuracy as well as adding armor piercing ammunition to better pierce the car. The murder of Biggie was professionally executed and it was covered up by the Los Angeles Police Department that continues to stonewall any true investigation.

But the fact is that the same agenda continued; Wallace was killed for no other reason than to allow Death Row to operate free from the influence of Knight; blame Knight for the killing of Wallace and thereby silence Knight.

But as we see in the March 18, 1997 Times article, preliminary findings are not congruent in the least with the theory of liability that Wright Junior and company need to keep, so that the true crime is not exposed. This time they succeeded in the hit, but there was a lot of work to be done to make the picture "fit the frame."

And this time they had a worthy adversary in an LAPD detective that singlehandedly surfaced the biggest corruption scandal in recent history for the LAPD—the infamous Rampart Scandal. And instead of an investigation lead by investigators who would go on to retire naturally, this investigation cost its lead detective everything. The stakes were never higher, and the risks appropriate for those stakes. Time to "double down." Casinos are built with that philosophy.

THE LAMB OF NEW YORK

"The biggest difference between the informants who implicated Suge Knight in the killing of Biggie Smalls and those who pointed blame toward the Crips, Russell Poole had noticed, were that the former gave their names." —Randall Sullivan, LAbyrinth.

To the music industry's shock and horror, Christopher Wallace is shot dead. Wallace's murder took place on the last day that he was spending in Los Angeles. Wallace and his associates did not decide until that very afternoon to attend the evening's Vibe Magazine party at the Petersen Automotive Museum in L.A.'s Miracle Mile District.

The party was a closed event for music-industry executives, they were told and security at the party would not be a problem. The scene at the Petersen Museum apparently had been quite mellow, especially given the complications suggested by the guest list.

Death Row rapper DJ Quik had shown up with ten fearsome-looking Treetop Piru Bloods in tow, while the dozen or so Crips who wangled invitations may have included Orlando Anderson. By midnight, the museum was crammed with many more people than it was permitted to contain, and a majority were smoking marijuana. At 12:30 a.m., the air was so thick with smoke that an announcer warned the crowd, "The fire marshal's gonna turn the party out!"

Speaking of fires, at 12:05am, a man pulls up near a fire truck directly across from the Peterson Museum and brandishes a gun firing 3 or 4 shots into the air. The Fire Department calls in a report of shots fired. A call goes out to LAPD and a dozen officers respond. Suspects are arrested a couple of miles down Wilshire. LAPD is now completely occupied with this incident as it appears to be completely random and no motive present. "Shots fired" in Los Angeles is taken very seriously. Most of the police on duty are distracted with this incident.

Meanwhile the Wallace entourage heads for the nearest exit. Wallace and Combs wait for valets to deliver their vehicles. Combs gets into a white Chevy Suburban next to his driver, Kenneth Story, with his three bodyguards in the back seat. Wallace is seated in the passenger seat of a green Suburban, next to his driver, Gregory "G-Money" Young, while Junior M.A.F.I.A. rapper James "Lil' Caesar" Lloyd, who had grown up with Wallace in Brooklyn, and Wallace's best friend, Damien "D-Rock" Butler, sit in the back seat.

Combs runs the light at Wilshire as the signal turned red and Wallace's car stops on the south side of the intersection. A white Toyota Land Cruiser inexplicably makes a U-turn and attempts to block Wallace's car from a trailing Chevy Blazer driven by Bad Boy's director of security.

At that moment, a black Impala SS pulls up on the Suburban's right side. The driver, alone in the sedan, was a black male whose blue suit, bow tie and fade haircut suggested Louis Farrakhan's Nation of Islam sect. He looks Wallace in the eye for a moment, then reaches across his body with a blue-steel automatic pistol held in his right hand, braced it against his left forearm and emptied the gun into the front passenger seat of the Suburban. Wallace is the only passenger in the vehicle hit by the bullets.

The Impala speeds away, heading east on Wilshire, and the White Land Cruiser makes another U-turn and drove off. The Combs Suburban slowed nearly to a stop when Story heard the gunshots. Everyone inside ducked, then someone shouted that B.I.G. was under attack.

Combs ran across Wilshire to the green Suburban. When he opened the passenger-side door, Combs saw Wallace bleeding through his jacket. Unable to elicit a response from Wallace, a terrified Combs jumped into the Suburban behind Wallace's car, while Story pushed G-Money aside and drove the vehicle to the emergency dock of the Cedars-Sinai Medical Center, less than five minutes away.

Doctors rushed him into surgery as Combs and the others dropped to their knees and prayed, but by then Wallace was dead. It was 1:15 A.M.

DEATH ROW AND KNIGHT LINKED TO WALLACE

In the aftermath of the Shakur killing there was a telemarketing effort to send investigators clues that pointed toward Orlando Anderson and the Crips. In the Biggie case there were confidential informants that said Knight, David Mack, Rafael Perez, Big Sykes, Wright Junior, and Amir Muhammad talked about their involvement. Unlike the Shakur homicide those confidential informants all had names. They were able to tell investigators where they heard the information. Though some would develop the aforementioned Death Row Derangements Syndrome, all of their testimony seemed to make sense. It was rational. LAPD jailhouse informant Waymond Anderson was the only one who completely recanted. Then he recanted his recanting.

Within one day of the shooting, there is already public speculation that Death Row is behind the killing.

"It's ludicrous for anyone out there to blame Death Row," said Norris Anderson, who took over as general manager of Death Row after Knight was jailed on a probation violation in October. "We do not condone this kind of activity, and Death Row certainly had nothing to do with it. Snoop and Biggie and Puffy have been in the press recently trying to quash all this media madness."

"This is a terrible tragedy," Norris Anderson said. "I got woke up with the news at 5 a.m. this morning and I am still blown away. Death Row knows how bad something like this can feel. It happened in our own backyard with Shakur just a few months ago. My condolences go out to Biggie's family. I feel horrible for them. This killing has to stop."

But one thing is certain: unless the conspirators could make Wallace's murder about revenge and give Suge Knight a motive, The Red Knight and company would not be able to take over Death Row. It was now Death Row vs. The Red King, because the interests of each were now conflicted.

The reason that this became such a weird balancing act, was because to blame Knight without blaming Death Row was difficult to do. But there were many who wanted to talk about this killing.

"MR. MILLER: No, I am just telling you. I am trying to get to a point here. During the Tupac shooting and his subsequent death, that night that it occurred, from that time for the next months, metro police and Vegas was just inundated with clues on, you know, information about the mall caper, the incident at the MGM, and so forth when Biggie was killed, nothing. Not clue one. Any insight?" —Interview with Kevin Hackie.

Insight? Gang members organized by Wright Junior killed Shakur. Professionals organized by Wright Junior killed Christopher Wallace. When professionals are hired to kill they cover their tracks up front. That doesn't mean they don't brag about their accomplishments.

Mario Hammonds was one of those. Hammonds previously assisted the FBI on a case in 1994. Using information provided by Hammonds the FBI obtained six search warrants that resulted in the seizure of narcotics, weapons, body armor, and cash. FBI Special Agent Robert Totten in the San Francisco Bureau Office confirmed this information and that Hammonds is considered confidential and reliable to their office because of the information he provided in 1994 being true and correct.

Hammonds was an inmate at the Men's Colony in San Luis Obispo during the time that Suge Knight was incarcerated there. Mario Hammonds provided information on Suge Knight being involved in the Biggie Killing. Speaking of Knight, Hammonds said, "he coordinated the hit from LA County Jail." Hammonds also said that "girls were used at the Soul Train Awards to infiltrate E. Coast and find out where they were going to party and try to influence them to go to the after party."

Hammonds was interviewed about his association with Suge Knight while incarcerated at San Luis Obispo. From the Affidavit we learn that, on the day that Marion Knight arrived at the Men's Colony at San Luis Obispo, Hammonds was working at the reception center for new inmates. He recognized Knight immediately as they had met previously, in Las Vegas, when Hammonds was involved in the music business. He also met Tupac Shakur at the same time. Hammonds and Knight struck up a conversation at the reception center and eventually became cellmates at the facility.

Later, during a cigar break in the music room at the institution Knight began to talk to Hammonds about the "Biggie Smalls" homicide. Knight informed Hammonds that he had conspired and coordinated the killing of Christopher Wallace while he was in custody at the Los Angeles County Jail. He stated that the murder had been coordinated via the use of cell phones. Knight told Hammonds that he had used "Big Sykes" and "Reg" to put the team together. They had followed through and set up the murder on the outside for Knight. He told "Big Sykes" and "Reg" where Wallace was going to be on the evening of the murder and "to take care of it." Knight related that he had waited a year to get Wallace back out on the west coast.

Knight told Hammonds, "That fat bitch took it like a bitch. Rolled up on his ass and smoked his fat ass. I got the fat ass. My people took care of it." Knight said, "Yeah, we wanted the West Side, we wanted to let them know "Damoo" (Swahili for Blood) got him on the West Side." Hammonds stated that they were alone in the music room when Knight began to discuss the Christopher Wallace incident.

According to Mario Hammonds, Knight called "Reg" believed to be Wright Junior, and "Big Sykes" from the Los Angeles County Jail to carry out his orders to kill "Biggie Smalls" in retribution for the death of Tupac Shakur in Las Vegas and Jake Robles in Atlanta.

Given the amount of press, which has been generated by the deaths of Tupac Shakur and Christopher Wallace, it would appear to Hammonds that the death of Shakur catapulted Wallace into the number one position in the rap music industry. According to Hammonds, Knight took the death of Shakur very personal. By removing Wallace it would not only avenge the death of Shakur but would hurt Bad Boy Entertainment with the loss of their top rap star.

Having it done on the West Coast was a private and personal matter to Knight. Knight has always aligned himself with the "Blood Gangster association. He often referred to this allegiance in the media. His reference to Hammonds that he wanted 'Them' to know that the Bloods had done him (Wallace) on the West Side (West Coast) and that he had waited a year to do it, indicates his personal grudge and intense hatred for those he held responsible for the revenge in the death of his friends Shakur and Robles."

Kenneth Boagni also wanted to talk. He relayed some of the information Ray Perez had told him about the murder of Notorious B.I.G. He told them about the phone calls that were made and what was said on those phone calls. He told them exactly how the killing took place and gave them several names. From Boagni's book he writes:

"He told them of clandestine meetings with Death Row's security team that Ray and Mack attended. He told them about some meetings in which the head of Death Row's security team relayed specific instructions to Ray and Mack. 'Instructions from whom?' Katz asked eagerly. 'From who?' Boagni said, as if the answer were only obvious. "'Who do you think? Their boss. Marion Suge Knight. Mr. Boagni, can you tell me about Perez's and Mack's involvement with Death Row Records?' 'They both work privately for Death Row Records security team. They party a lot with Death Row clients. They attend parties, recording sessions and video shoots for Death Row. And they were there the night that Christopher Wallace was killed. They were working security that night,' Boagni said. (Assistant City Attorney) Bogan leaned forward almost eagerly. 'Did Ray tell you anything else that night?' he asked. Boagni nodded his head slowly. 'Yeah… but I'm only willing to talk off the record.' (Assistant City Attorney) Bogan gestured for Boagni to go ahead. 'Ray and Mack played a huge part in the murder of rap star Notorious B.I.G.'"

"He stayed at the LA County Jail from December 10, 2000 through February 27, 2001, all the while testifying before the board. During that time, Boagni met with several detectives from the LAPD, attorneys for various officers and even City Attorneys. It was also during this time that Boagni first told Armas, off the record, that Perez had been at the scene when Biggie Smalls was murdered."

"The Board Hearing dragged on and on with more questions about Sergeant Byrnes and Ray Perez. Then Boagni saw Officer Armas whisper something to Mr. Seaman, Sergeant Byrnes' attorney. The attorney looked up at Boagni and addressed him. "Does Ray Perez work alongside David Mack as part of the security team for Death Row Records?"

"Immediately the board members stood up and halted the entire proceeding. They kicked everyone out of the hearing and made certain that the hearing was sealed. The board member who seemed to be in charge cleared his throat loudly. 'Mr. Boagni,' he said, 'This is an ongoing investigation. Please do not answer that question.'

"With that, everyone took a break for a few minutes. As Ken's eyes rested on Officer Armas, his face hardened. Boagni had previously talked about Ray's affiliation with Death Row Records, but had specifically told Armas not to mention that. He wasn't sure he wanted to go there yet. Officer Armas had agreed. So much for that. Boagni glared until their eyes met.

'Don't do that again,' he told Armas. 'Sorry,' Armas said. And the questioning resumed."

"When the hearing resumed, the administration asked a final question:"Mr. Boagni, what do you know of Perez's involvement with the record company known as Death Row Records?"

"The board members lost it. They shut the hearing room down again. They had everyone removed from the room, including Boagni, and were out of the room for at least forty-five minutes. Ken was starting to get a little worried. The Death Row Records thing kept coming up. When the Board Hearing reconvened, the captain of the board panel addressed Boagni, saying, "Please do not answer any questions related to Death Row Records or Perez's alleged affiliation with any record company."

"Okay," Boagni said. The captain stated for the record that the hearing was to be sealed and that only Boagni's initials were to be used in the transcripts." Boagni has never recanted his statements.

Kevin Hackie was in West Hollywood at the House of Blues when Hussein Fatal brought in a gun. An off duty Santa Monica Police officer had been hired as security and he seized the gun. He took the firearm into custody at the Santa Monica Police Station and conducted a ballistics test. The results were entered into the Federal Database. Wright Junior kept asking Hackie to keep tabs on the gun and a few weeks later it was cleared from having been involved in any crimes and ready to be picked up. Hackie retrieved the firearm and gave it back to Wright Junior After the Shakur murder the FBI interrogated Kevin Hackie. They claimed to Hackie that this weapon was the one that was used to kill Shakur. The FBI said that there was a positive match when the ballistics on file were compared to the bullets recovered from the Shakur murder.

Wright Junior was the last known person to possess this firearm. Perhaps he gave it to the shooter at the gang summit? We don't know. It is an area that requires further investigation.

Kevin Hackie worked undercover for the FBI and ATF. This might have given him more access to know things like a confirmation on the murder weapon used in the killing of Shakur. He also claimed to know that Christopher Wallace was under surveillance at the time he was killed. Hackie's attorneys talked to Assistant US Attorney, Ron Cheng, on July 25, 2001, where Hackie was forbidden from acknowledging that he had worked undercover during his testimony in the Christopher Wallace Wrongful Death Suit against the City of Los Angeles.

From a letter written by Wallace attorneys to FBI Agent Phil Carson we read, "Mr. Hackie will detail the role of Reggie Wright Junior, Wright Way Security, and off-duty law enforcement personnel as it relates to the operations of Death Row Records, the murder of Tupac Shakur, and the murder of Christopher Wallace. He is willing to meet with Reggie Wright Junior and to discuss with him the above referenced manners. He is willing to wear a wire while doing so. It is Mr. Hackie's strong belief that Reggie Wright Junior has sufficient information to procure indictments against Death Row Records personnel and that he could be instrumental in obtaining information."

Kevin Hackie had also done a staggering number of interviews with the LAPD both before and after LAPD Detective Russell Poole's departure from the department. His testimony did not change and he was clearly in possession of inside information that scared The Red Knight.

The Police report on James Lloyd states "Witness Lloyd has been interviewed on several occasions and his statements are pretty consistent."

Lloyd was a long-time friend of the victim and they grew up in the same neighborhood in New York. He was a witness in the 1994 shooting and had met Shakur before.

Lloyd stated that the only security they had was from New York and their security was provided by Paul Offord. Lloyd stated that Offord always provided security and to his knowledge they hired law enforcement officers as security officers. Lloyd said he had no knowledge of South Side Compton gang members providing security. In addition, he said he has no contact with anyone from Compton nor did "Biggie" to his knowledge.

Lloyd said he's been to Compton on one occasion. He was not sure of the month or date but it was in 1993. He met an unknown female, via "Biggie." She was from Compton and they went to her house which was in Compton. Lloyd could not recall the female's name, address, and telephone number nor could he provide her physical description at the time of the latest and last interviews with him.

Witness Lloyd said they ("Biggie" and his entourage which included Lloyd) arrived in Los Angeles a month prior to the 1997 "Soul Train Awards." They stayed in several motels/hotels during their stay, which included a stay at the Four Seasons, Niko, Montrose, Omni and finally the Westwood Marquise. They were in Los Angeles to promote "Biggie's" upcoming recordings. They had no problems with anyone prior to the shooting of "Biggie."

Witness "Lil Ceasar" Lloyd's most striking revelation (which would later be heavily attacked) was that other than going to northern California to conduct interviews with a radio station and visiting several malls, they pretty much remained in their room.

On the night of the shooting, they arrived at the party and entered without any problems. While they were there, Witness Lloyd was approached by a male (subsequently identified as "Keefe-D") that inquired about security.

He was approached by "Keffe-D" approximately twenty minutes prior to the shooting. He believes he saw him a second time when the party was ordered closed. "Keefe-D" said "What's up? You need some security, someone by your side?" Lloyd told him they were all right and had security. Lloyd had no explanation why "Keffe-D" approached him and inquired about security.

"Keffe-D" was accompanied by approximately ten other males. He could not provide further descriptions of them other than they were Black. After "Keffe-D" left Lloyd, he approached "Biggie" and spoke to him. Lloyd was not able to hear what the conversation was about. Lloyd was asked if security would allow people to approach "Biggie" and he said when "Keffe-D" approached "Biggie," security was there. "Biggie" told security (in reference to "Keffe-D") "He's cool, I know him."

Police note that Lloyd was interviewed on a prior occasion and identified "Keffe-D" as the male that inquired about security. He did not know "Keffe- D's" name.

Witness Lloyd said he saw "Keffe-D" in 1996 at a concert in the Anaheim. In Anaheim, "Keffe-D" was with a friend of "Puffy's" from New York. He did not know Puffy's friend name. They were back stage when he saw "Keffe-D."

Lloyd restated that their security was provided by Paul Offord,

Gene (subsequently identified as Eugene Deal), Kenny (subsequently identified as Kenneth Story) and other guys unknown to him.

But Lloyd never testified that "Keffe-D" did any type of security and did not detail in any way what the relationship was between "Keffe-D" and Wallace.

Sometime Later Kading would attempt to embellish this:

"First and foremost, there was the presence of Duane "Keffe D" Davis, the Crip kingpin Puffy had previously turned to for West Coast security. Keffe D had buttonholed Combs for a whispered exchange at Biggie's ringside table, but at the time Lil' Caesar had no idea what the conversation was about." Murder Rap: (p. 32)

Nowhere have we seen any evidence of the claim that Davis provided Security for Combs in this witness' interview. In fact in a March 20, 2997 interview, the following was documented:

"Witness stated he came out to Los Angeles with 'Big' as a back-up rapper... When asked if he had seen this person before he said 'yes.' He said he saw the person when he was shown the photo display folders. He said the guy was in frame #2 was the guy who approached him. He said he did not know the guy or the guys who were with him. Lloyd said that when the guy introduce himself to him, he said that he was from Compton... He described the shooter as a male, brown skinned, close fade type haircut, 24/25 years old."

Damian Butler stated he came to Los Angeles with "Lil Caesar" (James Lloyd) and his best friend Christopher Wallace aka 'Biggie Small" (victim) to promote his upcoming 'LP.' He did not remember the exact date they arrived, but they had been in Los Angeles for almost one month.

He stated prior to coming to Los Angeles Sean Puffy Combs setup Christopher Wallace's security through Paul Offord who is from New York. Paul Offord and Kenny Story, another bodyguard, picked them up from the airport and took them to Four Seasons Hotel, where they stayed for approximately eighteen days before the management of the hotel kicked them out. They were kicked out because of an altercation between Wallace and his girlfriend Tiffany Lane from Philadelphia. He, 'Lil Caesar" and 'Biggie Small' then went to the Nikko Hotel and stayed one night before being kicked out because the manager at the Four seasons may have called and told them about the incident between Wallace and Tiffany. They left that hotel and stayed 1-2 days in several other hotels before moving into the Westwood Marquis Hotel where they stayed for about one week.

He stated most of their time was spent inside of their hotel rooms, except when they were shooting videos and/or filming: which was done in the Marina and Downtown Los Angeles. There were always 3 to 4 security people at the filming locations.

Later they entered the museum and Wallace took a seat, inside of the party and never moved from his seat the entire night, until he got ready to leave. Butler noticed one guy walk from the street and stared at them, with a mad face. He described the person as being a male Black in his twenties wearing a blue/white pullover shirt, dark complexion.

Gregory Young's statement was of interest to police; it primarily focused on the shooter.

> "As he pulled up and stopped behind "Puffy's" vehicle at the red light a lone male Black driver pull up along the passenger side of the vehicle. He and "Biggie" simultaneously looked to their right and observed the driver pointing a gun at them. He had his left arm extended straight and his hand gripped to the steering wheel. The shooter had his right arm extended towards them and resting on the left arm with his upper biceps partially concealing the bottom portion of his face. The driver started shooting at them. He immediately ducked down and tried to get the vehicle's seat belts off. "Biggie" slumped in his direction. He exited the vehicle and hid behind the suburban, until the shooting stopped. Kenny drove "Biggie" to the hospital (Cedar Sinai)."

Young described the shooter as being a male Black, 25/27 years, old, medium complexion, wearing a bow tie with a light color jacket, possible gray or cream in color, clean cut with thin mustache.

Witness Ken Story also corroborated the Young statement and repeated Butler's statement about a guy with a "mad face."

"While 'Puffy' and 'Big' were standing in the parking lot, the witness observed a guy walk from the street and walk between the victim and 'Puffy.' The guy stood to the right of the witness. The guy stared at the witness with a mad face. This guy was checking out everything, so one of the victim's friend and witness started to watch this guy. The guy just stood there for a few minutes."

Story was interviewed several times: March 9th, 11th, 14th, and 15th of 1997. He did one last interview and added new information:

"While at the Vibe party, a lot of people came up to the table and talked to Biggy. In response to your question, a couple of guys that appeared to be gang members did come up to the table and talked to Biggy but I don't know them. Keeshawn (Johnson) or Paul (Offord) gave me an invitation flier to a Vibe sponsored after party. The party was located on Doheny Avenue, north of Sunset Boulevard, in the Hollywood hills. We had decided to attend that party.

"After the Vibe party, while standing in the parking structure, I noticed a lone male standing several feet away staring at us. I made eye contact with Damien indicating that we should keep an eye on him. This guy also walked right through our group and we just watched him. I think he could have been involved in Biggy's (sic) death because of the way he was "mad dogging us." He appeared to be a gang member and no one from our group knew him.

"He was a male black, 5'8" to 5'10," 185 to 205 pounds, mid to late 20's, dark complexion, short hair, no beard, unknown if he wore a mustache, blue jeans and a long sleeve blue and white stripe shirt. The shirt was a pull over type with a collar and he wore it loose and almost down to his knees. No visible scars or tattoos."

Marcus Nunn was a confidential informant that said that Knight hired a Mob Piru, a set of the Blood Gang, to take out Christopher Wallace. From Randall Sullivan's book LAbyrinth we read, "A slightly more persuasive account of Biggie's slaying was offered by an inmate at Corcoran Prison. This man said that Marcus Nunn, a Mob

Piru Blood who shared a cell with him at the time of Biggie Small's murder, had confided that Suge hired another Mob Piru to take the rapper out… Marcus Nunn denied everything."

Devin—from the book *LAbyrinth* we read, A Los Angeles County Jail inmate who gave only his first name—"Devin"—phoned the management company of Biggie's ex- girlfriend L'il Kim (after reading an article about the singer in People magazine), and said he knew for certain that the killer of Biggie Smalls was a Bloods gang member who had received $50,000 for the job from David Kenner. The shooter had fled to Chicago immediately after the killing, Devin said, but now was back in L.A. and working at Death Row Records.

Antoine Sutphen aka Boobie knows Rosanne Monique Smith who is familiar with Death Row Records. He was jealous of Heron. Sutphen provided information to the LAPD that Wallace had been killed by Suge's Goon squad. Also from the book *LAbyrinth* we read, "Two current Death Row Records employees, one male the other female had contacted LAPD during the first week after the Biggie Smalls' death… the male employee said he had heard Suge Knight boast about arranging Biggie's murder, while the female employee told police that she believed David Kenner had actually arranged the hit, and that she could provide information that Kenner was a "major drug dealer." (Randall Sullivan, LAbyrinth.)

Eugene Deal had impressed LAPD detectives as the most credible witness among those in the caravan of cars that had carried Sean Puffy Combs and Wallace to the Petersen Museum party on the night of the murder. In his interviews with the police, Deal, a New York State parole officer, had strongly denounced the theory that Crips had committed the crime, mainly because the members of the gang he met at the Petersen party that night had shown him "nothing but love."

And Deal's description of the "Nation of Islam guy" who seemed to be stalking Combs as they waited for their rides after the party had always been the most intriguing statement provided by any witnesses. As the Muslim approached from the sidewalk that evening, Deal said, he "seemed to be checking them out"—Combs in particular—before turning to walk north in the direction from which the black Impala would come less than ten minutes later.

"Puffy and Deal stayed until the end of the show. When

they were leaving the award ceremony, some Nation of Islam members stopped Puffy at the door. Puffy said something to him then said, "Yo Mustaffa tell him you and me are cool." Deal advised that he was not sure what was going on (Mustaffa is Farakhan's son). The unknown Nation of Islam member said to Puffy, "I want to talk to you because you be disrespecting brothers in the East." Then Puffy asked Mustaffa to tell him everything was cool and Mustaffa put his hand out and the conversation ended. Mustaffa and Puffy are close friends. (Deal believes that when the Nation of Islam members are working security for people other than Nation of Islam members, 'they are half-ass.')"

"Deal noticed a few Death Row people at the party. One of the people with a Death Row chain around his neck came up to Puffy and said, "Yo Puff man that's all bullshit and we all know it. He was wearing a blue suit and was kind of stocky 5'6" to 5'7." Then a girl with a Death Row chain around her neck came over to Puffy and said some unknown things."

"When they were about to leave. Deal told the drivers of their vehicles to go retrieve them and park them by the exit in the parking structure. When Puffy, Biggie and the rest of the group exited the party, they stood around the entrance having their pictures taken and talking to girls for about a half an hour. While they were standing around, Deal saw a person that looked like he was from the Nation of Islam walking through the parking structure. The Nation of Islam person was wearing a blue suit. Puffy then said a couple of minutes later, 'Let's get out of here.'

"As everyone entered the vehicles, Deal stood by the side of the truck. As he stood by the truck he was looking around for other Nation of Islam members, because they never work alone. But Deal did not see any other members. The Nation of Islam member in blue had a white handkerchief in his hand and started to walk north on Fairfax Avenue towards Wilshire Boulevard at a fast pace. The possible Islam member walked about (5) feet away from Deal he was wearing a medium blue suit, white shirt, a bluish green bow tie, had a football head with a receding hairline, 5'9," 165-180 pounds, brown skinned, light mustache and was about 26 to 35 years old."

Deal said that police never showed him a photo of Amir Muhammad, but documentary filmmaker Nick Broomfield did; with camera rolling, Deal was shown pictures of a half-dozen people who had been linked to the murder in one way or another. Deal immediately picked out one photo and said, "That's him right there." The man in the photograph was Harry Billups, a.k.a. Amir Muhammad.

When David Mack was arrested for the bank robbery, Amir was the first one to visit him in prison. He obtained entry by using a false name, a false social security number, and an out of service telephone number which will be discussed in more detail later. Amir and David Mack's friendship goes back 20 years to the University of Oregon where the two were college roommates and athletes.

Michael Robinson: According to Robinson he met Amir Muhammad at a stripper party in Compton where he meets Muhammad. Muhammad confesses to the murder of Wallace.

Michael Robinson a.k.a. "Psycho Mike" has proven to be highly reliable to the Sheriff's Department, FBI, and the DEA. All of the law enforcement agencies wanted Robinson's information kept confidential so they could continue to rely on his information. Therefore the judge in the case sealed his name. But in typical Chuck Philips style Philips and the LA Times attacked Psycho Mike's credibility and then revealed his name.

Randall Sullivan says in his Rolling Stone article, 'What the Times did not report was Psycho Mike's consistency and lucidity during his deposition. He had not been caught in a single contradiction by the city attorneys who tried to trip him up."

"Ten minutes into that deposition, I knew this guy was going to be an absolutely great witness for us in court," said Perry Sanders attorney for the Wallace Estate in the 2006 lawsuit against the City of Los Angeles. "He came across as someone who was just going to tell it like it was, and to hell with you if you didn't like it."

The portion of the LA Times article that embittered Sanders and Rob Frank, another Wallace Estate attorney, was the section in which Chuck Philips used Psycho Mike's February 3rd, 2005, deposition to suggest he was confessing that his information about the involvement of Mack and Muhammad in the murder had come to him secondhand.

In fact, he had never said it was anything else: Most of what he knew about this case, Mike explained, had resulted from trusted friends and family connections. One of Mike's own brothers had been a professional killer (until he himself was murdered in his bed) and, in that capacity, was familiar with Muhammad, whom he also understood to be a contract assassin. "He wasn't a stranger to my brother," the informant observed. "Two killers was in the same group."

When "Psycho Mike" finally met Muhammad at the house in Compton where a Death Row Records employee named Rick James lived, Robinson brought up the Wallace case. Muhammad immediately dropped his voice to a "killer's whisper" and said, "if my brother was alive, I'd be dead," apparently meaning that his own brother would have killed him for his insolence." (He said) 'I would not be here talking about it.'"

A distinction needs to be made here between confidential reliable informants and those gaming the system. LAPD jailhouse informant Waymond Anderson was clearly a person that was gaming the system. He originally said that Suge Knight inquired about putting a contract on Biggie Smalls and that statement was polygraphed.

Despite what Psycho Mike claimed to know about how dangerous Muhammad was, he went along with an FBI plan to get incriminating statements from him on tape in December 2003, driving south to San Diego and knocking on the door of the house where Muhammad was then living. But Muhammad "got spooked when he seen me," Mike recalled. "Thought I was coming there to kill him" and refused to let him inside.

This story would be later repainted by the lead detective in the failed 2006 LAPD "Murder Rap" investigation, Greg Kading. In his version of events, the moment that Muhammad saw Robinson he shut the door and called the cops. While Kading mischaracterizes this incident in its entirety it is a fascinating indictment that for all the trouble the FBI undertook to bring Robinson to Muhammad's house, they did nothing to protect Robinson after that event.

PART SEVEN:
THE WRECKING CREW

RE-ACTIVATING THE THIRD ELEMENT VIA CHUCK PHILIPS

Russell Poole, lead Wallace homicide investigator, believed that the shooter, Amir Muhammed, was assisted by off duty LAPD officers in the killing of Wallace.

The lead detective in the failed LAPD 2006 "Murder Rap" investigation has put out statements (2011, truthabouttupac.com) that Mario Hammonds was "discredited." But in the entire "Murder Rap" book, there is not one single mention of Boagni or Hammonds. Not one!

This silence is compelling, as on their own terms neither Hammonds nor Boagni have been refuted. It is probably smart not to mention Boagni in "Rap" because Boagni was used as a CREDIBLE KEY WITNESS for the Los Angeles Police Department in eight (8) Board of Rights hearings, where the LAPD had Boagni testify that Raphael Perez had lied about certain LAPD officers. The hearings were held at the Bradbury building and the L.A. County jail. Boagni stated that his testimony was based on the fact that he helped Perez "make up stories" about certain LAPD officers. Those officers, based on the CREDIBLE testimony of Boagni were cleared. It would be a strange place to now say that Boagni isn't credible about everything he wrote in his book, but is credible when it lead to eight (8) LAPD officers being exonerated.

It is demonstrably clear to The Red Knight that The Alchemist of Thieves had performed a stunning job with the El Rey Killing, the Broadus Murder Case and the Shakur Case. In the latter, the case was absolutely hung.

There were no real suspects—at least publicly. There was a rift between the Las Vegas Police and their neighbors to the west, because the Police in Compton had continually thrown their version of the suspect at Las Vegas Police, and when Vegas didn't agree, they were crucified in the media by The Kingdom of Thieves' own version of Vlad the Impaler—Chuck Philips.

Philips was the one man wrecking crew for Kenner. The conspirators needed to make the Wallace homicide stick to Knight, because it completed the image of Wallace being victim of a gang rivalry/East Coast vs. West Coast/Suge vs. Puffy—the same theory that was attempted by Brennan in 1996. If they couldn't get Knight in the deepest corner of prison, they at least could wave off investigators; this time the ones in Los Angeles, who in the El Rey homicide had "played ball" and dropped the investigation.

But Russ Poole was no regular pushover. Having cleared over eighty (80) homicides in Los Angeles, Poole was a formidable opponent, simply because Poole had an already "been there, done that" approach to homicides. He had been known for opening the "Rampart Corruption Case" and exposing corrupt LAPD officers. So Kenner was immediately going to have to move away from using police to interfere, to simply letting Philips off his leash to attack indiscriminately. It wasn't long after that Kenner separated himself from the Death Row organization.

Philips, who had been on the Shakur investigation from the beginning, siezed the opportunity to dive into the Wallace case. Michael Robinson aka Psycho Mike, a reliable FBI informant, was let out of prison to meet and identify a man Harry Billups, who the FBI believed to be Amir Muhammad. Immediately following this meeting, as stated earlier, Robinson began making claims that someone had leaked word of the FBI investigation of Billups to Chuck Philips, who promptly produced a story for the Times that Robinson said, "penned me out as the source of going down to San Diego with a wire."

Robinson was furious: "I confronted [FBI agent] Phil Carson, and I wanted to jump on him. I wanted to hurt him." Carson, though, insisted he wasn't Philips' source, and even signed an affidavit stating so.

Sergio Robleto, a private detective for the Wallace family described the release of the sealed unredacted Robinson deposition transcript as "tantamount to jury tampering." And the Times decision to reveal the informant's street name in the Philips article "Informant Admits Hearsay" was Robleto believes, like "signing his (Robinson's) death warrant."

Within days of the article's publication, Robleto says, Blood gang members found Psycho Mike's secret location, roughed him up on the street and promised to come back later and "take care of [him] for good." He disappeared immediately after this incident, and neither Robleto nor the attorneys he is working for have been able to contact him since. Sanders and Frank had expected the man to be one of their strongest witnesses but now would have to make do with a DVD of his deposition.

Robinson was an original informant who identified Amir Muhammad as the shooter in the Wallace killing. Robinson was given a pre-trial deposition about his second-hand knowledge of the Wallace murder. The deposition was done privately to protect Robinson's identity, but Philips "outted" Robinson after the transcript leaked, by divulging Robinson's "street name" in the LA Times. According to the Wallace defense team, as a result of that outing, Robinson was beaten by the Bloods and disappeared immediately thereafter, "electing" not to testify at trial.

Philips apologists think the divulging of Robinson was accidental. It could not have been; Philips knew the difference. In an interview in Hip Hop DX it was clear that Philips knew the danger he put Robinson in:

> "But when you're writing about a murder, some of the people who talked to me would be killed if they were identified in any way... Now I'm at the point where I can give my old stories to the people I approach and say, 'This is how I write, and this is how it will happen. I've never burned anybody, and I'm not gonna burn you."

Retired Los Angeles County Sheriff, Sargent Richard Valdemar, writes in Police Magazine's June of 2005 issue:

> "Times staff writer Chuck Philips wrote an article in which he identified my informant, Michael Robinson, by his gang moniker "Psycho Mike." Robinson was a Compton Lantana Block Crip and a Black Guerrilla Family associate who had defected from the gang in prison. Michael Robinson had become a reliable gang informant who had testified in federal court against the "Bounty Hunter Bloods" and worked as an informant for the Los Angeles County Sheriff Department's Major Crimes Bureau for more than 15 years.

> "I believe the reason Chuck Philips was willing to expose my reliable informant was that Robinson had given testimony in a deposition in which he identified Suge Knight, disgraced LAPD gang officers David Mack and Rafael Perez, and Mack's friend (also a former officer) Amir Muhammad. He implicated them in the murder of Brooklyn rapper Notorious B.I.G.

(Christopher Wallace).

"This deposition was given under seal because of the danger of possible retaliation posed from the police, other gang members and from the gangster-police security team employed by Mob Piru gang member Suge Knight and Death Row Records. But his sealed testimony was "leaked" to Chuck Philips.

"Times staff reporter Chuck Philips had been covering the hip-hop murders of Tupac Shakur and Notorious B.I.G. But his reporting tended to discount allegations against CEO of Death Row Records Marion "Suge" Knight. Later when Compton, Inglewood and Los Angeles cops who worked for Suge were implicated, he attacked the credibility of these sources. According to some sources, the daughter of then LAPD Chief Bernard Parks was supposedly partying with the cops and Death Row crew.

"But Chuck Philips did all he could to twist the witness statements, expose the sources and protect his pals at Death Row. His Los Angeles Times editors failed to see that obviously his view was biased. He wasn't being objective; he was selling papers.

"As a result of the Times articles and Chuck Philips, Michael Robinson was attacked physically on more than one occasion. He was shot at, cut in the face and head with a razor, and his front teeth were knocked out. The assailants even mentioned the Times article during one attack. Robinson's life was in constant danger after the publication of the article, and the FBI and sheriff's department had to relocate him several times.

"Michael Robinson died of a heart attack on Dec. 5, 2006. He was only 49 years old. It is my belief that Michael Robinson died as a result of the stress and anxiety caused by his exposure and identification in Chuck Philip's hit piece that ran June 3, 2005."

But Philips was not alone in making sure The Kingdom of Thieves was protected. The LAPD kept Boagni's testimony on the Board of Rights matters (not public) out of the media and away from the families of Shakur and Wallace. Philips helped control that. But The Kingdom of Thieves had declared war against all enemies, including Boagni and Hammonds. So how do you discredit them without discrediting their previous contributions as collateral damage?

You start by discrediting the way their information was being carried—you shoot the messenger. In this case, the messenger was Waymond Anderson.

WAYMOND IN WONDERLAND

The case of convicted murderer and arsonist, Waymond Anderson is a paradox. On the one hand, without Waymond Anderson we would have never known about witnesses in the Shakur and Wallace murders on the other hand he was the magic bullet to destroy the Wallace civil suit against the City of Los Angeles. Originally in 1997, Waymond Anderson came forth to LAPD Detectives with information implicating Suge Knight in the murder. By the time the story was fully spun in 2007, he had tainted the testimony of Mario Hammonds, Michael Robinson, Ya-May Christle, Kenneth Boagni, Ken Knox, Keith "Keefe-D" Davis, & Russell Poole. He spun the story to include JD Hawkins, Perry Sanders, David Mack, Rafael Perez, Violetta Wallace, Don Vincent, Christopher Wallace, Steven Katz, Chuck Philips and Suge Knight all with personal knowledge while sitting in his jail cell. His knowledge of the cases is incongruent with his reach from his jail cell without being fed information from the outside.

> "This became a pattern for Waymond Anderson: when confronted with statements he had previously made implicating Suge Knight in the Wallace murder, Anderson would admit having made the statements, but would say he did so at the behest of other inmates who were witnesses for the plaintiffs. Thus, Anderson was able to deny the statements he had made about Knight, and simultaneously raise questions about the credibility of other witnesses who had also implicated Knight."
> —Patrick Frey aka Patterico

Waymond Anderson originally claimed that LAPD Officers David Mack and Raphael Perez were conspiring with Knight to have Wallace killed. Waymond Anderson's biggest beef with the LAPD Detectives was their focus on solving the Shakur and Wallace cases and their lack of interest in helping Anderson with his own case. From the deposition of Waymond Anderson we read:

"I had never been in jail, I was having a nervous break-down. You know, scared as hell of being in—in jail. I was on medication at the time and diabetic and I have epilepsy. And, again, I guess it was just, you know, a mental breakdown from, you know, being taken out of a 10,000 square foot home and being put in a box, you know, every day. My life was dramati-cally, you know, changed. And I'm trying to get somebody to listen to me, and Los Angeles Police Department, they don't, you know, give a damn, nor any other detectives that have in-terviewed me. As soon as—they want me to tell them what I know, but they don't want to talk about my case. And this is the first time that I'm in a position that I finally got someone to investigate my case correctly.

"And so when detectives come and see you, you're trying to tell them that, "Hey, I'm innocent for a crime." They're say-ing, you know, "Yeah, yeah, yeah, we hear you, but, you know, tell us who killed the biggest rapper in the history of L.A., you know, we'll talk about that a little later." To me that's degrad-ing and disrespectful so, okay, if you guys think I'm a sucker or full of shit, then here you go. You want a story, here you go. So I have no respect for any law enforcement in Los Angeles. And any time they come to me thinking that I'm stupid enough to help them solve their—their case, I'm basically just giving them the bone that they wanted."

Waymond Anderson was convicted of the September 18, 1993 crime of busting into a converted garage to collect a debt. Armed with gasoline, he soaked the room, created a torch with a newspaper and lighter and ignited Robert Wellington and the dwelling. Two eyewit-nesses to the murder and arson testified against Anderson at the trial, which resulted in a conviction.

What would entice Waymond Anderson to recant a simple story by replacing it with a morass of impossible and improbable con-nections? In July of 2008, Anderson gives us the smoking gun. He tells a new story that the City Attorney's office and Chuck Philips had given him the false hope of freedom in exchange for his spoiler testimony.

Chuck Philips puts out an article attempting to exonerate Waymond Anderson, knowing he was using false statements and evidence but figuring he could deny his way out of any scrutiny by laying the information at the feet of Anderson and "just reporting the news, not making it."

That fooled no one. Anyone who knew Philips knew he manufactured the news and then reported it.

After Philips' article came out, Waymond Anderson in turn not only denied what he had alleged in 1997 relating to Mack and Perez and Knight, but alleged the entire Wallace estate with (Russell Poole) formed a conspiracy to defraud the City of Los Angeles, made up information and tried to pay Boagni and Hammonds to lie.

Philips 2007 LA Times article "Inmate recants story about LAPD link to rapper's slaying" in 2007, reports that Anderson was recanting his former statements which let the LAPD off the hook. Via Anderson's "credibility suicide," Boagni's and Hammonds' stories became suspect. Anderson claimed that they all conspired together to cook the whole thing up. That was all anyone needed to know—and that's all of the two hundred sixty one (261) page deposition anyone knew about.

However, the article "What the LA Times Never Told you" on the Patterico.com website, destroyed the Philips 2007 LA Times article the way thesmokinggun.com website would blow Philips' Sabatino Forgeries wide open.

This exposé revealed that Waymond Anderson no longer held that Mack and Perez were conspiring with Knight. Waymond Anderson alleged Wallace's killer to be the same man who framed Waymond Anderson for murder. And as unbelievable as it sounds even on its face, Waymond Anderson contended that even though the man framed him for murder, Waymond Anderson was still close to the killer, and was informed about details on both murders. This was on the phone, since Waymond Anderson had not seen the "free" light of day after late 1994.

Waymond Anderson said the killer was a man named Duane Keith Davis. And if that name seems familiar, think of him as the same person Brennan mentioned in his 1996 affidavit as Orlando Anderson's uncle, "Keefe-D."

Why didn't Philips mention anything more about Anderson's far-fetched stories, other than to state that he recanted about Perez? Because, when you read the explanation on who Anderson says was involved, you might as well have just asked Philips to tell you himself. In the L.A. Times article "Who Killed Tupac Shakur?" published in 2002, Philips was busily implementing the Kenner Alchemy's Element Three (the intervention). And per the story created by Tim Brennan and The Kingdom of Thieves, accompanying Duane Davis to Las Vegas was Orlando Anderson, whom Chuck Philips named as Tupac Shakur's murderer.

In that article, Philips made the allegation "The murder weapon was supplied by New York rapper Notorious B.I.G., who agreed to pay the Crips $1 million for killing Shakur." Philips never gave a source or witness name to verify that event, stating only there were "people who were present." Since that 2002 article was released to the public, no one has ever emerged to certify the claim that Wallace had paid for Shakur's murder. Wallace's mother was outraged declaring it as completely false.

And this story died off in 2002 until Waymond Anderson resurrects it in 2007 after visiting with Chuck Philips.

In his deposition in August 2007, Anderson claimed there was supposed to be a million dollar payment made for the murder of Tupac Shakur and Suge Knight, but only half of the money was paid. Waymond Anderson said he was on the phone when Wallace made the $450,000 payment:

From the 2007 Waymond Anderson Deposition (the one where he "recanted" and is supposed to be honest):

Q. "Okay. And to whom did Mr. Wallace pay $450,000?
A. He gave it to Keith Davis and one of the Hawkins people.
Q. And how do you know that?
A. I was on the phone when the money was delivered to Las Vegas.
Q. And by whom was it delivered?
A. Christopher Wallace himself.
Q. And to whom was it received, by whom was it received?
A. Keith Davis.

Q.   And you were on the phone when the delivery
      happened?
A.   Yes."

Of course, Waymond Anderson didn't originally claim that
Duane Davis was a conspirator in his original 1997 testimony. He
blamed that on a man known as J.D "Jerry" Hawkins. J.D. Hawkins
name shows up in US Department of Justice File R1-06-0417 as the
case file name "Jerry Hawkins."

DO YOU KNOW JERRY HAWKINS?

So what is the relationship between Jerry Hawkins and Keith
Davis? Why did the DEA want to talk to Keith Davis? And why would
the "lead" "Murder Rap" detective publish a document on a fan board
claiming to be his proof of Keith Davis' proffer deal as it related to the
killing of Shakur and Wallace, bearing the file name of Jerry Hawkins?
First, we review what Waymond Anderson's very scared and threatened
admissions about Hawkins, whom he just "fingered" for conspiring to
murder Shakur and Knight.

Q.   "Now, you mentioned Jerry Hawkins, who's Jerry
      Hawkins?
A.   I refuse to answer that question.
Q.   Okay, and what is the basis of that refusal?
A.   I just refuse to answer. I take the Fifth on that.

Q.   And I'm just trying to determine which one it is
      or whether it's a different reason?
A.   It's just a name that you, me and nobody in this
      room want to talk about.
Q.   Okay. Did Mr. Hawkins at any time have any cell
      phones that belonged to you?
A.   I take the Fifth on that.

Q.   Okay. Has -- has Mr. Hawkins paid for any of
      your legal counsel?
      A.   Keith Davis and Hawkins have

paid for some of my—not the legal counsel I have now. I mean, I don't even have any money. These guys doing my case pro bono. But they paid for my trial attorney who railroaded me on the case, yes, they did.

> Q.   Was Mr. Hawkins in any way related to the conspiracy to take over Death Row Records?
>
> A.   I've tried to -- I'm not going to say anything about Mr. Hawkins until I'm given immunity and moved to the Los Angeles County Jail. I told you that 40 minutes ago." (2007 Waymond Anderson Deposition)

The next step in understanding the J.D. Hawkins' relationship is to understand Jerry Hawkins' place in this entire story; turns out he interacted with Reggie Wright Sr.'s team and did business in the Death Row controlled area of Compton.

> "That's one of those things that I can point out to you that can be verified and proven. Where the Hawkins family does their business it used to be patrolled by the Compton Police Department." (2007 Waymond Anderson Deposition)

Jerry Hawkins is apparently a drug dealer on the DEA's list, and the "Murder Rap" task force was a part of this investigation, though nothing is mentioned about the it— not one word—about Jerry Hawkins—although it is clear that Tammy Hawkins, who is likely part of that same family, was "outted" in "Rap" by her description, as Theresa Swann. The Hawkins family did their business in Compton and by Waymond Anderson's 2007 recanted version of events, were passing million dollar transactions from Wallace to Davis for the killing of Shakur and Knight. Waymond Anderson was scared to death to talk about them.

When the dust settles, the Duane Keith Davis interview about the Killing of Tupac Shakur will reveal (if it is ever released) that most if not all of the questions were geared toward clarifying Jerry Hawkins role in the killing of Tupac Shakur and not Orlando Anderson, triggered by the Waymond Anderson allegations in the 2007 deposition.

The timeline is congruent; Duane Davis was not interviewed until December of 2008 and the DEA Report not filed until March 2009. This interview was about drugs and not the murder of Shakur. That explains why Davis was interviewed by the DEA, and not by Los Angeles Police detectives themselves; the "Murder Rap" cops were local law enforcement accessories used to bring in and question Duane Keith Davis; it was a federal case against Hawkins.

When Timothy Searight, Assistant US Attorney, is mentioned as the approving party for Keith Davis proffer deal, it seems incongruent at any look—Davis was not pending any federal charges against him at the time. When the "Murder Rap" cops confront Duane Keith Davis at his home and he asks them what they want, they do not discuss a plea deal or the pending charges, and Davis seems unaware of any pending charges.

> "Keffe D rose and hit the button to open the garage door. Sunshine flooded in and we squinted against the bright light. His skepticism had begun to fade. He was thinking now, figuring the angles and weighing his options. "What do you want from me?" he asked at last. I paused on my way to the car and turned to him. 'Let me put it this way,' I replied. 'We're homicide investigators.'" ("Murder Rap" p. 120).

And yet Philips never mentions what "Murder Rap" contends is the strongest lead ever in the killings—Davis' involvement in the killings of Wallace—in his articles in the Times about Waymond Anderson's new deposition.

> "Shortly before our follow-up meeting with Keffe-D, I received a call from Higgins. He had a simple question: what exactly was the nature of the information we were seeking from his client? I was equally direct in my response: we'd want to know what really happened outside the Petersen Museum on the night of March 9, 1997. In short, who killed Biggie Smalls and why?" ("Murder Rap" p. 122).

The incongruence between the need to investigate the Wallace killing as explained above, and the DEA's reported interrogation subject matter "The Killing of Tupac Shakur" is obvious; stranger than that, is the fact that in discussing the "Killing of Tupac Shakur," there was no one from Las Vegas Police invited to witness. Ironically, Detective Kading openly questioned why information collected by Poole and Bond in 2013 regarding the "Killing of Tupac Shakur" did not go to the Las Vegas Police. Internet anarchist Battaglia slammed Poole and Bond with claims that the LAPD told him in 2014 that the "LAPD has nothing to do with Shakur."

There is only one explanation that fits the following:

a. A document purporting to be Davis "confession" to the Shakur killing is entitled "Jerry Hawkins" and not "Duane Davis";

b. A document purporting to be Davis "confession" to the Shakur killing is redacted when it should be about exactly that; Davis' involvement in the killing of Shakur;

c. Davis was presented to a Federal Prosecutor for a proffer deal when there appeared to be no federal charges against Davis, Davis does not acknowledge one in "Rap" nor are any ever mentioned;

d. The LAPD detectives have no interest in a drug case, they are there as "homicide detectives" who tell Davis' attorney they are there for the Wallace killing and not the Shakur killing;

That explanation would be that the truth of the Keith Davis proffer deal was to find out what Davis knew about the killing of Shakur as it related to Hawkins and nothing more. The focus on the questions will no doubt show that while Davis may have offered a colorful allegory on his story of the killing, it was irrelevant.

The question that was answered independently outside of the 2008 interrogation, was whether Waymond Anderson parroted Philips' claims of Wallace paying a million dollars for a hit on Shakur and Knight. Since so much of Anderson's testimony imploded, it was unlikely anything new would appear, but the opportunity to get information from Davis on the Shakur murder was, and will probably be incidental to the larger DEA discussion—what was the nature of Davis relationship with Jerry Hawkins and if any of this had to do with

Shakur or Wallace. Of course it was found and dismissed quickly that Wallace was nowhere near Vegas when the Shakur killing happened, and ended that alegation in 2007 as quickly as it was dismissed in 2002.

Before this recanted position of Waymond Anderson, Duane Davis was never mentioned as part of the Wallace case. Again, all of these conversations supposedly took place while Anderson was incarcerated, facing murder charges for the murder Waymond Anderson claimed Davis had committed. But Waymond Anderson's attorney did admit that the FBI had actually questioned Waymond Anderson about his interaction with Philips. And representatives from the FBI were present at the court hearing where Waymond Anderson made these claims.

In spite of what Waymond Anderson said in his deposition, Wright Junior had his own Keith Davis Story. "They got beat up and they retaliated for one of their boys being beat up. That's all it was; retaliation for the beating of Orlando Anderson." —Wright Junior interview in AllHipHop.com:

But that is NOT the same Keith Davis story that Waymond Anderson tells.

Anderson says Davis killed Shakur over drugs and that his murder was pre- meditated the day before. Now like the Lakewood Mall Footlocker story, which seemed to vary by time, date and even city, the story in this case takes a substantial turn as to the dynamic of the motive. Waymond Anderson is even in conflict with Davis' own later testimony.

The story then turned from a revenge for the Orlando Anderson beating to a planned killing and purpose of their trip to Las Vegas. Waymond Anderson claims that Davis was going to kill Shakur regardless of the Orlando Anderson scuffle, which no one could predict would happen. This was the "truth" that Waymond Anderson concocted to replace what he had stated in the polygraphed interview with Russell Poole. So whom do we believe—Waymond Anderson or Keith Davis?

Davis himself also makes claims that he met with Biggie, but somehow that gets glossed over by Chuck Philips.

Do You Know Duane Keith "Keefe-D" Davis?

If anyone knows Duane Keith "Keefe-D" Davis, they need to contact a bail bondsman. As of December 3, 2014, Davis is a fugitive from the law, wanted on one of several charges he was facing (this one a felony). Clearly Davis has no intention on seeing a Courtroom anytime soon.

Not that he ever did. It can be safely established that "Keefe-D" will do anything it takes to avoid spending any serious time in jail—which means also physically moving to another state—which is what the bail bondsmen in Riverside County, CA believe to be the case.

In any investigation, one quickly becomes entrenched in a game called "who's credible?" The Kingdom of Thieves was populated with convicted felons of every color shape and size. It was also populated with people who should probably be convicted felons. Each one of them convicted for their own reasons—most of them claiming their innocence. So it is appropriate and fitting that the witnesses the citizens of The Kingdom associate with, would also be felons.

It is the job of the jury to try to get to the truth regarding a witness' "credibility," it does not have to be the investigator's role. However it helps to at least believe that the information you have is strong enough to take to the prosecutor. In this case, the amount of work necessary to build the "credibility pyramid" is probably greater than the amount of work it took to build the Great Pyramids themselves.

It is for this reason that many investigators take a "flat earth approach" to their investigation. It is detrimental to make a speedy judgment on the witness making a statement. So the "litmus test" is to frame the validity of the person's statement within the context of other supporting evidence. If a 4 time convicted felon (who would not be considered "credible" most of the time) states that he knew the tire was flat, and we have a picture of the car to which he refers, and that car has a flat tire, we do not doubt the testimony because there is something else to back it. This is called "corroborating evidence."

This applies in the reverse as well. Chuck Philips claimed that Kenneth Boagni's statements were false because Waymond Anderson told the police that Boagni had "conspired" with Waymond Anderson. Later, after being unsuccessful in his Waymond Anderson exoneration campaign, Philips suddenly found that Waymond Anderson was not credible; Philips then painted Boagni with that same bad tint.

And it's important to differentiate between someone (like a Duane Davis) making deals to avoid going to jail, and people already in jail who might (like Boagni) or might not (like Robert Soria) be looking for a way to get reduced jail time. And there are a few (like Sabatino and Waymond Anderson) who try to game the system; they are willing to say or do anything to get out of jail. But that has not frequently been the case. The reason that the "jail system" works, arguably, is because most of the prisoners know what they did to get to jail and have accepted it. Many are not looking for any reprieve. They just want to do their time and leave.

That sits in direct opposition to those who evade indictment or imprisonment—especially once they have been arrested and charged with a crime, it is usually a forced accountability; society holds them involuntarily to make the accused account for their alleged wrongdoing—with the faith in our judicial system that they will not be found guilty if they are not guilty. Bail circumvents that forced accountability and bestows faith in the individual to "do the right thing" and appear. Evasion to one degree or another becomes a statement about what lengths a party will go to, to avoid accountability. Such as the case with Davis.

Boagni, Hackie, Robinson, and Hammonds all gave interviews while in jail, and while they asked for return cooperation (Boagni and Hackie), the denial of that promised cooperation did not stop them from continuing to ask—and continuing to talk. And neither Boagni, Hackie nor Hammonds substantially changed their story. Robinson changed his story to some degree after having been attacked by gang members, which his 15 year LA County Sherriff handler blames as the cause of Robinson's eventual death. Boagni wrote a book about it and did not change his story. He said Raphael Perez was at the Peterson Museum the night of the shooting.

It is equally important to understand that none of these people have a reason to assume a story that alleges other convicted felons are doing something wrong—especially when it is clear they are not benefitting from what they are offering as evidence. As Soria wrote in a letter from prison "I won't recant" the only reason that Danny and Malcom (Patton) are saying what they are, is because they do not want to be where I am at."

What does all this have to do with Davis? Unlike someone who has no reason to tell a story that endangers them, Davis takes actions that change to keep himself free of indictment; which is why his recent evasion is a good reason to doubt his credibility. Davis did not simply volunteer information. According to the book "Murder Rap" the only way they could get Davis to talk about anything was to trap Davis and pressure Davis into taking a "proffer deal." So it became a matter of "act or take your chances in front of a judge" (which in itself is dubious because there weren't any formal charges on Davis at the time the proffer deal had been made—just the threat of charges from the US Attorney).

Davis dealt with the 2014 invitation to court the same way he dealt with the proffer deal—Davis pattern of behavior makes it clear that it was and is not important to Davis if the later penalties of lying under oath or contempt of court are threats. All Davis is showing is that Davis will do and say anything in the immediate to avoid the threat in front of him. This lack of foresight makes Davis a bad witness and dangerous to anyone who might rely on him; unless the person relying on him is so desperate for a lead that they will take anything.

But Davis had spoken before to Russell Poole, all the way back in 1997. Davis called his previous statements "all bullshit" that implicated Knight and Death Row in the homicides. His stories in the "Rap" proffer deal and in his 1997 interview were diametrically opposed. And like Wright Junior's recent surge of total recall regarding Death Row operations—operations he claimed to know nothing about in 2007 when interviewed by AllHipHop.com—Davis suddenly—ten years later—had 20/20 recall on the entire scope of both homicides—in living Technicolor—manna to the starving 2006 "Task Force." (Manna is the appropriate term, as the Hebrew translation for "manna" is "What is it?" which is what they must have been asking about Davis regurgitating of what was basically Waymond Anderson's story—which was also Chuck Philips' story. It is not clear if there is a Hebrew translation for "What the hell is this?").

Recently, the 2014 "Tupac" web boards have been filled with news of something in the air that is making witnesses to the 1996 Shakur Homicide—witnesses who knew little at the time—suddenly have that same recall that Davis had, and be so full of information on specific details of the Shakur homicide, their testimony can be used to recreate the events in 1996 to a "photo-real" standard.

Newsweek magazine published a November 2014 article relating to this very issue; can a witness actually remember events better over the years?

"Memory, as experts have been trying to teach judges and jurors, does not function like an iPhone camera recording. Memories can not only be deleted; they can be altered or invented without you even realizing it, as shown in a study published last year in the International Journal of Law and Psychiatry, which involved 861 U.S. soldiers enrolled in a survival school. As part of training, they endured abusive interrogations. Afterward, many were shown a photo of someone who looked nothing like their interrogator, and interviewers insinuated that the person depicted was the culprit. Eighty-four percent of the soldiers misidentified their interrogators after being misled, and some also remembered weapons or telephones that never existed.

"An extensive body of research with similar findings has become increasingly perplexing for the nation's judicial systems, leading the National Academy of Sciences (NAS) to release a sweeping report last month calling for an overhaul of how the courts and law enforcement deal with one of the most powerfully persuasive pieces of evidence that can sway a jury: eyewitness identification. Research has shown that leading questioning or suggestive behavior by psychiatrists, police or acquaintances, as well as accounts in the media, can result in 'planting' false memories in the mind of a witness. In some cases, this can lead witnesses to believe they saw incidents that never occurred. In lawsuits recently filed against Castlewood Treatment Center in St. Louis, plaintiffs have argued that therapists used hypnosis and psychiatric drugs to recover 'hidden' abuse memories that turned out to be false.

"Since 1983, there have been a string of reversals for cases in which courts excluded such expert testimonies. The first was an Arizona case in which eyewitness testimonies led to Dolan Chapple's conviction on three counts of murder; the ruling was overturned by the Arizona Supreme Court, which stated that the initial judge had 'abused his discretion in excluding expert testimony concerning eyewitness reliability.' Similar reversals followed in California and Washington."

—"The End of Eyewitness Testimonies" by Erika Hayasaki

In light of the evidence against 18 year memories being clearer than they were when they provided statements, it is an incredible—and somewhat naïve—belief that witnesses can remember more than they had years before. That is why investigators to interviews immediately, take notes and do as many follow-up interviews as necessary to document the entire testimony. It is almost impossible to "refresh" memories as clear as the original ones.

Another suspicious claim raised by Davis/Anderson apologists (and forwarded by the 2006 "Rap" investigation) is that the second (or third if you believe Waymond Anderson was actually coached by Davis) version of Davis' story—the "no bullshit" story, has been corroborated by other "eyewitnesses" at the scene of the crime. It is convenient that most of the key witnesses that might refute the accuracy of the recently revived recollections are dead. No one to dispute or take issue leaves unrefuted speculation. The 1996 Shakur Shooting 18 Year Reunion must have been missing most of its alumni.

There is simply no proving that these "witness corroborations" —are simply facts known 18 years later and the research in the Newsweek article tends to enforce that statement. The power of suggestion is an amazing thing. The question is about whether witnesses have been given information ahead of time to "jog" their memories—to a position convenient for the Davis/Anderson's apologists. Chuck Philips tried that with Frank Alexander as the recorded conversation demonstrates.

While Kading claims that the LAPD "cleared him" of any wrongdoing in the US Attorney's case against alleged murderer George Torres-Ramos, LA Weekly (prior to Kading's publicist intervention with Vogel) in the article "Numero Uno v. LAPD" June 23, 2009, spoke on the matter of certain former detectives trying to manufacture "corroborating" evidence to support Torres-Ramos' otherwise completely non-evidenced story:

"Now, attention shifts to Kading's controversial taped conversations with jailhouse snitches, and newly discovered jailhouse tapes that the defense team did not know existed. Although the new tapes are not believed to include Kading, previous tapes heard by the jury contained "numerous and repeated promises of leniency and providing numerous benefits," made by Kading in exchange for the two men's testimony against Torres, according to defense attorney Steven G. Madison. Madison says that in one conversation, Kading says, "It's always this way, man. I have to come up with the answers and tell you — and then you just say, 'Yeah, you're right.'"

The contention that "total recall" was planted also finds traction in the case of Waymond Anderson. How would Waymond Anderson—who sought to discredit Ya-May Christle, know anything about this LAPD officer—especially enough to try to smear her credibility by alleging Christle was in an affair? Remember, Waymond Anderson claimed years later that he was given entire case files from the LA City Attorney through Chuck Philips. So there is an overwhelming probability that the four women in the car—the "four girls" who are now supposed to be remembering details that just so happen to corroborate Davis story—have been "interviewed" by the same person that the LA Weekly reports may have influence earlier testimony.

To be clear, no one is calling the witnesses in the Shakur shooting "liars." It is just an unsupportable belief that after 18 years, witnesses, who when it mattered, had little to offer are now suddenly encyclopedias of fact. But a good and proven "witness whisperer" may get a witness to say anything. It is critical that if the new witness recall is actually that good, then police ought to immediately recall these witnesses for deposition!

As to Davis personally, he has done nothing to help himself. In addition to changing his testimony—not simply refusing to repeat it—Davis has made his testimony "multiple choice"—not unlike Waymond Anderson. Perhaps when he is truly behind bars for a long term, he might be able to offer testimony not motivated by his proven desire to stay out of jail. Until that time, he is on the "lam"—and remains in question—no matter what random corroborations may exist. A foundation built on Duane Keith Davis is suspect. Darnell Brim, one of the leaders of the Southside Crips knew that. Not only had Davis accused Orlando Anderson of pointing a gun and firing with deadly intent—Davis accused Brim in the same way, years earlier.

This is what Brim (who was himself shot) had to say about Duane Keith Davis:

"He's Baby Lane's uncle. He's part of the group that hangs on Burris, I'm not friends with him. He likes to talk a lot. He keeps stuff going; like hearsay stuff. Like when my homeboy Lee got killed he was saying that he saw what happened- including that he seen my car driving away from the shooting. He was saying that I was the guy who shot Lee."

"When he found out that. I was locked down, he changed his story and said that it was someone who looked like me. He keeps a lot of stuff going- like girls do. I asked him about it when I got out of jail. He said something like, "you know what's going on, you don't like us and we don't like you, just keep it like that." I told him that that was no problem."

"I don't know if he's selling dope, I don't know his business. I don't know if he has a job. I don't think that Keefy D would shoot anybody and I don't know if he had anything to do with killing Biggie."

It is hard to imagine a conspiracy theory involving Crips and other gang members when the leader of that very group is dubious on Davis' involvement in any homicide. But Brim is certainly clear on Davis and his "M.O."

THE DEATH ROW TIMES TURNS ON PHILIPS

Sabatino was the end for Chuck Philips' in his imitation of The Kenner Alchemy. It is likely because at that point the Alchemist himself was no longer directly involved; Frankenstein's monster loosed on the village without Dr. Frankenstein to try to stop the monster. All of the work for The Kingdom of Thieves was still expected to be performed, but without the proper instruction and strategic guidance there was no boundary.

It was when Waymond Anderson turned on Philips in July 30, 2008, that notice was taken publicly—Anderson came forward again, this time to claim that Philips, acting on the behest of Suge Knight, smuggled threatening letters from Knight into jail in order to force Anderson to commit perjury which he did when he recanted his earlier position. In this new third version of events, Anderson claimed that the City Attorney threatened him that if Anderson continued to claim that Perez and Mack were involved in the murders of Wallace, Anderson would never get out of jail.

He also said that the Assistant City Attorney, Don Vincent, handed Chuck Philips the entire body of the Christopher Wallace vs. City of Los Angeles case files for Waymond Anderson to get familiar with the case so he could disqualify Perry Sanders.

THE COURT:	Basically, they gave you all the deposition transcripts they had?
THE WITNESS:	Yes, sir.
THE COURT:	Why did the Times give them to you?
THE WITNESS:	They were trying to disqualify Perry Sanders. . . . They were trying to disqualify Perry Sanders from the Christopher Wallace case. . . . it was all a lie, sir.

Anderson also accused Chuck Philips of smuggling messages into prison from Suge Knight that contain threats to Anderson.

Q.	And was this Chuck Phillips, was he an L.A. Times reporter?
A.	Yes, sir. He's been fired.
Q.	But he came to visit you in advance of the deposition?
A.	Several times. I received threatening letters.
THE COURT:	Who did?
THE WITNESS:	I did.
Q. (By Mr. Bernstein)	From who?
A.	Suge.
Q.	Suge Knight?
A.	Yeah.
Q.	Was Suge Knight in prison with you?
A.	No.
Q.	How did you get these threatening letters?
A.	They were brought in by Chuck Phillips [sic].
Q.	Chuck Phillips gave you threatening

	letters that he said were from Suge Knight
A.	They were kites. They call them kites.
Q.	Kites. Can you describe that for me?
THE COURT:	Was Chuck Phillips in prison?
THE WITNESS:	No, sir.
THE COURT:	Kites are normally written transactions between prisoners, right?
THE WITNESS:	Right, but this kite — what Suge sent me was rolled up in paper like a prisoner would do it, and it was smuggled into the Corcoran visiting room. I turned over all the kites to the F.B.I.

One key witness at the Wallace vs. City of Los Angeles civil trial, Death Row insider, Kevin Hackie, who identified David Mack as attending Death Row functions, also stated in a pre-trial deposition that "Chuck Philips was frequently at Death Row functions and received payments from Death Row Records." Hackie backed off of this statement at trial, but he also tried to back away from everything he had told investigators, stating, convincingly, that 'I'm in fear for my life.' Asked what he feared, Hackie stated: 'Retribution by the Bloods, the Los Angeles Police Department, and associates of Death Row Records.'" This is reminiscent of the reason the Los Angeles Superior Court sealed the deposition of Michael Robinson stating, "This deposition was given under seal because of the danger of possible retaliation posed from the police, other gang members, and from the gangster/ police security team employed by Mob Piru gang member Suge Knight and Death Row Records."

The Times' questionable coverage of the Tupac Shakur and Notorious B.I.G. (AKA Biggie Smalls) murders had long been the subject of Internet gossip and speculation among reporters. But no one in the mainstream media had dared to address it until Rolling Stone Magazine hit newsstands in late 2005 with a lengthy, exhaustive piece re-examining the unsolved murder of Wallace. July of 2005, a mistrial was declared in Wallace's wrongful death lawsuit, which charges that gangster cops killed her son and the LAPD covered it up.

A U.S. District Court judge ruled that the Wallace plaintiffs were at least half right; the LAPD had in fact engaged in a cover-up, withholding tapes of a jailhouse confession, as well as 1000 pages of crucial documents. This information was turned over to Wallace's attorneys, who used that information in a retrial, and still believe that information to be credible.

Following the lead of the Los Angeles Times, the story of this mistrial was largely ignored or downplayed by the media. Few understood the potential impact of this court ruling. A victory in the lawsuit could literally bankrupt the city, as Wallace's potential lifetime earnings have been projected at over $350 million. The decision also served to re-open the LAPD Rampart scandal, as Rampart songbird Rafael Perez was implicated in the case by the suppressed evidence. City officials felt Rampart was behind them, having approved $70 million in settlements without any of the existing 200 lawsuits ever going to trial.

That buried evidence was bound to surface. "The Rampart scandal and the lengths to which police and city officials had gone to protect Perez from those who knew him as a fabricator were now an essential aspect of the case," stated Rolling Stone.

The Times had long backed Philips' implementation of the Kenner Alchemy and dismissed the theory behind the Wallace lawsuit. The man behind this theory, was former LAPD Robbery/Homicide Detective Russell Poole.

As reported by Frontpagemagazine.com, Poole was a cop "of impeccable reputation," who resigned from the force after 18 years in 1999 because, he claimed, the LAPD had suppressed his investigation of the Christopher Wallace murder. Poole first tried to take his story public that same year by going to the L.A. Times, which misreported what he told them and altered his story to discredit his testimony.

The Times has ignored or attempted to discredit Poole's theory ever since, and while this time Philips may have stepped over the line, it may have ultimately been the first time that the Times started to realize that more was being done by Philips to coerce and influence news, than they had ever believed. The Times has a conflict in their position; Waymond Anderson had now accused Chuck Philips of some pretty serious wrongdoing; wrongdoing that, if proven, could result in criminal charges. Wrongdoing that was apparently being investigated by the FBI. —(Waymond Anderson Deposition)

THE 2006 "MURDER RAP" "TASK FORCE" INVESTIGATION

"'Task Force" is a bad term to me." —Brent Becker in a 2007 interview.

Shortly after the Waymond Anderson and Sabatino debacles; by 2008 Philips was laid off at the Times and unable to carry out The Kenner Alchemy. But by that time the Third Element needed no further assistance. When The Kenner Alchemy is properly executed, the bi-product is the creation of the Fourth Element—the "train wreck." To get a picture of the train wreck, one must consider the state of the investigation and the key members involved.

- The witnesses originally good for the prosecution had been summarily and unfairly dismissed under the weight of Waymond Anderson fiasco.
- Kevin Hackie was still considered not credible while he was in jail (at least to the public, because the LAPD kept wanting to see him) and afterward on probation awaiting his appeal. He was called a "convicted felon" as if that mattered, and to the honest public that smear was enough to neutralize Hackie.
- Knight was out of prison but had spent so much time there, he wasn't a threat at that point; most of his inner circle Knights of The Kingdom of Thieves had been killed. There was a shell of a Kingdom to come back to.
- By 2006 Death Row had filed bankruptcy.
- The faith of the labels was gone.
- LAPD was embroiled in a lawsuit against the Wallace family, so houses were divided and everyone was looking out for themselves.

In other words, there was no uniform presence to combat Philips' previous runaway allegations and news-making articles, and everyone so busy picking up the pieces from the Philip's "bombs" that all parties were in need of getting their own acts together before any alignment of interests could happen.

The Fourth Element was perfected; the picture of the Shakur train wreck was much smaller; a split between Las Vegas and Los Angeles, and no movement or real cooperation in either. In the Wallace case the train wreck was exponentially uglier. It was in a "perfect moment"—before anyone could regroup and join forces.

So why were the efforts of Philips and Wright Junior in the Wallace case Third Element that much messier than Shakur's? The play looked the same. The players were the same. Different results. Worse results. So what explains this?

The answer lies in the quote of Johann Sebastian Bach—"There's nothing remarkable about it. All one has to do is hit the right keys at the right time and the instrument plays itself."

The reason the Wallace Third Element was messier than Shakur's was because David Kenner, the composer of chaos, The Alchemist of the Kingdom of Thieves, was gone by that time. There was no one to conduct the orchestra, to advise people like Philips on "what was enough" or the idea of "can we" vs. "should we?" As stated earlier, witnesses have characterized The Red Knight as a "bully." This meant that the Wallace orchestration was doomed to be blunt, brutal and direct. There was no Kenner "moderation" or "jurisprudence" left. And that is why the Philips and Wright Junior 2002-2006 karaoke was just a cheap copy of The Alchemy—and far less effective.

The Red Knight, long a student of the Alchemist, but never an alchemist himself, would attempt to conjure The Kenner Alchemy's Fifth Element—the act manufactured to leave a scar on the public psyche so great that they would not dare question the "facts." His effort, like most who are not true Alchemists, met with mediocre results, and ultimately failed. But it was a valiant try: instead of a national newspaper with Pulitzer Prize winning reporters they elected to write a book about it and set the "record straight" once and for all.

But to do that they, needed someone with more "crossover" appeal than Philips. They needed an insider voice that would appear credible, and yet a bit of a loose cannon.

The book was called "Murder Rap," the act: the "investigation" and the voice: retired Detective Greg Kading.

Before Kading and his 2006 failed "Murder Rap" task force could galvanize The Red Knight story into the public, they had to get their story straight. Without Kenner, that proved to be a mountain to move. If one looks objectively at Mr. Kading's very confused statements over the last few years and then objectively looks at the 2006 "Murder Rap" investigation, it is easy to see the corners that investigators painted themselves into.

To understand the 2006 investigation and it's champion, it is important to first understand the schizophrenic journey of its leader and the love/hate relationship with the Los Angeles Police Department. On the one hand Kading states that the LAPD gives him all the latitude to go where the case took them.

> "A free hand to do the job was my one non-negotiable stipulation, even if it meant exposing an LAPD conspiracy or cover-up." ("Murder Rap" page 67)

Kading then adds that they had almost solved the case: "I want to make it known how the case had almost been solved." ("Murder Rap" page 260).

> "As our futile fishing expeditions had already established, a case could chase its own tail for weeks or months at a time before finally breaking." ("Murder Rap" page 110)

On the other hand Kading gets into a series of blistering indictments about the very group that allowed him the "latitude" to "lead" a task force with LAPD and a multitude of Federal resources, like ATF, DEA, and the FBI for 5 years of tax payer money (2006-2010):

- "I want to make it known how the case had almost been solved and who was responsible for the failure to see it through. ("Murder Rap Page 260)."
- "But I wasn't buying it. I couldn't help but wonder if the LAPD might not be holding the ongoing IA investigation over my head as a way of silencing my objections to the fate of the task force." ("Murder Rap" Page 256).
- "The LAPD was trying to cover up the Biggie Smalls murder, not by protecting corrupt cops but by undercutting the ability of its own investigators

to solve the case." ("Murder Rap" Page
254-255).

So what caused the FIVE-YEAR investigation to ultimately yield
no new suspects or new information? The end result was just simply a few
witnesses who came forward to "blame the dead guy" (Orlando Anderson)
based on coerced confessions (Davis), falsified affidavits placed in front
of a witness to make her fear prosecution ("Swann") and a shooter whose
identity was derived from a letter from an inmate, Roderick Reed, and a
"sort of" confirmation from none other than Person of Interest, Reggie
Wright Junior—The Red Knight himself. The "sort of" part was an admission that the shooter and Suge Knight had "secrets" between them. The
task force exhausted at least 20,000 man-hours. At an average of $45.00-
$75.00 an hour, the cost to the tax payers was over a million and a half
dollars ($1,500,000). At some point, the LAPD had to shut off the tap.

The lead detective on the "task force" cited the need to quit the
LAPD, to pursue the "truth" of the case. Maybe he needed to. It was clear
that the LAPD was not giving him the access they had promised him. For
example, when asked about his access to Russell Poole (the original Wallace
Case Detective whose theories Kading claims to have discredited in their
entirety) he admits to the HipHopDX web site:

"It wasn't out of a desire not to talk to him, but because I was
an employee with the LAPD, with the City of Los Angeles, conducting an ongoing criminal investigation, and he was a witness
in a civil suit for the plaintiff against the city of Los Angeles. It's a
conflict of interest for us to go and try to compare notes or have
conversations. We're precluded from having any conversations. I
would've loved to have talked to Voletta Wallace during the investigation. I would've loved to talk to some of the other people
on the plaintiff's witness list, but we just simply couldn't because
the legal politics involved." (HipHopDX October 05, 2011 at
8:37AM)

Moreover it is disclosed that during his tenure with the LAPD
"Task Force," Detective Kading, was not exposed to any information on
the possible Mack/Perez/LAPD involvement or any other evidence in the
Wallace Civil Trial—which lasted the entire duration of the task force and
ended the day the Wallace suit ended:

"I have no reason to believe they were there, but I don't have any—I haven't seen the evidence that was in the civil case [brought by Voletta Wallace] regarding the LAPD; I was involved in the criminal investigation. We were kind of bifurcated away from the civil investigation." ("Murder Rap")

In other words the City of Los Angeles spent over a million and a half dollars to "go where the case went" and it went exactly where the LAPD wanted it to go—and nowhere else.

Yet in spite of having no access to thousands of clues and missing documents and interviews, in the promotion of his book "Murder Rap," LA Weekly claimed LAPD higher-ups pulled Kading off the double investigation "right when he was poised to drive it home."

Without new clues from the Wallace civil case, and no interviews (or re-interviews) with witnesses or former investigators from the case; how much information did the "Murder Rap" team really have to play with?

The declarations of Ya-Mae Christle and Kenneth Knox of the LAPD were both taken in the Wallace civil case, so it's hard to know if they were reviewed by the task force. Those declarations make reference to specific reclamation efforts of LAPD Internal Affairs to seize "Any and all information to the murder of Wallace." This included the confiscation of a "foot-tall" stack of documents related to Wallace, a computer, and all of Kenneth Knox's investigation notes in regards to a surveillance he was conducting from LAPD West Valley Division on the Death Row facilities in the Valley known as Can-Am Studios.

In the case of Knox, the documents were taken from him while he was out on an injury leave. He inquired about the matter to his superiors, who told him that the information had simply "disappeared." It was fortunate for the case that Russell Poole had copies of Knox' observation log; it's doubtful that anyone else had access to those notes, as they were taken from Knox before the "Rap task force" had been assembled.

Moreover, there is an admission in "Rap" that the task force got the "murder books" back after Internal Affairs had "processed them."

"Notwithstanding the city's frantic demand that the case be solved immediately if not sooner, IA hung on to the murder books, leaving the task force nothing to work with. Short of starting the entire investigation again from scratch, the team had little choice but to wait patiently for IA to laboriously copy the reams of documents and return them in a slow and frustrating trickle." ("Murder Rap," page 70)

It goes without saying that the "Rap" Task Force had no conceivable way of discerning the delta between what was originally in the murder books and what they were receiving back from Internal Affairs. In spite of not knowing what the original murder books looked like or what information the early investigators, such as Russell Poole had at their disposal, the Murder Rap Task Force had the hubris to make the following statement:

"Russell Poole's theory of course leads to the inevitable lawsuit about the police being involved because Russell Poole finds out that a guy named Amir had visited David Mack at the Montebello City Jail after his bank robbery arrest. And he's like, "Oh, shoot! Amir? Wait a minute, I have a clue with a guy named Amir on it." It was a very loose connection. It was definitely necessary to follow-up on it, but it wasn't enough to build a whole theory around." —Greg Kading Interview with HipHopDX.com 10/5/2011

What a sweeping blanket statement. What about the eyewitnesses to the killing? They had created with a Los Angeles Police Department sketch artist a sketch of the shooter that looked exactly like the DMV photo of Amir. Eugene Deal had identified Amir as the shooter. That is certainly much more than a mere coincidence of the man that visited David Mack in jail. Even though he had used a false name, telephone number, and social security number. That seems to indicate that he didn't want anyone to know his true identity.

So where does that leave us? Obviously an entire case being decided without ever having weighed or even examined the evidence against it. How does any respectable detective miss thousands of pages of witness testimony and deposition statements and not be able to interview witnesses that at least the attorneys believe have probative value, yet declare the case to be "closed"? There is so much left!

Kading's team couldn't see evidence from the civil trial.

Perhaps Kading is telling us that he was the recipient of a "one foot" stack of documents and computer runs relating to Wallace that disappeared from Sargent Ya-May Christle's desk. Kading, in his own book Murder Rap states that he was put on the investigation in May of 2006:

"'Brian,' I asked straight up when Tyndall called me on May 1, 2006, with his offer to join the team, 'are we supposed to solve this case or are we supposed to protect the department?' 'Greg,' he replied, 'we're going to go wherever this takes us. You have my word on it.'" (Murder Rap)

Tyndall probably didn't know or didn't tell Kading that "wherever" is a short road inside of LAPD. Not only would they not be able to "go" toward civil witnesses, but they were probably denied much more. Take the Sworn Statement of Christle:

"I have spent almost 17 years in the Los Angeles Police Department. I was a sergeant II until I complained about inappropriate conduct of Chief Berkow including my computer being taken after I input discovery information related to the lawsuit of Wallace vs. City of Los Angeles. The information was input following the mistrial.

"On August 4, 2005 Police Administrator Gerard Chalef sent a notice to all LAPD officers to provide all materials pertaining to the Christopher Wallace AKA Biggie Smalls... Homicide investigation.'

"After this memorandum was issued more than one foot worth of discovery information was received. I sat next to Lieutenant Bill Scott and input a summary of the information into a discovery matrix on my computer. Upon information and belief this material had not been turned over to the Plaintiffs, since there was no need after the mistrial to gather information already provided.

"The materials I was asked to summarize included information about the alleged involvement by LAPD officers, a Compton gang member, and others into the murder of Mr. Wallace.

The information matrix I prepared included information from computer runs, where people were during the murder and different witnesses with information concerning the murder of Wallace.

"After compiling this summary of information the Wallace case my computer was taken from me I complained to the Inspector General of misconduct the subject matter of my complaint included my suspicion that information regarding the Wallace murder was purged from my computer. The materials in my computer discovery matrix included claims of some witnesses that LAPD police officers and others were involved in the killing of Mr. Wallace.

"I was informed on April 21, 2006 from an officer in Risk Management that the investigation and recovery of documents pertaining to the Wallace Homicide is still ongoing by LAPD I believe that my having complained about the removal of my computer and potential destruction of evidence pertaining to the Wallace murder investigation was a reason why I was retaliated against by the LAPD—transferred and unjustly demoted from a coveted assignment with Internal Affairs"

—Declaration of Ya-May Christle

So unless Kading can account for the "one foot worth" of LAPD information, involving claims of some witnesses that LAPD Police Officers and others were involved in the killing of Mr. Wallace, how can he claim that the case is anywhere near closed or solved?

"We had very explicit orders that any developments regarding Mack, Perez or any other LAPD officer tied to Death Row, we had to make a special note of it and then hand that over. The problem was we never got any. Everybody that we would talk to and bring that up and ask those questions it was always the same answer: 'Well yeah' 'How do you know?' 'Well, it's what I read in the newspaper.' 'Well, why do you believe that?' 'I read it in the newspaper.' So everything about those guys was stuff that was hearsay information. Nobody ever had anything beyond that." ("Murder Rap")

And there you go, straight from the source. And the even more absurd extension of the absurd logic: I can't talk to anyone that might be civil related (they could not interview them), and no one having any information regarding the claims in the civil case were coming forward. There is a reason for that—there were no new leads on the case that advanced the "rogue LAPD cop" case because the LAPD was hiding the leads in the desk of Detective Katz—or taking them away from Ya-May Christle. In fact, Kading has probably never seen Christle's declaration before—it was civil and it was not pro-LAPD.

After this, "Rap" explains that Detectives Kading and Dupree (his partner) "reorganized the murder books." This leaves all types of room for speculation: what did they get back from Internal Affairs? How did they know what they were missing from the "original murder books?" It was not like there was a table of contents or an index. Without being familiar with the books before the I.A. "reclamation" how does one really know what data was actually "washed" from the books?

What makes it worse is the admission that Kading and Dupree apparently reorganized the Wallace murder books in a way "that would require an entirely new kind of investigative approach." What in the world does that mean? What kind of investigative approach is that? It must be the "three legged sack race" investigation—see how far you can run when hobbled and working out of concert. But one thing is absolutely clear; if it had to do with any subject matter involving LAPD involvement, it was not a topic that could be followed up on.

And what about Las Vegas Police, who we last saw retreating back to Las Vegas, humiliated by Philips' reckless smear of Becker and their investigation? If there was a murder of Shakur to be discussed at all, as explained earlier in the Jerry Hawkins DEA investigation, Las Vegas Police would certainly be involved... or should they?

According to former Shakur homicide investigator Brent Becker, there had not been much collaboration up until then. This will be important as time goes on. In fact, Kading states that he has never met or talked to Brent Becker, the original junior detective on the Shakur Homicide. When asked on chat board Makaveli.com "Greg did you talk to Detective Mike Franks and Detective Brent Becker?"

"I personally did not," Kading states "however, my colleagues were always in constant communication with Las Vegas over the years whenever mutual information had to be shared. There were lots of LAPD detectives besides myself working the cases." August 8, 2013 11:34 AM

Really? And not one of them was talking to Las Vegas Police, according to "Rap" on orders from LAPD top brass?

"It was his decision, along with Chief Bratton, that we were not obliged to notify the LVMPD of our findings... turf battles are regrettably common in law enforcement and we knew we couldn't just ask them to hand over the evidence we needed... So much for our carefully considered strategy to keep Las Vegas Police out of the loop for the time being." ("Murder Rap" pages 105-106, 167, 254)

So with no information trading hands between Las Vegas Police and LAPD it isn't any surprise to hear the following from Kading's supervisor,

McClure stated, "We followed every viable lead that we had at the time and pushed it to the point where we needed something else to occur in order to move the case forward. And that something—someone else coming forward to corroborate what we had—didn't happen."

LACK OF LEADERSHIP

Former LAPD Detective Kading's own lack of knowledge of the players in the game also tends to confuse his agenda. In his interview with Internet Anarchist, Anthony Battaglia aka Anton Batey, Kading erroneously states as fact that Michael Robinson was the man to put the name of Amir Mohammed to the media. Michael Robinson had little to do with anything. Michael Robinson was an informant and no one really put the name of Mohammed out to the media. It was Waymond Anderson who was the one who made the claims. Battaglia fails to catch this and in fact, does not bring Waymond Anderson up at all.

"Frank Alexander never blew a whistle on anything. Have you read his many police interviews? Everyone knows what Frank has said publicly, and if that's what you call a whistleblower, it's no wonder you can't prove anything.

"Russ Poole never blew the whistle on anything. He constructed a theory based on fallible information and when his supervisors and co-workers rejected his theory, he got frustrated. He was transferred off the Biggie case because of off-duty misconduct. Poole's theory has been discredited on every conceivable level. Your statement is ludicrous. "Dozens" of LAPD at Death Row"? Please! There was ONE guy from the LAPD—Richard McCauley. He was confronted, criticized, and disciplined for working off-duty at Death Row. Please get your facts straight." —Greg Kading's post on forum.

Kading must never have read LAPD Internal affairs document 96-1408. Page 16, where the report states: "At the conclusion of his interview, Reginald Wright, owner of Wright Way Protective Services, reluctantly provided investigators with the names of THREE additional department employees who possibly performed private security for Wright Way Protective Services/Death Row Records. The concerned employees were PO II Hurley Glenn Criner, Serial No. 25951, Valley Traffic, PO III David Love. Serial No. 27795, Hollywood Patrol, and possibly Kenneth Sutton (not verified). Wright was vague in explaining their actual roles with Wright Way Protective Services."

These names were verified with the Wright Way roster provided by Frank Alexander and in Russ Poole's documents.

"Perez never worked at Death Row and Poole knows that, so does everybody else (but you apparently). So now the Rampart investigation is a cover-up? John—take 5 minutes and do the math on how many hundreds of people would are necessary to be involved in your grand conspiracy. Every time you speak, the conspiracy gets bigger and bigger—now me and Anton are participants?"

We've covered Perez earlier. Boagni's testimony was in the documents Katz and the LAPD hid.

"Your so-called "whistleblowers" haven't exposed anything but their own continuous and provable lies. What gets me is why YOU believe them. When their lies have been exposed, and you continue to proclaim their lies, it gives the impression that you really don't care about the truth—or you are just sensationally naive."

"Back to my original request—can you please provide ONE co-conspirator who can substantiate your theory, even in-part. He doesn't have to know the whole thing, just his own role—just ONE. After 17 years—just ONE. I'm sure there would be a major book deal in it for him—just ONE brother John."

Battaglia also takes no time to correct Kading when Kading makes the allegation that Robinson recants his testimony. Remember that this was all public information in Chuck Philip's articles. It was Waymond Anderson that recanted his statements implicating Knight; Kading should know all of this. However the conspicuously absent Waymond Anderson from Battaglia's interview and the brief and incomplete mention of Waymond Anderson in the interview with hiphopdx makes it clear that Kading is "chipping in the rough."

This appears to be the problem: in addition to knowing the details of the theory you subscribe too, it is also equally important to understand the details of why untrue statements are untrue. Kading is well briefed in anything having to do with Orlando Anderson and Duane Keith Davis; his comments related to any other theory are characterized as a) vague, b) incorrect and c) challenging to the credibility of the person challenging a) or b). He is dismissive of certain elements and pays direct attention to others.

The disposition of the White Cadillac is a perfect example. Batey asks what happened to the white Cadillac and Kading discusses, for a moment, that they "ditched the Cadillac" in a parking lot, like it was a wadded up piece of Kleenex. Vehicles are a little more than that, yet Battaglia doesn't even ask Kading (and one may believe that his heavily edited interviews may contain this, but who really knows) what happened to the car after that. If Kading knew the disposition of the car, nothing more is mentioned—they merrily skip off to another topic.

There was plenty of opportunity to discuss Waymond Anderson. Why didn't they? As it was a critical piece of Philips' stories and Kading opened the door by mentioning Robinson. With Battaglia's penchant to make himself a source of authority in the matter, it's curious he does not beat up on Kading by calling out his inconsistency or ask for clarification on this inconsistency. He does not even push the matter more by asking about Chuck Philips or Waymond Anderson. They just pass it by.

The propaganda machine is in high gear. It is one thing to back a certain philosophy; but to place such hard lines on one side but not on another gives your position a decided lack of credibility. Battaglia never questions Kading on Waymond Anderson's revised statements, when he recanted, the contradictions against Kading's version of Keith Davis or Waymond Anderson's third statement recanting the Davis story. Battaglia fails to probe where the Anderson/Davis story came from if Davis was telling the LAPD that he had told no one about the matter. Did Waymond Anderson pull Davis' name out of a hat? Did Davis' actions in any way support Anderson's original claims that Davis had framed him for the crimes he was serving time for? What about the allegations that he and Davis talked all the time?

Maybe the "entirely new kind of investigative approach" is the "Inspector Clueseau" approach—just be uninformed about the case and hope something falls into your lap.

Right Location, Wrong Parties: In Clueseau fashion, misunderstanding takes on a new meaning, when Kading relays an evening at the House of Blues, which was actually videotaped. Like the storyteller he is, Kading actually re-casts the roles of the event and the people in them:

> "Yeah... when Keffe-D and his brother would entertain their out-of-town drug customers to a night on the town in L.A., the House of Blues was always on the list of places to party. On one particular night, Suge's brother in law, Norris Anderson, had a .40 cal Glock confiscated by security. Years later, Kevin Hackie would suggest this was the same gun used to kill Pac. It wasn't. The gun was test fired and the ballistics compared to the bullets/casings in Pac's murder did not match, but since it helped sell the "Suge killed Pac" theory for Hackie and Frank, they ran with it." —December 12, 2012 Makaveli Board

The truth is that the story Frank Alexander and Kevin Hackie tell is the one videotaped, where Hussein Fatal of the Outlawz was stopped by House of Blues' Security and the .40-caliber Glock was seized from him. Shakur was furious and the videotape shows Alexander, who was there, calming Shakur. Unfortunately, Kading was not there; Kading's confusion on events makes it difficult to understand his later allegation that "the gun was test fired and… did not match" as no one is sure if there were two identical events where one was with Shakur and Fatal and another with Keefe D' and Norris Anderson, where Norris Anderson's weapon was confiscated. Without supporting evidence a second similar event is dubious.

Confusion on Autopsy Photos: Next comes Kading's misinformation on the infamous autopsy photo published by author and friend of Kading's—Cathy Scott:

> "Therefore, we must work toward separating fact from fiction. The picture in Cathy's book is an authentic picture—I can assure you. It was taken AFTER September 13th (which is the day Pac died). It is one of many autopsy photos in the police file. A photographer at the morgue snapped a photo and leaked it to Cathy." (Makaveli Board, 06-20-2013, 11:05 AM)

Brent Becker of the Las Vegas Police, offers a conflicting story:

> "It wasn't released legitimately, it shouldn't have been out there, and I can tell you that it was not a police photo… It was taken post autopsy. We don't take post procedure photos. The only photos we take are of evidentiary value… We don't take pictures of dead bodies just to do it." (Interview Brent Becker on YouTube)

The Las Vegas Sun, Scott's former newspaper employer, claims that Clark County Coroner Ron Flud has said the photo, which shows Shakur dissected on a table at the morgue, is not an official coroner or police photo. Metro Internal Affairs Bureau Lt. John Alamshaw also said it appears that it was not an official photo.

But didn't Kading state it was "in the police file" made by a photographer at the morgue. (Is that the official title of the person taking a picture?) But Kading later says something different, calling the photo "unauthorized" which begs the question on if the photo really was in the police file?

"I talk to Cathy frequently. As a journalist, she has to protect her sources. Out of respect for the person who gave her an unauthorized photo of Tupac at the morgue, she will not reveal the person's name." (Makaveli Board 05-11-2014, 02:30 AM)

It appears that actual communication with Las Vegas Police might make Kading's apparent unfamiliarity with the autopsy photo make more sense. But perhaps we can give the benefit of the doubt that the photo made its way in with the rest of the many photos, after it hit Scott's book. Kading remains unclear as to what his access to Las Vegas Police files actually was especially in light of the orders from LAPD brass not to talk to Las Vegas Police. And it is good to understand that many of the Las Vegas Police files that Kading had access to were very, very old, and were original interviews given to LAPD by Las Vegas Police. The authors of this book have access to the same files. So he probably had no idea and was just covering for Scott who herself has never revealed the source of the photo, deflecting the matter to her publisher who claimed, "The source of the information wasn't relevant."

Mistaken Conclusions of Fact: MGM Scuffle: The following statement is made as if fact:

"Only a few hours earlier he and his Piru posse had dealt a painful lesson to Baby Lane in the lobby of the MGM Grand, punishing the Crip for the crime of stealing a Death Row medallion at the Lakewood Mall two months earlier."(Rap, p. 135)

The trouble is that an assumption is not a fact and the motive for the attack in the MGM is only that—an assumption:

"The story about Pac attacking Orlando over the mall incident is "assumed" to be true, but has not been established as fact." (Makaveli Board 04-19-2013, 03:28 P.M.)

Buntry's Car Damage: Kading claims that "It's a fact that someone from Buntry's car fired on the Cadillac... it's just not known for sure whether it was Buntry or his passenger Neckbone. Orlando shot back and actually hit Buntry's car." While someone said it years later, none of the original statements speak to this. No one says anyone from Buntry's car fired. The only one they thought fired was a man in black (presumably Alexander who did not have a gun).

Confusion on the Shooter Car in Wallace: In "Behind the Music: Notorious B.I.G" Kading makes a statement regarding an Impala the shooter used the night Wallace was killed. This was a claim that Kading would repeat throughout 2012; the shooter's car was a green impala, not a black one; an error he faults Detective Russell Poole for; "This is where Poole starts to go wrong." (LA Weekly, March 2012)

Kading repeats the claim so that there is no mistake.

"But what Russell Poole doesn't do is tell people about how every single witness that was in those cars denied it being a black Impala. They said that it was a green Impala." (djbishopradio.com, March 9 2012, from HipHopDX)

While it has been confirmed the car was indeed a mid-90s Chevrolet SS Impala:

- Lil Cease and Greg Young, who were both in the car with Biggie during the shooting, stated that the car was a dark green color.
- Kenneth Story told the police that the car was "a clean, black Chevrolet Impala Super Sport," and "had seen exactly such a vehicle parked on Fairfax Avenue as he and the rest of the Bad Boy group waited for their vehicles in the Petersen Museum's parking structure.
- A Metropolitan Transit Authority driver whose bus had been westbound on Wilshire when the shooting occurred confirmed to police that the shooter's sedan was black. So there were witnesses who attested that the car was indeed black.
- Reggie Blaylock, an Inglewood police officer in his words said the car was "a 94 or 95 Chevrolet Impala,

SS, black, with large wide tires."
- Kading himself in "Rap" agreed with the widely held belief that the car was a black Chevy Impala and made no mention of the car being a different color. Not one time. "We felt sure, suddenly and completely, that Wardell "Poochie" Fouse had shot Christopher Wallace from the driver's seat of a black Chevrolet Impala outside the Petersen Automotive Museum on March 9, 1997." ("Rap," p. 222).

The probable conclusion we could draw from all of this is that Kading was lying to "Behind the Music" when he claimed that Theresa Swann told him that Wardell Fouse was driving a Green Impala and this was merely a transparent attempt to draw attention away from David Mack, Amir Muhammad, Rafael Perez, and Reggie Wright Junior.

Eugene Deal's Interview: In "Clearing the Rubble," ("Rap," p. 90) Kading makes two arguably false statements. The first involves a composite drawing from Eugene Deal, Wallace's and Sean Combs' bodyguard the night of the shooting. Kading says that the composite only bore a passing resemblance to Muhammad. Fred Miller, Russell Poole's former supervisor and partner in the Wallace investigation said that the resemblance between Muhammad's driver's license photo and Deal's composite drawing was "very uncanny."

"It didn't help that he bore a passing resemblance to the figure with the bow tie and fade haircut outside the museum, or Bad Boy bodyguard Eugene Deal would tentatively identify him as the "Nation of Islam guy" behind the wheel of the Impala." ("Rap," p. 90).

The second conflicting statement is tied to the first and involves Deal's identification of the shooter. While Kading has put some DRDS on Deal, who now claims that the incident was staged and the claim false, at one point in the "Biggie and Tupac" documentary, Deal, in a very confident tone when he pointed to Muhammad's photo in a six pack said "That's the guy right there."

There was nothing tentative about Deal's identification of Muhammad. He said it with full confidence and went into a rage in the film because LAPD had not showed him this photo when Deal was interviewed. Deal also maintained his stance that Muhammad was the person he identified at the Petersen Automotive museum during his testimony in the wrongful death civil case back in 2005.

Ignoring Billups' Illegal Activity: There is a fundamental flaw in how Kading, who was not there to witness it, describes Amir Muhammad's visit to David Mack while he was in jail. He is completely obtuse to the detail of Muhammad's jailhouse visit that caused so many people to be suspicious of Billups. Kading prejudices the visit by stating Billups was only there "to see his childhood friend." What he fatally ignores, is that in a prison, Billups wrote a fake social security number and fake address in the jail's visitation log. To Poole and others this was a huge red flag. To Kading—nothing.

To the government it is, especially falsifying information in prison. 18 U.S.C. § 1001 says "whoever, in any matter within the jurisdiction of the executive, legislative, or judicial branch of the Government of the United States, knowingly and willfully (3) makes or uses any false writing or document knowing the same to contain any materially false, fictitious, or fraudulent statement or entry" shall be fined under the title, imprisoned not more than 5-8 years, or both.

Illegal activities aside, Kading then leans on his pal Philips to trivialize Billups. "I'm not a murderer, I'm a mortgage broker," he told the Los Angeles Times ("Rap," p. 90). After the housing collapse of 2006 it is curious that more suspicion wasn't placed on Billups because he was a "mortgage broker" after the generally bad press they got. Billups claim to be a priest? Maybe. Mortgage broker? Guilty.

So why would a "simple mortgage broker" knowingly risk violating Federal Law in a Federal prison, and use false information to check in? And why would that "simple mortgage broker" list to eight (8) prior addresses, each with no forwarding address? That is the mark of someone who doesn't want their troubles linked or following them. LAPD Robbery and Homicide detectives did a research on both of Billups's adopted Muslim name and legal name and it revealed this irregularity.

Moreover, why would a "simple mortgage broker" have a fake driver's license? In fact, why would anyone? Billups had a fake driver's license in the name of "Harry Muhammad."

Finally why are the police called to question a "simple mortgage broker" accused of (October 21st of 1998) "firearm brandishing?" Why does a "simple mortgage broker" carry a semiautomatic Beretta with an eight-round clip in his car?

Most importantly, why is none of this registering with Detective Kading or anyone else on the task force? Again—simple mortgage broker—fake names, fake Social Security numbers, fake driver's license with a fake name, brandishing firearms, multiple non-forwarded home addresses and carrying concealed weapons? "Rap" made a point of accusing Theresa Swann of using fake IDs as evidence of her criminal behavior. So how did the "simple mortgage broker" get a pass? What kind of mortgages was he brokering and to who?

Billups forgeries and irregularities could not have been harder to ignore, as the task force was involved in the FBI's Michael Robinson/Amir Muhammad set-up meeting and the fact that jailhouse informant Michael Robinson went to Billups home wearing a wire, which we covered earlier in this book. Yet he remained a "simple mortgage broker" and a shooter walked out.

Finally, there appears to be no evidence to suggest that Kading had any cleared homicides to his name. The closest thing to a homicide investigation Kading came into was in seeing dead bodies at the gangland murder scenes, in his involvement with CRASH.

So what happens when a million and a half dollar investigation gets handed to a team lead by a detective that doesn't know the difference (after 6 years) between an IRS audit and a royalties audit and has trouble remembering the fact—intensive case? What happens when the leader of the investigation declares the case "almost" solved, yet knows that half of its probative evidence—hundreds of documents and interviews, depositions and statements are not available to him?

What you get is what you see: inconsistent facts, contradicting and conflicting statements, ignored, or worse—intentionally overlooked—evidence and just plain being wrong about much of the investigation.

To The Red Knight's chagrin, the Kading—influenced Fifth Element fizzled out and died. Credibility issues and lost opportunities abounded. Again, without Kenner to guide the process it was only a bad imitation. It was time to take matters into his own hands and conjure the Fifth Element himself—and that's when The Red Knight "went Hollywood!"

REGGIE GOES HOLLYWOOD

Right in the middle of the 2014 LAPD leak of the Malcolm Patton Confession Letter, a certain event happens synonymous with the appearance of Hailey's Comet; Reggie Wright Junior comes out of his shell to speak.

The last time Wright Junior had anything to add publicly, was in 2007. At that time he gave a couple of interviews and was stating that "I didn't know what the financial arrangement was" and complaining about Frank Alexander, Kevin Hackie, and Michael Moore.

This time though The Fifth Element appears to be money driven—or maybe revenge driven. Wright Junior partnered up with a "businessman," (who had some bad dealings with Knight, and for some reason believed he was unique) by the name of Lloyd "TaTa" Lake. In what seemed like a moment—and what actually lasted for a moment, the two were everywhere, giving interviews on the Internet, speaking in a few podcasts and trying to raise money for a documentary they wanted to do.

In their documentary, tentatively called "Justice for Tupac and Biggie," Lake and Wright Junior publicly question if Death Row Records co-founder, Suge Knight, could be an informant for the government and if that possible connection played a part in the unsolved murder investigations of Shakur and Wallace.

This was an extraordinary opportunity to listen and learn; Wright Junior made a life of not talking. So, if he was, in fact, going to talk, it must have been important. But Wright's explanation of why he believed he would have been better at running Death Row than Knight just felt like the last drops in the 1996 "Death Row takeover plan's" fuel tank; there was no Death Row and Wright's "after-the-party" attempt to discredit Knight as a "snitch" just felt cheap—one hundred and fifty thousand cheap. Wright Junior put a bounty on his snitching and when the money wasn't rolling in—his interviews ceased.

In the end, they never got close to that amount; calling the documentary "finished" but holding out releasing it until they get paid $150,000. Allhiphop.com says "Lake is looking to raise $150,000 over the next 30 days. If the filmmakers are able to reach their goal in the allotted time, the documentary will be released to the public."

The reason they never got the money likely had to do with their interviews in which they gave their entire storyline away!

> Lake, From an Interview with HipHop Wired:
> HHW: So you believe Suge Knight is responsible for the killing of Christopher Wallace?
> Lloyd: His child's mother told that's what happened. When you look at the police reports and Reggie Wright says he believes Suge is responsible for it. And these are the people that are close to him. So I don't know what else you need.
> HHW: Are you familiar with Greg Kading?
> Lloyd: Yes, I spoke to Greg about three weeks ago.

So we know the agenda. Was the unnamed child's mother "Sharitha"?

> Wright Junior from AllHiphop.com:
> "My reasoning is for a couple of reasons. I have no desire to really talk. I know there have been different DVDs out there by guys that used to work for my security company that were so far away from the basis of the truth. Eventually, the truth has come out I believe.
> "My reasoning is number one, loyalty to Lloyd Lake. He asked me to help him with his project. The second reason is over the seventeen years a lot of things and different accusations have been said. My kids were younger at the time, so they weren't really on the Internet or reading, but now that they're on the Internet, every time these misquotes or misinformation come out. I just wanted to get it cleared up. I know that Suge and some other people are out there trying to do documentaries and movie deals. I want to get my side of the story out before they get their side of the story out.
> "And then my third reason, and probably the most important reason, is because Suge has been out there slandering my name recently. He also tried to have me incarcerated and had people file police reports against me for making terrorist threats. These things happened back in 2002-2003, but I just learned of them because of how the federal government does when they try to get you to speak on different situations that

they know you know about. So they try to show you things that he was doing to me back in those days that I wasn't aware of."

Wright Junior hasn't read the Death Row Times in a while.

Wright Junior from AllHiphop.com:

"He had me call the U.S. Attorney. I did. The U.S. Attorney advised me that, "I can't talk to you Reggie. You're not his attorney of record. I would have to hear from his attorney." Which at the time (the attorney) handling the federal matter was David Chesnoff out of Las Vegas. So I called David Chesnoff and told him Suge wanted to do the six months and cooperate against David Kenner. David Chesnoff told me, 'I represent tough guys from the Mafia. One thing I don't do is represent rats that would do any type of telling, so you tell Suge if that's what he wants to do then he needs to remove me or I'll remove myself as his attorney of record.'"

LA Weekly, the printed outlet for Kading's publicist, also interviewed Wright stating: "Wright advances the claims made in LAPD Detective Greg Kading's 2011 book, Murder Rap, which blew the case wide open and was the subject of an L.A. Weekly cover story. Murder Rap, for which a documentary of the same name is also in the works, implicates Southside Crip Orlando 'Baby Lane' Anderson for the murder of Tupac, and Mob Piru gang member Wardell 'Poochie' Fouse for the murder of Biggie Smalls. (Both Anderson and Fouse have since been murdered themselves.) The book fingers Sean Combs (aka Puff Daddy) and Knight, respectively, for setting the deaths in motion. Combs and Knight could not be reached for comment for this story. In a wide-ranging interview, L.A. Weekly spoke with Wright about the documentary and his time at Death Row Records."

LA Weekly: These murders may one day be studied in criminal-justice classes. Do you think there will ever be closure of the Tupac or Biggie investigations?

Reggie Wright: I don't think so. I think too much has
been done, and lost. I think closure is here.
If everything that Greg Kading reported
in his book is accurate, I believe law
enforcement agencies on both
investigations are satisfied. Both killers
are dead. Puffy and Suge Knight are
responsible for both of the killings, but
the people that can really talk against
them are no longer living."

The mutual admiration society speaks up.

Kading responds to Makaveli Board post: 07-08-2013, 12:22
P.M.

Q: Wow so cool Greg, what is Reggie doing these
days? Is he still talking with Suge? And of course
Pac was not a gang member, he was artist as
Lesane said!

A: Reggie is doing very good. He keeps things low
key and moving forward. He is one of the most
informed guys on what was happening around
Death Row during the 90's. Him and Suge
aren't on the best of terms, but it's nothing too
serious. They just don't have anything in
common anymore.

KEVIN HACKIE REVISITED

re·cant (r-knt) v: To make a formal retraction or disavowal of
(a statement or belief to which one has previously committed oneself).
v.intr. To make a formal retraction or disavowal of a previously held
statement or belief.

"John—you make this too easy man," "Murder Rap" Detective Kading states to an Internet fan. "When you use unreliable and discredited sources, you in turn discredit your own
theory.

"Kevin Hackie was not a whistleblower, Kevin Hackie was a desperate criminal facing multiple felony counts when he went to the FBI and told them he'd snitch on Death Row if they would help him with his court case. Period. Kevin Hackie was not "fired" by Reggie Wright Junior—Hackie got into trouble with his employer, the Compton School Police Department, because he was falsely impersonating a Federal Agent at the hospital in Vegas and refusing to give his credentials to the police there.

"They in turn called Hourie Taylor, his police chief, and told them about Hackie's behavior. Hackie eventually was fired, convicted of his crimes and went to jail. The FBI told Hackie to fuck off because he couldn't produce anything worthwhile and they were concerned that he had mental problems. Where's the FBI motorcade documents, John? Why did Hackie call Reggie Wright and apologize for all the false accusations he's made over the years (Asher is aware of this)."

—Comment by Greg Kading on August 6, 2013 at 9:34am

From this post, it looks like Mr. Kading is again incorrect about many things and doesn't seem to be very nice. The fact is that Hourie Taylor was not Hackie's boss. The Compton School Police come under the school district, which was not dissolved when the regular Compton PD was dissolved. They have their own leadership and hierarchy.

Because of the "Murder Rap" detective sequestration from Wallace Civil Documents, Kading was probably not aware of the letter from the Assistant US Attorney Cheng who forbade Hackie's attorneys from discussing Hackie's "work for the FBI and ATF" in Court, citing Federal Secrets protection.

There are many other mistruths in this posting, but it is important to explain them in line and in context. Paraphrasing is harmful. Witnesses are not compelled to testify. They do so because they have an inherent respect for the "system" and a belief that doing the right thing and telling the truth are what they owe society. Some testify because they can gain something from doing so. Some do so at the risk of their freedom and their lives.

One such witness had nothing to gain and everything to lose in testifying. His name is Kevin Raymond Hackie. And he paid a dear price for his desire to do the right thing. There is no evidence that he had any other motive. Hackie was openly mocked, slandered, libeled, criticized, and reviled in some fan communities. We go back to asking the question "why criticize Hackie if his only weakness is that he elected not to repeat what he had said previously in nine interviews?" Hackie simply quit being willing to cooperate and regardless of the impact to the Wallace case, their attorney, Sanders stated publicly that they understood.

When one looks at the entire body of work and takes nothing out of context, Hackie did not change his story or contradict the story he had given LAPD eight times. Hackie never said "you know all that stuff I gave LAPD? Yeah, that was all bullshit!" This book openly challenges a real fan of the case or interested researcher to show an example of Hackie actually changing the elements of his story. There is no evidence that he has!

Later, Hackie was charged and convicted of a felony involving the sale of firearms, but is anyone serious about the witnesses in the two killings really going to completely exclude Hackie when others have 2 strikes or worse against them? And that conviction gave apologists for the Kingdom of Thieves, an easy reason to toss Hackie's name aside.

The pattern here with Philips, Kading, Waymond Anderson and others is that only some of the story is told; only a part of the story is told. So what part of Kevin Hackie's story has not been disclosed?

Kevin Hackie's conviction was overturned on appeal. Not dismissed, not plea-bargained. Not part of a proffer deal. The case was adjudicated and OVERTURNED on its merits—not like the dozens of witnesses in this story who have deals brokered for their statement. And Hackie still cooperated with police before, during and after the appeal and overturn of his charges. However, it has not stopped the merchants of defamation and slander, who know the difference, from still trying to take baseless slaps at Hackie, who they feel, is some sort of Shakur and Wallace punching bag.

"Kevin Hackie was a never-ending disaster as a witness (caught in continual lies) until he changed his tune"—Greg Kading, Makaveli Chat board (May 28, 2014, 04:36 P.M.)

"He's staying clear of all this—which is smart. He knows stepping back into the conversation will be detrimental to whatever reputation he has left." —Greg Kading, Makaveli

Chat board (August 19, 2013 10:36 AM)

Easily the most maligned person in the entire investigation, Kevin Hackie was the poster child for the Kenner Alchemy Element Three—sabotage. This is directly proportional to the value and weight of his testimony.

Kevin Hackie was one of the first security guards hired by Wright Junior to work with him at Death Row Records and easily the one with the longest exposure to the misdeeds within the Kingdom of Thieves. Hackie's importance to the investigation was his introduction to Wright long before the Kingdom of Thieves was founded.

"I would say 1987, '88. I started working for the school district in '89. Prior to that I was a cadet with the Inglewood Police Department. I had met him—I remember it has been probably 12 years ago, I went out there to take some paper-work out there. At the time Reggie was a jailer. That is where I first really kind of met him. I got on with the school district back in '89. '89 or '88, I got on out there. Reggie was still employed as a jailer, because Reggie was only a policeman like five years. And him and I, you know, always hit it off. Occasionally on some calls out on the streets I backed him up, you know, here and there."

Hackie was well versed on the inner workings of Death Row and confirms not only the problems Shakur was having with the label, but also his tenure with Shakur and Death Row.

"Originally, I was the original bodyguard for Tupac from the get-go, because had been—out of all the guys, I had been working, quote, unquote, for Wright Way the longest, because I had known Reggie the longest. Actually my girlfriend called and said, 'Did you hear about it?' My ex-girlfriend. I said, 'What are you talking about?' 'Tupac was shot' probably going to try to hit me, too. I am like, it couldn't happen. That I believe that to be sincerely, he was Friday before we had just finished shooting Gang Related, that was the last picture he was in with Belushi, and he didn't want to go to Vegas. He told me, Suge, 'Man', he says, 'I am not going to Vegas.'"

On his relationship with Wright Junior:

"You know, Frank had called me in early November, Reggie wanted him to come out to the office. So, I was on duly that night. So. I drove over there and met Frank. And he says, you know, 'can you please stand by?'

"I said, 'You know, I really don't want to get involved with this mess.'

"So, whoever the attorney was in there with Reggie, they knew that I was out—I was on duty, they knew I was out there. He said 'don't bring fucking Kevin's ass in here' because he is all pissed off. And so, you know, I figured by that time, of course, his daddy started leaking things in. Well, of course, I had been talking with the FBI and so on and so on.

"And about. I would say March of last year March or February; I get a call from Reggie out of the blue. 'Kevin, I need a favor, can you drive for me' I am like, 'what? Can I drive for you?'

"I said, 'Reggie, what do y'all think I am, fucking stupid?' I said, "You know me well enough to know right now,' I said, 'if you want to do something to me, you want to go ahead and take me out,' I said, 'be a man, take me out." Because he knows if he comes up against me one-on-one he will lose.

"Reggie says, 'Oh, fuck you, mother fucker, I can have you killed at any given time.' I said, "Reggie, you know where I am at." I said, 'You know, it is your ballgame, do what you got to do.'

"But as I said again, hey, he is trying to set me up. He hadn't talked to me for four or five months, he said I was a snitch the whole shebang, this and that. And then all of a sudden he calls me up and he wants me to drive for him, you know."

On Orlando Anderson Chain Snatching:

MR. MILLER: When - you said earlier that you thought
               that the attack on Tupac's people, they
               were trying to get that medallion at the

mall, was a bullshit story.

MR. HACKIE: As far as I believe it was a bullshit story. I
was never told of it."

On Arriving in Las Vegas and Local Run-In:

Kevin's troubles started from the moment he arrived in Las Vegas, by what seems like more of a pissing contest that went south. But
it was more than that; Kevin was about to blow his cover and being as
distraught over the shooting of his friend Shakur as he was, really just
didn't care at that moment. However, Kevin's associates at the ATF and
the FBI did not want to waste all the money already sunk into building the drug and money laundering case against Death Row; outing
an informant at that time would not only have been dangerous for
Hackie, but it would have compromised the investigation—as in fact
it partially did.

MR. HACKIE: I was on the phone there at the hospital,
which at that time I was communicating
with a federal agent out here. Basically at
the time a doctor and I exchanged words.
I had the officer's permission to use the
phone. And basically turned into one big
mess. Metro police, one of those guys
pulled up, and they had the walkie-talkie.
I guess basically at the time of the
shooting, you know, metro police in Vegas
were considered to be the FBI of Las
Vegas. They are the cream of the crop.
They are like LAPD of Los Angeles

MR. MILLER: Okay.

MR. HACKIE: And the officer and I basically got into
a verbal dispute. I showed them my ID
at the time, this and that, and he says
what are you really doing here; why are you
on the phone; who were you talking to?
The FBI, and all this other mess. To make a
long story short, Vegas police told me I had
to be out of town by 8:00, 9:00 that night.

At the time they called, at the time the chief of police Mike Menez (phonetic), and basically a day after Las Vegas police learned there was some involvement with me and the FBI. So, of course, they sent the chief two or three days later. But I mean, it was all squashed thereafter.

At this point, the "feds" were not fully capable of containing the situation because the proverbial "cat" was out of the bag.

MR. HACKIE: So, by that time that night Reggie and Suge came to the hospital, Reggie became kind of suspicious of me. Well, who I was on the phone with and all this. It basically blew up in a big mess. And so, anyhow, after, about two or three weeks later we had a meeting of all of the security guys out at Can-Am Studios. And Reggie basically was still keeping everybody employed, and I guess by that time his dad, right after Tupac's shooting, about a week later in Compton they started having all the raids.

On the Possible Gun used to Shoot Shakur

MR. HACKIE: By the way, what caliber of gun was he shot with?
MR. MILLER: 9 millimeter.
MR. HACKIE: 9 millimeter. Tupac was shot with a .40. Are you guys aware of the .40-caliber?
MR. MILLER: Yep. What about it?
MR. HACKIE: It was a .40-caliber on Tupac.
MR. MILLER: Do you have something you want to say about that?
MR. HACKIE: I say, again, at this point I haven't heard any more, but the feds actually had the .40-caliber gun, which is…

MR. MILLER: They actually had it?

MR. HACKIE: I will bet you lunch, I will tell you
something, in July of 1996, I know it is
probably hearsay, and Hodgeman knows
who I am, July of '96, one of the Outlawz,
when we went to the House of Blues. One
of the kids, one of them went inside a place
and had a gun on him. Whatever reason, I
don't know. The guy, the Santa Monica
policeman, the detective took the gun off
of him, I went over and talked to him,
I was shocked, because I told them if they
had anything on them, don't bring no shit
with them. But they were all scared.

The Outlaw who had his gun removed as revealed by Frank
Alexander, who was present, as well as video footage shot by videographer Gobi Rahimi at the time the incident unfolded. The Outlaw was
"Hussein Fatal" and according to Alexander, a furious Shakur, who
Alexander had to physical calm down, sentenced "Fatal" to remain in
the limo for the entire time they were in the House of Blues.

MR. HACKIE: Reggie went over and talked to the Santa
Monica cop, whatever, and says, you know,
he apologized, this and that, so on and so,
to make a long story short, the detective
from Santa Monica, he is working off duty,
he is head of security, he is a real nice guy,
tall guy, he took the gun with him. And I
know he took it to his station in Santa
Monica, they ran it, see if it was stolen or
whatever.
"Reggie called me up about two, three
weeks later, because Reggie kept calling
them to see if they could pick the gun up,
it was a compact Glock 40, compact. Like
a fool, Reggie kept calling, kept calling,
and finally said it was ready, because I used
to work at Santa Monica, I went over and

picked the gun up. At that time, I go ahead and picked the gun up. The feds went and had the gun and everything, took a ballistics test fit. Come to find out, the gun that was used in the actual shooting. This is no assumption, I don't care who tells you otherwise, this is no assumption and Reggie is the one that had the gun, turned the gun over to Reggie. I don't know to this day where he was carrying it, it was at one time. It was a compact Clock. But I am sure by now, you know, the gun has been dumped.

MR. MILLER: You are saying Reggie shot Tupac?

MR. HACKIE: I am not saying Reggie shot him. I am saying the gun in question.

MR. MILLER: Okay, so are you saying that the feds had the gun and they tested it?

MR. HACKIE: I brought the gun into them.

MR. MILLER: Why did they release it?

MR. HACKIE: Dan McMullen. Dan McMullen and John Cissioni (phonetic), ATF.

MR. MILLER: Why did they release the gun?

MR. HACKIE: Turned it back over. At the time I was co operating, assisting him and everything, you know. They did what they had to do. And that was it. Took the gun back to Reggie.

MR. MILLER: July of '96?

MR. HACKIE: July, August of '96, around that time.

MR. MILLER: I will have to talk to Dan and see where the gun is at.

MR. HACKIE: Dan and I are on good terms. Dan has also got the photos I gave him.

Los Angeles Police Interview I

Hackie originally interviewed with Detectives Poole and Fred Miller in Van Nuys, California on a rainy day. The detectives brought a tape recorder and told Hackie that they were going to tape the interview. The interview lasted three (3) hours.

Poole showed to Hackie numerous photographs of LAPD Officers Rafael Perez, David Mack, and Sammy Martin. Hackie told Poole and Miller that Hackie recognized and identified these three officers as being present at numerous Death Row Records' events.

In this first interview, Hackie also told the detectives that Hackie met Perez during the Rodney King Riots of 29-30 April 1992. Hackie also told them that Hackie knew Perez and Mack on a professional level because we were law enforcement officers. Hackie also told these detectives that Hackie was knowledgeable of materially relevant information pertaining to Perez, and that information related to Perez's career. They then discussed Reggie Wright Junior, and his dealings with Marion Suge Knight, how Wright started up his security company, and that Knight financed "Wright Way Protective Services," in Paramount, California.

Even years earlier, Detective Miller asked Hackie if Hackie feared Knight or Wright, and Hackie responded that Hackie had some concerns but if the situation arose, Hackie would take appropriate action to protect Hackie and his family. Miller then inquired about Hackie's involvement with the FBI, and Hackie responded that his lawyer had filed an appeal to the California Court of Appeals to overturn his wrongful conviction.

Hackie told Poole that he would do some digging only if Poole would assure that Hackies identity would remain in "absolute confidence"—for fear of retribution, retaliation, recrimination, and reprisal to Hackie and his family. Hackie repeatedly stressed to Poole and Miller that absolute confidentiality had, and must, be maintained. Even years before the Wallace trial Hackie knew the stakes were high.

Poole assured him, "Kevin, you can trust me, this information and whatever help you can give us in solving this case will remain absolutely confidential, only my partner and I will know about our contacts with you."

The detectives then pressed Hackie to find out and if an Officer Martin and Ray (Raphael) Perez were involved with the Bank of America robbery. Hackie reiterated that he would only assist them if they agreed to absolute confidentiality. "Kevin, I know you could get killed. I guarantee this will be confidential."

MR. HACKIE:	Well, Junior, basically. Not Senior at the time. But Senior in a sense was still talking, telling police business, confidential stuff, thinking he is still one of the boys. But not knowing Reggie was in Suge's back pocket going back a couple of years even before he got to retirement. And then things Reggie has done throughout the years, I was a policeman before Reggie was, but Reggie was a jailer for the city. Reggie got caught stealing prisoners' money."
MR. HACKIE:	Well, while the normal homeboys are always home at 6:00 in the morning, it is all said and done. So, basically when the feds intervened, started talking to Chief Taylor, put two and two together, Reggie's dad was Lieutenant Wright, and basically at one time was like that with Hourie Taylor, but that is not the case anymore, because Reggie's father was dumbfounded to the fact that Reggie was involved deeper than what he believed to be. So, of course, his dad has been a cop 14, 15 years, management, and his son was medical retirement police officer they still talked. And so, of course, a lot of the actual raids, come to find out, information got to these guys prior to. That is why a lot of these guys and—
MR. MILLER:	Prior to what?
MR. HACKIE:	Prior to actual raids taking place—A lot of search warrants done.
MR. MILLER:	Right.
MR. HACKIE:	Okay. Brennan (phonetic)
MR. MILLER:	Tim Brennan?
MR. HACKIE:	Yeah, Brennan and Ladd (phonetic), gang guys out there. Of course, they did a majority of the affidavits, warrants, and everything. But at the time, I don't know

	if it is still the case, Reggie Wright, Sr., was the boss.
MR. MILLER:	Right.
MR. HACKIE:	And I don't know if you I know, one of our officers, Lawrence Finch, the school district, his brother was the first one shot. Bobbie Finch, he was shot over on Mayo.
MR. MILLER:	Uh-huh.
MR. HACKIE:	Finch has (inaudible) with me. And basically thereafter when all the raids started, there was a lot—they got information prior to. Now, to this day Finch believed, of course, that Reggie had something to do with it, which—
MR. MILLER:	Reggie, Sr.?
MR. HACKIE:	Well, Junior, basically. Not Senior at the time. But Senior in a sense was still talking, telling police business, confidential stuff, thinking he is still one of the boys.

Hackie Los Angeles Police Interview II

In May of 1998, Poole and Hackie again met at Hackie's office. Poole showed Hackie a video tape of the party at the Peterson Automotive Museum, located at the southeast corner of Wilshire Boulevard and Fairfax, before Wallace's murder. Poole brought a tape recorder and told Hackie that he was going to tape the interview. Poole asked Hackie if Hackie could identify or recognize any of the persons in the tape. Hackie identified a few persons. Hackie then told Poole that Hackie had a lead, but had to go to Parker Center to meet with LAPD Detective Miller and an unidentified detective.

They met in a room at the Robbery Homicide Unit. Hackie met LAPD Chief of Police Bernard Parks at that meeting and was then introduced by Detective Miller as Chief Parks was walking with Deputy Chief Gascon. Bull had convened the interview through William Hodgeman in order to have the weapons charges dismissed. Bull told Hodgeman that Hackie possessed relevant information; evidence that could possibly solve the Wallace murder. The interview was tape-recorded. LAPD Detective Miller operated the tape recording device; Poole asked Hackie if Hackie could find out for Poole and Miller if Perez and Officer Martin were involved with the Bank of America robbery.

Hackie reiterated that Hackie would only assist them if they agreed to his demand absolute confidentiality as stated above. Poole then said to your declarant: "Kevin, I know you could get killed. I guarantee this will be confidential."

The interview lasted approximately 3.0 hours.

MR. MILLER:	what was the relationship between the two?
MR. HACKIE:	Reggie and Suge?
MR. MILLER:	Right.
MR. HACKIE:	well, basically we always referred to Reggie as a little bitch, because he was Suge's little—basically a little pimp. And I knew about two months before—in June, June or July we had quote, unquote, a little security meeting, and basically I was—Reggie and I used to, or I gel in a sense fight, of course, you know... I am fired. I am fired. Fuck them mother fuckers. This and that. Reggie and I had that type of relationship. But, yeah, I told Reggie about two, three months before the shooting, I said to him, I said, Reggie, what is going on? I said, you know, (inaudible), you two are acting like some goddamn gang member, you know. So I said to him, you know, what is going on? 'You know, Suge has just got me doing all of these things.' Never would say what Suge had him doing. But I knew based upon the money Reggie was doling out, making 50,000, 80,000 this month, this and that. And I knew at that time just based upon Reggie had money all of a sudden, Reggie has about four or five apartment buildings

now and some other things. So. I knew at that time, of course, he was still tied in, but whether or not Suge had him money laundering, or out here actually setting up hits.

MR. HACKIE: Reggie has a good rapport in a sense with the Bloods and the Crips out in Compton, because they basically, you know, Reggie was the type of cop, there was rumor control at one time he was out here shaking the deals upside down taking the money and not booking them. I don't know if you remember Berrell (phonetic) and McDonald, the night they were killed. Okay. That answered that right there. McDonald, the kid had nothing to do with his reserve, he just got crap and he got caught in something. Berrell and Reggie used to be notorious for that. Pulling over the deal, shaking them up, taking whatever loose change they had, send them on their way. That was suspected originally that night, based upon the fact that night we had four or five drive-by shootings in Fruit Town that particular night with the red pickup truck.

So, I mean, all policemen going on quote, unquote, unofficial code 6 traffic stops without calling in. Based upon that night, you know, you have I had four or five drive-by shootings in a four or five-hour span, you pull over a truck which you have every reason to believe is the suspect vehicle; you are going to call off. Now, it has been rumored again that, of course, Berrell knew this guy. This is one of the guys they were shaking up. Taking his money for a long period of time.

And Reggie was in the same boat. Reggie,

Neckbone—Alton McDonald is Buntry. Neckbone's real name is Arthur—I can't think of his fucking name… Arthur something. He was popped over here on Beverly Hills Drive and no CDO, pulled up in a car. Neckbone's eye is all fucked up from Reggie. That happened in on-duty incident back in '91 or,'92, Reggie pulled him over supposedly…"

Hackie Los Angeles Police Interview III and IV

During this interview, LAPD Detective Miller stated to Hackie that Reggie Wright, Junior, controlled the dope trafficking in Compton, California and Wright's father, Reggie Wright, Sr., who served on the Compton Police Department, was concealing his son's involvement with the street crimes and that he believed that Reggie Wright, Junior, was calling the shots and having people murdered over drug transactions.

Approximately one month before this interview, LAPD Detective Miller had conducted a search of Death Row Records corporate offices and Wright Junior's home. Miller said: "Kevin, Reggie would possibly trust you" Hackie told Miller "I will bring the killer of Wallace to the door step of Parker Center. Have the DA dismiss the case."

Miller replied to Hackie as follows:

"Kevin, how is this going to look? An ex-has-been cop solving one of the most notorious killings in the City of Los Angeles. We can't have that. Look, help me with Reggie and I will help you."

Hackie asked Miller what was important: to bring in the killer of Wallace or to arrest Reggie Wright, Junior, which Miller only had hearsay evidence, at best. Hackie told Miller that Hackie believed Miller's motivation to arrest Wright Junior was personal. Miller replied that he would get Wright with or without Hackie's help. Hackie told Miller that his sole concern was obtaining the overturn and vacation of the conviction and having the case dismissed. Hackie also told Miller to talk with Hodgeman the next day so, the matter could be wrapped up, and Miller affirmed that he would call Hodgeman.

Approximately one week went by and Kevin did not receive any further contact or word from Miller.

Next, Hackie receives a call from Frank Alexander, who was present when Tupac Shakur was murdered in Las Vegas, Nevada. Alexander specifically told Hackie:

"The FBI Long Beach Office just interviewed me about Suge again. They also mentioned LAPD Detective Miller stated that you're trying to cut a deal for yourself."

Hackie then asked Alexander to specifically identify the FBI agents he spoke with about this matter. He declined to identify them, and that was the last time we spoke.

Hackie immediately contacted Miller and asked what was he doing talking to the FBI, and he replied they were lying. Hackie asked Miller if he wanted the murderer of Wallace or not, and he replied that he would call in a couple of days. That was the last time Hackie spoke with Miller

These several interviews lasted approximately 1 hour. Hackie made it explicitly clear at this interview that the information related had to remain and be maintained in absolute confidentiality. Hackie specifically said those words prefatory to each and every individual tape-recorded interview and a playing of each tape will reveal my voice and words to that effect

Hackie Los Angeles Police Interview V: December 9, 1999

Hackie provided the fifth interview on December 9, 1999. This interview lasted approximately five to ten minutes over the telephone. Hackie met with two LAPD detectives from Internal Affairs in his office regarding a complaint that he filed about his concerns that Poole had given the details of his confidential interview to the Los Angeles Times. The detective recorded this interview. A Caucasian female sergeant and a Hispanic detective sergeant stated that they had come from Burbank, California. Hackie repeated how he had consistently cooperated with the LAPD only because he was assured absolute confidentiality of the interviews and assured that that neither Hackie nor his family would be in danger. Hackie asked the detectives how Poole could give this information to the Los Angeles Times. He reiterated his promise to Miller that he would physically bring in the killer of Wallace to the Parker Center doorsteps, in exchange for a dismissal of the weapons case.

One of the detectives told Hackie that she would have LAPD

Detectives Katz and Martin meet with him, and she would meet with Hackie separate from that regarding his complaint. As of this day, Hackie never heard again from the detective.

Hackie Los Angeles Police Interview VI: January 15, 2000

Hackie provided the sixth interview on January 15, 2000. He received a telephone call from LAPD Detective Gregory Grant at his office and wanted to speak with Hackie regarding LAPD Officer David Mack and the Bank of America bank robbery. Grant told Hackie that the interview was being recorded. Grant told Hackie that he was from the LAPD "Rampart Task Force."

Hackie told Grant that he had previously been interviewed by the FBI, and if Grant wanted to talk with Hackie to contact Howard Price, Esq. Hackie made it explicitly clear on this phone call that the conversation and its details had to remain and be maintained in absolute confidentiality. Hackie again said those words prefatory to each and every individual tape-recorded interview and said, "A playing of each tape will reveal my voice and words to that effect."

Hackie Los Angeles Police Interview VII: Late January, 2000

Hackie provided the seventh interview in late January 2000 for one and a half hours (1,5 hours) with LAPD Detectives Katz and Martin at his office and discussed the Wallace murder. Hackie yet again—for at least the fifth time—reaffirmed that Hackie could resolve the Wallace murder but that Hackie wanted the weapons case dismissed, and the conviction overturned and vacated. This interview was tape recorded by the detectives. The detectives tried to elicit responses from Hackie about the Wallace murder, but getting increasingly tired of the one-way relationship Hackie reiterated the consistent demand for the weapons case's dismissal.

The detectives left, stating that they were not like Poole because they would keep information confidential and that they would contact Hackie again. To this day, Katz and Martin never contacted Hackie again.

Hackie Los Angeles Police Interview VIII: June 6, 2000

Hackie provided the eighth interview on June 6, 2000 while incarcerated at the Baker Community Corrections for the later-to-be-overturned weapons charge that was pending against him. LAPD Detectives interviewed him about the identity of the Wallace murderer. These detectives came to the facility the same day Hackie received a June 2000 LAPD Confidential Report from Charles Rappley, an investigative reporter for the LA Weekly. Stunned and surprised at yet another in what would become a long list of leaks, Hackie did not understand how Rappley obtained this LAPD document, which was supposed to be held in absolute confidence

Again, the detectives stressed that the interview would remain confidential. There were approximately four (4) taped telephone conversation interviews at that facility. During the course of one of these interviews, LAPD Detective Grant stated that he had been in contact with LA County District Attorney that had handled the state court action, and Grant told your declarant that based upon that contact, Hackie would be released within one week. That representation was specifically stressed by Grant to Hackie. Baker facility even assigned Parole Agent Beavour and California Department of Corrections Lt. Lewis to this matter because they were told the same.

In this two (2) hour interview, detectives asked if Hackie would wear a wire (a hidden transmitter for recording conversations) for investigative purposes of ascertaining where the stolen Bank of America proceeds were located. Hackie agreed to this.

The day after this interview, Detective Grant called and spoke to Hackie. Grant again assured Hackie he had talked with the District Attorney's Office regarding the weapons case dismissal and that within one week Hackie would be released. Instead Hackie was transferred to protective custody at Chino, California; no release was granted.

In spite of the recorded misrepresentations by the LAPD, Hackie still provided a ninth (9th) ninety (90) minute tape recorded interview on May 16, 2009. Two LAPD officers contacted Hackie to testify at a Board of Rights hearing for officers being disciplined by Perez allegations.

"The officers contacted Agent Behar of the F.B.I. to speak with your declarant." Hackie told Behar that LAPD had not kept its word as to what it assured it would do. Hackie also told him that the LAPD had dishonored its word of confidentiality and that Hackie had no confidence or reason to cooperate.

Hackie also told the two officers that the Wallace murder could have been resolved over 2½ years before had the LAPD been good at its word. Agent Behar also discussed with Hackie, Reggie Wright Junior, Death Row Records, and Suge Knight.

Kevin Hackie, like RJ Bond so many years later, had no reason at any time to doubt or question the veracity or truthfulness of the representations made by the LAPD officers when giving the tape recorded interviews. He reasonably believed that the factual information he provided would be maintained in absolute confidence. There was no question the LAPD had disclosed information to a variety of sources, or to one source who then told many sources. Eventually the second scenario was found invalid when confidential materials showed up in magazines and newspapers. Information was "leaked" (or more plainly stated—given) to Randall Sullivan, Peter Boyer, Rolling Stone, and the New Yorker. Only the LAPD and the City of Los Angeles could have disclosed that information because it is derived from the very individual taped interview sessions that Hackie provided to them as a result of their serial interrogations.

Hackie's Conviction Overturned, 2001

By 2001, Kevin Hackie's case was overturned with no help whatsoever from the Los Angeles Police Department or any other law enforcement agency. In fact he sued the city of Los Angeles and the detectives who he believed leaked the information. The case later settled.

Hackie was in no mood to cooperate when the Christopher Wallace family came knocking:

"And you know quite frankly I didn't want to be involved in that situation any more. That's where it came about with the informant (accusations), because they had all the documentation of course from the LAPD and privy of course to the tapes, because the tapes they finally had to handover the tapes to me obviously from a federal lawsuit in 2001. I don't know if you are familiar with the Wallace case and my case; Judge Florence Cooper is the same judge in both cases. She was the judge in my city case which settled out."—Hackie to AllHipHop. com, October 27, 2009

Hackie still maintains possession of the original taped interviews, and the allegations he makes in those interviews do not substantially change, and we have not seen evidence at press time to refute his consistency.

Letter to Agent Phil Carson, FBI, April 15, 2004: "It has become apparent that one of the of manners in which the LAPD has covered facts and circumstances relating to this murder is to refuse to conduct substantial investigation that may lead to proof of criminal conduct on the part of the Los Angeles Police Department officers. In this regard Los Angeles Police Department interviewed Kevin H shortly after the murder of Christopher Wallace. Mr. Hackie claimed to have substantial information of assistance to the case and offered to provide this information to the Los Angeles Police Department. The Los Angeles Police Department chose not to deal with Mr. Hackie, and the information he possesses regarding this murder has never come to light."

Then to help the Wallace case, on June 6, 2004, Hackie filed a declaration that he had "personal knowledge" that persons within Death Row Records offered $25,000 to a law enforcement officer to kill Wallace. He said it was "well known within Death Row" that Mack and other LAPD officers worked as "covert agents" for the rap record label. Hackie stated in the document that he had personally observed Mack at the 1995 Black Image Awards, a 1996 boxing match in Las Vegas and "numerous Death Row functions" that were reserved for Knight's close associates.

Hackie Stops Talking

Then seemingly inexplicably, Hackie came down with Death Row Derangement Syndrome.

"I will be in court to testify, but it is a matter of record that I am stressed out and have been on medication for the past five years," Hackie said during an extensive interview conducted in the presence of his attorney, Joseph L. Pittera of Torrance.

"My memory is bad. I'm going to answer questions to the best of my knowledge, what I remember. But this whole thing has put me over the edge. I am so stressed. I probably won't even remember our conversation tomorrow."

At the courthouse, Hackie said the Wallace family legal team had "altered" his statements before placing them in the declaration.

"My statements were taken out of context," Hackie said.

"Some things in there I never even said. They added them in. As far as David Mack attending private Death Row parties, I never said that. All I said was I saw him at some functions."

"I received about five or six different declarations to look over," Hackie said. "I signed off on it one day when (one of the Wallace family lawyers) said it was imperative that it be signed. The fact is, I skimmed through the papers, but I didn't really read it. I just signed it."

Though frustrated, the Wallace family and its attorneys were well versed in witnesses who get a sudden onset of Death Row Derangement Syndrome.

"Mr. Hackie and his counsel have recently expressed extreme fear and reluctance to voluntarily participate," said attorney Perry Sanders. "An earlier motion that we filed on his behalf to preserve his testimony because he was afraid was fought by the city, and the court denied it being taken. Now here we are on the eve of trial and it's no wonder he attempts to distance himself from statements he made long before a lawsuit was ever filed."

In other words, as in the previous 10 interview attempts, all Hackie wanted to do was keep his testimony sealed or confidential because witnesses around Death Row tended to have issues with—as Benjamin Ogletree stated—"their limbs and body parts functioning." Sanders went to the Court and the Court, defending their actions, treated Hackie with the same disrespect as the Los Angeles Police.

PART EIGHT:
THE TRUTH
STILL EXISTS

The entire story of the Shakur and Wallace cases is a rogue's gallery of liars, thieves, and profiteers. It didn't matter if you were crook or cop—red or blue— "good guy" or "bad guy," the lines of personal ethics and honesty have been redefined throughout this investigation. And after examining the truths relating to the shootings and the Five Element Kenner Alchemy, which heavily depended on the destruction of human credibility, there begs the obvious question of "what's left?" "Is there anyone who might be credible enough to have made it through the gauntlet of the Kingdom of Death Row? The good news is that the truth still exists and there are stones that have not been turned over, and other stones that need to be turned a second time.

Why shouldn't we re-examine each and every person that was disparaged and criticized by Philips from 1994 until 2008? The L.A. Times terminated Philips over one incident, but it was hardly the first incident they knew about. Even if the Times did not know about Philips' undue influence and coercion of witnesses and his tendency to make news and not report it, they knew about it when Philips produced bad information about Waymond Anderson, and were doubly aware of it by the time Waymond Anderson turned on Philips and claimed that (surprise) Philips was trying to coerce and influence a witness. Why should we NOT examine the testimony of people who Philips claimed, often via some vague and unnamed source, were "not credible?"

Philips sloppy journalism would soon catch up with him. On April 7, 2008 "Times Retracts Shakur Story" appears in the LA Times. The article states:

> "The article, titled 'An Attack on Tupac Shakur Launched a Hip-Hop War' and written by Times staff writer Chuck Philips, purported to relate "new" information about a 1994 assault on rap star Tupac Shakur, including a description of events contained in FBI reports.
>
> "The Times has since concluded that the FBI reports were fabricated and that some of the other sources relied on—including the person Philips previously believed to be the 'confidential source' cited in the FBI reports—do not support major elements in the story.
>
> "Consequently, The Times is retracting the March 17 Web publications as well as a shorter version of the article that ap-

peared on Page E1 in the March 19 Calendar section of the newspaper. Statements that Philips made in two online chats, on March 18 and 25, and on The Times' Soundboard blog on March 21 are also being retracted."

Philips is later laid off from the newspaper quietly. From Wikipedia we read, "Philips believes the retraction has ruined his reputation and career."

In an interview done for a documentary about Tupac's life, several of his closest friends recounted the injuries that Shakur had in the 1994 shooting, and how they knew that Shakur's injuries were largely self-inflicted and not at the hand of another, and that the injury came from an unsafe and immature handling of a dangerous firearm, sticking it down his pants loaded and cocked.

The words they expressed in unison were a regret about knowing the truth and not publicly sharing it—or worse—allowing false accounts of the injuries to get out. Because the story, once unleashed, became bigger than it should have been and lead to conclusions and myths that were untrue; myths that lead to a bigger rivalry and what came next. They all spoke of that regret as the one thing they were sorry for—above all.

It is a fact that there are still people who know the truth and are still willing to allow a lie to continue in spite of its toll. And what if we could simply "invite back" those who were provably slighted by Philips and Death Row, and allow them and their testimony a "second look." Would it be any different than it is now? Kading and his ilk would have the public stick to the old stigmas and disparagements, truthful or not. Kading says that Boagni was "discredited" but never explains how or why. Same is true for Mario Hammonds and Kevin Hackie. But without evidence to support discrediting the testimony of a witness, then is the witness not still credible?

CREDIBLE WITNESSES STILL EXIST

The Los Angeles Police Department would prefer not to discuss Kenneth Boagni. The Los Angeles Police Department would prefer not to discuss Mario Hammonds. They would also prefer to not discuss

Kevin Hackie. In fact, the Los Angeles Police Department took great pains to keep the testimony of these men hidden.

In the case of Kevin Hackie, the City of Los Angeles argued in Court against protecting Kevin Hackies' identity. A department that was using (and heavily relied on) confidential informants, and who tried at all costs to keep those names and the clues they provided, "open clues," from being revealed, was arguing to NOT protect the identity of a man who had, in at least nine previous occasions, gladly and at personal cost, tried to help the LAPD get to the bottom of both Killings.

There would have been no reason to do more than one or two interviews to know that Hackie was not credible, but in a pattern of behavior that continued for years, the LAPD without hesitation was unafraid to call back this "not credible" witness and solicit new information or clarification on old information. Arguing to the Court that Hackie's privacy and safety were irrelevant had to be the ultimate slap in the face!

In the end, the city's arguments against Hackie were nothing more than "sour grapes" for Hackie's lawsuit against the city—they were unwilling to forgive, and a need to punish Hackie for his suit was all the City of Los Angeles needed to unnecessarily hang Hackie out to dry. With the stigma against Hackie, Hackie's otherwise explosive testimony would be simply a footnote—except to the LAPD it was fatal.

The same can be said about the testimony and credibility of Kenneth Boagni. He was also treated the same way by the police, as far as access and multiple interviews, but the reason that Boagni's involvement with the LAPD was something the City of Los Angeles didn't want the public to know about is because in eight different official City hearings that dealt with police officer terminations, the City of Los Angeles found Boagni's testimony credible enough to acquit 8 innocent Los Angeles Police Officers of any wrongdoing.

So what killed Boagni's credibility? Nothing really. Boagni is every bit as consistent as he's ever been and there is no reason the LAPD cannot use his testimony to indict Perez or Mack.

Mario Hammonds is another name that gets beat up in the wake of Waymond Anderson. Like Boagni, it is interesting that the "Murder Rap" detectives ever admitted that Hammond's "credible" testimony was also used by the LAPD to get out of hot water. Notations on the Boagni evidence demonstrated that at least nine of LAPD Detective Katz's superiors going up to the rank of assistant chief—were aware of Boagni's existence and relevance. They were too blinded by Waymond Anderson's lies about Hammonds and Boagni to ask.

Waymond Anderson was "committing demonstrable perjury"—that is, clearly lying—when he accused the Wallace family; its lead attorney, Perry R. Sanders Junior; and several other individuals of witness tampering in connection with their wrongful death lawsuit against the City of Los Angeles.

In a 20-plus-page motion, the Wallace estate asked for access to Waymond Anderson's phone and prison-visitation records for the last ten years, arguing that these records will reveal who and what was behind Waymond Anderson's "wholesale assault on the truth"—and in the process "shed light" on who was responsible for Wallace's still unsolved murder.

Waymond Anderson made what the motion calls his "outrageous under-oath allegations" in an August 20, 2007, deposition in which he unexpectedly recanted previous statements he had made to Los Angeles Police Department investigators long before the Wallace estate sued the city. His prior statements implicated former LAPD officers Rafael Perez and David Mack in Wallace's murder. Waymond Anderson also claimed in the deposition that he and a fellow inmate Boagni, who was serving time with him at Corcoran state prison personally participated in conversations with Perry Sanders and LAPD officers Russell Poole and Ya-May Christle, in which they, supposedly, conspired to falsely implicate LAPD officers in the murder.

The court documents include certified prison records that prove none of this could possibly be true since the only time Anderson and Bogani were at Corcoran together—and thus could have had such conversations—was between Feb 27 and June 20, 2001. During that time period, none of the people Anderson accused of being part of the "scam" had anything to do with the Wallace case.

Indeed, as the official court record shows, there was no Wallace lawsuit during this time period and the estate had not even hired an attorney. Perry Sanders wasn't hired by the Wallace family until July 2001, and the estate's civil suit was not filed until 2002. Moreover, Officer Poole had retired in 1999 and Officer Christle didn't start working on the Wallace case until 2005.

Waymond Anderson also testified in the August 20th deposition that he witnessed Bogani and another inmate, Mario Hammonds, conspiring at Corcoran to make up stories tying Perez, Mack, and former Death Row Records CEO Suge Knight to the murder. Time-dated documents and statements attached to the Wallace family filings belie this claim, since they show that both Boagni and Hammonds gave such statements to the LAPD long before Feb 27, 2001, the earliest Waymond Anderson could have witnessed such a conspiracy.

In short, none of the individuals named by Waymond Anderson was in a position to do what he claims they did at the time he claims they did it. As the filing notes, "Although it is typically difficult to prove a negative, Anderson provided an empirical time line that allows Plaintiffs to do so." The filing also makes a case for third-party involvement in Waymond Anderson's "wholesale" perjury.

> "It seems clear that Anderson's outrageous under-oath allegations about innocent people were intended to intimidate the victims of his perjury and to attempt to provide a defamation-proof vehicle for wide dissemination of lies in the media in a way so as to negatively affect public sentiment and the jury pool. Anderson alone had no such obvious motive, which... indicates third-party involvement."

> "The things Plaintiffs and Plaintiffs' counsel have had to endure in this litigation go beyond the pale of what anyone engaged in civil litigation should have to endure while availing themselves of their constitutional rights of access to a Federal Court."

As to Hammonds, he possessed two (2) sworn affidavits from California Police Officers, confirming that Hammonds worked with the FBI. With Hackie, Assistant US Attorney Cheng who forbade Hackie's attorneys from discussing Hackie's "work for the FBI and ATF" in Court, cited Federal Secrets protection. With Hammonds, the government's assistant US Attorney Leticia Kim in a letter dated November 2006, refused to allow testimony of Hammonds' credibility in his work with the FBI, citing confidentiality of investigations. If this sounds familiar, it is. Hackie had the same resistance from the US Attorney, who forbade Hackie from discussing his work with the FBI or ATF. Hammonds also had a signed letter from a US Secret Service Agent who vouched for his credibility.

According to a 2011 Rolling Stone Magazine article written by Randall Sullivan, the author of the book LAbyrinth, "LAPD representatives clearly recognized how damaging Hammonds' testimony could be to them: like Boagni, they had not only withheld tapes and materials generated by his interviews with the police during their initial surrender of evidence in the case, but had blacked out his name in documents as well. Police officials relented only after Sanders and Alexander discovered an obscure reference to the man and threatened a court order, persuading the LAPD to turn over everything in its possession that mentioned Hammonds.

"This resulted in the production of documents that revealed the biggest problem for the LAPD; The department itself had vouched for Hammonds' integrity when it used his statements to obtain search warrants in its investigations of Knight. During his interrogation by the city's attorneys, Hammonds put it this way: 'I am an honest individual. Even though I'm a criminal, I do not lie. My credibility... must be good, because I've made a livelihood out of this. People are in prison... locked up from some of the information that I have contributed to government agencies.'"

"The LAPD has to be asking themselves how they're going to call him a liar now," Sanders says, "when they've already called him a credible witness. I can't wait to see how the L.A. Times tries to spin this one for them."

CREDIBLE JOURNALISTS STILL EXIST

According to Daily Variety, there is a journalist named Chris Blatchford. Blatchford is a 'highly lauded' investigative reporter from KTTV Fox 11 in the Los Angeles area. Blatchford became an L.A. household name that came into the living rooms of "Los Angelinos" when television consisted only of three networks and a few local television stations. The terms "local" and Los Angeles seem opposing—with close to 10 million people spread over 175 square miles of California, Blatchford had a wide canvass from which to gather stories.

So what does he do? He selects the Inglewood/Hawthorne/Compton area and becomes a mainstay investigative journalist there. He reported almost nightly from a location that eventually turned from a "white only" area to a war zone, infested with crime and gang activity. But fearless through it all, Blatchford stayed in the area and was well acquainted with many of the "O.G.'s" and shot callers from the old school gangs. He was also watched more than a fair share of them, die, victims to the way of life the area promoted.

Through it all, Blatchford is known in the community for his pragmatism, no-nonsense talk, and the gift of discernment when it came to the games on the street. Most of all, however, Blatchford enjoyed for many years the respect of the residents in the area, who felt that at worst case, one would get a "fair shake" with Blatchford.

Blatchford was friends with and knew many of the parents of the Knights of the Kingdom of Thieves, who were themselves upstanding people. He watched many parents face the reality that no parent desires; to outlive their children. He has interviewed The Red King and many others in the Kingdom.

On a larger scale, Blatchford won a Peabody Award for investigative journalism for his investigation into Mafia infiltration of MCA/Universal's music and home video divisions. As a journalist he has uncovered fraud and abuses in welfare, food stamps, and aerospace. But he is widely known for his exposes on street gangs, prison gangs, and organized crime. He is the recipient of 9 Emmy awards, 49 Emmy nominations, 14 RTNDA Golden Mikes, 2 Edward R. Murrow Awards, 9 Regional Associated Press awards, 10 Los Angeles Press Club awards and numerous other honors.

In 2009, he released "The Black Hand: The Story of Rene 'Boxer' Enriquez and His Life in the Mexican Mafia." The book is an intense look at the inner workings of the Mexican Mafia—the most powerful gang in America and one of the most brutal and ruthless criminal organizations in the world.

Unlike Philips, who lists no other claims like it, from Blatchford's bio on the Fox News website, "He has been a keynote speaker for: National Major Gang Task Force, International Latino Gang Investigators Association, International Outlaw Motorcycle Investigators Association, California Gang Task Force, Central Coast Gang Investigators Association, Oklahoma Gang Investigators Association, Colorado S.T.I.N.G., Arizona State Gang Task Force, New Mexico Gang Task Force, Los Angeles County Bureau of Investigation, Orange County Gang Investigators Association, San Diego County Gang Investigators Association, San Mateo County Gang Investigators Association,

Southern California Gang Conference, California Youth Authority Training Academy, Know Gangs, and the Heartland Law Enforcement Training Institute. He is a frequent panelist on gang issues, including several sponsored by the U.S. Department of Justice."

Sometime in 1998, a confidential informant Robert Soria who was outed by Internet Anarchist Anthony Battaglia, approached Blatchford, whom he had worked with in the past, and told him that he had information about "who killed Tupac" and offered to solve the mystery. Soria's previous confidential information was a fact that adds to the long list of things that "Murder Rap" Detective Kading and Battaglia did not know (or bother to find out).

Soria provided reliable information on several criminal related events for Blatchford before Shakur was killed. Most notable was information Soria provided about one of Soria's criminal associates, who was planning to burglarize the California Highway Patrol Museum in Sacramento. Soria gave the detailed plan to Blatchford, including date and time. Soria agreed to wear a wire during the heist and stated he would be a witness in the case. Blatchford notified the CHP and gave them the details. Law Enforcement deployed on the museum and arrested the suspects. Soria subsequently became a witness. In the end the suspect pled guilty and received a ten-year prison sentence. Soria trusted Blatchford and subsequently wanted to give Blatchford this information.

Internet Anarchist Anthony Battaglia, outed Danny Patton aka "White Boy" a man that lived next door to Robert Soria, aka "X-Con." Patton was identified in the 1996 Tim Brennan Search Warrant Affidavit as having Leuders' Park Bloods membership and the moniker of "White Boy." According to Soria, one of the shooters, (a man also "outted" by Battaglia) Malcolm Patton, is the brother of Danny Patton. Malcom Patton feared for his life as there was a steady stream of dead bodies that were turning up with ties to the Shakur/Wallace killings in the year prior. Patton cited this as his reason to come forward with information about how he had participated in the murder.

To get Blatchford to invest in this crazy claim, Soria not only advised Blatchford that he possessed a tape with Danny Patton confessing the killing, but actually played the tape for Blatchford, who had difficulty hearing it over the phone because of its poor recording quality. So Soria put a man on the phone who claimed to be Malcolm

Patton.

Blatchford interviewed Malcolm Patton while on the line. It is clear from the conversation that Patton repeated all of Soria's claims to Blatchford. A good investigative reporter covering the Los Angeles area, one could only hope to have a penny for every crackpot who called or wrote to Fox-TV and Blatchford claiming to have killed Shakur themselves, or knew someone who did. Crazy leads like this were not unknown; police had heard that Oprah Winfrey, popular television hostess, was a shooter. Obviously there is no evidence to indicate anything of the sort, and the claim is nonsense, but a television reporter has to have about "heard it all."

The point of this, is that Blatchford would have to put the "screws" to Patton, not only to validate his identity, but his story as well. There are only so many hours in the day and a veteran reporter like Blatchford knows how to cut through the bullshit with laser-like accuracy in moments. So Malcolm had to be good enough to captivate Blatchford, but also get the reporter to agree to assemble a camera and sound crew, and do a formalized interview.

From Chris Blatchford's interviews, he received additional information to corroborate the letter and confirm that those confessing to the murder were the actual shooters. The following is Blatchford's statement sent to Russell Poole:

"May 1998, a Five-Deuce Hoover Crip that I know came to me saying he knew who killed Tupac Shakur. He told me that Sharitha Knight and Reggie Wright were behind the murder.

"CI says at first there was a get together in Balboa Park in the San Fernando Valley for different gangs. This was disguised as a Blood/Crips truce meeting. But it was really a feeler for Wright to see how much it would take to get Tupac hit. Wright wanted rights to all Tupac's material.

"He says it was Wright who—on the night of Tupac's murder—told the killers where Tupac would be, along with Suge. Those not in on the plan that night were sent to the 662 Club in Las Vegas.

"There were 3 hitmen hired to do the job: Gregory Harris Smith aka "Lil Half Dead" (dob 11-28-79), Malcolm Shabbaz Patton (dob 1972), and Danny Eugene Patton aka "Whiteboy" (dob 1974).

"The CI lived next door to Danny Patton in Reseda and did some construction work with him. CI says Danny Patton told him, "I shot that Tupac motherfucker. I was there man!" He had a tape recording of the conversation but I couldn't understand a word of it because of the bad quality of the tape.

"In early June 1998, the CI told me that Malcolm Patton was "tired of hiding it" and believed he was about to get hit. So, he wanted to turn himself in and tell the whole story. I talked to Malcolm on the telephone and we set up a meeting. He said he would bring one of the murder weapons, and wanted to do an on camera interview to protect himself.

"June 5, 1998 I showed up for the meeting and was given a hand-written letter (this was written by the CI's sister who transcribed what Malcolm told her). The letter claimed Lil Half Dead was upset with Tupac because Tupac stole one of his songs, "Brenda's Got a Baby." Lil Half Dead was beaten down by some Tupac soldiers while in Las Vegas. The letter also said, Wright had a meeting with gangsters and put a bounty on Tupac's head. Malcolm said he was the shooter that was supposed to take out Suge Knight. Lil Half Dead was supposed to kill Tupac. It quoted Malcolm as saying, "i can call you on a safe number and give you details of clothing, cars, streets, and describe anything you need to know to prove that I was there, and the night 2 pac tryed to escape, like a little pee-on bitch." The letter also said that Malcolm would drop off one of the murder weapons at KTTV studios.

"Malcolm never showed for the Reseda meeting, but when I returned to the station, security told me a young black man had tried to drop off a package for me at the guard shack. Company policy prohibited them from accepting it. I never heard from Malcolm again.

"The CI also told me that Danny was paid 100-thousand dollars for the hit in the form of a cashier's check. Danny signed the check. The CI said the hit team trio had rented a pearl white Cadillac at the Stratosphere Hotel Las Vegas and later dumped it at a salvage yard in Baker, disassembled. Three guns were used: tech 9, .45, and a Glock. Danny's gun jammed. Malcolm shot twice and missed his target. He also said "Neckbone" would be killed later because he knew the identity of the shooters. Neckbone was, in fact, killed at a later date.

"CI said that Danny Patton's mother, who worked as a drug counselor in the Valley, was "scared to go against him." Malcolm, at the time, was recently released from prison.

"A year or so later, CI told me Danny Patton wanted to meet with me. Subsequently, he and the CI did come to the station and talked with me for about a half-hour. The Tupac murder was never mentioned. CI later told me that Danny just wanted to feel me out.

Lil Half Dead is already doing life for another murder."

"I have mad respect for Chuck Philips."
—Greg Kading, July 2013 Interview

Of course from the moment that Blatchford's statement was leaked by the Los Angeles Police Department in June of 2014 The Red Knight/Kading machine tried futilely to conjure the Kenner Alchemy on Blatchford, as if summoning the ghost of Philips to derail the Patton Confession and Blatchford statement. Unlike the work of Philips, who would not have been caught in the act except for the existence of Alexander's tapes, and the work of outlets like "The Smoking Gun," Kading was foolish enough to put his coercion in writing.

On Friday, August 01, 2014 at 6:34 a.m. Kading contacted Blatchford via email and tried to explain to Blatchford what Poole and Bond were doing with their book- before it comes out!

"Greetings Chris. I'm sorry we haven't been able to connect. I know you're quite busy and may be dealing with issues of much higher priority. I hope things are well with you and your family. If I'm being a pest, I certainly apologize.

"Here's the dilemma I'm trying to resolve: As you might know, I've spoken to Dan Leighton and Heidi Siegmund-Cuda (briefly) in regards to a 1998 confession letter you'd received from a Hoover Crip gang member. Some of what was discussed in the letter made it into the Las Vegas police files I had access to while investigating Tupac and Biggies murders. Jointly, an informant (don't know if its the same source you had) was providing parallel information to the Feds who were conducting a RICO investigation into Death Row Records in the late 1990's. I also had access to these files.

"Although most of the information in the confession letter was easily refutable, I conducted a follow-up investigation into the allegations and claims. I've interviewed all of the parties who are alleged to be involved in the conspiracy to kill Tupac (according to the letter) to see if I'd missed anything.

"I suspect you drew the same conclusions back in 1998 and 1999, at least that was my impression after speaking with Dan, who regarded the letter as "nonsense." Unfortunately, however, there were a couple questions Dan could not answer and he deferred to you ("Chris has an amazing memory and keeps copious notes on everything").

"Currently, there is an effort by a retired LAPD Detective (Russell Poole) and conspiracy theorist RJ Bond, to exploit the letter and publicly accuse people (who are factually and demonstrably innocent) of murder. Those persons have every intention of pursuing defamation, slander, libel, and invasion of privacy claims should Poole and Bond's project ever see the light of day. RJ Bond has already begun marketing the project making allusions to the "reporter" who was the recipient of the letter. Trust me when I say this Chris, you'll want to be a safe distance from these folks when things go sideways.

"My role in the matter is quite simple. I've been engaged in the Tupac Shakur and Biggie Smalls fan community since the release of my book Murder Rap. I have a committed intent to provide the family, friends, and fans, with factual information about what took place in the murders of these two rappers. I take the responsibility seriously and believe we all bear a social responsibility to set history straight. Your body of work would indicate you feel the same. You've done enough gang related work to know firsthand what occurs when people are falsely accused, especially of something as nefarious as murder. Poole and Bond do not share these sentiments. In fact, they seem to revel in patching together baseless theories in order to create confusion, regardless of the toll it takes on people's lives. Much of what was provided to them in the confession letter has already been bastardized to fit their agenda.

"Chris—if any of this compels you, I'd love to talk and ask a few questions. If you don't have time, perhaps we can communicate via email. I was hoping you might be able to give me a brief explanation about how you'd come into possession of the letter and what your opinion of it was/is. I would be grateful and insure you the information will used responsibly."

In this email, Kading employs the same tactic Philips uses to try to solicit the witness to buy his story and turn Blatchford. The coercion is part sale and part threat, as Dan Leighton's name (a co-worker) and Heidi Cuda's name (another co-worker and co-author of Frank Alexander's book "Got Your Back") are both mentioned by reference as part of Kading's vague information.

Unknown to Kading, Blatchford was in communication with Poole, who was known for managing his witnesses, and Poole was watching Kading like a hawk. He took it very personally when the LAPD leaked the confession letter, and more so when he found out that two years earlier there had been another leak that jeopardized RJ Bond.

Having made his appeal, and hearing nothing from Blatchford, Kading made a second attempt to "turn" Blatchford, On Sunday, August 17, 2014 at 3:49 P.M. Kading again attempted to solicit Blatchford:

"Chris—I hope this note finds you and your family well. Unfortunately, we've been unable to connect and discuss the "letter" Russell Poole, and his associate RJ Bond, intend to exploit to accuse innocent people of murder. I understand it is hardly of your concern, but since the letter was first given to you, you're inextricably bound to the matter, unfortunately.

"I suspect both Poole and Bond are ignorant of the actual source of the letter. I suspect they have no idea the producer of the letter was/is a clinically diagnosed paranoid schizophrenic child molester. To be fair, he didn't turn his attention to children until after you'd been dealing with him, however, his ticket onto the crazy train had been stamped long before 1998.

"I, along with others, have done our due diligence. We have factually and irrefutably disproven the claims the source had conjured up. It is our intention to publicly address the matter prior to the release of Poole and Bonds book, "Tupac:187" in September. The persons listed as conspirators in the letter, including "lil half-dead," intend to bring suit against any and all parties involved in the publication.

"I am reaching out to you as a matter of professional courtesy. I am a fan of your investigative work and wouldn't want to see your good name and reputation attached to the reckless and irresponsible actions of Poole, Bond, etc.

"In my opinion, it would behoove you to distance yourself from the letter and its source, as Dan Leighton did, calling it "nonsense" and "unsubstantiated." If you have a response, we would be happy to represent it."

Of course credible journalists are not swayed by these tactics, as they get them all the time. There are always people who would prefer their names stay out of the media, and after forty years, Blatchford had seen it all. Suggestive and non-objective, Kading attempted to get Blatchford to agree with a specific scenario favorable to Kading's Orlando Anderson/Keith Davos agenda, while disparaging Bond and Poole—not different than that fateful phone call from Philips to Frank Alexander where Philips tried to play Alexander against the Las Vegas Police, tantamount to witness tampering, Blatchford—the seasoned journalist who stood against the Mexican Mafia—is not taking the bait.

On Aug 18, 2014, at 10:35 AM, Chris Blatchford wrote:

"Thanks. But who are you referring to as a paranoid schizophrenic?"

Kading responded Monday, August 18, 2014 at 11:02 AM:

"Hi Chris—according to Danny Patton, he was with Robert Soria (he also went by "Roger" and half-a-dozen other alias') when they both came to meet you... Malcolm Patton was also interviewed about the whole letter ordeal... as was Gregory Harris Smith. Anyhow, Robert was diagnosed with paranoid schizophrenia and receiving SSI for his condition at the time. Robert and I are currently corresponding and I'm also communicating with his ex-wife regarding the subject.

"My objective here is to help the people who've been falsely accused in the letter from the public scrutiny, defamation, and libel being promoted by RJ Bond and Russell Poole. I was hoping to get your implicit support in that effort."

"Thank you for responding Chris—I've no doubt you got better things to do."

"I was hoping to get your implicit support."

Who does that sound like?

Earlier, Philips interference in the Pelicano case was discussed. Philips attempted to coerce a jailhouse informant that his testimony "could sink this case" for the prosecution, should he change his story to the one Philips proposed. Kading must have been reading the Philips playbook; he was similarly alleging that Blatchford's disavowal of the letter "could sink this case" for Bond and Poole—and the police who might investigate it.

So who cares? Who cares if Bond and Poole were turned into non-credible letter carriers? Why did Kading and Battaglia try so hard to "get in front of" a letter that they claimed was a fraud? The same reason the O.J. Simpson attacked the collection of the D.N.A. evidence and not the evidence itself. The Simpson defense knew that attacking the D.N.A. evidence was too hard for an unsophisticated jury to understand. It was easier (and more understandable) for them to attack the people who brought the D.N.A. evidence to light—the police and technicians, who are imperfect creatures.

Simply stated, the push was on to try to discredit Poole, Bond and Soria (the person who brought Patton to Blatchford) before the evidence itself was attacked and Patton was asked too many questions. And to a limited degree Battaglia was successful in painting an imprisoned Soria as a "clinically diagnosed paranoid schizophrenic" and fallaciously calling Soria "the source of the letter" publicly, to an unsophisticated audience. And for a time, the public swayed to his false arguments.

Apparently Battaglia didn't learn from Julian Assuage and Edward Snowden of the "WikiLeaks" and NSA scandals. Both are fugitives from their homes. Living abroad in fear for their personal safety, they are always looking over their shoulder for having stood on their shaky ethical ground, and not finding the broad-backed support they believed they might have, when they acted. Of course, neither he nor Kading were thinking rationally, as Kading persisted in pushing Blatchford. Blatchford, for his part was standing pat. In fact, obviously aware of these tactics, Blatchford's forty years of investigative bullshit detection started to sound an alarm about the agenda driven emails.

On Aug 18, 2014, at 11:10 AM, Chris Blatchford wrote:

"My question would be. How do you know anything about the Pattons or Soria?"

On Monday, August 18, 2014 at 12:29 P.M. Kading wrote:

"Fair question Chris. The impetus was the Las Vegas police files that I had access to dating back to the time the subject was being discussed by LVMPD. In addition, we had federal sources from the Leuders Park and Mob Piru gangs that affiliated with Suge Knight and Death Row."

What Blatchford didn't know, was that on July 7, 2014, in connection with Battaglia's release of the Patton Confession Letter, Kading had already publicly claimed his source to Makaveli-board.net fan board members—and it was different than what he was about to tell Blatchford. At 4:52 P.M. Kading wrote:

"This is just more of the same from the Bond camp. The information in the letter was brought to Las Vegas PD's attention in 1999... The problem is RJ and his troupe "think" this is all "new" information. Its not. All you have to do is read the 16 year old Las Vegas Investigation Report on the matter. It will be another rabbit trail to lead naive Tupac Fans down in hopes of making a few dollars. The only difference between this nonsense and the prior disproven theories is the lawsuit that will arise by those falsely accused."

Who was Kading's "federal source?" And what exactly is a "federal source?" Could that "federal source" have been The Red Knight? Was Kading inadvertently admitting then that The Red Knight was a DEA federal informant? "Affiliated with Suge Knight and Death Row" kind of narrows the field, because Hackie never mentioned any of it.

Remember that Kading already used his peripheral involvement with the Jerry Hawkins DEA probe to foist a redacted DEA document marked "case: Jerry Hawkins" about Duane Davis claiming it to be proof of all Kading claimed about Davis and his alleged confessions. Kading did the same thing with a redacted Las Vegas Metro Police document which the F.B.I. detailed a conversation in 1999 with Frank Alexander. In this conversation, Alexander claims that Cuda and Leighton approached the L.A. Times about a person attempting to bring a gun to the Fox TV station. NO mention of the Patton Confession letter was made, and it appears likely that it was the fourth handed conversation from Blatchford to Leighton about the last part of the Patton story—the attempt to deliver the gun—without any background.

It is critical to note that Blatchford never gave anyone the letter, and did not go into it with Leighton. Even if he did, the information was never passed to the Las Vegas Police, because often times the work of an investigative reporter exists in the absence of police work, and Blatchford made it clear in later interviews that he was holding onto the letter with little confidence it would be followed up on.

Blatchford had to have sensed the inane, conflicting claim at work. Kading states what he thinks about the (incorrect) source of the letter, claims it a fraud, then insults Blatchford by claiming that Blatchford knowingly gave the fraud letter to Bond and Poole.

What Kading was unaware of is that Chris Blatchford has never given the letter or the names of the Pattons to the Las Vegas Police to this day, according to Chris Blatchford.

Blatchford stated that he called the Las Vegas Police and asked about Little Half Dead, when they seemed disinterested Blatchford claims he pursued the matter with them no further.

It was clear Kading had a compulsion to want to tell a story, so Blatchford asked further.

On Aug 18, 2014, at 1:02 P.M., Chris Blatchford wrote:

"Or how would the feds have those names?"

Blatchford was incorrect about Kading's compulsion, because this question appeared to annoy Kading, who wrote Monday, August 18, 2014 at 2:02 P.M.:

"There were a variety of sources Chris... some of them anonymous and some of them known. Not sure how the obtainment of the information is relevant. What is relevant is that the information is being used without regard for the impact it has on personal lives. I have to assume you've seen the toll false accusations can take on a person's life, family, safety, etc. That is why I've been persistent in trying to contact you. If your preference is to avoid the matter, I'll respectfully refrain from contacting you further."

On or about August 18, 2014, the picture of the letter from the Shakur Document, along with other material, such as the statement from Chris Blatchford—outing the witness was posted online by Battaglia in a series of YouTube videos. ("Tupac 2014: The 'confession letter' and the white Cadillac.") The names of all the persons of interest and a majority of the information in Blatchford's account were now public. Worse, Kading claims he took the time to contact the suspects and warn them.

Blatchford was warned of the video and made his own complaint with the LAPD He tested to see if Kading had actually contacted Soria after calling him a "clinically diagnosed paranoid schizophrenic," the same claim Kading made about Waymond Anderson and the same claim Reggie Wright Junior made about Bond in an August 2014 interview.

On Aug 19, 2014, at 10:27 AM, Chris Blatchford wrote to Kading:

"Do you have contact information for Robert?"

That same day, at 12:08 P.M., Kading responded to Blatchford. It is easy to see the tenor of the note change to terse, because now that the information in Patton's confession letter was out and quickly losing traction (they found out their reach is extremely limited), there was nothing to leverage Blatchford's assistance.

Kading wrote:

"Good morning Chris. I believe I saved the envelopes from his letters which have the return address. Unfortunately, I'm not at home. I expect a call from Robert and I'll ask his permission to forward his info. He asked me to respect his predicament (protective custody status due to the nature of his crimes). I seem to be on the receiving end of your questions, but can't get you to acknowledge mine. You're welcome to call me anytime, but our correspondence must be mutually responsive."

Blatchford had no further interest in contacting Kading. He knew what was happening and as a credible journalist, Blatchford did not discuss or exchange a lengthy debate on the matter of his story or his source. Blatchford did the right thing and contacted the police who saw the coercion for what it was.

CREDIBLE NEW "OLD EVIDENCE" STILL EXISTS

Blatchford was given the letter in 1998. It is a time capsule of sorts. Back in 1998 it gives many facts about the murder that were not generally known back then. It cites a specific place where Little Half Dead handed his demo to Tupac—the Bonaventure Hotel—three months before Tupac released "Brenda's Got a Baby." Little Half Dead is confirmed to be sold off to Priority in the letter, which is, in fact, what happened. It also speaks about a meeting with ICG, Gear Gang, Gost Town, Front Street, 52, A Try Hoover's, and South Park. Meetings like this are confirmed to have happened in the Brennan Affidavit.

There were a few meetings and a confession letter was written. As part of creating credibility for this story there was also an attempt to drop off the murder weapon at the journalist's office. Security at the building has a policy against receiving packages from anonymous sources so the package was refused.

The confession letter is rife with typos but the exact transcription is as follows:

"There was a major problem with demo stilling. 2 song's that 2 pac came out with were written by little half dead. little half dead was a up and coming rap singer. He gave 4 demo's to 2 pac to look over, because he meat 2 pac at the bonavenchur Hotel. 2 pac promised that he would look over the demo's. little half dead never heard from 2 pac, and 3 months later, after 2 pac revised the demo's the song brenda's got a baby was released. Brenda's got a baby was written by little half dead. little half dead let that slide. But he continued to go to different recording studios. Finally in 94 little half dead started making money. And he was sponsord mostly by Sh Night. What Night did not know was that little half dead found out that he was being sold to Priority 1. There was a meeting in Reno. And little half dead and 2 pac had dispute about song's that were taken. little half dead was beaten down by 2 pac Soldiers. As day's went by there was meeting's with ICG—gear gang—ghost town—front street—52 - A Try hoover's - and South Park, A bounty was put on 2 pac and Night. Mr. Writh Jr. gave Info where 2 pac was going to be. There was 6 different barri- cades that no matter what would of happened no one would of made it out. I was the shooter that was told to take Night out. little half dead was the one that took 2 pac out. As for gun that was used, will be dropped off at the security booth at fox 11. please do not have stop or talk to one of my drop- pin off the gun.

"Tell X-con how you whant it deliverd. I don't whant to put it in a box cause I don't whant you thinking it's a bomb. If you need any other Info, give X-con a list so I can meet him were I feel I am in more control. If you would like, I can call you on a safe number and give you details of the clothing, cars, streets, and discribe any-thing you need to know to prove that I was there, the night 2 Pac tryed to es- cape, like a little pee-on bitch."

Think of the brilliance of this letter. It is written by the Soria's sister and not by the hand of the shooter. She wrote it because she could "write well" but it is not particularly well written. The gun was supposed to be dropped off at Fox 11 where it was possibly known that it would be refused. There was a man who approached Fox security with a paper bag and something heavy in it, asking for Blatchford. Since Blatchford was away, the package was in fact refused.

Is this letter credible? Is it part of the continuing drama to obfuscate the truth? Is this an attempt by Little Half Dead to sell more records? It very well could be. However, there are some very salient points about the letter and notes from the journalist that have given us pause for reflection.

The first work to be done is to see that the letter may have some degree of credibility. One must try to define the letter's data points, and then corroborate them or try to find like events or like behavior on the part of the Persons of Interest. This is critical; it is easy to laugh off a letter like this and immediately claim it a "fraud" and "not credible" as Kading and Battaglia, who are trying to fill the void that Philips has left in the "smear journalism" department. The allegations are completely unique, the names never heard in this context, except for Danny Patton. The details are a little too specific to be shrugged off as generalities. But because they were so unique, they have already been exposed to ridicule from those who simply wish it not to be true. So they must be defended.

It is also important to get petty and non-critical information out of the way, lest anyone like Battaglia or Kading, whose failed investigations may be challenged by this book, try to do like Philips and hand pick a few lines and use those few lines to gain and foothold and misdirect the public in discrediting the letter's allegations.

For example, like any witness statement, some details may be confused. The Blatchford statement contradicts the confession letter. He states that Gregory Harris Smith is "Little Half Dead" and that he is already doing life for another murder. In 1998 Gregory Harris Smith was tried and convicted of murder. He may, in fact, be one of the shooters and what was being told to Blatchford was confusing. But it is doubtful because of Gregory Harris would have been almost too young to have committed that crime. The Lil' Half Dead who was the rapper could mean Donald Smith. Perhaps there were four shooters instead of three or there were three shooters and a driver. The Blatchford statement also speaks of Neckbone being killed. Neckbone was sent to prison on a drug possession charge and is rumored to have been killed in Texas. He is one of the Death Row insiders. But no one can confirm or deny Neckbone's death at press time.
With those details out of the way.

The Likelihood of a Gang Summit

"As day's went by there was meeting's with ICG—gear gang—ghost town—front street—52—A Try hoover's—and South Park, A bounty was put on 2 pac and Night."

- ICG= Long Beach Insane Crip Gang.
- Geer Gang = West Adams District of South LA.
- Ghost Town = Bloods in Wilmington
- Front Street = Watts Crips
- 52 = Five Deuce at 52nd Street and South Broadway
- A Try Hoovers = Eight Tray Hoovers - 83rd Hoovers
- South Park = 51st and Avalon

This was a Crip/Blood summit. Is there any precedent for Crips and Bloods working together? Death Row signed Snoop Dogg who was affiliated with Crips and DJ Quick who was affiliated with Bloods. In Ken Knox's Police log he noted that both Bloods and New Jersey Crips were hanging out at the studio in the immediate aftermath of the Tupac murder when there was supposed to be a gang war. Many have speculated that Crips and Bloods would never be in the same room. The evidence does not support this claim. Money from drugs or record albums can erase even hardened rivalries.

Freeway Rick Ross says, "[The courts] wanted to relate the drugs to the violence but that wasn't the case. When we started selling drugs it was the first time you could see a Crip on a Blood's block. And they're getting along because they're working. They're trying to get money. And when you trying to get money you don't want no violence. You don't want the killing and the police coming around because that interrupts your cash flow."

According to the confession letter and the journalist's statement one of the shooters was a Crip and two were Bloods. Reggie Wright Junior, affiliated with the Bloods, attends the gang summit and asks permission to take out Suge and Tupac. A bounty is set and the wheels are put in motion. If Kevin Hackie is to be believed about the ballistics on Tupac's murder weapon, this summit may also be where Reggie Wright Junior passed the weapon to the shooter.

The Hood

There is a great novel written about life in the Hood called "The Playground," where two of the characters are Lil' Half Dead and Brenda. In this book a single mom moves from the suburbs to the project after her husband is killed by white supremacists. The day after she moves in her apartment is robbed and all of her stuff is taken. The lesson learned is that you only own something in the Hood if you are able to keep it.

Suge Knight, Sharitha Knight and David Kenner signed artists when those artists were in prison or facing legal trouble. There were so many examples that should have been huge billboards to Knight to avoid legal entanglements at all costs. But life in the Hood isn't simple. Knight once said that he grabbed the hood on his back and tried to take it to Beverly Hills where it didn't work. But whether you are in Beverly Hills or the Hood, as Eazy-E learned, you only own something as long as you can keep it. In Beverly Hills the swords are pens and the bullets are legal briefs. If Knight brought the Hood to Beverly Hills— David Kenner descended into the gangs and played with people's lives.

Suge Knight built a mega-record label in a short period of time. He was able to attract top talent and create revenue streams. Those around him saw an opportunity to take what he had created. They thought they could do what he was doing. It didn't look that tough but in the end all they could do was steal money while he was in prison. They had no ability to attract new talent, navigate record distribution or weather the storm of peer-to-peer sharing that transformed the industry.

Knight built it. But those around him took it from him. They set him up to be killed and when that failed they set him up to do prison time to effectively take what he created. Immediately after the September 7th shooting there were related shootings to cover up their plan. The shootings began again when Knight was about to be released. The people responsible for Tupac's murder wanted to make sure that Knight couldn't assemble muscle to retaliate for what was taken from him. Those closest to Knight are all dead.

But Knight still has that knack to find talent. He still can navigate the often treacherous waters of music distribution or tough negotiations. He may yet create another music revenue stream. But eclipsing the success of Death Row Records is a tough hill to climb. Perhaps he has learned the lesson that crime doesn't pay. Perhaps a kinder and gentler Knight will create something that cannot be taken away from him… again.

I have a picture that I took of all of the guys - one night we were doing a video shoot… and it was Suge and all of his henchmen. And all the henchmen are dead today. Every one of 'em is dead; Suge is the only one alive. So those were his friends. And if you really think about it you'll be like, Hmmm, that's kinda weird.
—Simone Greene to AllHiphopDX- December 2011

Danny Patton is "White Boy"

Police make lists of known gang members. They do this because gang members use aliases to hide their identities. Michael Moore says someone admonished an excited, but foolish proclamation of a successful "hit" over the radio, in fear of others inadvertently hearing as Moore did. Moore says the person's voice was likely Caucasian, it is not an irresponsible leap to believe the author of the confession letter was also the voice on the radio declaring "Got 'em."

Many years later, this confession letter surfaced and was not silent on who the shooters are. Further, in the supporting interviews done with the television investigative reporter, the information unknowingly adds volumes of color to Moore's testimony; one of the alleged shooters named in the letter was Caucasian. In fact his gang name "White Boy," carries that distinction in it.

This was not the first time Danny Patton's name came out from the Shakur Investigation. From the Tim Brennan Affidavit:

"On Sunday afternoon on September 9, 1996, the following gang members met at Leuders Park to discuss retaliation against "S.S.C": "MOB PIRUS"--"S-Ru" (Eugene-19 years old), "Mikey Ru" (Michael Payne), Khalif Perkins, aka "Black," "Bear"-21 years old, "Mar-Ru" (Marvin-20 years old); "LEUDERS PARK PIRUS"--"O.G. Money" (Lamont Akens), "C.K. Vell" (Lavell McAdory), "Ace" (Shawn Verwtte), "Hack" (Ephram Burgie), "Mack" (George Mack), "White Boy" (Danny Patton)."

The Mob Piru have been around for several decades and boasts about 200 members. Their territory stretches from Bullis Road in the West to Atlantic Avenue in the East with the 105 Freeway as their Northern border and Rosecrans Avenue as their Southern border. This gang also controls much of the area along Long Beach Blvd. in Lynwood, north of Compton. The Mob Piru began gaining notoriety in the 1990s with alleged connections to Suge Knight and Death Row Records, who funneled large amounts of money to the neighborhood by employing known gang members from the Mob Piru to his company, along with members of the Leuders Park Piru.

It is critical to understand that the Tim Brennan Affidavit for a Search Warrant was NEVER meant to be public, and was intended for an audience of one- the judge signing the approval for the search warrant. No one else in the public was ever intended to read what Tim Brennan made up. The fact that part of the affidavit ended up in the hands of the public in 2002, was almost as bad as the Patton letter being leaked by the L.A.P.D. and broadcast by Battaglia on the internet in the year 2014. Neither document was ever given context. The Patton Confession letter is being given in this book—but what about the Brennan Affidavit? Is there more to the rest of the Brennan Affidavit that has relevance?

Turns out there is. The Brennan Affidavit is only about one-third of the whole package submitted to the judge—who pragmatically never read the entire affidavit- and that is the reason that many cops write long affidavits; at 3am, the judge signing the order is woken out of a sleep to sign a warrant, and trusts the officer is telling the truth. The other two thirds have never been made public. Upon reviewing the undisclosed portion of the search warrant "package," there are two required pieces of information provided- a list of locations to serve the warrant and search, and a list or items or information being searched for.

Strikingly, the list of locations Brennan wanted to search—under the watchful eye of Reggie Wright Senior, the Officer in Charge—each corresponded to a gang member that was mentioned in Brennan's (public part of the) Affidavit.   They were all accounted for—all that were named gang members were tied to an address that needed to be searched. Some gang members Brennan couldn't get a real name for. However, if you were named in the Tim Brennan affidavit, your residence or safe house was being raided.

Of course, unless your name was Danny Patton aka "White Boy". All of the people listed in the same paragraph in Brennan's Affidavit as Patton, were on the list to be searched. That list has never before been revealed to the public. Nor has the fact that the Brennan Search Warrant that lead to dozens of seizures and arrests somehow completely passed by Patton, just as Biblical Angel of Death passed by the homes of the Israelites who had smeared sacrificial blood on their doorway thresholds. Perhaps the metaphor is more literal that that.

What would be the odds that a person named in Tim Brennan's affidavit as a person of notice, and specifically ignored in the search location lists would also end up the named shooter in the "Confession Letter" and Blatchford statement? Is it a coincidence that the "confession letter" throws a random name as a shooter and yet that exact person be exempted from a gang sweep? The odds would be staggering and the likelihood of coincidence infinitesimal.

It is also to be noted that in the book "Have Gun Will Travel" by Ronin Ro, it is stated that there were actually two sweeps performed by the Compton Police that comprised the Brenan "Search Warrant." The book claims that only people in the neighborhood being searched, knew that a week before the news-covered sweeps of a dozen or more locations, there was an earlier "pre-sweep" of those same locations.

In this earlier sweep, all of the guns were confiscated—likely to keep officers from being shot in the later, more public sweep. However, it noteworthy that this earlier sweep was not broadcast to the media, and the two searches "blended into one." This may have also been a free preview to the Compton Police as to what they needed to draw the media to—and what to stay away from—to paint the public portrait of the "gang problem" for the cameras.

And somewhere in the shadows, the actual shooters were laughing about the spectacle.

The Letter's "Demo Stealing" is Not a New Concept

"Rest in Peace EZ-E. One thing about Eric. Eric told me one day, I thought Andre did all the music with all the beats. You know what Eric told me? People would send our demos in. Andre redo 'em. We redo the raps. That's the song. I took that same getdown. I took it from Eazy. I did the same shit. Took it from EZ. Took it to a another level."—Suge Knight.

The other element of the letter raises a specter that terrifies true Tupac aficionados: the question of whether any or all of Tupac's music "bit off of," "was an homage to," "borrowed from" or "sampled"—the nice way of explaining the act of using anyone else's material. A very broad and unsophisticated way of saying the same thing (and Patton and Soria and others composing the letter probably qualify as "less sophisticated" in this context) is "stealing"—which also happens to be the legal word for it. The other phrases have been invented to soften the stigma of the theft.

"Brenda's got a Baby," (the song the confession letter claims was stolen from Half Dead) was not, for history sake, the first release off that album. The first single released was "Trapped" which did only about 60,000 units, and Interscope was vocally concerned (and this came out in interviews with his management) about its poor performance. "Brenda" comes out and skyrockets to the moon.

What is interesting is the human nature of the selection; Tupac would want to put out first his own creation (he knows he wrote music and verse) before anything he knows he got from someone else. "Brenda" may not have even been Tupac's choice to release, for him it may have been filler as it was the tenth track on the "2pacalypse Now" album. But Interscope picked that one, and not Tupac, because it just sounded better and Tupac's own original work didn't do so well.

Little Half Dead aka Donald Smith (DOB 9/13/1972) grew up in Long Beach, California. At the time of the shooting, he was a member of "Long Beach Crips." He is the cousin of Nate Dogg, Butch Cassidy, and Calvin Broadus aka Snoop Dogg. Keep in mind that just a few days before the shooting in Las Vegas, Broadus had his security detail stripped from him in New York over a beef with Suge Knight and Tupac Shakur by Reggie Wright Junior. Remember also that Broadus' manager was Sharitha Knight.

The confession letter goes on to say that Little Half Dead was sponsored "by Sh Night" which probably means Suge Knight. He found out that his contract was being sold to Priority 1. This would seem to indicate Donald Smith aka "Lil Half Dead" who was briefly with Death Row Records and whose contract was sold off to Priority. Lil' Half Dead is in fact with Priority Records and according to Wikipedia partially with Death Row Records. We know that several of the Death Row albums were distributed through Priority Records so it is conceivable that Lil' Half Dead's contract may have been sold to Priority as stated in the confession letter. Lil' 1/2 Dead was part of the Hip-Hop group 213. When Snoop and Nate were signed to Death Row Records in 1993 the group broke up. Lil' Half Dead released his album "The Dead Has Arisen" through Priority with a reference to being partially released on Death Row Records. How would a letter written in 1998 contain such an obscure fact?

Tupac Trip to Reno

The letter tells of a confrontation that occurred in Reno where Little Half Dead had a dispute about the stolen songs. This conflicts with the Blatchford statement that says this was Las Vegas. Since we do not know where Patton heard his story about Reno or where Blatchford heard Las Vegas from, we can only believe that it was the same place that Patton heard the Priority Records details from—Smith himself. Now as to witnesses, there are no witnesses we have interviewed that can attest to whether Tupac had ever been to Reno or if an additional altercation occurred in Las Vegas.

Atron Gregory Tupac's former manager claims to not be sure, but comments that when it was hot, Tupac would not go, because Tupac did not like the heat. Shakur must have learned to like the heat, because he was in Las Vegas frequently, so his tolerance for hot places, may not have precluded him from going to Reno— maybe it was fall or winter.

Some find lyrical meaning in Tupac's songs, to the point of using them to predict his "return" ("alive theorists") to the fans. In the song from the album "better days" called "Late Night," produced by "Jonny J" and featuring "DJ Quick" (yes the DJ Quick that has been present at about every violent Death Row event) Tupac writes the following:

"Runnin' through the street lights, 'cause we like, yo nigga
Get your mobb on show 'em what a G like
Around the corner it's like Vegas, or better yet like Reno..."

Tupac as an Instigator

"Little Half Dead was beaten down by Tupac's soldiers."

Of all of the claims in the Patton Letter, it appears that the statement that "Tupac's soldiers" beat Smith is probably the most easy to establish. However, when there is a group activity, and Tupac is in it, it has been rather difficult to say who started what; many of the violent Death Row activities Shakur was in the middle of were not directly invoked or provoked by Shakur. But the Orlando Anderson event clearly showed that all it took was the well placed comment in the ear of the Hip-Hop giant, to send him off and running to beat a guy "just standing there." More witness interviews reveal that this was not the first time Shakur beat up an innocent person—if Orlando Anderson was in fact innocent. It can also be proven that anyone who knew Shakur's hair trigger violent temper could invoke it with a planted idea. Perhaps that was the entire purpose of the Orlando Anderson fight.

Gregory "Shock G" Jacobs in an interview for an upcoming Tupac Biographic Documentary speaks about a situation where Tupac was defending "Queen Latifah" (another rap artist) and was picking a fight with a group of armed and offended men. "Okay we're all about to throw down with these cats... but we ain't got no guns..."

Jimi Dright, co-founder of Digital Underground, did an interview for his own uncompleted documentary about Tupac based on his forty page book "Static: The Apprenticeship of Tupac Shakur" (at forty pages, must have been the crash course).

Dright wrote, "Six sets of sexy supple breasts and bootys couldn't pacify Tupac's overwhelming need to beat-down defenseless sound engineers for the unforgivable sin of messing up DU's onstage monitor mixes."

According to Dright, "This guy had fucked up our stage sound. We got feedback for a few seconds and at that point Tupac made up his mind that he was going to beat the engineer's ass for fucking up.

"Tupac wanted to fuck him up right after our set and there were still two other acts that needed their sound mixed that night. So we had to explain to Tupac that if he beat the engineer's ass, nobody else would have sound for the rest of the night. Tupac didn't want to understand that. He didn't care. He wanted to beat the engineer's ass and that was it. So, Tupac had to be held backstage by DU's security for the next two nights to prevent him from beating down the tour's only sound engineer!"

Later on, Dright tells a story that Tupac had been walking around "very annoyed" that someone had broken into their tour-mate

Public Enemy's dressing room. Shakur was shouting, "We got to get them muthafuckas!" and "We got to get that punk, we can't have that!"

When Digital Underground arrived at their hotel in Oklahoma Saturday August 18, 1990, the lobby was packed with people, police and news reporters.

> "Tupac, in his never ending need to bond with another crew, looked and pointed at some guy. We were more than 100% sure that this was not the guy that broke into the dressing room, but 'Pac just picked any motherfucker out of the crowd and said, 'That's him!'"

> "Tupac took it upon himself to run over there and beat this defenseless hotel guest down. 'Pac knew that, as soon as he started beating him down, that we would all run over and grab him to prevent him from killing this man. But by this time Chuck-D and Public Enemy saw that Tupac was down for them. That night 'Pac rode on the Public Enemy bus to the next show."

Sunday August 26, 1990 was one of the last concert dates for the Public Enemy tour. Digital Underground was in San Diego, California. According to multiple witnesses, during sound check, Shakur again lost his cool when a local stagehand yelled at him. "In retaliation," Dright wrote "'Pac decided to punch him in the mouth. So Tupac reached around, punched the guy, and then took off running backstage."

Moreover, Tupac's temper tantrums and violent acts toward parties—guilty or just perceived that way—not only affected artists and engineers, but also affected his management company as well—threatening to fire his managers every day. Dright commented on the change he saw, already referring to 'Pac as a "shit starter."

> "'Pac went from being the sweet, nice, wild little shit starter, to being completely off the hook. He would make phone calls to our manager saying shit like 'Motherfucker, if you're not down to the Benz dealership by 4 o'clock, you're fired!' Tupac was riding our manager to death and none of Digital Underground's other business was getting handled."

There clearly did not need to be a reason to incur Tupac's wrath, and if someone was confronting him with the allegation that he had used—unconsciously or intentionally—their music, it takes no visionary to predict what happened next.

Baker California is a Legitimate Lead

The letter tells us that one of the shooters is willing to provide additional information about cars, guns, clothes, and anything else to prove he was there. He provides the journalist with information about dumping the car in Baker. This is such a random piece of information. But if you were planning a Las Vegas hit one of the key pieces of evidence would be the shooter's car. There could be so much evidence collected if the vehicle fell into the hands of law enforcement. Shell casings, fingerprints, hair samples, receipts, or many other items could be collected that could lead to a successful prosecution. Where would you stash such a vehicle? Baker California?

Baker is outside of Nevada jurisdiction. It is outside of Los Angeles jurisdiction. It is in the middle of nowhere. It is eighty-eight miles from the shooting. If the shooters drove directly there they could have been dumping the car less than ninety minutes. Las Vegas Detectives didn't arrive on the scene until two hours after the shooting had occurred. Within a few minutes of the shooting the car would have been outside of Las Vegas. If roadblocks were established the car would certainly evade them as establishing roadblocks takes time.

There is a checkpoint for fruits and vegetables inside California, the "Yermo Station," where all cars must stop. Dropping the car in Baker avoids this checkpoint. So if the car were dumped in Baker California it would seem to indicate that someone with vast knowledge of law enforcement, investigations, and jurisdictions was part of the planning. Baker California tells us that gang members didn't plan this. Who would possess this type of knowledge? Was it a person that received a degree in Justice Administration? Or a criminal defense attorney?

The Six Barricade Detail

Why on earth would someone think to add a detail like this into a letter? At this point in the analysis of the letter, and all of the details about Lil Half dead, Priority Records, contracts, meetings in other cities—one starts to understand the virtual impossibility of faking this information by an unsophisticated group. The amount of work it would take for non-record company individuals to piece together just the details on the Priority records issues, and understand what they imply just by making the statement alone can only be because the source knows what they were told.

The same can be said about the "six barricades." The letter claims Wright Junior gave everyone details of the events of the evening and that there were six (6) "barricades" set up, so "no one made it out alive."

How implausible is this? Jeff Braley, former Hamilton Township Homicide Detective says not implausible at all.

"Once again, you know, we're going back to the planning. Where they're going to be, where you're going to plan your hit? Now, you're going to look for an optimum target.

"I mean, you're going to look for the perfect place and you're going to make sure that that victim travels across that place. You know, you're not going to want it to be where there's just throngs of public or cars or where you can't get close to things such that, you're going to want it maybe to be a little bit more isolated or you're going to want it to be in an exact place to give you maximum exposure for a shot.

"You're going to want him to be a target, not a hidden target, a target and if you can get them to a spot across in a path where you already have people in place, it's got your plans going to fall into place so to speak and you're going to have that shot availability to you."

And why make so many "barricades" in the first place? Opportunity and contingency! If there were deviations in the plan, and there actually weren't too many to consider in the events of the evening, there would need to be alternative locations. What is interesting to contemplate is whether Knight's decision to choose the route he chose, was driven by his being told about one possible location that he was made aware of. In other words, what if the route Knight chose to drive was to put Tupac at a location at a certain time to arrive at a "barricade" he was told about?

Consider this: if you want someone who is an unwilling victim to go to a certain place, and be sure he goes that route, what better way to get him to go that route than to tell him, "be here, at this location, and we'll take it from there." Knowing that Knight was heading along a specific route that passed by one of the other FIVE barricades he was unaware of is one sure way to know he will be where he is wanted.

Suge Knight was known to make a grand entrance. He obviously didn't take the most direct route. He traveled along the strip with his entourage to bring attention to himself and Tupac. He was sure to take a circuitous route.

According to Frank Alexander in his book, "Got Your Back" there was a couple of ways to get to Club 662 from Knight's home, and in fact there are several ways to get there.

As discussed earlier, and to recap, LOS (Or Line of Sight) is what allows a person to actually see what they are shooting at. Line of Sight says that we need to acquire a target at some point. Knight passed the following streets;

- E Diablo Avenue
- Giles Street
- East Reno Avenue
- East Tropicana Blvd.
- Rue de Monte Carlo
- East Harmon Avenue

Six opportunities to barricade the suspects. Perhaps six other barricade locations were chosen, but to signal out just that detail and be so specific is one thing, to not likely know that there were only about six points to intercept the entourage, and that that specific information was give to them by Wright.

Anyone wanting to catch the procession would have had to sit waiting to make a right on Las Vegas Boulevard. Similarly, if the shooters wanted to catch the procession, and were waiting for it, they would have been waiting to make a right on the following street:

- Audrie Street

CREDIBLE "NEW" EYEWITNESSES EXIST, BUT ARE STILL AFRAID

One never knows who might come forward as a witness when they had not done so before. Most people who witness a crime are unafraid of reporting it. However, in certain circumstances, it is perfectly normal to not want to provide information about someone you know has a reputation for violence. One such case is a witness that stepped up to testify; she had been advised not to offer witness testimony by an attorney who was afraid for her. Many years later, like several other witnesses, she came forward to tell her story:

The witness was a woman working for a company that organized the Vibe Party at the Peterson Museum event; it was one of her first jobs. She stated that in her role, she would be at Peterson the day before the Vibe Party to coordinate events with artists and their entourage (she would make sure that everyone who wanted to be there got there, and it was her job to know who was attending the event.

The witness claimed to have seen a man at the museum the day prior to the Vibe Party. He was very well dressed and well-manicured. He was working some degree of security for the event, but it was hard for the witness to know if it was venue security or security of one of the artists. What stuck in the witnesses head was the fact that this man, for not being one of the event organizers, seemed to be very "detail level" knowledgeable about things that were not yet public information. He was very conversant with her about the timing of the night's events, which is a conversation that is normally saved for event management. He was also in her words "very slick" in his manner of speech and the way he presented himself.

At the Vibe Party the next evening, the witness ran into the man again. The witness was in a bit of a hurry and could only say a few words to the man, but was there in conversation long enough to recall they had one, and it was not a "Hi how are you?" type of conversation.

The witness remembered the man until the day she saw the man on TV, a few months later. The man was Raphael "Ray" Perez and he was at the Peterson Museum both the day before and the night of Wallace's killing. She immediately panicked and called her father, an attorney in LA. She explained to him that she could place Perez at the museum both days.

Her father appropriately advised her that there was much danger ahead if her name was exposed. She agreed with the assessment and until Bond interviewed her, she was not willing to discuss anything at all.

CREDIBLE POLICE STILL WORK THE STREETS
Old Habits Die Hard

Becoming a confidential informant for the Los Angeles Police Department has a high price tag. Your name will most likely be handed to the people you implicate. Paul Lewis aka Lucky provided information to his public defender about Waymond Anderson writing letters to witnesses offering them money to change their testimony in his murder trial. That information is passed right over to Waymond Anderson's attorney. Mario Hammond's name is leaked by LAPD as is Kenneth Boagni and Kevin Hackie. There was a history of an organized LAPD cover-up in regards to Wallace, and attempts to coerce witnesses by leaking their names and confidential information.

It had been ten years since the LAPD cover-up resulted in a mistrial of the Wallace civil suit; certainly things had changed by now. Russell Poole believed that the LAPD had changed. There had been two new reformer police Chiefs since Bernard Parks left. Poole felt he could trust the department. As Poole would find out, as long as bad cops exist, there is no such thing as confidentiality with the LAPD

Armed with the information and belief that this might spur interest in the investigation, Bond and Poole were invited to the New Parker Center by LAPD Deputy Chief of Police. On June 24th 2014, Russell Poole and Richard Bond parked in the Police Garage and went up to the conference room.

In attendance were the following, and only the following: Deputy Chief Kirk Albanese, Commander Kevin McCarthy, Captain William Hayes & Detective I Daryn Dupree, who was introduced to Bond in 2007. Bond knew of Dupree as having worked with LAPD Detective Greg Kading. The others Bond had never met before.

In this meeting, a hard copy printed version of an overview of the case was passed out to all in attendance. Russ Poole passed out a copy of Chris Blatchford's statement, which was corroborating one of the pieces of evidence displayed in the printed overview of the new leads. There were only four people who had received a copy of this printed document.

In the document there were pictures of pieces of evidence in the case. One of the pictures was of a letter that had been lent exclusively to us by Blatchford, who still owns the original. No copy of the letter itself was given but a clear picture of the letter was given so that it was clear we had the evidence.

The purpose of the meeting was to book into evidence the Malcom Patton confession letter that was written in 1998. The meeting was confidential and the information passed to LAPD was supposed to remain with the people in the room. There were assurances given by Chief Albanese, at that meeting, that the letter would be handled carefully, and that it wouldn't find its way from LAPD to the streets. The letter was given formatting that if leaked would be immediately traced back to the LAPD

From the moment Daryn Dupree had his hands on the new information Bond and Poole had introduced, Bond let Poole know it was going to leak to Kading. And on or about July 7, 2014, within 2 weeks, the first public statements about the letter and Blatchford's statement surfaced from Greg Kading. Kading started off by saying that the matter had been discussed in Las Vegas and quickly dismissed it in spite of there having been no Las Vegas investigation of the letter.

The Patton Confession Letter is Leaked and Posted

On August 18th Battaglia posted the Patton Confession Letter; sure enough it has the special formatting; it was leaked by the Los Angeles Police Department. The Confession Letter alleges that Reggie Wright Junior contracted gangs to kill both Tupac and Suge Knight on the night of September 7th 1996. The leak is a clear attempt to derail the credibility of the letter before it can ever gain traction. In case the letter's contents rang true to anyone countermeasures were set in motion. It is a play right out of the Death Row playbook —Third Element—derail the investigation.

Early on the 24th of August, just six days after the letter leaks publicly, Suge Knight is shot. Knight was the clear target of the shooting. Keith Middlebrook said, "Two gang members showed up and accused Suge of killing Tupac and called him a traitor. I think they were two guys from Compton. They yelled at Knight, 'You killed Tupac.'" Why would the shooters mention Tupac? They were trying to tie Knight to the Tupac killing to steer the public opinion away from those responsible for the murder.

But this time, other than the bad cop who leaked the confession letter, there were other officers who did not bury the case. They are currently investigating the matter and intentionally put "new faces" on the leaked confession letter, because there are those within the LAPD who do not feel like continuing to be the cleanup crew for a party they didn't throw.

When Bond received word that the letter had leaked and he was being targeted for the Philips/Kading smear campaign, he was concerned. Some years earlier Kading, who has clearly shown his alliance with Wright Junior had publicly commented that Bond should have been glad that Wardell "Poochie" Fouse (whom he believes killed Wallace) was not alive still—implying that Kading believed Bond would—or should—be dead.

This time around Kading attempted to incite others to action with the public comment "RJ Bond is trying to Frame Lil Half Dead for Murder!" Of course this is typical of the lies that this corrupt ex-cop puts out, because Bond was not trying to do anything of the type. Bond was merely repeating what Blatchford had claimed Patton stated. But what chilled Bond is the fact that Kading tipped his hand to the truth: that Kading must have believed the Patton statement about the capabilities of Smith. Otherwise there would be no point in making that kind of statement.

If Smith were not capable of or desirous of implementing a response to the Patton letter, Kading would not have publicly asked that someone put the word out to Smith. "The logic was irrefutable" as Kading stated in "Murder Rap"; Kading believed Bond should be dead for his daring to comment on Wright, Knight and go to the police about Patton and Smith. For this reason, he asked that Smith be notified because he believed Smith to be capable of doing what he believed Poochie Fouse would have done to Bond.

Since Bond was aware that Kading was not particularly discriminating on who was hurt by his comments—this was his concern that he stated in his 2011 Internal Affairs complaint against Kading. This "confidential" report, which was leaked to Kading by the LAPD

(Bond believes it again to be Dupree) angered Kading to the point wishing "Poochie Fouse" on Bond. The claims of reckless endangerment of Bond was also an independent observation of Random House that cost Kading his book deal

"I didn't make money off the book. It was self-published. I had a very lucrative offer from Random House, and after they legally vetted it, they decided they could not publish it because of what they termed 'reckless endangerment.'

"Random House felt that it would put people in harm's way. They wouldn't want blood on their hands, and particularly, they thought that by outing [Suge's girlfriend], Suge might retaliate against her. So Random House decided not to publish it and this was after we had written a complete manuscript." (Kading, Complex.com, 3/12/2012)

"I was offered a very lucrative publishing contract which I accepted. I had a considerable publishing deal with Random house and they had bought the rights to the book and I had delivered the manuscript and everything was great. And then once their lawyers got their hands on it, and they realized the controversy that it might create, they decided to decline on publishing and their explanation was it was reckless endangerment. They thought that putting people like Suge Knight's girlfriend and Keefe D and all those people on blast, something might get messy and then Random House would have blood on their hands. They were concerned about the welfare of the crooks actually." (Kading, Planetill.com, 3/22/2012.)

LAPD Responds

Bond knew that Kading was producing a documentary based on his book, and in fear of doubt being cast on its claims, was now making wild gestures to do everything he could to disparage Bond and the letter. Of course, this was nothing new. Since the leaked IA report—where Kading asked websites to publish Bond's un-redacted home address—Kading took practically every opportunity where he was interviewed to smear Bond.

This time it was different. Kading was asking someone believed to be capable of murder to be called and told Bond was "trying to frame him." Bond became concerned for his family's safety. Bond and Poole reached out to the LAPD and the staff in their meeting other than Dupree.

Immediately, an Internal Affairs investigation was launched into the leak, IA: CF NO. 14-001995, and detectives are assigned to investigate the case.

Los Angeles Police Deputy Chief Kirk Albanese correctly stated it this way: "The LAPD has the responsibility to properly conduct the homicide investigation. That means to do our best to identify the person or persons responsible for committing the homicide that occurred in our city. There should be no bias just objective fact finding as we strive to solve the crime. This is our responsibility and I will ensure this is what we do."

He was right. Not all of LAPD want the stigma of old and many still want to do the right thing. Bond was visited right away—at his home outside of Los Angeles—by the three detectives from the LAPD Threat Assessment Unit, who deal with cyber-stalking, Internet harassment and stalking in general. They were concerned as Bond was about the solicitation from Kading. They launched an investigation into the matter and briefed Bond as new information surfaced. At press time both the investigations are ongoing.

Leaks still continue, but it is a source of pain for the LAPD that they wish (from the top down) to be a part of the past.

Russ Poole on Kading's Defamation

"Greg Kading devotes an entire book and writes numerous Internet posts disparaging previous investigations including the investigation conducted by former lead investigator Russell Poole. Poole responds,

"For several years now, I have not responded to former disgraced LAPD Detective Greg Kading's barrage of insults, lies and distortions of my career and investigations that I was assigned too. I don't know Kading, I never met him, nor have ever talked to him. As far as I know, he has never made an effort to contact me in regards to my role in any investigation. My record, reputation and experience stands for itself.

—Russell W. Poole Retired LAPD Homicide Detective.

Tim Brennan of the Compton Police department releases an affidavit for a Search Warrant. In this affidavit, many statements alleged to be fact are made. We determine at face value that several statements are just factually incorrect; where victims' car was positioned in the procession, where the shooting actually happened geographically—small things like that. So we turned toward the bigger allegations with a jaundice eye. Was there a series of gang shootings related to the Shakur Killing, was there a "gang war" fueled by gang members affiliations, to the point were victims were getting killed daily—all because of the gangs' alleged hatred of each other?

So what do we do to test the validity of Brennan's assertion that the gangs would just as soon kill each other as look at each other? (a theme that Kading later embellishes to operatic levels with Orlando Anderson and Keith Davis patrolling the neighborhood looking for other gang members to kill).

We turned to other police reports of the alleged period of time. Do they confirm gang run-ins and killings?

There are police reports that sustain both the killings of gang members in Compton. We're not saying the killings didn't happen. And we're not even willing to dispute that they may have been killed by shooters from another gang. But we are correct in dismissing the allegation that there was a "gang war" and that this alleged rivalry fueled many of the killings in that time period—including Wallace himself. There is documented evidence to sustain a counter argument that there was no problem of that nature present. Police reports are accepted as documents and not witness statements, but even if they weren't—ten officers as witnesses? We'll take that.

In saying all of this, as you read this book, understand that when we make a claim, we do not simply have an unnamed "irrelevant" source for the information. In the majority of the cases, we have names for our witnesses and documentation to evidence it or corroborate the statement.

The "confession letter" we speak much about was leaked this year, and caused, as we knew it would, some tongue wagging by uninformed Wright apologists like Anthony Battaglia, whose alter ego Internet alias is "Anton Batey." Battaglia grossly mischaracterized the "source" of the information in the letter as Robert Soria, and then proceeded to publicly flog his (unproven) medical condition and claim publicly the letter to be a fraud. Soria was the courier of the letter, like the mailman.

The actual source of the letter was Malcom Patton, who was named ("outted") by Battaglia just weeks before this book went to press. We were going to reveal the identity of Patton using an assumed name. Battaglia assumed we were taking the more direct route, and decided to beat us to the punch. Patton dictated the letter to Soria's sister. Soria had nothing to say about the letter or its contents. So why blast him? Shoot the messenger, it appears.

But why not go after the source of the letter, and defame him as not credible? Is he credible? We don't know. When he was interviewed by Kading (allegedly, as he wrote to Blatchford) Patton said that "he didn't do it."

However, if a detective's job is to determine if something didn't actually happen, the person of interest in the commission of an alleged crime's denial of wrongdoing is one piece of information only. They are a suspect and not a witness—unless they claim to be at the crime scene, and Patton, according to Kading, has clearly stated he wasn't involved at all. So the detective has to rely on other facts—circumstantial or direct—including interrogation of the suspects to determine if the statement made by the source of the information—the letter—is credible or not. This has not been done. Not by Kading, who summarily dismisses the claims in the letter.

In "Murder Rap" (which is used so strongly in this book by reference not as a personal attack, but as the most recent incarnation of the fatally flawed Anderson/Keith Davis/Gang Killing theory) Wardell "Poochie" Fouse is nominated by Roderick Reed (a "lifer" inmate with some apparent insider information on Death Row and its associates) to be the shooter of Christopher Wallace aka Biggie Smalls. Kading and his task force seem leery of the letter (which is a written witness statement, or actually not even that—it is information only).

So what do they do to test its validity? They call upon Reginald Wright Junior, former head of Death Row Security and well documented Person of Interest in both the Wallace and Shakur killings, and ask him about the letter? He confirms that Poochie Fouse had a secret relationship with Marion Knight, and will not say much more than that. Both of the investigators, according to the book, resolve somehow from that testimony that Reed's letter is legitimate, and Poochie was the shooter.

PART NINE:
MAKING SENSE
OF IT ALL

THE LIE

Over the next couple years, there will be several projects that will come out. Many of them will posit other theories, such as the one about Shakur still being alive, and one about the government being behind the killings. The most common theory that will come out will be the "Orlando Anderson/South Side Crips/Keith Davis/Gang War/East and West Coast Rivalry/Puffy Combs" theory. It has the most velocity behind it and is more fully developed because of all the water that has passed under the bridges in this book. Chuck Philips may not be the most honest person, but he is a good—no make that great—writer. Kading is smooth and personable and wears the "game show host" mantle very well. He comes off as warm and caring about the subject matter.

The "Orlando Anderson Myth" that has evolved into a bigger story, however, is a fabrication based largely on the "blame the dead guy" philosophy. Here's the irony: that same philosophy was created by the Alchemist, The Red Knight and Red Queen of Thieves. They wanted to blame The Red King for all of the theft, overspending, loss of record deals, waste and the increasing heat they were getting from everyone from Michael Harris to the DEA to the artists themselves. Because Knight was larger in image than Death Row, he was an easy icon to use to "blame the dead guy." That's why they wanted to kill Knight, and probably still do.

From the same hypocrisy that points a shaky finger at Poole and others who believe a certain few players (less than 10) "gamed the system" and laughingly calls it a "Grand Conspiracy Theory" comes a tale that has evolved to become a story with hundreds (if not thousands) of participants. Most of those participants are conveniently ambiguous: unknown informants, anonymous informants/participants and "gang" entities. The rest are dead.

From the earliest examples of the El Rey intervention by Brennan, it was made clear that you can't go arrest "the Crips" as an entity, no more than you can arrest the Church. Can't arrest a dead guy either. But to hear the final version of the story that started almost 20 years ago, you are going to be immersed into the entire drug culture and drug wars of the 80-90's and the gangs who worked for the east coast power brokers. Other gangs worked for the cartels from the south. The entire music industry was founded on this drug trade and its founders all drug dealers. Rappers were killed because of beefs related to gangs or drugs.

And the story goes: One such rivalry was a dead guy who stole another dead guy's chain. The one dead guy bragged to his other group of other dead guys about it. Meanwhile one guy on the east coast with a rap label who is still alive controlled a bunch of other guys who are all dead now that were part of an amorphous entity who distributed drugs, and those guys who are all dead now had a tenuous truce with their west coast rivals, the other dead guys.

Now, those dead guys were involved with a west coast rap label who had ties to an amorphous entity. The head of that label was protected by a bunch of dead guys and had artists who are now dead protected by a security company whose bodyguards for the dead guy who got shot are both dead. The witnesses, two dead guys saw the shooting of the one dead guy in Las Vegas, so they can't talk. The one guy who is alive, but was supposed to be dead, called on a dead guy to kill the east coast amorphous entity's favorite popular rapper, the other dead guy. The witness who claimed the dead guy shot the other dead guy in Las Vegas and has information about the LA dead guy's killing, because he claimed a bunch of dead guys from the east coast amorphous entity were providing security for the LA dead guy, has now skipped (at press time) on $100,000 bail and may himself be a dead guy.

Wow. Just Wow. An entire drug culture, dozens of drug guys, and a hundred witnesses who have absolutely no firsthand knowledge about what happened, and a few witnesses who knew the dead guys, but the dead guys aren't here to confirm how well these people knew the dead guys to make a credible statement. There will be many police interviewed who have tons to do—generically—with the drug trade and gangs in general. But few of them have any personal knowledge. There will also be authors who have been reporters covering the story by reading it in the magazine and then reporting on it.

Now the involvement of the entire drug trade? That's a grand conspiracy.

Tables have turned.

THE TRUTH

The simple truth of the matter is that Shakur was killed over money. This was nothing more than a heist. He was killed because to some people Shakur was worth more dead than alive. He was in transition and that created uncertainty. Those who were benefiting from Shakur's revenue stream and who might soon lose it had the most to gain from Shakur's death.

Our opinion about what happened that night, based upon a newly surfaced confession letter, supporting interviews and the facts, is that David Kenner, Reggie Wright Junior, and Sharitha Knight were pulling the strings. Michael Moore was next to Wright Junior immediately after the shooting and told of hearing "Got 'em" coming over Wright's radio. After that "Don't say nothin' over the radio" was heard being said by someone else. David Kenner and Reggie Wright Junior had orchestrated the bodyguards being disarmed through attorney George Kelesis. Sharitha Knight, Suge Knight's wife, would inherit all of Suge's shares in Death Row Records if Suge were killed.

Reggie Wright Junior was the last person to possess the gun used in Shakur's murder. It had been confiscated from Hussein Fatal, one of the Outlawz, at the House of Blues and the gun was ballistics' tested and entered into the Federal Database. Kevin Hackie picked up the gun and handed it over to Wright Junior.

According to the confession letter Wright Junior went to a gang summit. He inquired about killing Suge Knight and Tupac Shakur. The green light was given and soldiers were chosen. Reggie gave them information about where Knight and Shakur would be and they were given the tools necessary to carryout the assassination including the murder weapon. The men rented a white car from a rental car agency inside the Stratosphere Hotel. They carried out the attempted hit and drove to Baker California where they partially disassembled the car and made their way back to Southern California.

The shooter has been alleged to be rapper, affiliated with the Crips, who had a motive—the theft of his songs by Shakur. He had approached Shakur earlier about the theft and was beaten down by Shakur's soldiers. He had an axe to grind and determined to exact revenge.

The other shooters were Bloods, one given the responsibility to shoot Suge Knight. Gang Bangers often get high or drunk before a crime and this often leads to a botched job. Also, they were not very good shots and were using regular ammunition to shoot through a vehicle. This all contributed to Knight walking away that night. For their role the shooters were given a cashier's check as payment. Their motive was money and revenge. But the conspirators' motive was theft of Shakur's money and music as well as stealing the ownership and management of Death Row Records.

With Knight out of the way they could set a new course for the record label and replace the climate of fear, intimidation, and thugary with a more corporate and business friendly face. Shakur was going to be a problem soon that nobody wanted to face. He would create a public stir about the theft of his money that had already occurred and that would be bad for business. Knight's gangster image created legal entanglements at the same time the initial funding from a criminal enterprise was reaching up from the underworld. The various criminal investigations into Death Row could easily be closed upon Knight's death. The murders would solve so many problems!

"Got'em" came over the radio as a pronouncement of success by the shooter because who could imagine that up to thirteen bullets could possibly be launched without killing Suge Knight and Tupac Shakur? And Knight weighs in at 315 pounds and is 6' 3" a pretty hard target to miss. But the hit was pure failure. In the immediate aftermath Shakur wasn't dead and Knight wasn't even really hurt. Shakur was given a 50/50 chance of survival. He was being cared for in the hospital. The puppet masters were busy doing damage control. Strategic shootings and hits were carried out in Compton to silence possible leaks and a very coordinated and evolving cover story was being concocted. The disinformation machine was spinning the truth. Reggie Wright Junior sat in every interview with those close to the shooting when they were questioned by the Las Vegas Police Department.

What seemed like a botched assassination soon began to yield results. Several days later Shakur died. On October 22nd Knight's probation was revoked because of the testimony of Detective Richardson from Compton Police.

"By the time Suge Knight was sent to prison several years later, the Task Force had nothing to violate him on, and he ended up being violated due to his part in the assault of Orlando Anderson (the night Tupac was shot), based on the interview of Anderson by the Compton Police Department's Gang Unit." —ComptonPoliceGangs.com a website hosted by Tim Brennan and Robert Ladd.

Wait!!!

The Compton Police interviewed Anderson? And that interview along with the video footage was used in court as the reason to send Suge Knight away? Remember the name Reggie Wright Sr. who was running the Compton Gang Unit? Was Reggie Wright Junior orchestrating Knight's probation violation? Wrap your mind around the fact that Orlando Anderson actually testified at Knight's hearing as a character witness. This was a direct contradiction to the testimony given by Anderson in the Compton Police Department interview.

David Kenner, in the coolest passive aggressive style, entered the surveillance tape into evidence and orchestrated Anderson's testimony knowing that this would backfire and send Knight to prison. Kenner had already cleared the way for harsh treatment of Knight by orchestrating the replacement of the Assistant District Attorney and Judge in the case. Knight was probably unaware he was being played.

The conspirators were left to run the record label and the theft of Shakur's and other Death Row artist's money continued, and remained hidden for a while. Litigation would uncover much of the theft but so much of what was stolen from Shakur and the others will never be fully known.

On the night of the hit the bodyguards were disarmed. The route was set. Resistance was limited. The confession letter talks about six different barricades limiting the route. It talks about "Mr. Right Junior" giving specifics about where Knight and Shakur would be. It talks about gang meetings. More specifics were provided to the Chris Blatchford who received the confession letter. But it was clear that Shakur and Knight had to go.

Shakur was attempting to remove his masters from the vault. He already fired David Kenner. There might be additional opportunities to eliminate Shakur but so many more complications might exist by then. Time was running out. Once the "Shakur exiting Death Row media spectacle" began it would be hard to contain and Shakur's plans had been set in motion. Here was an opportunity to eliminate Shakur and Knight at the same time. 200 songs were in the vault. The contract surrounding those songs was vague. Possession was on the side of Death Row. Death Row Records was pretty certain they would be able to release many albums under the Shakur brand.

What is known is that in any criminal enterprise there is order. Gang killings or mob killings are not carried out randomly. There is only ever a killing after permission has been granted. Those that act alone end up dead. Even a Coues d'état is only successfully orchestrated when factions are united to topple the existing leadership. There had to be meetings to orchestrate a killing like this. There was planning. There were telephone calls. There was organization. And in the aftermath of a failed operation there had to be consequences. They had to hide the truth from investigators. They had to hide the truth from Knight. The killings in the immediate aftermath focused on those that knew something. When Knight was about to be released the killings focused on Knight's inner circle. They had to prepare for that day when Knight got out. They had to emasculate him so that he couldn't retaliate.

A campaign was begun to manage the Shakur Murder investigation. Red Knight Reggie Wright Junior escorted and listened in as the police interviewed every single material witness to the murder of Shakur. But it was also important that Suge Knight was kept from knowing the truth of what happened on September 7, 1996. Knight held many meetings with bodyguards and others to get to the bottom of it. Red Knight Junior Wright instructed the bodyguards to lie to Knight. Because Knight must never know that those closest to him had planned to take everything from him. Wright Junior's original plan to kill Knight had failed. King Knight was taking precautions. In the immediate aftermath he wasn't an easy target. There were rumors about the price on his head. There were predictions that King Knight would be dead by Christmas. But there was a strategy put in place to send him away thereby neutralizing him even if he wasn't killed. Under California law that meant he would not be able to conduct business. He would have no choice but to entrust those closest to him, who plotted to kill him, to handle his kingdom.

"'Suge Knight has made a lot of enemies over the years,' said Tim Brennan, 'Some of the very people who worked for Suge have now turned against him.'"

Immediately after Shakur's death Red Knight Reggie Wright Junior was complaining that Death Row owed him $60,000 and they were not paying him. At $15,000 every two weeks from the Death Row Check Register—that would equate to not being paid in two months. He was not able to pay the security guards… and they were some scary people to hold off for two whole months. Legal fees were mounting as civil and criminal cases piled up. Two of the three bread-winners, for the label, had already left; the third was dead. But Wright Junior wasn't fazed. He spoke of the coming time when the coffers would once again be flush with cash. There were rumors about a $50 million dollar Lloyds of London life insurance policy on Shakur naming Knight as the beneficiary. Overhead was being cut and all of the equipment, furniture, and assets of Death Row were being put into storage.

The conspirators whispered in Knight's ear fueling the East Coast/West Coast rivalry. They played on the hatred that Knight had for Sean Puffy Combs. They pinned the murder of Shakur on Combs in Knight's mind. Remember they only needed one person to believe that Combs was responsible. Knight took the bait. Lt. Knox was patrolling the Can-Am Studios in Tarzana and receiving reports directly from Reggie Wright Junior that Knight had violated his probation. Wright Junior told Knox that Knight was now rolling with Bloods as his bodyguards—a clear probation violation. Knox was also told about Knight's trips out of the country—another violation. Knox, a responsible cop, reported all of that back up the chain of command. Suge Knight was on a collision course with the law. 45 days after Shakur was shot, Knight was taken into custody for violating his probation.

The Larry Longo trap had been set by Kenner. When this all bubbled up, Knight was going to get no mercy from the court. He was headed to prison for a nine year sentence, he would spend five years locked up, where he would be sidelined from the music world. His revenue streams were now fair game: the vultures were circling. But Knight had muscle; he had resources; he would strike back. He would be ruthless. They sold Sean Puffy Combs as the man responsible for the death of Shakur.

So why kill Biggie? In retaliation! The hard sell was underway.

Knight already blamed Combs for the death of his close friend, Jai Robles, in Atlanta. Knight was starting to have doubts. Conflicting stories about what happened on September 7th were beginning to surface. Knight found out about the guards being disarmed. He found out about Wright Junior asking the bodyguards to lie. The time had come for a bold move—misdirection—an act of furtherance. They needed to create a distraction. They needed to keep Knight's mind occupied with avenging the death of Shakur and of Jai Robles. They set their sights on taking something from Sean Puffy Combs—his top artist! They hatched the plot to kill Biggie Smalls. It became an obsession. Who could sell this to Knight? One of the Outlawz was brought on board. His voice would become the rallying cry for the mission to kill Biggie; Shakur's death must be avenged! Big Syke had wanted closer ties with Knight. This would bind them all together in ways that transcend normal friendship. It would heal any deep fracture to the childhood friendship of Wright Junior and Knight. It would put Wright Junior back in the driver's seat.

The campaign was begun to send Knight away. He was sentenced to nine years in prison but he was still alive. It became complicated. Knight didn't really believe all that he was being told in the immediate aftermath of the Shakur shooting. He was in the car that night. He easily could have been killed. Wright Junior had been caught in lies. Wright Junior was trying to convince him that Frank Alexander needed to be killed. Norris had smoothed things over with Alexander but it wasn't quite adding up. Who could Knight trust? Wright Junior sowed seeds of mistrust in David Kenner and there clearly was a fracture there. It had been so easy. Kenner rented the Longo house and moved Knight in. The perception of manipulating a Deputy D.A. was the real reason Knight was offered no mercy by the court. David Kenner blamed health problems as his reason for dropping out of the Knight's cases but it was much more than that. He no longer felt comfortable around all of the Death Row people. He feared he would be next to disappear. Wright Junior's seeds of distrust for Kenner were sprouting and taking root. Kenner felt that distrust and distanced himself.

Knight felt the isolation. He felt the betrayal. He wanted to get to the bottom of everything and establish the bedrock of truth but he had to settle his affairs. He was leaving for a very long time. He needed to put people in charge. Everything he had built was crumbling and he had his future to think about. His immediate future was prison where people he may have upset were quite powerful. He had his fans and connections but a single wrong move could have grave consequences.

Control of his empire on the outside might mean safety on the inside. He needed to test those around him to determine loyalty. Wright Junior came to him with a plan to even the score with Sean Puffy Combs who Knight held responsible for the murder of Jai Robles. The plan seemed like a plausible way to accomplish quickly what Knight needed to determine—who to trust.

Now Wright Junior who participated in the conspiracy to kill Knight and Shakur could cozy up to Knight continually painting a picture of hope that this next hearing would mean freedom or that he could appeal but Knight was beginning to sense that he was going to do a lengthy stretch in prison. Wright Junior's acting job, feigning to work tirelessly to get Knight out of jail was wearing thin. He advanced to helping Knight obsess in planning the murder of Biggie Smalls. Knight was adamant that the hit happen in Los Angeles where a message would be sent. East Coast rappers felt safer knowing Knight was in jail. They began trips out west. Biggie was in Los Angeles for almost a month before he was killed. Security precautions grew lax and opportunity would come to Knight, Wright Junior, Big Syke, Billups, Perez, and Mack. There was no room for mistakes. This wasn't going to be handled by kids fronting for a gang. This was going to be handled by professionals.

For Wright Junior it was clear that this could put him in the driver's seat for good. He could regain Knight's trust and set him up all at the same time. If Knight was ever believed to be the murderer of Christopher Wallace, Knight would be locked up for life. Since Knight hadn't been killed during the Shakur shooting locking Knight up for good would be the next best thing. Knight's hatred for Sean Puffy Combs would be his undoing. There was one thing Wright Junior knew about Knight, no matter how many fingers were pointing at Knight and no matter how much heat the authorities put on him, Knight would never speak directly to law enforcement and he would never rat on Wright Junior. Knight would take the murder rap himself without ever implicating any other participant. Wright Junior knew the people he selected would do the same. Rafael Perez never implicated the police officers he was close to when he was caught stealing and distributing drugs. David Mack never told where the money was or who the two other participants were in the bank robbery. Wright Junior had finally learned that using the wrong people led to far too many entanglements. Shakur was the Coup d'état, Biggie would be the swan song. Biggie was on the West Coast getting comfortable. He was getting careless. Kenner's reign had been undermined. Now it was time for the Coup de grâce.

Knight, the exiled king, was so much easier to manage when he was in county jail. Inside he was treated like royalty. There were guards that wanted music deals who provided Knight with special privileges. Cell phones, not usually allowed in the jail, were smuggled in for Knight. He was able to communicate with Wright Junior and his team on the night of Biggie's killing.

Women had been sent into Biggie's camp to monitor the big man's movements. They encouraged Biggie to attend the party at the Petersen and they received confirmation that he was going. Inside the party there were spotters who kept the team apprised of Biggie's every move. Those spotters were familiar with tactics used by police as they were police themselves. They had attended on the night previously to make all of the necessary last minute adjustments to the plan. On the night of the murder they fanned out and knew their roles. Each executed the plan flawlessly. As Biggie's entourage moved toward the cars the elements were in place for action.

To create a distraction a man pulls up alongside a fire engine in front of the Petersen Museum and gets out of his car. His gun drops on the ground where it is in clear sight of nearby firemen. In an act of theatrics he picks it up and cocks it to see if the gun is still working and then he fires a few rounds into the air. There is no hurry or attempt to conceal his identity from the firemen who copy down his license plate number and radio it in. "Shots fired" is taken seriously in Los Angeles and that would keep the few squad cars, on patrol, occupied for quite some time as they pulled over the driver and made an arrest. Late at night on the Westside of Los Angeles, this single action takes most of the patrolling cars out of circulation.

There are eyewitnesses that saw David Mack and Rafael Perez at the Petersen. They were monitoring Biggie. They were using cell phones to relay all movements. They kept close watch on him as he approached the parking structure and notified the team when Biggie was in the SUV. His vehicle approached Wilshire.   Amir was alone in the waiting SS Impala; he made the U-turn and pulled up alongside. Amir was both driver and shooter. His arm came down and shots with armor piercing GECO ammunition hit only the door of Biggie Smalls. Nobody else in the car was hit. This was precision. A moment later the

SS Impala made a quick right and then a left and vanished into the night. Cedars Sinai Hospital was only a few minutes away and there was a rush to get Biggie to the Hospital but the damage was done. Biggie was dead!!!

By plotting to kill Biggie the relationship of Wright Junior and Knight was rekindled: renewed by the thirst for blood. Wright Junior was back in Knight's good graces. The chaos of the million shattered pieces continued until Reggie Wright Junior was put at the helm of Death Row Records and then magically the chaos ended.

But in the end it was too late; like Studio 54 of the Seventies and so many other larger than life enterprises, the Kingdom of Thieves collapsed and sunk into Bankruptcy Court like the Titanic. Few got paid; lawyers got paid and Sharitha got paid. Death Row assets were sold for pennies on the dollar, its memorabilia relegated, so meaningless, it became fodder for a reality television shows about scavenging storage facilities for less than pennies on the dollar.

Knight is recovering from getting shot at. He has no record company, but may be looking for the next demo tape to come in. The former Red Knight, has not only had restraining orders placed on him but also placed one on his children's mother. All of the apartments and property he claimed in the Brian Watt deposition are gone. He claimed in Court paperwork that Wright Way is for all intents and purposes making no money. Sharitha is living on the money she received from the Bankruptcy Court.

David Kenner dropped out of the official Death Row business not long after Knight went to prison, citing health issues. The timing is interesting; the McPherson law firm racked up over one million dollars in the Brumfield beating case and handling other matters for Knight and The Red Knight who was the attorney's liaison with Knight. Of course they never saw any of that money save a small piece of the Bankruptcy.

Dre went on to become a billionaire with Jimmy Iovine at Interscope, by lending Young's name to headphones and "ear buds" for the cell phones, and applying the hip hop "cool image" to the headphones. If they wanted to be true in their branding, they should have made the headphones kill the person who put them on. Hip-Hop has become more known for violence, crime, death and disparagement than any other expression of music on the planet.

And while there are good social commentators who use the

medium to legitimately express themselves, their futures are bleak. The entire culture was based on and encourages theft and dishonesty. The last hundreds of pages prior to this attest to this fact, as well as this fact: of all the over 200 "unreleased" Shakur songs he worked so hard to produce, there have been so many released illegally, or "leaked" that the estate would be hard pressed to release anything that was "truly unheard."

The Shakur Estate remains to this day, looking for the rest of the "masters" to make Shakur's original recordings whole. Original film prints of Shakur's "Gangsta Party" and "2 of Amerika's Most Wanted" languished in a downtown L.A. storage facility not owned by Death Row, whose custodian allegedly lost the facility due to non-payment; the prints are either destroyed or in the hands of someone who has no idea of their value—and who can't use the footage anyway because of likeness rights and unclean copyright on the music. Footage shot of Shakur "behind the scenes" remains a quagmire of tied up and confusing copyright. In some cases the footage has never been shown publicly, one of the necessities for a Copyright (Publication), yet the copyright registrant spends much time threatening others over "leaked" versions of his unpublished videos. We do not know of the Wallace Estate and can only hope they fared better. Wallace's label did not go out of business and that is a good sign.

There was so much more that could be done with the Shakur and Wallace legacies, but even that remains an issue of confusion and lack of direction. We hope that one day that will get resolved. Shakur and Wallace gave us their beats, their storytelling, their view of the world. They have both been silenced. They lost their lives. The world lost everything they would have created. The perpetrators got away with this theft. They got away with cold-blooded murder.

RELEASE OF THE INFORMATION—YOUR TURN

What we have written is based upon information that is not in general circulation. We are going to release all of the documents we have collected and let all of you draw your own conclusions. There has been way too much sequestering of information by those with subjective opinions who harbor an agenda. Everyone should look at this information objectively.

What we have is a mere fraction of the documents that exist. We encourage all who have documents to release them through us or on your own—simply release them. Let the public have them. It has been an onerous task to pour over what we have, and it will not be an immediate release as scanning and posting takes time but we vow to all our readers that each document we possess will be posted.

No more lying. Don't post a picture saying that a mugshot of Michael Moore taken in 2003 was one taken in 1996 right after Shakur's shooting just to try to lie about your allegation that Moore was talked to. No more. It has to stop sometime. How about now?

Bibliography

This book was the result of searching and reviewing literally tens of thousands of pages, much too numerous to be mentioned here.

This bibliography is by no means exhaustive, but the major points of conversation are covered herein.

All Hip Hop, I. W. (2007, October 31). AllHiphop.com.

Application for Wiretap Affidavit of Brian Tyndell, Application for Wiretap Affidavit of Brian Tyndell (Superior Court of California Los Angeles July 30, 1998).

Arnold, P. F. (2011, October 25). Arnold, Paul: Former Detective. Retrieved from http://www.hiphopdx.com/: http://www.hiphopdx.com/index/news/id.17118/title.former-detective-greg-kading-clarifies-his-explosive-claims-regarding-the-murder-of-the-notorious-big

Associated Press & Robert Macy, N. e. (1997, March 12). Associated Press & Robert Macy, No evidence of link in rapper slayings. Retrieved from AP: http://www.2pacmania.de/fanlife-presse-lv_8.php

Atlanta PD, (. (1997, November 7). Internal Memorandum re: Jai Robles. Internal Memorandum re: Jai Robles.

Beale, B. R. (2006, August 18). Bond. Richard: Interview with Mutah Beale.

Becker, B. (2009, September 3). Murder of Tupac - Interview with Detective Brent Becker (Youtube). (A. Battaglia, Interviewer)

Blaylock, R. (1997, April 28). Statement of Reginal Blaylock DR 97-0711963. (J. G. Police, Interviewer)

Boagni, K. (2013). Prison Secrets: The LAPD's Notorious Cover Up of Biggie's Murder . Los Angeles: Urban Gold.

Bomb1st.com: Reggie Wright Jr. Discusses 2pac taking Reels From Death Row, I. (2011, March 6). http://www.youtube.com/watch?v=w700_GFXfwQ. Retrieved from Reggie Wright Jr. Discusses 2pac taking Reels From Death Row: http://www.youtube.com/watch?v=w700_GFXfwQ

Bond, R. (2006, June 18). Raw Interview Brett Becker (Tupac Assassination Tapes).

Bond, R. (2006, November). Raw Interview Cathy Scott (Tupac Assassination Tapes).

Bond, R. (2006, December 18). Raw Interview Donald Erath Jr. (Tupac Assassination Tapes).

Bond, R. (2006, November). Raw Interview Frank Alexander (Tupac Assassination Tapes).

Bond, R. (2006, December). Raw Interview Michael Allen (Tupac Assassination Tapes).

Bond, R. (2008, August 23). Raw Interview Gloria Cox (Tupac Reckoning Tapes). (R. Bond, Interviewer)

Bond, R. (2008, Jan 15). Raw Interview Larry Spellman (Tupac Reckoning Tapes). (R. Bond, Interviewer)

Bond, R. (2008). Raw Interview Tracy Robinson (Tupac Reckoning Tapes).

Bond, R. (2009). Raw Interview Frank Alexander (Tupac Reckoning Tapes).

Bond, R. (2009, April 15). Raw Interview Leila Steinberg (Tupac Reckoning Tapes). Not Broadcast. (R. Bond, Interviewer) Retrieved from AllHipHop.com.

Bond, R. (2012). Raw Interview with Papa G (George Pryce).

Brennan, T. (1996, September). Affidavit in Support of Search Warrant. Compton PD.

Brennan, T. (2009, June 21). Who Murdered Tupac? Interview w/ Detective Tim Brennan . (A. Battaglia, Interviewer)

Brennan, T. (2014, September 23). Compton History. ComptonStreetGangs.com.

Brennan, T. A. (1996, September 25). Brennan, Tim Affidavit of Probable Cause.

Broadus Adversarial Suit, U. B. (2009).

Broadus Adversarial Suit, U. B. (2013, April 17). Broadus Contract Case 2:06 BK-11205-VZ Exhibit Page 2 of 49. Retrieved from PACER Document Retreival System:http://www.pacer.gov

Broadus v. Sharitha Knight, C. L. (1997, July 21).

Bruck, C. (1997, July). Takedown of Tupac. New Yorker Magazine.

Campbell, R. (2009, July 24). Interview with Orlando Anderson's Lawyer (Youtube). (A. Battaglia, Interviewer)

Cathy Scott: Death of Tupac Shakur One Year Later, L. v. (1997, June 9).

Christle, Y.-M. (2006, May 27). Declaration of Ya-Mae Chrsitle. Declaration of Witness, pp. 1-3.

Death Row v. Tucker, C. S. (1995, August 15). www.pacer.gov. Retrieved from Death Row v. Tucker.

Dept of Corrections, S. o. (1997, July 30). Mario Hammonds Reliability re: Black Guerilla . Mario Hammonds Reliability re: Black Guerilla .

Donald David- Estate of Tupac Shakur, F. (1997, April 19). www.pacer.gov- Afeni Shakur v. Death Row Records. Retrieved from www.pacer.gov.

FBI Report, W. M. (2003, January 6). FBI Report, Wallace Murder Investigation. Retrieved from fbi. gov: http://vault.fbi.gov/Christopher%20%28Biggie%20Smalls%29%20Wallace%20/christopher-biggie-smalls-wallace-part-1-of-3/view

Finke, N. (2007, August 18). Why Didn't LA Times' Chuck Philips Use U.S. Attorney Statement About Seagal. Retrieved from Deadline.com: http://deadline.com/2007/08/why-didnt-la-times-chuck-philips-use-us-attorney-statement-about-steven-seagal-3118/

Frank, R. (2004, April 15). Letter to Agent Phil Carson (FBI) re: Hackie. Wallace v. City of Los Angeles.

Green, S. T. (2012). Retrieved from Golden Girls Publishing; Time Served My Days and Nights on Death Row Record.

Gregory, A. (2002). Raw Interview Lena Sunday (Tupac: Tha Early Years Tapes).

Gregory, A. (2007). Raw Interview Charles Fuller (Tupac: Tha Early Years Tapes).

Gregory, A. (n.d.). Raw Interview Yasmyyn Fula (Tupac: Tha Early Years Tapes). (L. S. Gregory, Interviewer)

Hackie, K. (Various). Nine (9) Transcripts of Kevin Hackie Inteviews. (L. A. Police, Interviewer)

Harris, J. (2002). Raw Interview Kennth Archer (Tupac Assassination Tapes).

Harris, J. (2002). Raw Interview Leslie Gauldin (Tupac Assassination Tapes).

Harris, J. (2002). Raw Interview Michael Moore (Tupac Assassination Tapes).

Hilburn and Crowe, L. T. (1996, September 14). Hilburn and Crowe, LA Times: Rapper Tupac Shakur, 25, Dies. Retrieved from LA Times: http://articles.latimes.com/1996-09-14/news/mn-43719_1_rapper-tupac-shakur

James Prince, D. o. (2006, April). James Prince, Declaration of James Prince.

KadafiLegacy.com. (n.d.). Interview with Yasmyyn Fula. (KadafiLegacy.com, Interviewer)

Kading, G. (2011). Murder Rap. One Time Publishing.

Kading, G. (2013, September 3). Greg Kading 2Pac Forum Postings . Retrieved from http://www.2Pac-forum.com: http://www.makaveli-board.net/showthread.php?30727-Greg-Kading-s-Murder-Rap-Thread/page24

Kading, G. (2013, September 2). Greg-Kading's-Murder-Rap-Thread Pages 1-144. Retrieved from http://www.makaveli-board.net/: http://www.makaveli-board.net/showthread.php?30727-Greg-Kadings-s-Murder-Rap-Thread/page23

Kading, G. (2013, July 31). Interview with Greg Kading by "Anton Batey". (A. Battaglia, Interviewer)

Kenner, R. (2012, March). Compex Interview with Gregory Kading. Retrieved from www.complex.com: http://www.complex.com/music/2012/03/interview-former-lapd-detective-says-he-knows-who-killed-the-notorious-big

Knox, K. (1996, May 5). LAPD Can-Am Surveiilance Log. LAPD Can-Am Surveiilance Log, pp. 1-16.

Knox, K. (n.d.). Declaration of Kenneth Knox- Wallace v. City of LA. Declaration of Kenneth Knox-Wallace v. City of LA.

Kugel, A. (2005, February 25). PR.com. Retrieved from Dina LaPolt and Afeni Shakur Keep Tupac Shakur's Indelible Legacy Alive: http://www.pr.com/arrticles/1010

LA District Attorney Office. (1998, March 19). (Cosper) Report on SID # 100-8226/97 OIS 029/97 to William Garland. Gaines Lyge Shooting Investigation.

LA Times. (1992, September 23). (John Broader) Quayle Calls for Pulling Rap Album Tied to Murder Case. Retrieved from LA Times.com: http://articles.latimes.com/1992-09-23/news/mn-1144_1_rap-album

LA Times. (1996, September 18). (Huber) Police Find No Shakur Tie to Compton Slayings. Retrieved from LA Times: http://articles.latimes.com/1996-09-18/local/me-44974_1_shakur-s-death

LA Times. (1996, February 21). (Tina Daunt)Rapper Snoop Doggy Dogg Is Acquitted of Murder. Retrieved from LA Times.com: http://articles.latimes.com/1996-02-21/news/mn-38322_1_rapper-snoop-doggy-dogg

LA Times. (1997, February 10). (Chuck Philips) Rap Mogul's Lawyers Contend Detective Lied. Retrieved from LA Times.com: http://www.latimes.com/news/local/la-me-tupacsuge10feb1097,0,1623507.story#axzz2mFb1Vseu

LA Times. (2002, September 7). (Chuck Philips) How Vegas police probe floundered in Tupac Shakur case. Retrieved from LA Times.com: http://www.latimes.com/news/nationworld/nation/la-fi-tupac-7sep07,0,6002100.story#axzz2mFb1Vseu

LA Times. (2002, September 6). (Chuck Philips) Who Killed Tupac Shakur. Retrieved from LATimes.com: http://www.latimes.com/news/nationworld/nation/la-fi-tupac6sep06,0,5543346.story#axzz2mFb1Vseu

LA Times. (2003, July 1). (Chuck Philips) As Associates Fall, Is Suge Knight Next. Retrieved from LaTimes.com: http://www.latimes.com/news/local/la-fi-suge1aug01,0,1646381.story#axzz2mFb1Vseu

LA Times. (2006, July 31). (Chuck Philips) LAPD Renews Search for Rapper's Killer. Retrieved from LA Times.com: http://articles.latimes.com/2006/jul/31/local/me-biggie31

LA Times. (2007, January 16). (Chuck Philips) Chorus of protests seeks to free singer locked up for 1993 killing. Retrieved from LA Times.com: http://www.latimes.com/news/la-me-suave16jan16-story.html#page=1

LA Times, (. (2008, April 7). Times retracts Shakur story . Retrieved from LA Times.com: http://www.latimes.com/entertainment/news/business/la-naw-quad17mar17-story.html#page=1

LA Times, (. L. (2007, September 26). Inmate recants story about LAPD link to rapper's slaying . Retrieved from LA Times.com: http://www.latimes.com/local/la-me-biggie26sep26-story.html#page=1

LA Weekly. (2011, October 3). (Simone Wilson) Greg Kading: Tupac and Biggie Murders... Retrieved from La Weekly.com: http://www.laweekly.com/informer/2011/10/03/tupac-and-biggie-murders-an-up-to-date-list-of-characters-given-new-evidence-from-ex-lapd-detective-greg-kading

LA Weekly, (. V. (2011, October 3). Greg Kading: The Internal Affairs Report that Cleared... Retrieved from LA Weekly: http://blogs.laweekly.com/informer/2011/10/greg_kading_the_internal_affai.php

LA Weekly, (. V. (2011, October 6). Los Angeles Cop's Book Says Sean Combs. Retrieved from www.laweekly.com: http://www.laweekly.com/2011-10-06/news/cop-s-book-says-sean-combs-suge-knight-ordered-tupac-and-biggie-killings/

Ladd, B. (2009, November 19). Who Killed Tupac Shakur - Interview with Sgt. Ladd (Youtube). (A. Battaglia, Interviewer)

LAPD. (1996, January 4). (Cooper) Follow Up Investigation Report DR 950714398. El Rey Theater Homicide, pp. 1-9.

LAPD. (1997, December 24). (Banks) David Mack Arrest Recovery Item List. (Banks) David Mack Arrest Recovery Item List.

LAPD. (1997, December 26). (Correctional Systems, Inc) Visiting Application and Approval Form (Muhammad). (Correctional Systems, Inc) Visiting Application and Approval Form (Muhammad).

LAPD. (1997, June 9). (Gollaz) Statement of Corey Lamont Edwards. Statement of Corey Lamont Edwards.

LAPD. (1997, April 28). (Inglewood PD) Voluntary Statement of Reginald Blaylock 2. Voluntary Statement of Reginald Blaylock 2.

LAPD. (1997, September 17). (Katz/Martin) Vountary Statement of Ingrid Johnson 2. (Katz/Martin) Vountary Statement of Ingrid Johnson 2.

LAPD. (1997, September 10). (Katz/Martin) Vountary Statement of Lauren Hart 2. (Katz/Martin) Vountary Statement of Lauren Hart 2.

LAPD. (1997, September 9). (Katz/Martin) Vountary Statement of Shelayne Turner 2. (Katz/Martin) Vountary Statement of Shelayne Turner 2.

LAPD. (1997, June 4). (OIS Division) Confidential Report on Kevin Gains, to Captain Carter, LAPD. Confidential Report on Kevin Gains, to Captain Carter, LAPD, pp. 1-9.

LAPD. (1997, December 16). (Poole) Davd Mack Search Warrant and Inventories, Pictures. (Poole) Davd Mack Search Warrant and Inventories, Pictures.

LAPD. (1997, March 9). (Poole) Death Investigation Report (Wallace). (Poole) Death Investigation (Wallace).

LAPD. (1997, March 18). (Poole) Kevin Gaines Pager Log. Kevin Gaines Pager Log.

LAPD. (1997). (Poole) Raphael Perez Search Warrants and Inventories and Documents. (Poole) Raphael Perez Search Warrants and Inventories and Documents.

LAPD. (1997, March 9). (Various) Arrest Report Harrell. (Various) Arrest Report Harrell.

LAPD. (1997, March 03). (Various) Christopher Wallace Murder Book . (Various) Christopher Wallace Murder Book .

LAPD. (1997). (Various) Chronological Records (Investigation) re: Wallace DR 97-0711963. (Various) Chronological Records (Investigation) re: Wallace DR 97-0711963.

LAPD. (1997, March). (Various) Crime Scene Log (Wallace) Personnel List. Crime Scene Log (Wallace) Personnel List.

LAPD. (1997, March). (Various) Dispatch Logs for Patrol Units. (Various) Dispatch Logs for Patrol Units.

LAPD. (1997, June 6). (Various) Forensic Fingerprint Reports. (Various) Forensic Fingerprint Reports.

LAPD. (1997). (Various) Gekko Ammunition Report. Gekko Ammunition Report.

LAPD. (1997, March 15). (Various) Leads from America's Most Wanted (hundreds of pages). (Various) Leads from America's Most Wanted (hundreds of pages).

LAPD. (1997). (Various) Vehicle Investigation Impound Reports (Many) . (Various) Vehicle Investigation Impound Reports (Many) .

LAPD. (1997, March 19). Voluntary Statement of Damien "D-Rock" Butler. Voluntary Statement of Damien "D-Rock" Butler.

LAPD. (1997, June 12). Voluntary Statement of Darnell Brim. Voluntary Statement of Darnell Brim.

LAPD. (1997, April 17). Voluntary Statement of Dewey West. Voluntary Statement of Dewey West.

LAPD. (1997, March 20). Voluntary Statement of Dewey West 2. Voluntary Statement of Dewey West 2.

LAPD. (1997, May 1). Voluntary Statement of Earnest Anderson. Voluntary Statement of Earnest

Anderson.

LAPD. (1997, April 22). Voluntary Statement of Eugene Deal. Voluntary Statement of Eugene Deal.

LAPD. (1997, March 20). Voluntary Statement of Gregory Young. Voluntary Statement of Gregory Young.

LAPD. (1997, March 10). Voluntary Statement of Gregory Young 2. Voluntary Statement of Gregory Young 2.

LAPD. (1997, October 9). Voluntary Statement of Henry "Hen Dog" Smith. Voluntary Statement of Henry "Hen Dog" Smith.

LAPD. (1997, April 4). Voluntary Statement of James "Lil Cease" Lloyd 3. Voluntary Statement of James Lloyd 3.

LAPD. (1997, March 9). Voluntary Statement of James Lloyd 1. Voluntary Statement of James Lloyd 1.

LAPD. (1997, March 20). Voluntary Statement of James Lloyd 2. Voluntary Statement of James Lloyd 2.

LAPD. (1997, March 9). Voluntary Statement of Kenneth Story. Voluntary Statement of Kenneth Story.

LAPD. (1997, March 15). Voluntary Statement of Kenneth Story 2. Voluntary Statement of Kenneth Story 2.

LAPD. (1997, March 9). Voluntary Statement of Paul Offord. Voluntary Statement of Paul Offord.

LAPD. (1997, September 8). Voluntary Statement of Recarter Gross re: Deandre Smith/Anderson and Davis in Car. Voluntary Statement of Recarter Gross re: Deandre Smith/Anderson and Davis in Car.

LAPD. (1997, March 12). Voluntary Statement of Reginald Blaylock. Voluntary Statement of Reginald Blaylock.

LAPD. (1997, May 14). Voluntary Statement of Rosanne Smith re: "Herron" Palmer . Voluntary Statement of Rosanne Smith re: "Herron" Palmer .

LAPD. (1997, March 20). Voluntary Statement of Sean "Puffy" Combs. Voluntary Statement of Sean "Puffy" Combs.

LAPD. (1998, March 12). (Bright) Preliminary Investigation Robbery George "Papa G" Pryce. (Bright) Preliminary Investigation Robbery George "Papa G" Pryce.

LAPD. (1998, June 8). (Miller) Six Month Progress Report (Wallace). (Miller) Six Month Progress Report (Wallace).

LAPD. (1998, July 3). (Tyndall) Application and Affidavit Raphael Perez Wiretap. Application and Affidavit Raphael Perez Wiretap.

LAPD. (1998, January 13). (Various) Misc Files re; Amir Muhammed (Harry Billups). (Various) Misc Files re; Amir Muhammed (Harry Billups).

LAPD. (1998, April 28). Voluntary Statement of Frank Alexander 3. Voluntary Statement of Frank Alexander 3.

LAPD. (1998, February 19). Voluntary Statement of Gerard Brooks. Voluntary Statement of Gerard Brooks.

LAPD. (1999, November 9). (Katz) Change of Investigating Officers. (Katz) Change of Investigating Officers.

LAPD. (1999, August 18). (Poole) Biggie Smalls Timeline. (Poole) Biggie Smalls Timeline.

LAPD. (1999, April 20). (Various) Receipt fot Property Taken Report- Death Row Records Search Warrant. (Various) Inventory Property Report- Death Row Records Search Warrant.

LAPD. (2002, April 4). Death Row Records LASO Search Warrant Re: Alton "Buntry" McDonald. Death Row Records LASO Search Warrant Re: Alton "Buntry" McDonald.

LAPD. (July, 17 1997). Voluntary Statement of Norris Anderson. Voluntary Statement of Norris Anderson.

LAPD, (. (1998, April 28). Inerview with Frank Alexander - DR-970711963. Interview with Frank Alexander, pp. 1-2.

Las Vegas Sun, (. S. (n.d.).

Las Vegas Sun, C. S. (1996, October 2). Arrest made in Tupac Shakur killing. Retrieved from Las Vegas Sun: http://www.lasvegassun.com/news/1996/oct/02/arrest-made-in-tupac-shakur-killing/

Las Vegas Sun, C. S. (1996, November 13). Shakur shooting witness found dead in N.J. Retrieved from Las Vegas Sun: http://www.lasvegassun.com/news/1996/nov/13/shakur-shooting-witness-found-dead-in-nj/

Las Vegas Sun, C. S. (1997, September 6). The death of Tupac Shakur one year later. Retrieved from The death of Tupac Shakur one year later: http://www.lasvegassun.com/news/1997/sep/06/the-death-of-tupac-shakur-one-year-later/

Las Vegas Sun, C. S. (1997, March 3). Tupac witnesses' stories conflicting. Retrieved from Las Vegas Sun: http://www.lasvegassun.com/news/1997/mar/03/tupac-witnesses-stories-conflicting/

Las Vegas Sun, C. S. (2002, November 15). Rap kingpin's former Vegas home is raided. Retrieved from Las Vegas Sun: http://www.lasvegassun.com/news/2002/nov/15/rap-kingpins-former-vegas-home-is-raided/

LASO, (. (2003, November 21). Supplemental Report: Avenue R Little Rock. Additional Information re: Frank Lyga.

Lopez and Hubler, L. T. (1996, September 17). LOPEZ and HUBLER, LA Times 2 Slayings May Be Linked. Retrieved from LA Times: http://articles.latimes.com/1996-09-17/news/mn-44642_1_shakur-attack

Los Angeles Superior Court, r. D. (2004, May 3). Los Angeles Superior Court, re: Dwayne Baudy Judgment (LC 062730).

Los Angeles Superior Court, r. H. (n.d.). Harris vs. Knight Case BC340196.

LVMPD. (1996). (Becker) Club 662 Premise Check Results Report. (Becker) Club 662 Premise Check Results Report.

LVMPD. (1996, September 6). (Becker) Monte Carlo Hotel Receipts Corey Edwards. (Becker) Monte Carlo Hotel Receipts Corey Edwards.

LVMPD. (1996, September 7). (Becker) Voluntary Statement of Frank Alexander. (Becker) Voluntary Statement of Frank Alexander.

LVMPD. (1996, September 8). (Becker) Voluntary Statement of Malcom Greenidge. (Becker) Voluntary Statement of Malcom Greenidge.

LVMPD. (1996, September 11). (Becker) Voluntary Statement of Marion Hugh Knight. (Becker) Voluntary Statement of Marion Hugh Knight.

LVMPD. (1996, September 7). (Becker) Voluntary Statement of Yafeu Fula. (Becker) Voluntary Statement of Yafeu Fula.

LVMPD. (1996). (Becker) Work Cards Issued for Club 662. (Becker) Work Cards Issued for Club 662.

LVMPD. (1996, September 10). (Various) Gate Logs for Marion Knight Residence September 1996. (Various) Gate Logs for Marion Knight Residence September 1996.

LVMPD. (1997, March 19). (Becker) Voluntary Statement of Frank Alexander Number 2. (Becker) Voluntary Statement of Frank Alexander Number 2.

LVMPD. (1997, March 20). (Becker) Voumtary Statement of Gregory Johnson. (Becker) Voumtary Statement of Gregory Johnson.

LVMPD, (. (1996, September 7). 28 Field Interview Cards. 28 Field Interview Cards (Copies), p. 10.

LVMPD/LAPD. (1997, June 9). Voluntary Statement of Corey Edwards. Voluntary Statement of Corey Edwards.

Makaveli Board & Kading, T. K. (2012, December 12). Makaveli Board. Retrieved from http://www.makaveli-board.net: http://www.makaveli-board.net/showthread.php?27532-The-Keefe-D-Tapes&p=216918&highlight=proffer#post216918

Manning, K. (1996, September 10). Videotaped Press Conference. (N. B. Vegas, Interviewer)

Mark Anthony Bell Robbery (Follow Up Case Closed "Other"), 950648425 (LAPD) (April 30, 1996).

Matthews, ". R. (2014, June 15). Interview with Death Row Dave Volume 1. (R. Poole, Interviewer)

MGM Hotel, H. S. (1996, September 7).

MTV, (. (1996, September 4). Interview with Master T. Retrieved from MTV news MTV.com: http://www.youtube.com/watch?v=Tr3EU6C2yyE&noredirect=1

MTV, (. C. (2001, August 9). Interview with Suge Knight. Retrieved from mtv.com: http://www.mtv.com/news/articles/1446517/suge-knight-talks-about-freedom-who-killed-pac.jhtml

MTV, (. M. (2002, September 6). Philips Interview Biggie Paid Gang To Kill Tupac, Report Says. Retrieved from www.mtv.com: http://www.mtv.com/news/articles/1457346/report-biggie-paid-tupac-murder.jhtml

MTV, (. R. (2008, March 21). L.A. Times' Chuck Philips Defends Method Behind Tupac, Diddy Story: 'I Know All Kinds Of Stuff I Don't Write About' . Retrieved from MTV.com:http://www.mtv.com/news/1583921/la-times-chuck-philips-defends-method-behind-tupac-diddy-story-i-know-all-kinds-of-stuff-i-dont-write-about/

Nevada Financial Disclosure Statement, r. G. (2008, December 8). Nevada Financial Disclosure Statement, re George Kelesis.

Orange NJ PD, (. (1996, November 12). Incident Report re: Yafeu Fula . Incident Report re: Yafeu Fula , pp. 1-3.

Patterico's Pontifications, (. F. (2006, January 6). More on Hiltzik from Comrade Patterico. Retrieved from Patterico's Pontifications: http://patterico.com/2006/01/06/more-on-hiltzik-from-comrade-patter-ico/

Patterico's Pontifications, (. F. (2008, January 2). Another Pro-Suge Knight Article by Chuck Philips. Retrieved from Patterico's Pontifications: http://patterico.com/2008/01/02/another-pro-suge-knight-article-by-chuck-philips/

Patterico's Pontifications, (. F. (2008, November 16). Inmate Who Was Close to Chuck Philips. Retrieved from Patterico's Pontifications: http://patterico.com/2008/11/16/

Patterico's Pontifications, (. F. (2008, March 26). L.A. Times Admits Documents in Tupac/Sean Combs Story Were Fabricated. Retrieved from Patterico's Pontifications:http://patterico.com/2008/03/26/breaking-la-times-admits-documents-in-tupacsean-combs-story-were-fabricated/

Patterico's Pontifications, (. F. (2008, April 3). Protecting His Own Dishonest Sources While Risking the Lives of Law Enforcement Informants. Retrieved from Patterico's Pontifications: http://patterico.com/2008/04/03/the-interesting-ethics-of-chuck-philips-protecting-his-own-dishonest-sources-while-risking-the-lives-of-law-enforcement-informants/

Phillips, C. R. (1997, February 10). Rap Mogul's Lawyers Contend Detective Lied. Retrieved from http://articles.latimes.com/1997-02-10/local/me-27295_1_las-vegas-police

Poole, R. (2003, July 10). Deposition of Russell Poole (Wallace v. City of Los Angeles). Deposition of Russell Poole (Wallace v. City of Los Angeles).

Poole, R. I. (1997). Interview Notes re: Kevin R Hackie .

Records, D. R. (1999, May 21). Release of Property Request. Release of Property Request.

Reed, R. (2004, July 7). Letters to Kevin Hackie re; help with case. Death Row Police.

Reggie Wright: Was Tupac Leaving Death Row, B. (2011, June 15). http://www.youtube.com/watch?v=40BoRPHGPts. Retrieved from Bomb1st.com: 2011
Ro, R. (1998). Have Gun Will Travel. Doubleday Publishing.

Robinson, T. (1996). Creative Session Tapes, Tupac.

Scott, C. (2009, January 15). Who Killed Tupac? Interview with Cathy Scott . (A. Battaglia, Interviewer)

Shakur, S. V. (1997, December). Shakur, Sanyika" Vibe Magazine Interview Orlando Anderson.

Shakur, S. V. (1997, December). Vibe Magazine Interview Suge Knight. Retrieved from vibe.com.

Shooter Letter, H. L. (1996, November).

Sullivan, R. (2003). LAbyrinth: A Detective Investigates the Murders of Tupac Shakur and Notorious B.I.G. Los Angeles: Grove Press.

Surrat, J. (2013, April 14). Interview with Lance Pierre (Raw). (J. Surrat, Interviewer)

Surrat, J. (2013, June 16). Interview with Simone Green (Raw).

Totten (FBI), R. (1996, August 22). Letter of Recommendation for Mario Hammonds as Reliable Informant. Letter of Recommendation for Mario Hammonds as Reliable Informant.

Tupac Fans.com, I. w. (2013, 10 22). www.tupacfans.com/interviews/cathy1.php. Retrieved from www.tupacfans.com.

US Bankruptcy Court, r. A. (2006, June 5). Adversarial Complaint Lydia Harris.

US Bankruptcy Court, r. A. (2007, December 21). Adversarial Complaint of Nathan Hale (a.k.a. Nate Dogg).

US Bankruptcy Court, r. A. (2007, August 12). Adversarial Complaint of Andre Young (a.k.a. Dr. Dre). Retrieved from www.pacer.gov.

US Bankruptcy Court, r. A. (2008, February 27). Adversarial Complaint Koch Entertainment.

US Bankruptcy Court, r. A. (2008, February 20). Adversarial Complaint of Shakur Estate.

US Bankruptcy Court, r. A.-1. (2013, 4 18). Amaru Settlement of Claims Case 2:06-bk-11205-VZ.

US Bankruptcy Court, r. D. (2006, April 4). Debtor Examination of Marion Knight. Retrieved from www.pacer.gov: http://www.pacer.gov

US Bankruptcy Court, r. D. (2006, June 5). Declaration of Alvin Mar ins support for Motion for Trustee.

US Bankruptcy Court, r. D. (2007, July 20). US Bankruptcy Court, re: Death Row vs. Afeni Shakur.

US Bankruptcy Court, r. D. (2007, July 26). US Bankruptcy Court, re: Death Row vs. Eagle Rock Entertainment.

US Bankruptcy Court, r. F. (2009, January 22). US Bankruptcy Court, re: First Interim Fee Application fo Kaye Scholler.

US Bankruptcy Court, r. F. (2013, May 21). Filing of Redacted Objection to Claim 59 (Toussant).

US Bankruptcy Court, r. M. (n.d.). US Bankruptcy Court, re: Matter of Clear Channel v. Death Row.

US Bankruptcy Court, r. M. (n.d.). US Bankruptcy Court, re: McPherson v. Death Row.

US Bankruptcy Court, r. O. (2008, November 19). US Bankruptcy Court, re: Order Approving Fourth Stipulated Agreement (Amaru).

US Bankruptcy Court, r. R. (2006, June 06). Richard Diamond Motion to Appoint Trustee. Retrieved from www.pacer.gov.

US Bankruptcy Court, r. T. (2006, August 31). US Bankruptcy Court, re: Tammie Hawkins. Retrieved from Trustee Request to Turn Over Property.

US Bankruptcy Court, r. T. (2008, April 03). US Bankruptcy Court, re: Trustee Complaint against Maxine Knight.

US Bankruptcy Court, r. T. (2008, November 6). US Bankruptcy Court, re: Trustee Complaint against Stormy J Ramdhan.

US Bankruptcy Court, r. T. (2008, June 20). US Bankruptcy Court, re: Trustee's Reply to Opposition of Afeni Shakur.

US Bankruptcy Court, r. T. (2012, October 23). US Bankruptcy Court, re: Trustee's Objection to Claim of Demetrius Shipp.

US Bankruptcy Court, r. T. (2012, October 23). US Bankruptcy Court, re: Trustee's Objection to Claim of Ricardo Brown ("Kurupt").

US Bankruptcy Court, r. T. (May, 21 2013). US Bankruptcy Court, re: Trustee's Objection to Claim 22 and 28 by Calvin Broadus.

US Bankruptcy Court, r. T. (October, 23 2012). US Bankruptcy Court, re: Trustee's Objection to Claim of David Chesnoff.

US Bankruptcy Court, r. T. (n.d.). Trustee Motion to Approve Settlement Agreement with Reginald L Wright.

US Bankruptcy Court, r. T. (n.d.). US Bankruptcy Court, re: Trustee's Objection to Claim of Jewell Lynn Caples.

US Department of Justice, (. (2002, June 6). Confidential Report on Testimony of Hackie. Confidential Report.

US District Court, A. M. (2003, March 24). US District Court, Amanda Metcalf v. Death Row Records.

US District Court, K. R.-C. (2001, June 4). US District Court, Kevin R Hackie v. Los Angeles, City Of-Central District of California. Declaration of Kevin R Hackie.

US District Court, S. v.-S. (2007, July 16). Shakur v. ZNO- Southern District of New York. Retrieved from www.pacer.gov: www.pacer.gov

US District Court, U. V. (n.d.). Retrieved from www.pacer.gov.

US District Court, U. V. (2008, November 12). Retrieved from www.pacer.gov: www.pacer.gov

US District Court, W. V. (2005, July 5). Order Granting Plainitff's Motion for Mistrial. Order Granting Plainitff's Motion for Mistrial.

US District Court, Y. F.-C.-1. (2001, April 19). US District Court, Yaasmyn Fula v. Death Row records-Central District (99-1206 JSL).

US v. Nino Durden Plea Bargain, CR-11-256 (US Disctrict Court March 29, 2001).

Webb, D. (2001, July 25). Letter re: Conversation with Ron Cheng. Kackie v. City of Los Angeles.

Webb, D. (2002, June 6). Letter: re: Dan Mc Mullin and Ciccione. Hackie v. City of Los Angeles.

Williams/Alexander, R. W. (2008). Williams/Alexander, Rollin' With Dre: The Unauthorized Account. Los Angeles: One World/Ballantine.

Wright, Reginald Jr. Deposition of, NC028423 Watt v. City of Compton (California Superior Court March 12, 2002).

Wrightway Protective Services, C. o. (1996, October 26). Wrightway Protective Services, Copy of Schedule for Can Am Studios.

Wrightway Protective Services, P. L. (1996, November 2). Wrightway Protective Services, Personnel List.

www.ingramcontent.com/pod-product-compliance
Lightning Source LLC
Chambersburg PA
CBHW072103040426

42334CB00042B/2172